For Evie Blue

<hr/>

Let me tell ya a coupla three things.
—Phil Leotardo

OFF THE BACK OF A TRUCK

UNOFFICIAL CONTRABAND *for* THE SOPRANOS FAN

NICK BRACCIA *and some* FRIENDS OF OURS

TILLER PRESS

New York   London   Toronto   Sydney   New Delhi

An Imprint of Simon & Schuster, Inc.
1230 Avenue of the Americas
New York, NY 10020

First Tiller Press hardcover edition December 2020

TILLER PRESS and colophon are trademarks of Simon & Schuster, Inc.

For information about special discounts for bulk purchases, please contact
Simon & Schuster Special Sales at 1-866-506-1949 or business@simonandschuster.com.

The Simon & Schuster Speakers Bureau can bring authors to your live event.
For more information or to book an event, contact the
Simon & Schuster Speakers Bureau at 1-866-248-3049 or
visit our website at www.simonspeakers.com.

Interior design by Jennifer Chung
Rat icon by Peter van Driel/The Noun Project
Crosshair icon by Creative Stall/The Noun Project
Star icon by Ahmad H/The Noun Project
Badge icon by Joana Pereira/The Noun Project
Crown icon by corpus delicti/The Noun Project

Manufactured in the United States of America

1   3   5   7   9   10   8   6   4   2

Library of Congress Cataloging-in-Publication Data

Names: Braccia, Nick, author.
Title: Off the back of a truck : unofficial contraband for the Sopranos fan /
by Nick Braccia (and some friends of ours). | Description: First Tiller Press hardcover
edition. | New York: Tiller Press, 2020. | Includes bibliographical references. |
Identifiers: LCCN 2020009832 (print) | LCCN 2020009833 (ebook) | ISBN 9781982139063
(hardcover) | ISBN 9781982139087 (ebook) | Subjects: LCSH: Sopranos (Television
program) | Classification: LCC PN1992.77.S66 B73 2020 (print) | LCC PN1992.77.S66
(ebook) | DDC 791.45/72—dc23 | LC record available at https://lccn.loc.gov/2020009832 |
LC ebook record available at https://lccn.loc.gov/2020009833

ISBN 978-1-9821-3906-3
ISBN 978-1-9821-3908-7 (ebook)

CONTENTS

Contents

Contents

Contents

VIII

INTRODUCTION

I'll make this short and sweet, because I know you're here for *The Sopranos*, not some *paisan* tapping on his keyboard in Washington Heights. I believe *The Sopranos* is arguably the greatest television show of all time, and most certainly the greatest of my lifetime.

I produced this book so that it'd feel different from other books (and there are some great ones) that focus primarily on the show's episodes. This book isn't a guide, it's a party. *With* fuckin' ziti, so don't worry, A.J. It was conceived to feel like you're walking into an apartment filled with a collection of smart, fun fans of the show, each with their own areas of expertise and passion. Most chapters have a chorus of voices that riff on themes, argue on topics, and pontificate from a position of complete mastery of David Chase's material. You should feel permitted to bounce around within the book, to spend more time with some voices and less with others. Roam around as though you're in Tony's backyard for a BBQ. While you're here, you can do any damn thing you'd like, *capisce*? And if you disagree with us, that's fine. We like to argue and we're easy to find online, but remember, if you come, come heavy.

Thanks for stopping by.

Nick Braccia and Friends

CHAPTER I

The FAMILIES

ighty-six episodes of *The Sopranos* aired on HBO from January 10, 1999, to June 10, 2007. Across its six seasons, we meet hundreds of characters, from Salvatore "Big Pussy" Bonpensiero (Vincent Pastore) to producer Bernie Brillstein, who plays himself in one of the DiMeo crime family's executive card games. While we watch Tony Soprano (James Gandolfini) navigate his tumultuous home life, we also keep tabs on the ever-evolving dynamics within two Mafia families (New Jersey's DiMeos and New York's Lupertazzis) and their internal factions. These frequently shifting collectives are rife with betrayals, murders, reentries into society, and fresh indictments.

There's a reason why the FBI uses big thumbtack boards that they plaster with mugshots, index cards, string, and Sharpie scribbles—there's a lot of sausage to juggle! We've constructed this chapter to provide orientation (or reorientation) to the hierarchies in place at the beginning of each season as well as the new ones that emerge at season's end, once the body count is tallied and the smoke has cleared. As you read through this book, you can always flip back to this chapter for a reminder as to who works for whom and when characters get promoted or planted.

Season One:

THE DIMEO FAMILY

When the series begins, the official boss of the DiMeo crime family is its namesake, Ercole "Eckley" DiMeo. The seventy-four-year-old DiMeo is never seen on-screen; he's serving a life sentence in a Springfield, Missouri, federal penitentiary. In his absence, the acting boss is Jackie Aprile Sr. (Michael Rispoli), who suffers from terminal stomach cancer. The DiMeo family has several *caporegimes* aka capos. These are the captains who serve underneath Aprile: Tony Soprano, Tony's uncle, Junior Soprano (Dominic Chianese), Jimmy Altieri (Joseph Badalucco Jr.), Larry Barese (Tony Darrow), and Raymond Curto (George Loros). A power struggle ensues between Tony and his uncle that upends the FBI's charts and gives northern New Jersey's undertakers plenty of fresh business. We'll also briefly meet Lupertazzi underboss John "Johnny Sack" Sacrimoni (Vincent Curatola), whose New York–based organization plays a more expansive role as the series progresses.

DIMEO FAMILY (NJ)

LEGEND

Natural Death		Promoted	
Whacked		Busted	
Death by Suicide		Rat	

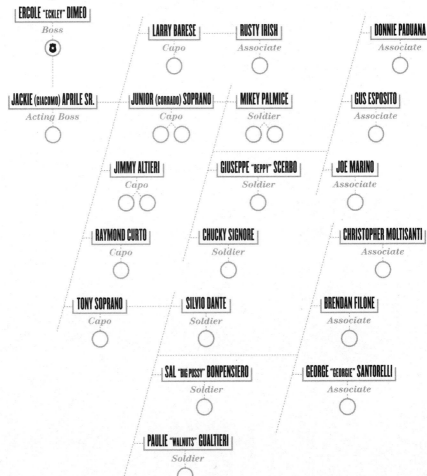

ERCOLE "ECKLEY" DIMEO
Boss

LARRY BARESE
Capo

RUSTY IRISH
Associate

DONNIE PADUANA
Associate

JACKIE (GIACOMO) APRILE SR.
Acting Boss

JUNIOR (CORRADO) SOPRANO
Capo

MIKEY PALMICE
Soldier

GUS ESPOSITO
Associate

JIMMY ALTIERI
Capo

GIUSEPPE "BEPPY" SCERBO
Soldier

JOE MARINO
Associate

RAYMOND CURTO
Capo

CHUCKY SIGNORE
Soldier

CHRISTOPHER MOLTISANTI
Associate

TONY SOPRANO
Capo

SILVIO DANTE
Soldier

BRENDAN FILONE
Associate

SAL "BIG PUSSY" BONPENSIERO
Soldier

GEORGE "GEORGIE" SANTORELLI
Associate

PAULIE "WALNUTS" GUALTIERI
Soldier

OUTSIDE ASSOCIATES

DICK BARONE
Barone Sanitation & Cartage

ARTIE BUCCO
Vesuvio

ADRIANA LA CERVA
Hostess

HESH RABKIN
Loan Shark

VIN MAKAZIAN
Newark PD

LUPERTAZZI FAMILY (NY)

JOHN "JOHNNY SACK" SACRIMONI
Underboss

DIMEO FAMILY (NJ)

LEGEND

- ▮ ········ *Natural Death*
- ✛ ········ *Whacked*
- ✖ ········ *Death by Suicide*
- ♛ ········ *Promoted*
- 🛡 ········ *Busted*
- 🐀 ········ *Rat*

*

ERCOLE "ECKLEY" DIMEO
Boss
🛡

LARRY BARESE
Capo
🛡

RUSTY IRISH
Associate
✛

DONNIE PADUANA
Associate
✛

JACKIE (GIACOMO) APRILE SR.
~~*Acting Boss*~~
▮

JUNIOR (CORRADO) SOPRANO
Acting Boss
♛ 🛡

MIKEY PALMICE
~~*Consigliere*~~
♛ ✛

GUS ESPOSITO
Associate
○

JIMMY ALTIERI
Capo
🐀 ✛

GIUSEPPE "BEPPY" SCERBO
Soldier
○

JOE MARINO
Associate
○

RAYMOND CURTO
Capo
○

CHUCKY SIGNORE
Soldier
✛

CHRISTOPHER MOLTISANTI
Associate
○

TONY SOPRANO
Actual Boss
♛

SILVIO DANTE
Consigliere
♛

BRENDAN FILONE
Associate
✛

SAL "BIG PUSSY" BONPENSIERO
Soldier
○

GEORGE "GEORGIE" SANTORELLI
Associate
○

PAULIE "WALNUTS" GUALTIERI
Soldier
○

OUTSIDE ASSOCIATES

DICK BARONE
Barone Sanitation & Cartage
○

ARTIE BUCCO
Nuovo Vesuvio
○

ADRIANA LA CERVA
Hostess
○

HESH RABKIN
Loan Shark
○

VIN MAKAZIAN
Newark PD
✖

LUPERTAZZI FAMILY (NY)

JOHN "JOHNNY SACK" SACRIMONI
Underboss
○

Season Two:

THE DIMEO FAMILY

Junior Soprano is technically boss but under house arrest, so Tony Soprano runs the family, day to day, with the help of some new players, like Bobby Baccalieri (Steve Schirripa), who is tasked with assisting Junior. Richie Aprile (David Proval), brother of the late boss, is released following a decade in prison and bristles against the new pecking order. Gigi Cestone (John Fiore) defects from Junior to work among Tony's crew, which soon includes Furio Giunta (Federico Castelluccio), a Napoletano heavy with aquiline features. There are a few new players on the lower rungs of the ladder, too. Tony's "nephew," Christopher Moltisanti (Michael Imperioli), charged with managing a boiler room, recruits two young wannabes, Matt Bevilaqua (Lillo Brancato Jr.) and Sean Gismonte (Chris Tardio). Finally, Salvatore "Big Pussy" Bonpensiero, who mysteriously disappeared at the end of Season One, returns.

02/01

" GUY WALKS INTO A PSYCHIATRIST'S OFFICE..."

DIMEO FAMILY (NJ)

Legend

🪦	Natural Death	👑	Promoted
⊕	Whacked	🛡	Busted
✕	Death by Suicide	🐀	Rat

*
ERCOLE "ECKLEY" DIMEO
Boss
🛡

JUNIOR (CORRADO) SOPRANO
Acting Boss
🛡

RICHIE APRILE
Capo

VITO SPATAFORE
Soldier

MURF LUPO
Soldier

TONY SOPRANO
Actual Boss

PHILLIP "PHILLY SPOONS" PARISI
Capo

DONALD "DONNY K." AFRANZA
Soldier

GIUSEPPE "BEPPY" SCERBO
Soldier

SILVIO DANTE
Consigliere

ALBERT "ALLY BOY" BARESE
Capo

PETER "BEANSIE" GAETA
Associate

BOBBY BACCALIERI JR.
Soldier

RAYMOND CURTO
Capo

SUNSHINE
Associate

CHRISTOPHER MOLTISANTI
Associate

PAULIE "WALNUTS" GUALTIERI
Capo
👑

PASQUALE "PATSY" PARISI
Soldier

GEORGE "GEORGIE" SANTORELLI
Associate

SAL "BIG PUSSY" BONPENSIERO
Soldier

SEAN GISMONTE
Associate

GIGI CESTONE
Soldier

MATTHEW BEVILAQUA
Associate

OUTSIDE ASSOCIATES

RONALD ZELLMAN
Newark Assemblyman

DICK BARONE
Barone Sanitation & Cartage

ARTIE BUCCO
Nuovo Vesuvio

ADRIANA LA CERVA
Hostess

HESH RABKIN
Loan Shark

DAVEY SCATINO
Ramsey Sports & Outdoor

ZUCCA FAMILY (ITA)

ANNALISA ZUCCA
Acting Boss

LUPERTAZZI FAMILY (NY)

JOHN "JOHNNY SACK" SACRIMONI
Underboss

DIMEO FAMILY (NJ)

LEGEND

⬛ ·········· *Natural Death*   ♛ ·········· *Promoted*

◈ ·········· *Whacked*   ᛟ ·········· *Busted*

✖ ·········· *Death by Suicide*   🐀 ·········· *Rat*

ERCOLE "ECKLEY" DIMEO *
Boss
ᛟ

JUNIOR (CORRADO) SOPRANO
Acting Boss
ᛟ

RICHIE APRILE
Capo
◈

MURF LUPO
Capo
♛

VITO SPATAFORE
Soldier

TONY SOPRANO
Actual Boss

PHILLIP "PHILLY SPOONS" PARISI
Capo
◈

GIUSEPPE "BEPPY" SCERBO
Soldier

DONALD "DONNY K." AFRANZA
Soldier

SILVIO DANTE
Consigliere

ALBERT "ALLY BOY" BARESE
Capo

BOBBY BACCALIERI JR.
Soldier

PETER "BEANSIE" GAETA
Associate

RAYMOND CURTO
Capo

SUNSHINE
Associate

CHRISTOPHER MOLTISANTI
Associate

PAULIE "WALNUTS" GUALTIERI
Capo

PASQUALE "PATSY" PARISI
Soldier

GEORGE "GEORGIE" SANTORELLI
Associate

SAL "BIG PUSSY" BONPENSIERO
Soldier
🐀 ◈

SEAN GISMONTE
Associate
◈

FURIO GIUNTA
Soldier

GIGI CESTONE
Soldier

MATTHEW BEVILAQUA
Associate
◈

OUTSIDE ASSOCIATES

RONALD ZELLMAN
Newark Assemblyman

DICK BARONE
Barone Sanitation & Cartage

ARTIE BUCCO
Nuovo Vesuvio

ADRIANA LA CERVA
Hostess

HESH RABKIN
Loan Shark

DAVEY SCATINO
Ramsey Sports & Outdoor

ZUCCA FAMILY (ITA)

ANNALISA ZUCCA
Acting Boss

LUPERTAZZI FAMILY (NY)

JOHN "JOHNNY SACK" SACRIMONI
Underboss

Season Three:

THE DIMEO FAMILY

Tony Soprano gets a double dose of agita. Ralph Cifaretto (Joe Pantoliano), a new face with a mercurial personality, is moving up in the family, but not fast enough for his liking. Meanwhile his late friend's son, Jackie Aprile Jr. (Jason Cerbone), requires mentorship if he's to stay out of the family business, as his father wished. Other new characters include made man Vito Spatafore (Joseph R. Gannascoli) as well as associates Eugene Pontecorvo (Robert Funaro) and Benny Fazio (Max Casella). All three will play larger roles as the series evolves. We also see considerably more of John Sacrimoni, who moves to New Jersey, as well as other Lupertazzi family members, including their boss, Carmine Lupertazzi Sr. (Tony Lip) and his malapropping son, Carmine Jr. (Ray Abruzzo).

DIMEO FAMILY (NJ)

LEGEND

🪦	Natural Death	♛	Promoted
⊕	Whacked	🔋	Busted
✖	Death by Suicide	🐀	Rat

*
ERCOLE "ECKLEY" DIMEO
Boss
🔋

JUNIOR (CORRADO) SOPRANO
Acting Boss
🔋

MURF LUPO
Capo

DONALD "DONNY K" KAFRANZA
Soldier

BOBBY BACCALIERI JR.
Soldier

TONY SOPRANO
Actual Boss

GIGI CESTONE
Capo

RALPH CIFARETTO
Soldier

GIUSEPPE "BEPPY" SCERBO
Soldier

SILVIO DANTE
Consigliere

ALBERT "ALLY BOY" BARESE
Capo

VITO SPATAFORE
Soldier

SUNSHINE
Associate

RAYMOND CURTO
Capo

DINO ZERILLI
Associate

JACKIE (GIACOMO) APRILE JR.
Associate

CARLO RENZI
Associate

PAULIE "WALNUTS" GUALTIERI
Capo

PASQUALE "PATSY" PARISI
Soldier

GEORGE "GEORGIE" SANTORELLI
Associate

CHRISTOPHER MOLTISANTI
Soldier

BENNY FAZIO
Associate

FURIO GIUNTA
Soldier

PAUL "LITTLE PAULIE" GERMANI
Associate

OUTSIDE ASSOCIATES

RONALD ZELLMAN
Newark Assemblyman

DICK BARONE
Barone Sanitation & Cartage

ARTIE BUCCO
Nuovo Vesuvio

ADRIANA LA CERVA
Hostess

HESH RABKIN
Loan Shark

GLORIA TRILLO
Globe Motors Salesperson

LUPERTAZZI FAMILY (NY)

CARMINE LUPERTAZZI SR.
Boss

JOHN "JOHNNY SACK" SACRIMONI
Underboss

CARMINE LUPERTAZZI JR.
Capo

DIMEO FAMILY (NJ)

*

ERCOLE "ECKLEY" DIMEO
Boss

Legend

🪦	Natural Death	👑	Promoted
✛	Whacked	🔒	Busted
✖	Death by Suicide	🐀	Rat

JUNIOR (CORRADO) SOPRANO
Acting Boss

MURF LUPO
Capo

DONALD "DONNY K" KAFRANZA
Soldier

BOBBY BACCALIERI JR.
Soldier

TONY SOPRANO
Actual Boss

GIGI CESTONE
Capo

RALPH CIFARETTO
Capo

GIUSEPPE "BEPPY" SCERBO
Soldier

SILVIO DANTE
Consigliere

ALBERT "ALLY BOY" BARESE
Capo

VITO SPATAFORE
Soldier

SUNSHINE
Associate

RAYMOND CURTO
Capo

DINO ZERILLI
Associate

JACKIE (GIACOMO) APRILE JR.
Associate

CARLO RENZI
Associate

PAULIE "WALNUTS" GUALTIERI
Capo

PASQUALE "PATSY" PARISI
Soldier

GEORGE "GEORGIE" SANTORELLI
Associate

CHRISTOPHER MOLTISANTI
Soldier

BENNY FAZIO
Associate

FURIO GIUNTA
Soldier

PAUL "LITTLE PAULIE" GERMANI
Associate

OUTSIDE ASSOCIATES

RONALD ZELLMAN
Newark Assemblyman

DICK BARONE
Barone Sanitation & Cartage

ARTIE BUCCO
Nuovo Vesuvio

ADRIANA LA CERVA
Hostess

HESH RABKIN
Loan Shark

GLORIA TRILLO
Globe Motors Salesperson

LUPERTAZZI FAMILY (NY)

CARMINE LUPERTAZZI SR.
Boss

JOHN "JOHNNY SACK" SACRIMONI
Underboss

CARMINE LUPERTAZZI JR.
Capo

Season Four:

THE DIMEO FAMILY

Tony's position is strong as Junior Soprano heads to trial, Bobby Baccalieri's promoted, and Paulie "Walnuts" Gualtieri (Tony Sirico) is a guest of the state in Youngstown, on a gun charge. The DiMeo and Lupertazzi families are in business together on the Newark Riverfront Esplanade, as well as in several schemes with Assemblyman Ronald Zellman (Peter Riegert). Ralph Cifaretto's insufferable behavior grates on Tony.

DIMEO FAMILY (NJ)

LEGEND

🪦 Natural Death		👑 Promoted	
⊕ Whacked		🛡 Busted	
✖ Death by Suicide		🐀 Rat	

*

ERCOLE "ECKLEY" DIMEO
Boss
🛡

JUNIOR (CORRADO) SOPRANO
Acting Boss
🛡

BOBBY BACCALIERI JR.
Capo

MURF LUPO
Soldier

DONALD "DONNY K" KAFRANZA
Soldier

TONY SOPRANO
Actual Boss

RALPH CIFARETTO
Capo

GIUSEPPE "BEPPY" SCERBO
Soldier

EUGENE PONTECORVO
Soldier

SILVIO DANTE
Consigliere

ALBERT "ALLY BOY" BARESE
Capo

VITO SPATAFORE
Soldier

CREDENZO CURTIS
Associate

RAYMOND CURTO
Capo
🐀

STANLEY JOHNSON
Associate

CARLO GERVASI
Capo

PASQUALE "PATSY" PARISI
Soldier

GEORGE "GEORGIE" SANTORELLI
Associate

PAULIE "WALNUTS" GUALTIERI
Capo
🛡

BENNY FAZIO
Soldier

PETER "PETEY BISSELL" LA ROSA
Associate

CHRISTOPHER MOLTISANTI
Acting Capo

FURIO GIUNTA
Soldier

PAUL "LITTLE PAULIE" GERMANI
Associate

OUTSIDE ASSOCIATES

RONALD ZELLMAN	DICK BARONE	ARTIE BUCCO	ADRIANA LA CERVA	HESH RABKIN	GLORIA TRILLO
Newark Assemblyman	*Barone Sanitation & Cartage*	*Nuovo Vesuvio*	*Crazy Horse Owner*	*Loan Shark*	*Globe Motors Salesperson*

LUPERTAZZI FAMILY (NY)

CARMINE LUPERTAZZI SR.	JOHN "JOHNNY SACK" SACRIMONI	CARMINE LUPERTAZZI JR.	JOE "JOEY PEEPS" PEPARELLI
Boss	*Underboss*	*Capo*	*Soldier*

DIMEO FAMILY (NJ)

Legend

- 🪦 ——— Natural Death
- ⌖ ——— Whacked
- ✖ ——— Death by Suicide
- 👑 ——— Promoted
- 🛡 ——— Busted
- 🐀 ——— Rat

*

ERCOLE "ECKLEY" DIMEO
Boss
🛡

JUNIOR (CORRADO) SOPRANO
Acting Boss

BOBBY BACCALIERI JR.
Capo

MURF LUPO
Soldier

DONALD "DONNY K" KAFRANZA
Soldier

TONY SOPRANO
Actual Boss

RALPH CIFARETTO
Capo
⌖

EUGENE PONTECORVO
Soldier

GIUSEPPE "BEPPY" SCERBO
Soldier

SILVIO DANTE
Consigliere

ALBERT "ALLY BOY" BARESE
Capo

VITO SPATAFORE
Soldier

CREDENZO CURTIS
Associate
⌖

RAYMOND CURTO
Capo
🐀

STANLEY JOHNSON
Associate
⌖

CARLO GERVASI
Capo

PASQUALE "PATSY" PARISI
Soldier

GEORGE "GEORGIE" SANTORELLI
Associate

PAULIE "WALNUTS" GUALTIERI
Capo

BENNY FAZIO
Soldier

PETER "PETEY BISSELL" LA ROSA
Associate

CHRISTOPHER MOLTISANTI
Soldier

PAUL "LITTLE PAULIE" GERMANI
Associate

OUTSIDE ASSOCIATES

RONALD ZELLMAN
Newark Assemblyman

DICK BARONE
Barone Sanitation & Cartage

ARTIE BUCCO
Nuovo Vesuvio

ADRIANA LA CERVA
Crazy Horse Owner
🐀

HESH RABKIN
Loan Shark

GLORIA TRILLO
Globe Motors Salesperson
✖

LUPERTAZZI FAMILY (NY)

CARMINE LUPERTAZZI SR.
Boss

JOHN "JOHNNY SACK" SACRIMONI
Underboss

CARMINE LUPERTAZZI JR.
Capo

JOE "JOEY PEEPS" PEPARELLI
Soldier

Season Five:

THE DIMEO AND LUPERTAZZI FAMILIES

Several high-profile New York and New Jersey guys are released from prison: old-timer Michele "Feech" La Manna (Robert Loggia), Lupertazzi capo Phil Leotardo (Frank Vincent), retired New York consigliere Angelo Garepe (Joe Santos), and Tony Soprano's cousin Tony Blundetto (Steve Buscemi). This influx of old blood creates complications for Tony, as a turf war brews between warring Lupertazzi factions in New York. The moment stability returns the Feds further complicate Tony's life when a shocking arrest aids the ascension of a vengeful Leotardo.

DIMEO FAMILY [NJ]

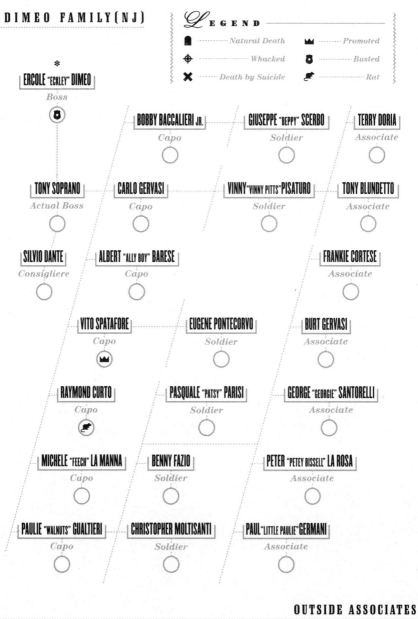

LEGEND

- 🪦 ········· Natural Death
- ⊕ ········· Whacked
- ✖ ········· Death by Suicide
- 👑 ········· Promoted
- 🛡 ········· Busted
- 🐀 ········· Rat

*
ERCOLE "ECKLEY" DIMEO
Boss
🛡

BOBBY BACCALIERI JR.
Capo

GIUSEPPE "BEPPY" SCERBO
Soldier

TERRY DORIA
Associate

TONY SOPRANO
Actual Boss

CARLO GERVASI
Capo

VINNY "VINNY PITTS" PISATURO
Soldier

TONY BLUNDETTO
Associate

SILVIO DANTE
Consigliere

ALBERT "ALLY BOY" BARESE
Capo

FRANKIE CORTESE
Associate

VITO SPATAFORE
Capo
👑

EUGENE PONTECORVO
Soldier

BURT GERVASI
Associate

RAYMOND CURTO
Capo
🐀

PASQUALE "PATSY" PARISI
Soldier

GEORGE "GEORGIE" SANTORELLI
Associate

MICHELE "FEECH" LA MANNA
Capo

BENNY FAZIO
Soldier

PETER "PETEY BISSELL" LA ROSA
Associate

PAULIE "WALNUTS" GUALTIERI
Capo

CHRISTOPHER MOLTISANTI
Soldier

PAUL "LITTLE PAULIE" GERMANI
Associate

OUTSIDE ASSOCIATES

DICK BARONE
Barone Sanitation & Cartage

ARTIE BUCCO
Nuovo Vesuvio

ADRIANA LA CERVA
Crazy Horse Owner
🐀

HESH RABKIN
Loan Shark

BRIAN CAMMARATA
Financial Adviser

DIMEO FAMILY (NJ)

LEGEND

🪦	Natural Death	👑	Promoted
⊕	Whacked	🛡	Busted
✕	Death by Suicide	🐀	Rat

ERCOLE "ECKLEY" DIMEO *
Boss
🛡

BOBBY BACCALIERI JR.
Capo

GIUSEPPE "BEPPY" SCERBO
Soldier

TERRY DORIA
Associate

TONY SOPRANO
Actual Boss

CARLO GERVASI
Capo

VINNY "VINNY PITTS" PISATURO
Soldier

TONY BLUNDETTO
Associate
⊕

SILVIO DANTE
Consigliere

ALBERT "ALLY BOY" BARESE
Capo

FRANKIE CORTESE
Associate

VITO SPATAFORE
Capo

EUGENE PONTECORVO
Soldier

BURT GERVASI
Associate

RAYMOND CURTO
Capo
🐀

PASQUALE "PATSY" PARISI
Soldier

GEORGE "GEORGIE" SANTORELLI
Associate

MICHELE "FEECH" LA MANNA
Capo
🛡

BENNY FAZIO
Soldier

PETER "PETEY BISSELL" LA ROSA
Associate

PAULIE "WALNUTS" GUALTIERI
Capo

CHRISTOPHER MOLTISANTI
Soldier

PAUL "LITTLE PAULIE" GERMANI
Associate

OUTSIDE ASSOCIATES

DICK BARONE
Barone Sanitation & Cartage

ARTIE BUCCO
Nuovo Vesuvio

ADRIANA LA CERVA
Crazy Horse Owner
🐀 ⊕

HESH RABKIN
Loan Shark

BRIAN CAMMARATA
Financial Adviser

LEGEND

🪦	Natural Death	👑	Promoted
⊕	Whacked	🛡	Busted
✖	Death by Suicide	🐀	Rat

LUPERTAZZI FAMILY (NY)

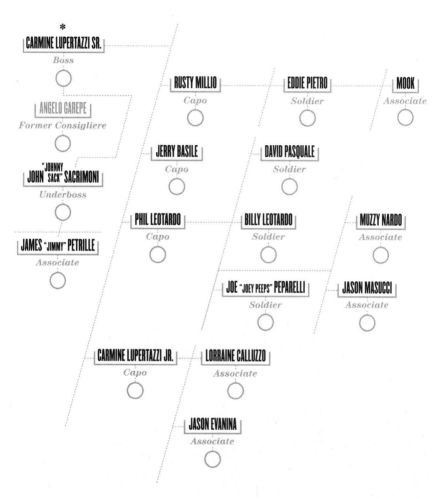

*
CARMINE LUPERTAZZI SR.
Boss
○

RUSTY MILLIO
Capo
○

EDDIE PIETRO
Soldier
○

MOOK
Associate
○

ANGELO GAREPE
Former Consigliere
○

JERRY BASILE
Capo
○

DAVID PASQUALE
Soldier
○

JOHN "JOHNNY SACK" SACRIMONI
Underboss
○

PHIL LEOTARDO
Capo
○

BILLY LEOTARDO
Soldier
○

MUZZY NARDO
Associate
○

JAMES "JIMMY" PETRILLE
Associate
○

JOE "JOEY PEEPS" PEPARELLI
Soldier
○

JASON MASUCCI
Associate
○

CARMINE LUPERTAZZI JR.
Capo
○

LORRAINE CALLUZZO
Associate
○

JASON EVANINA
Associate
○

LUPERTAZZI FAMILY (NY)

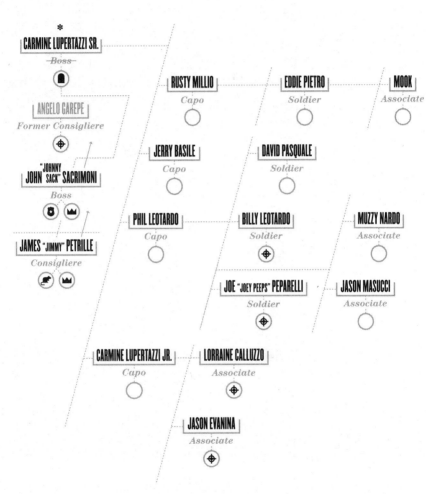

Legend

- Natural Death
- Whacked
- Death by Suicide
- Promoted
- Busted
- Rat

*
CARMINE LUPERTAZZI SR.
Boss

ANGELO GAREPE
Former Consigliere

JOHN "JOHNNY SACK" SACRIMONI
Boss

JAMES "JIMMY" PETRILLE
Consigliere

RUSTY MILLIO
Capo

JERRY BASILE
Capo

PHIL LEOTARDO
Capo

EDDIE PIETRO
Soldier

DAVID PASQUALE
Soldier

BILLY LEOTARDO
Soldier

JOE "JOEY PEEPS" PEPARELLI
Soldier

MOOK
Associate

MUZZY NARDO
Associate

JASON MASUCCI
Associate

CARMINE LUPERTAZZI JR.
Capo

LORRAINE CALLUZZO
Associate

JASON EVANINA
Associate

Season Six:

THE DIMEO AND LUPERTAZZI FAMILIES

Tony's the undisputed ruler of the roost, and his Uncle Junior, suffering from dementia, has been deemed unfit to stand trial. Bobby Baccalieri, Tony's new brother-in-law, gets a promotion to underboss, and Christopher, though no longer Tony's heir apparent, is bumped up another peg, getting to run his own crew as capo. For the Lupertazzis, John "Johnny Sack" Sacrimoni is in prison awaiting trial, which means that Phil Leotardo, still furious over the death of his brother, Billy (Chris Caldovino), is making the moves.

DIMEO FAMILY (NJ)

LEGEND

⬛	Natural Death	👑	Promoted
✛	Whacked	⬛	Busted
✖	Death by Suicide	🐀	Rat

*
ERCOLE "ECKLEY" DIMEO
Boss
🛡

TONY SOPRANO
Acting Boss

CARLO GERVASI
Capo

TERRY DORIA
Associate

SILVIO DANTE
Consigliere

BOBBY BACCALIERI JR.
Capo

BENNY FAZIO
Soldier

PERRY "MUSCLES MARINARA" ANNUNZIATA
Associate

CHRISTOPHER MOLTISANTI
Capo

BURT GERVASI
Soldier

JAMES "MURMUR" ZANCONE
Associate

VITO SPATAFORE
Capo

EUGENE PONTECORVO
Soldier

PETER "LITTLE PAULIE" GERMANI
Associate

RAYMOND CURTO
Capo
🐀

PASQUALE "PATSY" PARISI
Soldier

PETER "PETEY BISSELL" LAROSA
Associate

LARRY BARESE
Capo

WALDEN BELFIORE
Soldier

PAULIE "WALNUTS" GUALTIERI
Capo

GIUSEPPE "BEPPY" SCERBO
Soldier

GEORGE "GEORGIE" SANTORELLI
Associate

OUTSIDE ASSOCIATES

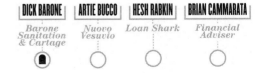

DICK BARONE
Barone Sanitation & Cartage

ARTIE BUCCO
Nuovo Vesuvio

HESH RABKIN
Loan Shark

BRIAN CAMMARATA
Financial Adviser

"MADE IN AMERICA"

DIMEO FAMILY (NJ)

LEGEND

⬤ Natural Death		♛	Promoted
✚ Whacked		🛡	Busted
✖ Death by Suicide		🐀	Rat

ERCOLE "ECKLEY" DIMEO *
Boss
🛡

TONY SOPRANO
Actual Boss
◯

CARLO GERVASI
Capo
🐀

TERRY DORIA
Associate
◯

SILVIO DANTE
Consigliere
◯

BOBBY BACCALIERI JR.
~~Underboss~~
♛ ✚

BENNY FAZIO
Soldier
◯

PERRY "MUSCLES MARINARA" ANNUNZIATA
Associate
◯

CHRISTOPHER MOLTISANTI
Capo
✚

BURT GERVASI
Soldier
✚

JAMES "MURMUR" ZANCONE
Associate
◯

VITO SPATAFORE
Capo
✚

EUGENE PONTECORVO
Soldier
✖ 🐀

PETER "LITTLE PAULIE" GERMANI
Associate
◯

RAYMOND CURTO
Capo
🐀 ⬤

PASQUALE "PATSY" PARISI
Soldier
◯

PETER "PETEY BISSELL" LAROSA
Associate
◯

LARRY BARESE
Capo
◯

WALDEN BELFIORE
Soldier
◯

PAULIE "WALNUTS" GUALTIERI
Capo
◯

GIUSEPPE "BEPPY" SCERBO
Soldier
◯

GEORGE "GEORGIE" SANTORELLI
Associate
◯

OUTSIDE ASSOCIATES

ARTIE BUCCO
Nuovo Vesuvio
◯

HESH RABKIN
Loan Shark
◯

BRIAN CAMMARATA
Financial Adviser
◯

LUPERTAZZI FAMILY (NY)

LEGEND

- 🛡 .... Natural Death
- ⊕ .... Whacked
- ✖ .... Death by Suicide
- 👑 .... Promoted
- 🛡 .... Busted
- 🐀 .... Rat

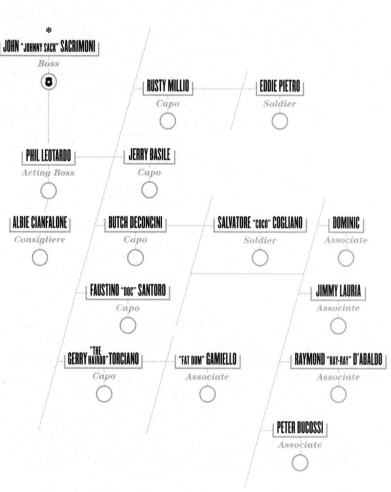

*

JOHN "JOHNNY SACK" SACRIMONI
Boss

RUSTY MILLIO
Capo

EDDIE PIETRO
Soldier

PHIL LEOTARDO
Acting Boss

JERRY BASILE
Capo

ALBIE CIANFALONE
Consigliere

BUTCH DECONCINI
Capo

SALVATORE "COCO" COGLIANO
Soldier

DOMINIC
Associate

FAUSTINO "DOC" SANTORO
Capo

JIMMY LAURIA
Associate

GERRY "THE HAIRDO" TORCIANO
Capo

"FAT DOM" GAMIELLO
Associate

RAYMOND "RAY-RAY" D'ABALDO
Associate

PETER BUCOSSI
Associate

LUPERTAZZI FAMILY (NY)

LEGEND

- Natural Death
- Whacked
- Death by Suicide
- Promoted
- Busted
- Rat

JOHN "JOHNNY SACK" SACRIMONI
Boss

RUSTY MILLIO
Capo

EDDIE PIETRO
Soldier

PHIL LEOTARDO
Boss

JERRY BASILE
Capo

ALBIE CIANFALONE
Consigliere

BUTCH DECONCINI
New Boss

SALVATORE "COCO" COGLIANO
Soldier

DOMINIC
Associate

FAUSTINO "DOC" SANTORO
Boss

JIMMY LAURIA
Associate

GERRY "THE HAIRDO" TORCIANO
Capo

"FAT DOM" GAMIELLO
Associate

RAYMOND "RAY-RAY" D'ABALDO
Associate

PETER BUCOSSI
Associate

CHAPTER II

INSPIRED CRIMES
INVESTIGATING *the*
Schemes of THE SOPRANOS

T he life of Tony Soprano (James Gandolfini) is spent at the center of a large organized crime operation in one of the wealthiest regions of the world's richest country. This means there's *a lot* to steal, so it's notable that the crimes on *The Sopranos* (excepting the murders) are almost always in the periphery. We see envelopes exchange hands, deadbeats and patsies catch beatings (or worse), but the show doesn't spend much time exploring crimes at the procedural level. There's none of the nuance or pleasure that we may enjoy in a heist movie. This isn't what the show's about, and we don't necessarily miss it, but *The Sopranos* frequently alludes to schemes that the average, law-abiding viewer might not fully understand. In this chapter, we're going to uncover and explore real-world incidents that likely inspired some of the *Sopranos* crimes and break down the mechanics of each scam.

I'll be honest: I don't have the street cred to write this chapter solo, so I've enlisted my old friend Eddie McNamara to lend a hand. We met in the mid-'90s, two tri-state area kids from blue-collar backgrounds studying abroad at an English university. Far from home, it helped to have a buddy to talk New York sports and pro wrestling and make jokes about Curtis Sliwa or references to Michael Musto's *Village Voice* column. A Brooklyn native, ex-cop, crime fiction writer, and chef, Eddie's been around the block. As part of this assignment, he pounded the pavement, looking for the truth and chatting up guys with real street experience, including Frank DiMatteo, a former organized crime associate and the acclaimed author of *The President Street Boys: Growing Up Mafia* as well as *Carmine the Snake: Carmine Persico and His Murderous Mafia Family*. Frank knows how it all goes down (his father was Larry Gallo's bodyguard) and he ran with the Genovese and DeCavalcante families (the latter being Jersey-based and the alleged inspiration for Tony Soprano's DiMeo family). Frank was a tremendous help and we appreciate his candor. His books are terrific. If you enjoy Nicholas Pileggi's work or Evan Wright's *American Desperado* (with the late Jon Roberts), or simply want an inside look at the gang that (allegedly) couldn't shoot straight, pick up one of his books for true stories of big scores, close calls, pet lions, and Liza Minnelli.

The bulk of this chapter represents the "how" of the DiMeo family's criminal rackets, but near the end, we'll shift focus to consider the "who" and "why" in the short essay "Sad Sacks, Suckers, and the Squeeze: The Victims of Tony Soprano." The series, taken as a whole, is much more concerned with the psychology of sharks and marks than the crimes themselves, so it'd be an injustice to consider Soprano's handiwork without examining the nature of the wounds inflicted.

THE CRIMES

WASTE MANAGEMENT CONSULTING —Nick Braccia
Episode 1.1, "The Sopranos"

In the first minutes of the first episode, Tony Soprano sits in the office of psychiatrist Jennifer Melfi (Lorraine Bracco). He's had a fainting spell and was referred by his family physician, Dr. Cusamano (Robert LuPone). She asks him what kind of work he's in and he responds, "Waste management consultant." For Melfi (and the audience) this is code for organized crime. In fact, there's no other W-2-providing job in the United States that's as synonymous with corruption. I'd argue that, in 2020, even Teamsters officials don't carry the same baggage as our friends in the garbage business. Has it always been this way? Not entirely.

Heather Rogers's excellent, well-researched book *Gone Tomorrow: The Hidden Life of Garbage* explains how in the '50s, Italian Americans came to control the carting industry. According to Rogers, New York City's Italian-American Mob learned by watching Jewish gangsters take over the trucking and restaurant industries. In these businesses, Jewish strongmen "infiltrated labor unions and formed corrupt professional associations." This means workers, managers, and competitors united to screw their customers via price-fixing. If there's no cheaper option for the services needed, then there's no choice but to pay—it's collusion. The Italians benefited from the Jewish mob's strategy, because "Jewish gangsters did not allow their children into the business." With no Jewish heirs apparent, the Cosa Nostra stepped in to take over these existing rackets and scale their business model—using the requisite muscle—across other industries, like garbage, by mid-century.[1]

Until the cusp of the new millennium, the carting business ran as we might assume. The Mob had "extensive control" over stops, and if a new player tried to undercut their price or otherwise attract customers, they'd catch a beating, have their trucks torched, or worse.[2]

But it didn't last forever. Returning to his first session with Melfi, Tony, ostensibly talking about his business, tells her, "Lately, I'm getting the feeling that I came in at the end." Any *Sopranos* fan can project a multitude of meanings onto the line, but it can unequivocally be applied to the Mafia's place in the tri-state area garbage business, where a great consolidation was happening. Remember, by the end of the series, Tony is essentially out of the garbage business, as Barone Sanitation & Cartage is sold out from under him to Lupertazzi family interests.

Here's how the Mob got pushed out: Rogers describes how the national garbage corporations, suffering the pangs of the national recession, mustered the extra chutzpah needed to take on the New York–area Mob. There was just too much money at stake ($1 billion to $1.5 billion annually). Once big business moved in and teamed up with the city (including Mayor Rudolph Giuliani and D.A. Robert Morgenthau) indictments dropped and the rackets were busted. Customers, sick of being "held hostage" by the Mob for as much as triple the rates of carting costs in Chicago and Philadelphia, welcomed their new corporate overlords. Unfortunately, the two main businesses that took over—Waste Management and Browning-Ferris Industries—didn't provide much relief. "Thus the criminal cartel was replaced with a two-firm oligopoly. . . . And by 2002, the city's disposal rates were up 40% from six years earlier, rivaling the inflated fees of the mafia cartel."[3] Meet the new boss, even worse than the old boss.

Since *The Sopranos* aired, the garbage business has been further corporatized and regulated, but the New Jersey Mob, ever on the hustle, has worked to adapt. A 2017 report from the New Jersey State Commission of Investigation concluded:

> Elements of New Jersey's recycling industry remain vulnerable to corruption and intrusion by criminal elements because of glaring loopholes in the State's solid-waste regulatory and oversight system, the State Commission of Investigation said in a report issued today . . . that unscrupulous operators profit by covertly dumping contaminated soil and construction debris at inappropriate and unregulated sites that now pose serious environmental and public-health threats. Masquerading as seemingly legitimate recyclers, they are able to evade any form of background vetting and licensure simply because no such requirements exist for those engaged in the business they purportedly conduct. . . . According

to sworn testimony and documentary evidence obtained by the Commission, the participants in this toxic trafficking included organized crime associates and convicted felons.[4]

It's good to hear that gangsters, not known for being progressive, have gone green.

THE HASIDIC GOON SQUAD —Nick Braccia
Episode 1.3, "Denial, Anger, Acceptance"

Growing up in the New York–New Jersey–Connecticut tri-state area, I was an Italian-American kid with plenty of exposure to Jewish culture. Hell, we had a summer membership to the local Jewish Community Center from '84 to '89. But this doesn't mean I had any understanding of the customs of Hasidim and certainly no knowledge of religious marital laws, so, like most guido goyim, I had no idea what Silvio Dante (Steven Van Zandt), Hesh Rabkin (Jerry Adler), and crew were talking about when they brought up the "get" in the opening minutes of "Denial, Anger, Acceptance."

By parsing DiMeo crime family conversations at Jackie Aprile Sr.'s (Michael Rispoli's) hospital bed and outside Satriale's Pork Store we're able to understand that a get is an important religious document that one must obtain to dissolve a marriage in Orthodox culture. But for real details, we need to dig deeper. Albert Samaha, in his 2013 *Village Voice* piece "Bad Rabbi: Tales of Extortion and Torture Depict a Divorce Broker's Brutal Grip on the Orthodox Community," describes it as follows:

> a *get*, a document without which an Orthodox Jewish marriage cannot be dissolved. The rule can be traced to the biblical Book of Deuteronomy, and its sway remains stifling: Without a *get*, a woman who remarries is considered adulterous. Any children fathered by her new husband are illegitimate under Orthodox law and prohibited from marrying within the faith.
>
> The patriarchal nature of Orthodox marriages can lead to particularly contentious divorces. With custody and alimony at stake, a man may be tempted to use his biblically granted lever-

age in negotiations: No *get* until his terms are met. Though the practice is frowned upon, it is so pervasive that there's a word for a woman whose husband refuses to grant a *get*: an *agunah*, which translates from Hebrew as "chained woman."[5]

Silvio presents a scenario to Tony, as he believes there's money to be made in exchange for using Soprano muscle to facilitate a get. Always hungry for more money, Tony ignores the advice of his Jewish friend Hesh, who warns him not to get involved—"Run!" Instead, he meets Shlomo Teittleman (*Goodfellas* veteran Chuck Low), a motel and property owner with a daughter who is the alleged victim of abuse at the hands of her husband, Ariel (Ned Eisenberg). Ariel will only grant a get in exchange for 50 percent ownership of the Teittleman motel. The real estate mogul offers Tony 25 percent if he can convince Ariel to walk away from the marriage with nothing but his life.

With the Hasidic community being insular and unlikely to involve outsiders in mitigation (Teittleman's son, Hillel [Sig Libowitz], strongly objects to enlisting Tony's assistance), it's curious that they'd approach the Mafia. We better understand their outreach when Silvio explains, "The rabbi goon squad that used to smack these husbands around to get a divorce, they've been put out of business by the D.A.'s office." As it turns out, this is mostly true. There's been a great deal of media coverage on this convergence of faith and violence. Many pieces, including Samaha's aforementioned *Voice* article and two episodes of the popular Wondery podcast *Over My Dead Body*, cover the story of a man known as "The Prodfather," Rabbi Mendel Epstein. The Brooklyn rabbi earned his nickname by using a high-voltage cattle prod as a negotiation tool to persuade husbands to provide gets and free their wives. Epstein, who authored a 1989 book titled *A Woman's Guide to the Get Process*, could be viewed as an antihero feminist fighting back against extortionists who target their own wives and in-laws, but he sounds less heroic once we learn that rates for his services ran upward of $70,000. Rabbi Robin Hood he is not.

Did Epstein's exploits influence the writers? Well, in 1996 Abraham Rubin, a victim of Epstein and his crew, received multiple electric shocks to his genitals. When Tony finally gets Ariel to agree to the get, it's because he's willing to—on the advice of Hesh—"make like a mohel and finish his bris." The weapons are different (bolt cutters vs. high voltage) and it *could* be a coincidence, but it's more likely it's a nod to Epstein's strategic and anatomically focused approach. What's amazing is that "Denial, Anger, Acceptance" aired in 1999 but this "goon squad" that Silvio suggests is out of business actually continued to operate through the aughts. While Epstein and several members of his squad finally went down following a 2013 undercover sting (they were hit with lengthy prison terms, a dime for the Prodfather), it's likely similar services can be found in the Hasidic community today. If at any point they're permanently closed for business, they can always outsource to the Italians.

HIJACKING AND ROBBERY —Eddie McNamara
Episodes 1.2, "46 Long," and 1.10, "A Hit Is a Hit"

In Season One's "A Hit Is a Hit," Tony gives Dr. Cusamano a box of Cuban Montecristo cigars as a thank-you gift for referring him to Dr. Melfi. Cusamano, a straight arrow whom Tony gives the unfortunate nickname Cooz, adopts a working-class patois: "I bet these motherfuckers were hard to come by, huh, Ton?" and Tony plays along, responding that "they fell off a truck." If you're reading this book, you probably know what it really means when something "falls off a truck." But you might not realize how often it happens, or that it's likely you've handled some hot goods without knowing it. For example, how did it come to be that my grandmother had a kitchen full of fine china, high-end crystal, and mismatched tableware that appeared to be from five different restaurants? Or consider my grandfather, a Brooklyn dockworker, who had a closet full of suits and coats worthy of a film noir villain. They'd laugh and explain it away by saying that those things fell off the back of a truck, and even as a kid I wasn't buying it. Author and retired Mafia associate Frank DiMatteo tells us, "In the old days, nobody bought nothing." Most working-class immigrants, like my grandparents, received stolen goods that were due to be delivered to the buyer but got *cough, cough* *rerouted* just like the shipments of DVD players and Italian suits Christopher Moltisanti (Michael Imperioli) and Brendan Filone (Anthony DeSando) steal from Comley Trucking.

DiMatteo explains that most guys who do stickups are part of a crew: "Not too many independent guys are doing that. The crew has somebody inside that would tip you off on what's coming in. *If* there's something that you know you can move, you would go rob it. Stick up the truck, rob the warehouse. You would take it in and you would give it to a fence. If it's fenceable he would pay you less than half on the price of the stuff. Then he would sit there and hustle it out. If it's diamonds and jewelry, you usually don't sit on that because you're not going to sell a diamond ring in the middle of the street. If it's liquor you can move ten cases here, five cases there. It's all on what products you can sit on and what you have to fence off completely."

Hijacking shipments is one of the purest, oldest rackets in the game and the margins are unbeatable. Next time you're visiting with your grandparents, take a look around and try and figure out what fell off the back of a truck.

RECORD ROYALTIES FRAUD IN THE MUSIC INDUSTRY —Eddie McNamara
Episode 1.10, "A Hit Is a Hit"

Herman "Hesh" Rabkin: "I wrote six gold records."
Tony: "No, a couple of black kids wrote six gold records. You owned the company. You gave yourself a cowriting credit."
—*Episode 1.6, "Pax Soprana"*

Hesh Rabkin's character on *The Sopranos* was (not so) loosely based on real-life Mob associate and record mogul Morris Levy. Levy was a tough Jewish kid from the Bronx who, at thirteen, knocked out his seventy-five-year-old homeroom teacher,[6] ran away from home, took to the street life, and started working as a nightclub photographer. Eventually, he opened the legendary Birdland jazz club in New York City. In 1956, he founded Roulette Records, one of the most successful and influential independent rock 'n' roll labels. But deep down inside, despite all the gold records, all the music clubs, and literally owning the phrase "rock 'n' roll,"[7] what Mo Levy really was was a gangster.

Levy was so cutthroat that in 1975 he managed to shake down John

Lennon of all people, forcing him to record a corny oldies album for him, called, you guessed it, *Rock 'N' Roll*.[8] Naturally, the album featured three songs to which Morris Levy owned the rights. Lennon recorded it rather than battle Levy over whether the Beatles' "Come Together" ripped off an obscure Chuck Berry tune released on Roulette Records—*that's* power. But it gets even crazier. Lennon handed rough tapes of the recording session over to Levy (big mistake) and the gangster scooped the Beatle, releasing the recordings early as a mail-order special called *Roots*.[9] Months later Capitol released the real version of *Rock 'N' Roll*.

The more famous copyright case involved Levy's cowriting credit on the African-American and Puerto Rican group Frankie Lymon & The Teenagers' worldwide mega hit, "Why Do Fools Fall in Love." The song was written and recorded in November of 1955 for a label called Gee Records, and—once it became a hit—Morris Levy somehow showed up as a cowriter even though he didn't meet the group until months later.[10] He had bought the record company and added his name as a songwriter. Despite selling millions and millions of records, The Teenagers were only paid $1,000[11] by Levy and when they went to see him to get their money, they were told by one of his goons/music execs, "Don't come down here anymore or I'll have to kill you or hurt you."[12] It took thirty-six years and a court of law for the group to get their songwriting credits and $4 million owed to them from the Levy estate, only to have the ruling overturned on appeal a couple of years later.

Sixties rock idol and Roulette hitmaker Tommy James (of Tommy James & The Shondells) details his wild ride with Levy in his book, *Me, the Mob, and the Music*. James revealed that Roulette Records was a front for the Genovese crime family and he was told to leave New York for his own safety. He also shares how Mo Levy stiffed him out of $30 million in songwriting money (making the $400,000 Hesh owed Little Jimmy seem like pennies in comparison). James quipped that at Roulette Records royalties were only paid out when they were "owed to that famous songwriter Morris Levy."[13]

The law eventually caught up to Levy and his Genovese associates. The FBI alleged that Levy was operating as a front man for Vincent "The Chin" Gigante and running a major East Coast heroin distribution network via his record label.[14] Those charges didn't stick, but the Feds got him on extortion and brought the Mob's infiltration of the music industry to light. Levy sold his record label for $55 million and his retail operation for $40.5 million. In one final "fuck you" to the law, Levy died at his horse farm (remind you of any *Sopranos* character?) while out on bail without serving a single day of his ten-year sentence.

PUMP-AND-DUMP IPO SCANDALS —Eddie McNamara
Episode 2.1, "Guy Walks into a Psychiatrist's Office . . ."

When a gangster wants to make money in the stock market, he doesn't buy shares and hope for the best like us schmucks. He's got an army of aggressive salespeople working the phones, driving the price of his stock up (the pump) until he's ready to sell (the dump) at the expense of the poor suckers who thought they were buying a legitimate investment. This is perfectly illustrated in *The Sopranos'* second season, during which Christopher fraudulently obtains his Series 7 license and runs a boiler room focused around a stock in a fugazi company called Webistics. This is a case of life imitating art imitating life, as A. J. Discala (former husband of Meadow Soprano actress Jamie-Lynn Sigler) got pinched by the Feds in 2014 for running a pump-and-dump scam that defrauded unsuspecting investors out of millions of dollars. The stock market might not be the first place that comes to mind when you think of Mob business, but it probably should be. Wall Street has access to all the money in the world and is just a stone's throw away from the Mafia hotbeds of Brooklyn, Staten Island, and Hoboken, New Jersey. It's a marriage made in heaven.

So, how does it work? Funny you should ask. In 1999, when Season One of *The Sopranos* aired, I was a twenty-one-year-old recent college graduate sending out résumés looking for a job. I was having no luck. My old man was waking me up at 6 a.m. to force me to into sheetrock slavery, a sadistic ritual that continued until I found a job. Desperate, I'm skimming the local Bay Ridge paper and come across a "Train to Be a Stockbroker" ad in the classifieds. Seemed legit. And they didn't care about a résumé—just come down tomorrow and start working. I was in. Halfway to Gordon Gecko, I thought. The firm had a WASPy name like Cadbury and

Worthington, and their office was in the heart of the financial district. The receptionist was one of the most beautiful women I had ever seen, and the secretaries were all solid runners-up. The honeymoon lasted as long as I would have with one of the girls: about eleven seconds. The first red flag came when I noticed that half the guys working the phones looked nothing like Michael Douglas or Charlie Sheen (okay, maybe a couple looked like Charlie Sheen). Instead, they reminded me of the knockaround neighborhood guys I grew up with in South Brooklyn. I get a warm welcome from the boss (think Chazz Palminteri, if he fell asleep in a tanning bed). He takes me to his office and starts gassing me up: "You're a sharp kid. You're not nervous. We're gonna get you the books for the Series 7, and we're gonna make a lot of money together."

He hands me the day's script and the second red flag waves right in my face. We're in the middle of the tech bubble and they're pushing a Hungarian telecom company that's going to be the "American Online" of Europe, he says. He keeps adding the "n" to "America Online" and reads the script as if he's Andrew Dice Clay. It took all the strength in the world to keep a straight face. I mention that it's AOL or America Online without the "n," and he brushes that off, explaining that the people I'm going to be cold-calling only care about two things: me sounding like a guy who knows what he's talking about—so turn the Brooklyn accent up—and them feeling like they're getting on the ground floor of something big.

Minutes later I'm sitting in the middle of a phone bank with a list of qualified leads (people with at least $500,000 in the market), passing myself off as a stockbroker when I'm literally just a guy off the street. I'm cold-calling people, using their first names like I know them, and executing verbal judo to get around uncooperative secretaries. I'm saying shit to rich people like "We made a lot of money together the last time we did business" (we didn't) and "Do me a favor—if you're content to sit on your hands and let this opportunity pass you by, just hand the phone to one of the other doctors in your practice. Make sure it's somebody you like so you're not jealous of the car in their parking spot six months from now." Amazingly, this crap actually works sometimes. If the person is interested in talking again or wants more information (I had exactly zero information besides what was in my imagination), I'd bring my lead—now a prospect since they bit—to one of the brokers. It's up to the broker to close the deal, and when he does, he gets a commission, and I get a little something as a finder's fee.

The firm likely owned a HUGE number of shares in the company they were touting (Mr. Meadow Soprano's company owned three million shares of something called CodeSmart at 2.3 cents a share). Companies like these didn't qualify to trade on the New York Stock Exchange or NASDAQ. They were usually garbage IPOs underwritten by the firm, or penny stocks traded on the OTC or pink sheets. The boiler-room salespeople did the grunt work and primed the pump. The real pumping of the stock (that's just a nice way of saying "price manipulation") begins when the marketers started spamming online investment forums with hot tips and posts creating buzz. Faxes are (still!) sent out with exciting news about the stock. The firm buys more and more shares, and since it's a micro-cap company, this drives the price up significantly. Investors see a penny stock on the rise, and they start buying. Others are influenced by the hot tip panning out and jump in, and the stock price inflates even higher. Now the firm might do a 2-for-1 split, giving them six million shares.

Everybody loves a winner and as the price soars, even more investors buy in, chasing the get-rich-quick rush like a crackhead with a scratch-off ticket. The firm uses hype to sell more and more shares to hungry investors. And then one day, when the price is high enough, the firm cashes out and dumps their shares. Let's go back to the case of Mr. Discala: CodeSmart traded as high as $6.94 per share in 2013, almost 6,000 percent more than he paid for his shares. Then his company dumped all their shares and left the marks holding the bag when the price took a dive.

If the company is mobbed up, good luck finding somebody to complain to about losing your life savings. They vacate the office, change their firm's name, and set up shop elsewhere. The unaffiliated brokers will find themselves in debt or badly in need of some start-up capital because they lost their shirts, too. To get back into business they'll find a friendly mobster willing to lend them money and set them up. Once the broker is in debt to a wiseguy, he's threatened with physical or financial ruin if he doesn't do what he's told, and the cycle repeats. He sells their front-man shares of the next target stock for pennies, sets up his own boiler room, and gets people to pump up the stock, and the gangsters get out once the price hits the ceiling. Again the poor slob investors lose everything.

The Ben Affleck/Vin Diesel film *Boiler Room* gave a fairly accurate representation of turn-of-the-millennium boiler rooms. Martin Scorsese's *The Wolf of Wall Street* shows the aggressive sales tactics used to pump up penny stocks through the *Goodfellas* lens. Matt Taibbi wrote a great piece for *Rolling Stone* about the scams, and Gary Weiss's book *Born to Steal: When the Mafia Hit Wall Street* is worth picking up if you want to know everything the Mafia taught the white-collar crooks.

UNDERGROUND POKER GAMES AND CASINOS
—Nick Braccia and Eddie McNamara
Episodes 2.6, "The Happy Wanderer," and 5.11, "The Test Dream"

In *The Sopranos'* second season, we get a look at the underground "Executive" Poker Game—an all-night, high-stakes card game for high rollers, like the urologist Dr. Fried (Lewis J. Stadlen) and Frank Sinatra Jr. (who plays himself and takes Sambuca in his coffee). Later in the series, we'll see NFL legend Lawerence Taylor and Van Halen lead singer David Lee Roth participate. In Season Five, Soprano cousin Tony Blundetto (Steve Buscemi) is named boss of a full illegal casino operation with table games like craps and roulette. Gangsters love gambling: doing it, running it, and providing loans for it at unfavorable terms.

That said, it's not always the case that underground casinos and card games are Mafia-affiliated. "It's free enterprise, man," DiMatteo says. "You and me could get a card game going, and that's nobody's business." As long as you've got a pile of money for start-up and operational costs, you're free to give it a shot. They follow a familiar business and organizational structure, like you'd see in Atlantic City or Las Vegas. However, if neighborhood gangsters were to hear of such an operation, there's a good chance somebody might come down and try to muscle in on you. It's no secret that the Mob is not a fan of competition. "If you open a craps game in a neighborhood that already has craps games going, then you have a problem," DiMatteo says. "That you can't do."

Mob-run or Mob-affiliated casinos have the advantage of protection—unless Jackie Aprile Jr. (Jason Cerbone) and friends hit it—and a proven track record, so some type of relationship should be expected. "Generally, it's the boss's money and his soldiers work for him. They get paid like employees," says DiMatteo. "If an outside individual brings the game to the family, it's his to run (minus a percentage, of course). You're either an employee or your kicking up to the boss."

If you live in or near a city and are looking for action, just (quietly) ask the right people and you're likely to find a game for you no further away than the nearest laundromat. As always, we recommend you play only with what you can afford to lose, lest you end up sleeping in a tent or in the ground beneath it.

BOOKIES, SPORTS BETTING, AND THE NUMBERS RACKET
—Nick Braccia and Eddie McNamara
Episode 3.13, "Army of One"

Sportsbooks are a substantial part of the DiMeo family business, with area bookies connected or kicking up to the family. The importance of this revenue stream is made clear in "Army of One" when there is a pitiable turnout for young Jackie Jr.'s wake, which happens right before the Super Bowl. Rosalie Aprile (Sharon Angela), the grieving, heavily medicated mother of the deceased, turns to Tony Soprano and remarks, "Look at this place. Two days before the Super Bowl and nobody shows up. . . . What happened, Ton? Vegas moving the line?" You're probably related to or know somebody who has a bookie (even if you don't know it), but do you really have an idea how the business of bookmaking operates?

The bookie is not just the person who takes bets; he's the one responsible for having the cash to pay out winners. "The bookie is the money guy," says DiMatteo. "He's the banker." A bookie's cost of operations depends on whether he's working for a family or not. "If he's part of a crew, he has to kick up to the boss," he says. "If he's independent, he doesn't pay anybody, but he has to be able to back himself up." (Both financially and otherwise.)

With sports betting, bookies use the "juice" to maintain an advantage over bettors. DiMatteo calls the juice a "tax on losing" built into every bet, ranging from 10 percent to 25 percent. If you make a hundred dollar bet that the Mets will beat the Braves, and the Mets lose (because that's what the Mets do), you gotta pay the bookie $110–$125, depending on the juice. The bookie always sets the odds so he makes money, regardless of the outcome of a game.

The oddsmaker (who can be a different guy, but not always) is part statistician and part behavioral scientist. His mathematical model is as sophisticated as anything you'll see at the trading desk of a Wall Street firm. Like Robert De Niro's Sam "Ace" Rothstein in *Casino* (based on Frank "Lefty" Rosenthal), he has to know everything there is to know about the teams, the players competing, and their various aches and pains, plus high-level math equations to determine the probability of the outcome. He weighs that with the money line.

The money line works like this: Say you want to bet $100 on the Yankees (–130) against the Red Sox (+120). Those numbers are the "line." Since the Yankees are the favorite, you'd need to bet $130 to clear $100. If the Yankees win, but you only bet $100, the bookie pays you $77 plus your original $100 for a total of $177. If you'd bet on the underdog Sox, you'd have won $120 on that $100; the bookie would hand you a total of $220.

In this situation, the bookie is looking for action and a lot of bets— he's only concerned with the juice and making a profit. Oddsmakers also closely monitor the legal odds set by Vegas sportsbooks. If a lot of money comes in on the Yankees, they'll "move the line" and change the odds to rebalance them. The bettor, however, is paid based on what the line was when he placed his bet.

In many parts of the country (and the world), sports betting goes hand in hand with the numbers game—also known as Policy, the Italian lottery, and Bolita—which is still prevalent in poor and working-class neighborhoods. "Numbers" is the original version of the lottery. It was such a good idea that the New Jersey government stole it from the Mob in the late '70s, legalized it, hired toothy young ladies to call out numbers on TV, and has made billions of dollars to pad its budgets.

"The bookie takes numbers from people on the street, and if the number comes in, he pays 500 to 1. That means you get $500 for every dollar you bet," DiMatteo says. There are no smiling TV models, but the winning numbers can be found in the newspaper, hidden in the horserace results (usually the last digit in the listed total amount bet in three races—say the third, fifth, and seventh races at Aqueduct).

How does the bookie make money? He pockets the difference between the money he takes in minus the money paid out to winners and 25 percent split for the runners (gofers who actually take the money and the numbers from the customers). The odds of picking a winning number are 1,000 to 1, so the house advantage ensures that the bookie makes out like a bandit. Since the advent of legal, state-sponsored lotteries, Mafia bookies have transitioned away from numbers games and embraced sports betting. Latino organizations and independent operators run the majority of similar Bolita games out of barbershops, beauty salons, and bodegas. But as long as there's a bookie somewhere paying out 500 to 1 with no questions asked, no taxes taken out, and no government eyes on you as you pick up your winnings, there's money to be made (and lost) with the numbers.

We're never presented with evidence that the DiMeo family bookies are running a Policy game in 1999, but we can be certain that Tony's father, Johnny Boy, Junior Soprano, Dickie Moltisanti, and the many saints of Newark had their hand in it in the '60s.

ORGANIZING A BUST-OUT —Nick Braccia
Episode 2.10, "Bust-Out"

The bust-out is a Mob special and a gangster movie staple. Remember the Mob takeover of Bamboo Lounge in Martin Scorsese's *Goodfellas*? That was a bust-out. When Tony Soprano's childhood friend Davey Scatino (Robert Patrick), owner of Ramsey Sports and Outdoors, gets in over his head with gambling debts to both Tony and Richie Aprile (David Proval), Tony sets up shop in the sporting goods store and uses its good line of credit to order as much merchandise as possible. But Tony's not going into the bats, balls, and bass fishing business. He has every intention of selling the acquired goods on the street at a discount and zero intention of paying the store's creditors. Ultimately, Tony's actions force Scatino's business into bankruptcy.

Since the show aired, fraudsters have evolved the bust-out, taking advantage of globalization and the digital economy to perpetrate crimes against banks rather than people. Today, criminals create fake businesses on paper solely for the purpose of busting them out. And they don't have to move all that pesky merch. Instead of finding a patsy like Davey Scatino and driving up charges against his business, they create their own businesses. Phony businesses, fake credit cards, REAL MONEY. In 2013 the United States Justice Department and the (where else?) New Jersey State District Attorney uncovered a $200 million bust-out scam (with at least twenty-two co-conspirators!) and handed out indictments and prison sentences like they were candy. This particular case, Daniel Gross of *The Daily Beast* explained, "involved the creation of 80 fake companies, more than 1,800 mailing addresses, 7,000 false identities, and 25,000 credit cards."[15]

This was an extremely intricate scheme designed to circumvent all the checks and balances set up by banks and regulatory bodies eager to maximize their own profits while maintaining security. The broad strokes of the enterprise included using fake identities and identification to get a credit profile on the books. After obtaining credit cards for these identities, they'd use the cards at fake and real businesses, making modest purchases that they would pay back. This would improve the credit rating and extend the limit on the cards. When high limits were achieved, they'd max out the cards on goods, cash, and gold, with no intention of paying off the balance. Rinse. Repeat. They'd also set up sham companies with merchant accounts so that they could run up phony charges on the credit cards, and then the fake companies would get real money from the banks. When a fake card or business was sniffed out, they'd just remove it from circulation and keep the scam going.[16] It's a lot bigger than ordering a few picnic coolers and airline tickets against the credit line of a family-owned sporting goods store.

NO-SHOW JOBS AND BID-RIGGING —Eddie McNamara
Episode 2.11, "House Arrest"

"If it wasn't for the Mob, there would be no union," says DiMatteo. "In the old days, all the owners were paying cops or gangsters to bust up guys fighting for workers' rights. The boys would come down and they'd help the owners for money. But then they realized, whoa, what are we doing? If *we* organized them, *we'll* make the money."

In "House Arrest," Episode 11 of Season Two, the perfectly named Mob lawyer Neil Mink (David Margulies) informs Tony that the FBI is looking at him for the murder of Matthew Bevilaqua (Lillo Brancato Jr.) and he should spend more time at his on-the-books "waste management consultant" job at Barone Sanitation rather than ogling strippers and sipping scotch at the Bada Bing. So why does Tony need to pretend to be Johnny Lunchpail, and why do so many of the guys in his crew sit around construction sites on beach chairs? The answer is very simple: everybody needs health insurance and wiseguys are no different. Their line of work doesn't exactly come with a generous benefits package, so the best way to get the guys covered without having to buy an out-of-pocket health care plan like Joe Schmuck is to get a union job. And the best kind of union job is one where you don't have to actually show up for work. No-show jobs might not even pay much, but they get the gangster on the books and show legitimate employment and a source of income, should the Feds come a-knockin'. They also provide the benefit of setting his (actual) family up with the benefits that come with a union job.

Just because you have a no-show job doesn't mean there isn't work to do. Union construction is by far the gold standard of the industry. The members earn a solid middle-class living, work under very safe conditions, and do the best-quality construction in the business. But even a legit enterprise could use a little help from their friends when it comes to actually winning the bid for the job. DiMatteo tells us, "A gringo doesn't know what the bids are. If you got an inside guy who knows what everybody bid, and you know that the lowest bid is $4 million, you come in below, with something reasonable like $3.8. You get the contract. It's who you know, man. If I was a legitimate guy, fuck, I would pay a ton of money to know what that bid is to get that job, they're lucrative." Winning the game is a hell of a lot easier when you've rigged it.

PHONE CARD SCAMS —Nick Braccia
Episode 2.13, "Funhouse"

I'd love to know how David Chase and cowriter Todd A. Kessler put together the plot of "Funhouse." Which idea came first? 1) the alleged food poisoning that fuels Tony's fever dreams; 2) the big-mouth fish motif; or 3) the phone card scam. Regardless, it all comes together beautifully and gives us a look at a new scheme that'll put a fat envelope in everybody's pocket on a weekly basis.

While most DiMeo and Lupertazzi scams cross multiple episodes (airbags) or even seasons (the Esplanade), the phone card angle dramatizes how the crews are always on the make and looking to earn. Career crooks aren't lazy; they love the hustle, especially a fresh one. Early in the episode, a man named Sundeep (Ajay Mehta) brings Tony and Sal "Big Pussy" Bonpensiero (Vincent Pastore) in on an opportunity in the fraudulent phone card racket. While they meet at an Indian restaurant over whole fish and other delicious-looking fare, The Rolling Stones' "Thru and Thru" plays on the soundtrack. Keith Richards sings: *We're waiting on a call from you.* As is often the case on the show, the lyrics are rich with irony, as the phone cards they're slinging aren't going to help anybody reach out and touch someone.

Here's how Bonpensiero describes the logistics in one of the only scheme breakdowns laid out on the show:

> Telephone calling cards. You find a front man, who can get you a line of credit. You buy a couple of million units of calling time from a carrier. You become Acme Telephone Card Company. You're now in the business of selling prepaid calling cards. . . . You sell thousands of these cards to the greedy pricks, cards at a cut rate. But you bought the bulk time on credit, remember? The carrier gets stiffed. He cuts off the service to the cardholders, but you've already sold all your cards.

How accurate is his spiel? Not bad. In early 1997, Selwyn Raab, the acclaimed investigative journalist and author of the exhaustive *Five Families: The Rise, Decline, and Resurgence of America's Most Powerful Mafia Empires*, wrote an article for the *New York Times* that included phone card scams as one of several major new Mafia revenue plays. The idea is that these new schemes would help make up for losses in their traditional rackets, like bid-rigging and labor extortion. Raab wrote, "The new Mafia focus is primarily on multimillion-dollar frauds in three lucrative businesses: health insurance, prepaid telephone cards and small Wall Street brokerage houses, according to law enforcement experts on organized crime." It's notable that all three endeavors factor into *Sopranos* plotlines during the show's first two seasons. With respect to the phone card mechanics, Raab's anonymous sources describe the details of the scheme a little differently than Bonpensiero, but much of his explanation could be paraphrasing this very article:

> An agent, who spoke on the condition of anonymity because the matter was still under investigation, said that each card supplied by the Gambinos was typically sold for $20 in calls, but that most cards became worthless after $2 or $3 in calls because they had not been programmed for the listed amounts.
>
> The agent said that Gambino gangsters "ripped off millions in small amounts from thousands of customers who bought semi-worthless cards." The telephone carriers that handled the calls also lost money, he said, "because they made the deal almost entirely on credit to the phony distribution company, which never passed along the money for the calls that were actually made with the cards."[17]

Sadly, the phone card scam is Tony and Sal's last job together. By the end of "Funhouse," their connection is permanently severed and Bonpensiero is unable to come to the phone.

HOUSING AND URBAN DEVELOPMENT CORRUPTION
—Nick Braccia
Episode 4.7, "Watching Too Much Television"

Of all the DiMeo family schemes—and there are some doozies—the exploitation of the U.S. Department of Housing and Urban Development is the one that hurts the most. The gangsters' conspirators—Newark's East Ward assemblyman Ronald Zellman (Peter Riegert) and his friend, community leader and nonprofit executive Maurice Tiffen (Vondie Curtis-Hall)—are exactly the people who are meant to be serving the public. Activists in the '60s, their cynicism (and lifestyles) have made them susceptible to offers from Tony and Ralph Cifaretto (Joe Pantoliano). When they gather to plot in the sauna of a Russian spa, it doesn't feel like we're in New Jersey any longer. These are the last days of Rome.

Originally, Tony gets the idea to scam HUD from Carmela Soprano's (Edie Falco's) cousin and financial planner, Brian Cammarata (Matthew Del Negro). Sitting at breakfast after the "Welcome Home" party for Paulie Gualtieri (Tony Sirico), Brian explains:

> We worked one summer for this not-for-profit housing group. . . . You ever heard of HUD? . . . HUD was set up in part to help minorities and low-income families become homeowners. As long as the Feds are guaranteeing the home mortgage, the banks figure what the hell, they'll loan the money. You get a front man to buy houses in some crummy neighborhood. Talkin' about some real shitboxes. Maybe they're worth like 100 grand a piece. Next you tie up with some nonprofit organization says they intend to buy these houses from your stooge . . .

The conversation trails off, but we can put together the rest. Once the stooge (in their case, the poker-playing urologist Dr. Fried) buys up property, the nonprofit (Maurice Tiffen) steps in to have the properties assessed by a crooked appraiser who vastly inflates their value. It's this new cost that's brought to HUD, and subsequently the bank, by the nonprofit, which is going to buy them at the new, higher price. And with a letter of endorsement from Assemblyman Zellman, nobody's going to sniff around. Nothing happens with the houses, the conspirators slice up the dough, and the project slides into "dissolution" while the federal government is on the hook to the bank. In a roundabout way, Zellman and Tiffen *do* end up sticking it to The Man—like they planned to in college—but the only people they really help are themselves.

Like most of the vile crimes committed by Tony and friends, this one is ripped from reality. HUD was pillaged by corruption throughout the '90s, but a 2001 *New York Times* article by Alan Feuer is the story most contemporaneous to *The Sopranos*. It covered the indictment of a Lucchese soldier, Ray Argentina, and several co-conspirators for mortgage fraud in Brooklyn, upstate New York, and Long Island. It's a serpentine scheme, but closely parallels the opportunity Cammarata outlines:

> [Federal prosecutors] said at least seven businesses, from an appraisal company to a mortgage lending concern, were involved, and they added that Mr. Argentina's crew somehow got fraudulent loans that were insured by the Department of Housing and Urban Development.
>
> The indictment charges that in July 1999, for example, Michael Palmieri, a real estate appraiser approved by Housing and Urban Development, prepared bogus appraisals to get financing to buy a property at 625 Franklin Avenue in Brooklyn.[18]

There's still corruption in HUD today, though maybe not as brazen as the initiatives in the early aughts. In 2019, former HUD employees from Virginia and Hawaii were indicted for their part in real estate scams.

AIRBAG SCAMS —Nick Braccia
Episode 5.2, "Rat Pack"

To help his cousin Tony Blundetto get back on his feet following a lengthy prison stint, Tony Soprano offers him point position on an airbag scam. Writer Matthew Weiner didn't have to look very far for inspiration for this plot point: in 1998, federal and local officials shut down a ring that spanned New York, New Jersey, and New England and brought in $1.5 million by charging consumers (and insurance companies) top dollar for what they believed were factory airbags, "certified as new and direct from a manufacturer." The bust was covered by Robert D. McFadden for the *New York Times*.[19] To summarize: over 5,500 hundred airbags were stolen over a three-year period. And these crews got *good*. They hit one Long Island car dealership and nabbed sixty airbags from cars on the lot in an hour—consider the manpower and skills required to break into cars and remove airbags at the rate of one per minute. The ringleader, Maurizio Percan, operating out of the Bronx and Long Island, would give thieves $100–$200 per airbag and either install them in cars serviced in his own Bronx body shop (for up to $2,500) or distribute them across the country (orders were taken from all fifty states) for a few hundred dollars of profit. This mail-order component was the majority of the business, as it netted approximately $100–$200 profit per order for Percan with little labor—just small ads in trade magazines and a toll-free phone number. How much these nationwide dealers marked up the costs to improve their margin we'll never know, but I'd suspect that Percan's own price tag of $2,500 isn't far off the mark.

The ring was taken down by an elaborate sting with undercovers posing as thieves and customers. When Percan was busted, he was on his honeymoon in Kauai. It's not in McFadden's report, but we'd bet when they slapped the cuffs on, he felt a little deflated.

While this story dates back prior to *The Sopranos'* premiere, airbag scams are still a moneymaker. In 2019, Frank DiMatteo told us, "Airbags are very expensive. You take them out of a car and you sell them to a shop. People blow their airbags and they're very expensive. I think up to $2,000 a pop or better." Want to be safe? If you need a new airbag, take it to the dealership. We can't say it's guaranteed legit, but it's better than Willets Point.

POINT SHAVING —Eddie McNamara
Episode 5.2, "Rat Pack"

In "Rat Pack" Junior Soprano (Dominic Chianese) thanks Manhattan Mafia kingpin Carmine Lupertazzi (Tony Lip) for inventing point shaving with "CCNY versus Kentucky, 1951. Nobody beat the spread. I bought myself a black Fleetwood." The Mafia's ability to control the CCNY (City College of New York) team with bribes on their way to NIT (National Invitation Tournament) and NCAA championships in '51 was one of the most legendary sports-fixing scandals,[20] but it was far from the only one. As the sports axiom goes, "If you ain't cheating, you ain't trying."

Have you ever watched a sporting event and thought to yourself, "This is so ridiculous, it can't possibly be on the level"? Chances are your gut feeling was right and you were watching some sort of fix, dive, or manipulation of the outcome. Illegal sports betting in the United States is a $150-billion-a-year industry and, with respect to Mr. Hyman Roth of Miami, that's not only bigger than U.S. Steel; it's seventy-five times bigger than U.S. Steel. As long as there's money to be made, cheating and sports will be linked together. Some sports fans experience a Santa-isn't-real type of feeling when their favorite athletes are caught shooting steroids and blood doping to gain an advantage on the playing field. Considering that wiseguys have 150 billion reasons to mess with the integrity and honor of sports, how could you ever trust that the game or fight you bought a ticket to is legit? If this sounds like some crazy conspiracy-theory talk to you, open your paper to the sports section and check out the betting lines and point spreads. If you can't legally gamble on sports in your state, why the hell is the local paper publishing that? You know why.

The relationship between the Mob and the world of sports isn't exactly a secret. Eliot Asinof's classic 1963 book *Eight Men Out* tells the story of how Arnold Rothstein and a syndicate of gamblers were able to pull off "the most gigantic sporting swindle in the history of America" by paying eight members of the heavily favored Chicago White Sox to lose the 1919 World Series. Hall of Fame boxers like Jake LaMotta (*Raging Bull*) and Sonny Liston (*The Devil and Sonny Liston*) took famous dives on behalf of their Cosa Nostra benefactors.

In 1978, a couple of guys you may have heard of—Henry Hill and Jimmy "The Gent" Burke—recruited some players from the Boston College basketball team into a multi-game point-shaving scam. The players were broke college students, who were playing for free while making their universities, coaches, and gamblers rich. If financial incentive and righteous indignation weren't enough to motivate them to "play ball" the way the gangsters wanted them to, legend has it that Hill reminded them that "you can't play basketball with broken hands." The scam was brilliant in its simplicity. For example, if Boston College were 15-point underdogs to UCLA, the connected guys bet against BC, and all the players had to do was make sure they lost by more than 15 points. Throw a couple of bricks, create a bunch of turnovers, let the other guy get the rebound, and the job is done without anybody being the wiser. The scam went along fine until BC player Ernie Cobb scored 8 points in the last minute of a game against Holy Cross, costing the Mob (especially Burke) a small fortune. Shortly after, Henry

Hill turned state's evidence and testified against Jimmy Burke and the Lucchese family about every crime under the sun, from the Lufthansa heist to the point-shaving fix. An ESPN *30 for 30* documentary called "Playing for the Mob" explores this matter further. Henry Hill even spilled the beans to *Sports Illustrated* in February 1981 with his article "How I Put the Fix In."[21]

Having players on board is great, but a corrupt referee in your pocket is even better. Fans almost expect officials to blow calls and make mistakes, so who's going to notice when a shady referee is secretly dictating the game with what looks like run-of-the-mill ineptitude? Tim Donaghy was an NBA referee for thirteen seasons (1994 to 2007: this type of thing isn't a relic of the Mob's glory days); he was also a gambling addict who bet tens of thousands of dollars a game and found himself in the hole to low-level gangsters for God knows how much. To work off his debt, Donaghy gave tips on basketball games to James Battista for $2,000 a pop, and this Battista guy made so much money using Donaghy's info that he bumped his pay up to five grand for a winning tip. The FBI eventually crashed the party. Donaghy alluded to a much larger network of NBA executives collaborating with referees to favor playoff teams who drew big television ratings and ticket sales. According to the defendant, league officials leaned on dirty refs to manipulate scores by not calling technical fouls on star players and ensuring that easy baskets from free throws went to the right team. Of course, the NBA denied his accusations and the commissioner even dropped some gangster talk, calling him a "singing, cooperating witness."

Next time you see an oddball interception or a 7–1 favorite MMA fighter basically putting himself into a submission to lose, ask yourself if it was just a simple mistake, or are guys like Junior Soprano going to buy new Caddys?

CIGARETTE SMUGGLING —Eddie McNamara
Episode 5.5, "Irregular Around the Margins"

Smuggling cartons of cigarettes is an organized crime staple, as much a part of their twentieth- (and twenty-first-) century diet as Sunday gravy. In "Irregular Around the Margins," the writers needed to get Christopher out of town so Tony and Adriana La Cerva (Drea de Matteo) would be alone.

Sending the full-time murderer and fledgling movie producer on an overnight trip to North Carolina for a haul of smokes was the perfect—and most realistic—move.

Cigarette smuggling has always been a Mob cash cow, but it might be the only *Sopranos* racket that's become more lucrative since the series ended. Today, New York state's cigarette taxes are ridiculously high—the highest in the country at $4.35 per pack, not counting an additional local New York City tax of $1.50. (Contrast that with North Carolina's tax of $0.45 per pack and it makes a lot of sense that Moltisanti had to pack his bag and head for tobacco country. And in 2004, when the episode aired, they were taxed even less.) Unsurprisingly, the illegal cigarette trade in New York has increased by 59 percent since 2006. Even the most upstanding citizen knows that $13 for a pack of cigarettes is a rip-off.

DiMatteo says, "It's big business right now. You buy them for $50 a carton, which is five bucks a pack, then you sell them up here for nine bucks a pack, you make $40 a carton." It doesn't sound like a major payday until you factor in the quantities—you're moving them by the truckload. And you can't beat the risk/reward ratio. Sure, you're taking a chance driving across state lines, but "it's not like murder or drugs or anything like that." It's a class E or D felony (A is the highest), which means you're unlikely to see jail time unless you've got a bunch of priors.

THE LOAN SHARK —Eddie McNamara
Episode 6.16, "Chasing It"

Throughout the series, there are countless references to loansharking, the "shy" business (short for shylock), and paying the "vig," or interest. This ancient business and its practices are central to the plot of "Chasing It" and the dissolution of the friendship between Tony and Hesh Rabkin. Tony hits a string of bad luck and borrows $200,000 from his loan shark friend to cover his losses. He takes his time paying him back and, when Hesh grumbles a bit about the lack of repayment, a passive-aggressive tit-for-tat over the vig ensues. It escalates to the point where it's hard to believe the men were ever truly friends. Loansharking is still big, big business, and for many, these crooks may seem less criminal than predatory payday loan companies. We wanted to get a sense for how it works on the street, so we talked to Frank DiMatteo.

Let's say you get a hot stock tip but you have no cash, and the bank laughs in your face. If you borrow a grand from a loan shark, what happens after he gives you the money? "Say you have to pay the vig at five points—that's $50 a week until you pay off the whole $1,000," DiMatteo says.

Now, let's say the stock tanks and you can't pay him back. Does the guy start muscling you like in the movies? Don't kiss your kneecaps good-bye just yet. From a wiseguy's perspective, "you wait as long as you can because you don't want to hurt nobody for money," DiMatteo says. The reasoning is more pragmatic than pacifist. "It's a last resort to hit anybody. If you do, nine times out of ten, you're not going to get your money or they'll run to the law. If they get hit, it's because you know you're not gonna get the money anyway."

No industry standard exists for kicking up to the boss in the shy business. For example, in Season One, Hesh only needs to kick up 2 percent to Junior, and he still complains until Tony helps him lower it to 1.5 percent. Later in the series, the underlings in the Sopranos crew need to kick up to Tony, and the percentage varies according to whether they compiled the book of debt and debtors themselves, bought the book from someone else, or were just handed the book and told to take care of it by the boss. As in any other business, the more risk you take, the more reward you can earn—and the more you're taxed, too.

WIRE ROOMS —Nick Braccia
Episode 6.12, "Kaisha"

After virulent homophobe Phil Leotardo (Frank Vincent) murders Vito Spatafore (Joseph R. Gannascoli) for his homosexuality, Tony wants payback. Vito, after all, was a made man in Tony's crew, and if anybody was going to murder him (as Tony had planned) it would be on *his* orders. Rather than start a bloodbath (which happens a few episodes later), Tony decides to hit Phil where it hurts—his wallet—by blowing up his Sheepshead Bay wire room.

So what's a wire room and why would this matter to Phil? A wire room is the central nervous system of an illegal gambling operation. Today, "wire room" may as well be synonymous with "internet offshore gambling hub," but we could write an entire book on that history, which parallels the advent of telecommunications. It's only a little hyperbolic to suggest that as soon as Samuel Morse finished tapping his first code, an off-track gambler pushed him out of the way so he could play the ponies. It's likely that, in 2006, when the episode "Kaisha" aired, a wire room would be filled with computers, hard drives, and paper records (remember this is before cloud storage!) to process and detail all the action across the Lupertazzi family sports gambling business. Without these records, bookies can't collect. Losing bettors can get off scot-free, and winners who go unpaid can take their business elsewhere. It's upheaval. Imagine if your bank's computers went down and they had no backup. That's what happens when you blow up a wire room in 2006.

Even though today's wire rooms are offshore and distributed, raids still go down. In the summer of 2019, cops took down a gambling headquarters in Astoria, Queens (where men took bets, collected money, and managed payouts), connected to a digital wire room in Costa Rica.[22]

It's important to remember that, for the first half of the century, telegraph wires were *the* way gambling operations scaled their business. This was ended by JFK and RFK's 1961 Interstate Wire Act, which states:

> Whoever being engaged in the business of betting or wagering knowingly uses a wire communication facility for the transmission in interstate or foreign commerce of bets or wagers or information assisting in the placing of bets or wagers on any sporting event or contest, or for the transmission of a wire communication which entitles the recipient to receive money or credit as a result of bets or wagers, or for information assisting in the placing of bets or wagers, shall be fined under this title or imprisoned not more than two years, or both.[23]

The president and his attorney general brother didn't exactly endear themselves to the Chicago Mob (the Outfit) that had worked to win Illinois for Joe Kennedy's war-hero kid. The Wire Act and other anti-gambling, anti-

Mob legislation crippled the illegal gambling industry. A 1962 *Sports Illustrated* article titled "The Bookies Close Up Shop"[24] speaks to its impact: a "bitter Vegas bettor says, 'They lost in Laos, they lost in Cuba, they lost in East Berlin, but they sure are giving the gamblers a beating.'" Gambling was down, but not out. Evolving beyond the seedy OTBs and onto myriad mobile and digital platforms today, "global sports betting market capitalization is estimated at 250 billion dollars."[25]

CREDIT CARD FRAUD AND TERRORISM —Eddie McNamara
Episode 6.6, "Live Free or Die"

> **Tony**: Let me ask you somethin'. Those, uh, two Arabs. With the credit cards, Fazool or whatever his name is—
> **Christopher:** Yeah?
> **Tony:** You think there's a chance they could be, uh, I don't know, al-Qaedas, somethin' like that?

The very real shadow of paranoia and fear of terrorism in the post-9/11 world extended everywhere—even the Bada Bing. Beginning with Season Four, the establishing shots of the Twin Towers were removed from the show's opening credits, and, as expected, the crew's distrust of outsiders grew. When Christopher's associates, Ahmed (Taleb Adlah) and Muhammad (Donnie Keshawarz), mirror the behavior of some of the 9/11 terrorists (drinking alcohol, conspicuously hanging around the strip club), Tony definitely raises an eyebrow. To his point, their motivations extended beyond lap dances and bottom-shelf booze—they need Christopher's help buying TEC-9s and stolen credit cards.

Agent Harris (Matt Servitto), newly appointed to the Terrorist Task Force, visits Tony at home to inquire about Middle Eastern men and suspicious shipments to Port Newark. Tony's first instinct is never to rat to the Feds, but then Harris goes right for his weak spot—he brings up how Meadow has to drive through the tunnels that connect New Jersey with New York City every day for college. When she becomes a potential target, Tony finally seems to consider the gravity of being even marginally involved with terrorists.

It's common knowledge that terrorism is funded by state sponsors and through bogus charities, but most people don't grasp how stolen credit card numbers keep terrorists in business. Buying stolen credit cards (or numbers that are then turned into cards) is necessary in the world of international terror because you can't just hand a would-be terrorist wads of cash and send him about his mission. It's much easier to slip him a plastic card, and it attracts far less attention.

In real life, money for al-Qaeda fuckery is provided by men like cell phone business owner Nuradin Abdi. He pled guilty to providing stolen credit card numbers to a man who bought gear for al-Qaeda to carry out attacks on the Brooklyn Bridge and a shopping mall in Columbus, Ohio. (The plans were thwarted when one member of the terror cell ratted.) Plus, they need propaganda, and they use websites to target recruits, get their jihadi message out, and show off beheading videos. To cover their tracks, they use credit card numbers bought on the black market or stolen from gambling sites. Much like the Irish Republican Army, these cells blur the lines between terrorist group and criminal syndicate—robbing banks, smuggling cigarettes, counterfeiting money, running protection rackets, kidnapping for ransom, killing for hire, blowing up businesses for insurance money, and running massive credit card frauds. The Mob wrote the book on this. Safe to say, if the Mob is running a scam, so are terrorists.

When Tony sees Ahmed and Muhammad dressed in traditional Muslim garb outside the Bing, he begins to get even more suspicious and confronts Christopher about his gun-nut pals. Christopher defends them, but Tony's not convinced. Eventually, Tony has a sit-down at Satriale's with Agent Harris and provides information against them. Does Tony do it because it's the right thing, or does he help because Harris would write him a 5K letter that would take his cooperation into account if he were ever taken down? The same question could be asked about the American Mafia "protecting" the New York waterfront from Nazi sabotage during World War II; legend has it that Lucky Luciano paved the way for the Allied invasion of Sicily in return for deportation back to Sicily (without serving a prison term). The Mob plays both sides of the coin when it comes to terror, providing weapons to terrorists and providing information to the Feds. It all comes down to money, even why the FBI never brings down Tony Soprano. Post-9/11, most FBI resources were funneled away from organized crime and into antiterrorism.

SAD SACKS, SUCKERS, AND THE SQUEEZE:
THE VICTIMS OF TONY SOPRANO
—Nick Braccia

There are no crimes without victims. And there are no gangsters without patsies to exploit or indebted civilians to juice, whether for information, favors, or interest on the principal. When Tony Soprano's high school friend Davey Scatino, bankrupt and broken by gambling debts to Tony, whines, "You told me not to get in the game. Why'd you let me do it?" Tony explains, "It's my nature. The frog and the scorpion, you know?" But Tony's misappropriating the fable. In the story, the scorpion sacrifices its own life so it can kill the frog. Tony *isn't* like the scorpion when he bankrupts Davey and preys on others. He uses his cunning to assess each person's weaknesses so that he can profit the most with the least amount of guilt and personal risk. He's a master of transactional and moral arithmetic with an innate ability to size up and squeeze value from people, especially the desperate and the damned. David Chase and his writing team shape these victims as fully drawn characters to be portrayed by master actors who induce both our disgust and our sympathy. When we see the human source of Tony's income—how his sausage is made—we understand the cost.

In the very first episode, Chase expresses Tony's symbiotic relationship to his victims in his brief interaction with Alex Mahaffey (Michael Gaston), an insurance adjuster with gambling debts. Later in Season One we meet corrupt cop Vin Makazian (John Heard) and, in Season Two, the aforementioned Scatino, a sporting-goods store owner, who are pushed to suicide and madness by choices Tony enables. If Tony's a kind of vampire who feeds off these and other victims, then his childhood friend, the chef Artie Bucco (John Ventimiglia), is in his thrall; Artie idolizes Tony, even as the Mob boss feeds from his veins (or at least his restaurant). Tony's practice certainly runs in the family blood—just watch any scene with his sister Janice (Aida Turturro)—but it's also learned by others through the behavior he models, as we see when Carmela Soprano applies strong-arm tactics on Robert Wegler (David Strathairn) to get A.J.'s (Robert Iler) grade bumped up. Since the Sopranos are representative of aspects of society, consumerism, and corporate culture, Chase makes sure to spread the predatory behavior around, so we see shakedowns and scams abound, from schools to nonprofits to the church. Still, it's Tony who is the master. This is, after all, his "bread and butter."

THE DICE ROLLERS

David Chase illustrates the codependent relationship between Tony and his victims eight minutes into the very first episode. In "The Sopranos," when Tony and Christopher spot insurance adjuster Mahaffey, they're ecstatic. He's a degenerate gambler who owes the loan shark Hesh Rabkin a lot of dough and they need to remind him of his debts. As they administer his beating, the soundtrack song plays like a doo-wop haiku for Tony's relationship with these self-destructive men: Dion DiMucci sings, "I wonder why, I love you like I do/Is it because I think you love me, too?" Mahaffey's appearance in "The Sopranos" is brief (he's a precursor: our victim zero), and while his situation is played for laughs, it introduces the absurd, dark, and ultimately tragic dynamic Tony has with his marks throughout the series. As Dion's lyrics suggest, these victims do love Tony and all he peddles: vice, fantasy, the hope of escape. Even death. Like Season Three's Gloria Trillo (Annabella Sciorra), some are moths to the flame, with existential pain so unbearable they seek the surest way to snuff it out. Suicide by wop.

Detective Makazian isn't hapless like Mahaffey. He's a man deep in anguish, but he knows his role and the stakes. He and Tony go through the motions in their debtor-and-indebted relationship—they have no pretenses—and Makazian understands that his worst enemy is the one he sees in the mirror. In fewer than ten scenes over four episodes, we get a strong sense of Makazian's internal decay and self-disgust. He laments his existence ("Bustin' whores and junkies, plus it's a super huge thrill to pay two alimonies on a $40,000-a-year income") and bemoans his bad luck ("By the time I get to take the sergeant's exam, the pay scale is frozen by law"). Tony doesn't hide his repugnance at the perpetually disheveled Makazian. He throws a crinkled bill at him, telling him to "go buy an iron." This cop is so thoroughly corrupt, the rot seeps through his body, even into his clothes.

Makazian doesn't humor the idea of any path back to respectability.

He's too far gone. He places bets when he's already in deep. "That'll solve all your problems," Tony jokes. And he lashes out in futile anger, as when he brutally beats Dr. Melfi's date, Randall (Mark Blum), during a contrived traffic stop. By the time we've met Makazian, he's got stage 4 cancer, and, as John "Johnny Sack" Sacrimoni (Vincent Curatola) later teaches us, there's no stage 5.

His suicide isn't a direct result of his debts. He kills himself because he loses his only safe harbor: the brothel run by Debbie (Karen Sillas), a clean, quiet mansion with hot water, good whiskey, and a madam who mothers him. In one of Heard's remarkable scenes, he shares with Tony a story of his childhood about how he'd hide under the bed "until everything was normal" when his alcoholic father beat his mother. The brothel is this grown man's "under the bed," and when he loses it, he loses his last pleasure in living. Stuck in traffic, waiting to jump off a New Jersey bridge, his screams convey how intolerable he finds each moment. He's burning alive, and only a lethal dive into water can extinguish the flames.

Vin Makazian may be indebted to Tony through gambling, but we get the sense that it's just one of his many vices, any of which could lead to his destruction. Davey Scatino is very specifically a compulsive gambler, and he works Tony just as much as Tony works him. A seasoned, resourceful addict, Scatino sneaks, simpers, and waxes poetic about the high school glory days with Tony—whatever he needs to do to get past the guard of a man who generally likes to keep his civilian friends out of his line of fire. But Tony's no fool. He does the math and, if Scatino insists, Tony can accommodate his wagers. He's given him fair warning and, if worse comes to worst, he can make money by taking Davey's livelihood *and* avoid the guilt of having to hurt or kill his old football buddy. Tony's not the type to think too much after the bet has been made, but we get a much deeper understanding of Scatino, who, with a similar scene count to Makazian, shows us all the hunger, hope, shame, and anger a gambling addict experiences. We see a brief lucky streak, his terrible losses, the subsequent denial, and his rage and his hopelessness that build to a near suicide. And while his addiction (and debts) eat away at him, it couldn't be more rote for Tony, who has been "busting guys out" for years. It comes so easily to him that Davey's woe barely registers. "When this is over, you're free to go!" a frustrated

Tony explains. Scatino doesn't understand that he's getting the *nice* version of the bust-out. If Richie Aprile, to whom he also owes thousands, were running the show, Scatino would be turtle food below Paterson Great Falls.

Makazian and Scatino have a commonality aside from being into Tony for big bucks. Like Makazian, Davey longs for a safe space, similar to the cop's brothel. One night, Tony finds him sleeping in a tent on his showroom floor. "It's easier than going home," he explains. Both gamblers are trying to escape their lives, to escape themselves. Neither has a happy ending. While Scatino's fate isn't as grim as Makazian's, he leaves his family in shambles and heads out West to be a ranch hand in close proximity to Vegas. But his fantasy is short-lived. We learn later that he's in a mental institution. Tony's able to rationalize it all away: "A grown man made a wager. He lost! He made another one. He lost again!" The cop and the store owner were well on their way to self-destruction, though Tony's happy to speed up the process for a reasonable rate.

A TASTE FOR THE LIFE

These gamblers could be cautionary tales for Tony's best friend, Nuovo Vesuvio proprietor and head chef Artie Bucco, a man who aspires to the wiseguy lifestyle but doesn't possess any of the requisite chutzpah or stomach for cruelty. Artie's a wannabe and a soft mark, but he's also the closest thing Tony has to a brother. Tony's predatory nature and Artie's gangster fantasies make for a turbulent friendship, but it's one of Soprano's only relationships that isn't completely transactional. Over the show's six seasons, Artie's character arc is one of the most satisfying as he struggles to reconcile his contradictions, and he often provides Tony opportunities to display his usually obscured humanity.

Early in the series, we see how much Artie envies Tony's magnetism, the easy way Tony sates his appetites, and what he thinks is Tony's control over his emotions. His sharp, shrewd wife, Charmaine (Kathrine Narducci), is a knockout—Artie's scored way out of his league—but this doesn't stop him from coveting every gangster moll and overseas import who takes up the hostess role at his restaurant. It's all part of his hidden desire to live like one of the knockaround guys who populate the Nuovo Vesuvio bar. And while he's impressionable—in Season One's "Boca," he joins his murderous friends in calling for the head of a soccer coach who commits statutory rape—he can also inspire Tony to acts of decency. He shows his mettle in a confrontation with Tony at the Bing, where he gets in his friend's face and convinces him to spare the coach's life. Artie's intervention allows Tony to feel like he's done the right thing, for once. Tony doesn't even know how to process this emotion, so he gets blotto and takes pills before confessing to Carmela, "I didn't hurt nobody." But this kind of fortitude isn't the norm for Artie. He spends much of the series placating Tony as his pal runs up his endless tab or lusting around the Bada Bing rather than being home with his family. "It's funny, 'cause guys like me, we get drunk and stare," he laments in Season Six's "Luxury Lounge," contrasting himself with Tony, who can (and does) sleep with any of the dancers he desires.

When Artie metaphorically tries on Tony's leather jacket and operates his own loan business, it goes as badly as one might expect. The doe-eyed chef is the perfect rube for the Armagnac scheme by Jean-Philippe (Jean-Hugues Anglade), especially once the Frenchman's gorgeous sister, Elodi (Murielle Arden), gets him on the hook. When Tony, who backed the loan, tells Artie to "get his arms around this thing," Artie practices his tough talk in the mirror. Unfortunately, Artie cooks better than he fights. He gets his ass kicked, loses the money, and, like Makazian and Scatino before him, turns to suicide. It's Tony who saves his life, but Artie, embarrassed, lays out the complicated truth: "You saw this whole thing, didn't you? You can see twenty moves down the road. I don't blame you. I envy you. It's like an instinct. Your mind goes through all the permutations at like internet speed. . . . 'Worst case scenario, I eat for free.'" Artie's assessment—not the frog and the scorpion fable—reflects the truth about Tony, and it pains Tony that Artie, a person he loves, sees his nature so clearly. Artie's clarity begets a troubling question: Can Tony be a real friend when the whole world is his mark?

Artie's gangster fantasies and weakness will cost him his marriage for a period and nearly his business, but, with Charmaine's love and Tony's brute honesty, he's finally able to straighten out. One of Tony's goons, Benny Fazio (Max Casella), persuades the restaurant's Albanian hostess, Martina (Manuela Feris), to distract the flirtatious Artie and steal customer credit card numbers, further imperiling his already staggered business. Wounded

Artie confronts and beats Benny, who later burns Artie's hand in a pot of boiling sauce. With Tony's protection, he survives this trial and earns some scars, having fought for his pride and his restaurant. Tony rewards him for it. He gives Artie a selfless and honest appraisal: he should get back in the kitchen and ditch the overfriendly front-of-house banter. (A restaurant review once mentioned his "convivial" manner, and it went to his head.)

Artie's character arc ends in triumph when he rediscovers his identity in his grandfather's old recipe notebook. For the first time in the series, we get the sense that he's most at home when he's in the restaurant's kitchen. He's got his special place, the one that Makazian and Scatino desired but never found. In fact, it's always been there, but he was too enamored with his pal's gangster lifestyle to realize it. Sautéing that delicious-looking rabbit, Artie Bucco finally understands that he's a very lucky man and, at long last, nobody's patsy.

CHAPTER III

The Craft of
THE SOPRANOS

There are great and influential television shows that aired before *The Sopranos*, programs where all the aspects of filmmaking artistry (writing, acting, editing, cinematography, music, costume design, location, set design, etc.) converged to form a perfect dramatic or comic vision. Still, the level of craft employed by David Chase and his team over eight years and eighty-six episodes is a remarkable and lasting achievement. The scenes may come off naturally, but the actors are clear that every word was scripted, each scene carefully designed. This was not a freewheeling production where ad-libbing actors dropped "gabagools" at will. *The Sopranos* has many scenes that required complex setups and are extremely cinematic—think of the killings of Joe "Joey Peeps" Peparelli (Joe Maruzzo) and, later, Billy Leotardo (Chris Caldovino) by Tony Blundetto (Steve Buscemi). I view the show as novelistic: the balance of every scene hinges on a careful arrangement of elements, as precise as a paragraph by John Updike or Philip Roth, or a conversation written by George V. Higgins.

For this chapter, a collection of experts has contributed essays and assessments that speak to the level of craftsmanship brought to the show— how every perfectly executed detail contributes to a fully realized world that feels organic and true, not overstylized. Holy Cross professor Steve Vineberg, author of *Method Actors: Three Generations of an American Acting Style*, examines the show's key performances in his essay "Method Acting and *The Sopranos*." Mark Dellelo, who teaches filmmaking at Brandeis University, shares his thoughts on editing and cinematography in

The Sopranos, then partners with Boston musician Andy Cambria to generate a *Sopranos* Top Forty: a look at how soundtrack choices are made for thematic resonance and, more often than not, irony. Cookbook author Eddie McNamara writes about the show's use of food and even provides a recipe, then Eddie and I combine forces to pick the ten best food moments on *The Sopranos*. Next, fashion and beauty expert Meirav Devash covers how the show's costumes work and offers up tips on how to achieve FBI Agent Deborah Ciccerone-Waldrup's (Lola Glaudini's) undercover "Danielle from Whippany" look.

Toward the end of the chapter is a trio of interviews. First, I sit down with Dr. Jonathan Hastings, a Dartmouth-Hitchcock health system psychiatrist, for a conversation on the use and theme of psychotherapy on the show, including, but not exclusive to the interactions between Tony Soprano (James Gandolfini) and Dr. Jennifer Melfi (Lorraine Bracco). Then, I connect with Professor Fred Gardaphé, Distinguished Professor of English and Italian American Studies at Queens College, CUNY and the John D. Calandra Italian American Institute to chat about Italian-American culture, masculinity, and language, as presented on the show. Finally, after a full day at SopranosCon at the Meadowlands, I tour Jersey locations from the show with film producer Heather Buckley to get her take on her home state, the importance of setting, and what it means to be "Jersey."

METHOD ACTING AND *THE SOPRANOS*
—Steve Vineberg

Francis Ford Coppola changed the face of the gangster genre forever in *The Godfather* and *The Godfather, Part II* when he threw away the stereotypes that had inhabited gangster movies since the early talkies. In the most memorable ones, like *Little Caesar, The Public Enemy,* and Howard Hawks's *Scarface,* the charisma of the stars (Edward G. Robinson, Jimmy Cagney, Paul Muni) infused the characters with dynamic force but not exactly emotional resonance; the combination of the inbred flashy stylization of the genre, the boldfaced, stripped-down story lines, and the moralistic subtext kept audiences at a firm distance. Coppola replaced this approach with a narrative as complex as a nineteenth-century novel's and psychologically realistic characters who bore no significant resemblance to the types audiences had been looking at on the screen for the previous four decades, and his amazing assembly of actors—prizing emotional veracity over showmanship—helped him do it. These two movies, released two and a half years apart in 1972 and 1974, are, among their other achievements, the most staggering display of American Method acting in the history of motion pictures.

Nearly thirty years later, the HBO series *The Sopranos* finds a different path into the genre. David Chase returns to the conventions that Coppola overturned. We recognize Tony Soprano, his crew, and his adversaries as latter-day versions of the figures in studio-era gangster pictures, but the key male performers—James Gandolfini as Tony, Michael Imperioli as his cousin and protégé Christopher Moltisanti (whom he likes to refer to as his nephew), and Dominic Chianese as Corrado, or Junior, the brother of Tony's dead father and sometime puppet head of the Soprano "family"—dig underneath the stereotypes on which their characters are constructed. So do two of the key female performers, Nancy Marchand as Tony's mother, Livia, and Drea de Matteo as Adriana La Cerva, Christopher's live-in girlfriend. What Edie Falco brings to the drama as Tony's wife, Carmela, is the most original character development in the series.

Whereas in the *Godfather* pictures the surprise for us is that Vito and Michael Corleone have any generic link to their cinematic antecedents, in *The Sopranos* the surprise is that characters whose cinematic legacy is transparent can have so much going on inside them. And again, it's their Stanislavskian commitment to emotional truth that allows the actors to reveal it all. The other major female character in the show, Dr. Jennifer Melfi (played by Lorraine Bracco), who spends six years as Tony's psychiatrist, can't be discussed in gangster-movie terms; his decision to seek therapy for panic attacks and depression is the weird comic premise of the series, which is presumably the reason Chase holds on to it long after it's ceased to make dramatic sense. After the first season the interactions in Melfi's office are only useful in bringing out new colors in Tony, and thus in Gandolfini's performance (and, for the brief time when Carmela comes along to her husband's sessions, in Falco's).

THE MALE CHARACTERS, ESPECIALLY TONY

In a sense, *The Sopranos* divides the old-style alpha-male movie gangster, as Robert Warshow described him in his classic essay "The Gangster as Tragic Hero," into three characters, each representing a different generation. Tony is the sociopath, what Warshow calls the professional hurter of people, arrogant, defiant, and imperiled (Warshow would say doomed) by his own success. Junior is the peacock, flamboyant and obsessed with, even paranoid about, how others see him. Christopher is the ambitious young hotshot, the one who plays with fire (he moves from cocaine to heroin) and gets burned. This setup works with the ensemble ideal of Method acting to ground the drama in the relationships among the characters, which was always of secondary importance in the early-talkie gangster films, where most of the supporting actors don't stick in the memory. Here we're continually being reminded of how Tony views each of the other two men, highly changeable perspectives as he either feels close to his uncle and his young cousin or feels betrayed by them, and on the flip side, as they feel favored or undervalued by him. The intricate tangle of these relationships, where love and hate, comfort and jealousy, are in a constant push-pull tension, gives rise to some of the most extraordinary and ambiguous moments in the three performances: when Tony asks Junior, "Don't you love me?"

and Junior is turned away so his nephew can't see the tears he's fighting; and when Junior shoots him; when Christopher, certain that Tony has slept with Adriana (he hasn't, but he considered it), draws down on him; and when Tony suffocates him as he lies in the car he wrecked on the highway under the influence of drugs.

Chianese's acting is inflected with a bruised old-world grace; he's like a cross between two of the most unusual supporting performances in *The Godfather, Part II*, that of the Method playwright Michael V. Gazzo as Frankie Pentangeli and that of the iconic Method acting teacher Lee Strasberg as Hyman Roth. And Imperioli, whose work on the series has been, I think, underappreciated, is a little like James Dean and the very young, open-faced Paul Newman.

But, of course, it's Gandolfini we have to focus on. His portrait of Tony may begin with a great joke: that this man, immense in every way, on the cusp of becoming boss of the New Jersey Mob, is twisted into so many knots by the influence of his gangster father, his guilt over the incarceration of his cousin and best friend Tony Blundetto (Steve Buscemi), and especially his emotional abandonment by his joyless, unloving mother that he winds up in a shrink's office. But though the actor draws on deep resources of charm and is an accomplished comedian whose grin is reminiscent of Oliver Hardy's, it's not a comic performance. It's often playful, though Tony's notion of play is usually dark, like that of a cat with a mouse. He's mostly ironic rather than funny, treating most of the people he deals with and often even those he loves as if he were looking down on them from a superior perch, an attitude that often seesaws without warning into fits of terrifying fury and—for those he doesn't love—violence, some of it incomprehensible (like his attacks on the harmless, none-too-bright manager of Bada Bing, the strip club where he transacts most of his business). When the situation calls for him to perpetrate or order violence on those he loves, like Salvatore "Big Pussy" Bonpensiero (Vincent Pastore), who he figures out has been talking to the FBI, it tears him apart.

Tony's immensity is in his physical size and strength, as well as in the size of his personality; when a panic attack knocks him on his ass, or when Junior's gunshot puts him in a coma, we're struck (and moved) by the unexpected draining away of that physical prowess. We all know that greed, along with power, is the main motivator of Mob crime, but no one before Gandolfini has ever given such a detailed and broad account of all the ways in which covetousness operates for a man like this. It's not just that he demands his "taste" of every theft or scam that transpires in his jurisdiction, accepting it without thanks like a medieval lord pocketing his share of the produce of his lands. It's also that in his appreciation of his creature comforts, he's voracious. He's almost always eating something; it's a credit to the subtlety and freshness of Gandolfini's acting that he plays the scenes where Tony enjoys his food so that he doesn't come across as merely gluttonous or, like his associate and eventual brother-in-law, Bobby Baccalieri (Steve Schirripa), the victim of an unmanageable appetite. He loves good wine: in one episode, he and Christopher liberate some stolen cases of red when they come across a motorcycle gang preparing to transport it, and he knocks back several bottles. And his sexual desire is insatiable, though it almost costs him his marriage. Carmela, who has put up with his philandering for years, finally gets disgusted when he goes to bed with his aging uncle's one-legged Russian nurse, Svetlana Kirilenka (Alla Kliouka), and throws him out. Rarely does a woman turn him down, though one of them, Gloria (Annabella Sciorra), whom he meets in the waiting room of Melfi's office, turns out to be almost more than he can handle. So when Melfi herself rejects his advances, despite his persistence, he's baffled, then hurt, then angry.

Gandolfini balances Tony's unpretentiousness—his pride in his Italian-peasant ancestry, his New Jersey plainspokenness—with his awareness that he's very smart, smarter than almost anyone he knows, with a genius for business and undeniable leadership skills. So he can't decide how he feels about being in therapy, both in the early days when he keeps it a secret from everyone except Carm and later when the cat's out of the bag. But he needs help: he feels low much of the time and he keeps passing out. So he's grudgingly accepting, except when he gets impatient and determines that it's useless bullshit—or when he erupts at some of Melfi's questions and observations, especially about his monstrous mother. That's when the old-world taboos kick in (as they do when his daughter, Meadow, played by Jamie-Lynn Sigler, dates a biracial fellow student during her freshman year at Columbia) and the barricades go up, with frightening force.

There are times when Gandolfini reminds us of the Marlon Brando of *A Streetcar Named Desire*: Tony's bullying side has a distinct measure of Stanley Kowalski in it. His sister Janice (Aida Turturro), a drama queen par excellence and a narcissist who has her own therapist convinced (if no one else) that she's a profoundly compassionate woman, takes an anger management class and boasts that she has her temper firmly in control. So Tony, over dinner, needles her about the son she deserted years ago until she boils over and starts breaking the furniture, then he slips out of the house with a sneaky smile on his puss. He's like Stanley yowling like a cat in heat to unsettle Blanche.

As Gandolfini plays him, everything about Tony runs deep, even what might seem like a sentimental impulse in another character, his love for the racehorse that he and one of his captains, Ralph Cifaretto (Joe Pantoliano), own together; the horse's unhappy fate gives rise to one of Tony's most unsettling acts of violence. When it comes to his children, especially his self-centered, directionless son, A.J. (Robert Iler), he's almost crucified on his love for them. Near the end of the final season, A.J. tries to kill himself in the backyard pool and Tony has to pull him out of the water. His inability to do anything to help his son gives rise to some of Gandolfini's most complicated and impassioned acting.

THE FEMALE CHARACTERS

The conventional gangster movie generally contains only three types of women: the good-time girl who shows off what she's got; the good girl who goes wrong; and the weary, exhausted, long-suffering mother who is repulsed by her son's life. The fact that a gangster protagonist, for all his money, can't make his mother happy is a sign that he's living out a diseased version of the American dream.

Nancy Marchand's Livia, who doesn't have a kind word for anyone but her grandchildren, a masterly manipulator who succeeds in getting Junior to put out a hit on her own son in revenge for his putting her in a retirement home, a woman so steeped in denial that she can convince herself that she's not doing what she's doing even at the moment when she's doing it, is a brilliant reversal of the conventional gangster's mother—and Marchand, at the end of her career, is brilliant in the part.

Drea de Matteo's heartbreaking portrait of Adriana shuffles the elements of the good girl gone wrong. She's a sweet and rather uncomplicated beauty, a playgirl at heart but devoted to Christopher, and her association with the underworld—which consists mostly of enjoying the perks (like cocaine) and allowing its denizens into her club, the Crazy Horse—makes her an ideal target for the Feds, who are mounting a case against the Soprano "family." They hound her literally to her death; her story line is a Peckinpah-like narrative where it's very tough to measure the bad guys against the alleged good guys.

But just as any discussion of the principal male performers has to concentrate on Gandolfini, any exploration of the leading actresses has to land primarily on Edie Falco, his most frequent and most memorable scene partner and his acting match. Falco has the role that didn't appear in the old gangster movies until Diane Keaton played Kay in *The Godfather I* and *II*: the Mafia wife. Kay's character serves as the counterpoint and the uncomprehending element to the Sicilian culture she's married into, in dramatic contrast to her mother-in-law, Mama Corleone (Morgana King), who is unstintingly loyal to her husband, and is absent, by tradition, from the business dealings of the family, pretending not to know what's really going on.

Carmela is neither a Mama Corleone nor a Kay; she is acutely aware of what kind of work her husband is involved in (even if she doesn't know the details), and she negotiates her indirect participation in it through the material benefits she gains from it. This is especially evident in the episode where she sees a therapist on her own, Dr. Krakower (Sully Boyar), who tells her point-blank to walk out on her husband and refuses to take what he calls "blood money" in payment for their session. Earlier, when she tells her parish priest, Father Phil (Paul Schulze), that she has contemplated leaving Tony, he presses on her the vow she took to God when she married and urges her to help her husband become a better man; Dr. Krakower refuses to allow her to cherish any such delusions. But Carm has a much harder time negotiating Tony's infidelities: they make her feel cheap and bested, and the only way she can put up with them is not to think about them. Yet she's too conscious and too sensitive to carry on for very long in that way.

The role of Carmela is every bit as complex as the role of Tony, and Falco fills every corner of the character. She has a ferocity—a fishwife side—that you see when she curses him out or hurls the expensive ring he's just bought her across the room. But that's merely one area of an emotional response to her circumstances that is remarkably broad *and* deep. She certainly enjoys her lifestyle—she likes nice things—but not in the unconsidered girlish way Adriana does; an unabashed romantic, Carmela has genuine appreciation for their beauty, just as she is moved by art and, on vacation with her best friend, Rosalie Aprile (Sharon Angela), by the architecture and history of Paris. She isn't intellectual, and she can't overcome certain prejudices stemming from her upbringing: when both her kids convey their English teachers' reading of *Billy Budd* as a fable of repressed homoeroticism, she protests, and when A.J.'s guidance counselor (David Strathairn), with whom she has a brief affair while she and Tony are separated, encourages her to read *Madame Bovary*, she admits that it's over her head.

But she takes everything in and feels it to her bones, whether it's the careless and sometimes hateful treatment she has to put up with at different times from one or the other of her teenagers, or the grief of her friends as they lose husbands and sons, either to illness or to violence. We don't always like the way she behaves; she's too immersed in the Soprano lifestyle to be immune to gaining advantages that are morally compromised, as when she asks a judge, the sister of her next-door neighbor, for a letter of recommendation for Meadow's college file in a way that makes the woman (who barely knows her daughter) understand it would be unwise to refuse. But she's also capable of astonishing insights, like her identification of Father Phil's habit of flirting with women who go to him to satisfy their spiritual needs while letting them mother him by proffering homemade food.

Falco's and Gandolfini's performances have become legendary, and there's much more to be said about them than this essay has space for. It should be standard that in a six-season television drama, actors get the opportunity to explore their characters in a way that they can't in a two- or three-hour movie, yet it isn't always the case. It is in *The Sopranos*, however. These eighty-six hours of viewing turn up one high point after another.

In closing, I'd like to single out one episode that Falco and Gandolfini share, during "Whitecaps," the finale of Season Four. That's the one where Carmela finds out that Tony slept with Svetlana, Junior's nurse, and the news makes her physically ill, giving rise to hysteria, made up of equal parts of rage and disgust, that is unlike anything we've seen from this character before. When she spits it out at Tony, Gandolfini plays a scene in which the character has to confront his sexual betrayal while denying it at the same time. Their breakup is dragged out over two anguished arguments; it's *Scenes from a Marriage*, but way better than Bergman's. A better analogy would be to what I think is the greatest American movie ever made about the dissolution of a marriage, Alan Parker's 1982 *Shoot the Moon* with Diane Keaton and Albert Finney. "Whitecaps" is as staggering an hour of television as I've ever seen, and though the writers (Chase, Robin Green, and Mitchell Burgess) and the director (John Patterson) deserve to be lauded, it's in the performances of the two stars of the show that their ideas come to fruition.

IRREGULAR AROUND THE MARGINS:
PSYCHOLOGY, POINT OF VIEW, AND METAPHOR THROUGH THE CINEMATOGRAPHY AND EDITING OF *THE SOPRANOS* —Mark Dellelo

David Chase establishes a visual style for *The Sopranos* in the very first shots of the pilot episode, which he directed and wrote (the cinematographer, Alik Sakharov, would go on to shoot about half of the episodes, sharing duties with Phil Abraham). It's a style that relies heavily on wide-angle lenses and low camera angles, much like the show that served as its spiritual forebear: David Lynch's *Twin Peaks*, which premiered nearly a decade earlier and was, until the arrival of *The Sopranos*, the most daring and cinematic series in the history of television.

In the opening sequence of the *Twin Peaks* pilot, Pete Martell (Jack Nance), exits his kitchen through a door in the background behind a counter that recedes on a long diagonal line from foreground to middle ground. We then see him walking along a diagonal stone wall from middle ground to foreground outside the house, which is now in the deep background. A point-of-view shot reveals that he sees a body on the beach. Meanwhile, a shot taken from the bottom of the staircase in the victim's home shows her mother, Sarah Palmer (Grace Zabriskie), scrambling up to see if Laura is still in bed. There's a practical reason this shot is taken with the camera tilted up, as this angle emulates the point of view we'd expect the character to see just before she ascends the stairs. But Lynch's decision to hold this shot for as long as he does is a stylistic one, as it no longer works as a realistic estimate of Sarah's point of view by the time she gets to the top of the stairs. Lynch will often begin a shot or a sequence in a way that anchors us realistically in a character's viewpoint or environment, but then push or prolong the result in order to achieve distortion and thereby evoke an irregular psychological mood. And sometimes, as in those ultrawide shots of Pete *before* he discovers the body, that mood is an omen.

It's easy to understand why Chase would adopt this style as a model for *The Sopranos*, given that it's premised on the psychotherapy sessions of a sociopath and that so much of the action unfolds directly from this character's point of view. It's also unsurprising that Chase, like Lynch, would before long pursue it into the psychological netherworld of dreams. Our first glimpses of Tony, in Dr. Melfi's waiting room, are shown through wide-angle lenses, which have a distorting power over both the space and his figure. In a sequence constructed entirely of low-angle shots, we watch him study the statue of a naked woman. In the first of these shots, Tony is in the background, diminished in relation to the statue's legs, which tower above him and form a frame-within-a-frame around him (a metaphor for the way in which the women in his life—his wife, his mother, and soon his therapist—hold him in thrall). But then the camera dollies toward him, and as his figure becomes foregrounded, the wide and low angle makes *him* appear massive. When he enters Melfi's office, the lighting sharply falls off on the right side of his face, chiseling out a low-key mood that evokes the menace of film noir. As he begins to narrate the events of the day when he collapsed, the editing shuttles us back into the sunlight and establishes a cross-cutting pattern. And here we see the first instance of the bird's-eye shot that will appear again and again whenever he wakes up in bed.

Though this first instance of cross-cutting keeps the action firmly anchored in Tony's point of view, as the show develops, this editing strategy will become a vehicle for shuttling among multiple characters' points of view and creating an omniscient, novelistic texture. In Episode 1.2, we begin to see some scenes unfold from the points of view of the other mobsters, but they are essentially proxies for the boss here—the cross-cutting in this early episode primarily works to juxtapose Tony's domestic life (mostly at home, where the lighting is always sunny) with his work life (out on the streets at night or in the Bada Bing, where the lighting is always shadowy, even in the middle of the day). This is the first clear reference to *The Godfather*, which opens with a sequence at the Corleone home in which the kitchen windows bathe the women in daylight, while their mobster husbands whisper about their business in darkened rooms. There are a few scenes that show Tony at work in the daylight, sitting outside Satriale's butcher shop, but these are shot with the wide lenses and low angles I described above, which create a menacing mood.

OTHER POINTS OF VIEW

Episode 1.3 is the first one in which events that Tony doesn't know about become significant—where the cross-cutting is used to create dramatic irony. Early on there is a scene that unfolds from the point of view of Uncle Junior, who is angry at Christopher Moltisanti and Brendan Filone (Anthony DeSando) for hijacking one of his trucks. A few scenes later, Livia Soprano manipulates his anger and takes her first step toward undermining her son by encouraging Junior to do something about it. He delivers his payback while Tony attends Meadow's school recital. This sequence is the series' first small masterpiece of editing, pulling us inside multiple opposing points of view. Tony looks up at his daughter in pride right before her big solo, and an eyeline match moves us in to a close-up of Meadow hopped up on the speed he's unaware that Christopher has given her (a secret she shares with her girlfriend Hunter, played by Michele DeCesare, whom we see next as the camera follows Meadow's sly sideways glance). Meanwhile, Tony reaches for Carmela's hand and she pulls it away, angry that he's shown up late. And elsewhere, down on the docks, two Russian thugs hired by Junior are busy roughing up Christopher, while Junior himself stands outside the door to the bathroom where Brendan is shot dead in the tub. The blood that flows into the bathwater is an allusion to Frank Pentangeli's suicide at the end of *The Godfather, Part II*, which was an allusion to the baptism sequence in *The Godfather*. It's no accident that the soundtrack here is a Christmas carol, or that the entrance to the auditorium is shaped like a chapel, or that the thug who fires an empty chamber at Christopher crosses himself with a grin.

We first see Chase hit on the full potential of this cross-cutting technique in Season One's "College," where we're presented with two story threads, anchored in opposing points of view, in parallel with each other: while Carmela recovers at home from the flu, Tony drives Meadow through Maine to visit colleges. This is Chase's first opportunity to explore Carmela's point of view, particularly the marital neglect she feels, which makes her receptive to the attention Father Phil shows by dropping in on her.

Tony, distracted when he glimpses a stool pigeon (played by Tony Ray Rossi) who disappeared into the Witness Protection program, hangs up the phone on her shortly before Phil's arrival. The POV shots in this episode introduce another visual motif that will recur throughout the series, which mostly limits the use of telephoto lenses to moments of surveillance. A sequence in which Tony cases the stoolie's travel agency in the dead of night includes several shots of this kind. The silhouette lighting here—he leaves on his car's headlights, which illuminate him from behind—is quintessential film noir. The parallel action multiplies when this sequence gets juxtaposed with a simultaneous one in which the stoolie cases Tony's motel. These two threads converge when Tony arrives back at the motel and is caught in a telephoto shot from behind the long barrel of the stoolie's gun, and the suspense gets ratcheted higher when a rack in focus shifts the emphasis from the gun barrel onto Tony—though the stoolie, distracted by a bickering couple as they enter their room a few doors down, misses his chance to pull the trigger. The stoolie's anxious point of view is further evoked by some jittery handheld camerawork that is all the more striking in contrast to the arching dolly shots that show Tony's movements.

Tony dodges this bullet, so to speak, at the very moment Father Phil hears Carmela's confession back at the Soprano home. Right after she delivers a line about how much she fears God's wrath, Chase cuts to a close-up of the stoolie loading his gun. The great Russian filmmaker Sergei Eisenstein theorized a hierarchy of possibilities within the techniques of juxtaposition that film editing makes possible, with suspense at the lowest level and metaphor at the highest (which he called "intellectual montage"). Though there is certainly some suspense here, I don't think any of us is really afraid that the show's protagonist is about to get whacked halfway through the first season. We're as serene about the outcome as we are during the baptism montage in *The Godfather*. Chase alluded to this sequence previously, but here he really *gets* it. This kind of associational cut actually throws us momentarily out of the mechanics of the plot and makes us reflect on the themes of the show, writing them large as a metaphor about sin and fear of punishment. The portentous tone is leavened with some humor—Chase uses handheld camerawork not only to capture the stoolie's nerves, but also to evoke intoxication, both Meadow's and Father

Phil's. A cut away from the drunk priest scrabbling toward Carmela's bathroom matches to a shot of Meadow stepping out into the daylight with a hangover—a telephoto shot that we soon learn is perceived through a pair of binoculars the stoolie can barely hold steady after having staked out Tony's motel all night.

The contradictions between Tony's domestic and business lives are often thrown into sharp relief by this kind of juxtaposition. One moment he applauds Meadow's soccer team on the field, and the next we see the bare breasts of a pole dancer at the Bada Bing, where he's brought the coach to celebrate victory. As the show develops and the web of relationships becomes more complex, there are often elements of dramatic irony in these juxtapositions. In Season Three there's a match cut between two shots of Ralph Cifaretto pitching forward in laughter: in the first one he's at the home of his *comare,* a pole dancer from the Bada Bing, and in the next he's at the dinner table of his girlfriend, Rosalie Aprile. His laughter begins as a response to Silvio Dante (Steven Van Zandt) smacking the stripper around for having failed to show up to work and is then transformed by a smash cut into benign dinner party laughter—once again in response to Silvio, who's sitting there with his wife to cultivate the appearance of domestic bliss along with everyone else at Rosalie's table. The women, of course, don't ask what their husbands were up to earlier in the day, choosing to keep the conversation mostly about food—it's the editing that makes the point about the work that put that food onto the table.

There's a beautiful little sequence, near the end of Season Four, that shares some of the same dark humor but also layers in something more rueful by emphasizing Carmela's absence. Tony leaves his *comare*'s house to come home for dinner only to find Carmela gone, and a note that she made some pasta he can heat up. He pops it in the microwave and the editing takes us into Furio Giunta's (Federico Castelluccio) kitchen, where he's preparing a simple, solitary meal in an elegant old-world style, pining for Carmela, who'd rather be eating with him than making rigatoni for a husband who can't be bothered to show up on time for dinner. By this point in the series, the cross-cutting has evolved into something more subtle and emotionally rich than the earlier juxtapositions I've described. It has become a means of connecting moments of acute feeling among a broad network of characters who are each, by now, embroiled in their own private dramas. The episodes have less of a standalone quality in this season, as these dramatic through-lines tend to evolve rather than resolve by the end of each hour. Tony himself begins to feel less like the main protagonist and more like an equal player in a dramatic ensemble.

The sequence I've described above is from Season Four's tenth episode ("The Strong, Silent Type"); earlier in the same episode, a close-up of Furio shows him alone in the frame, crying, and when Tony enters and asks him what's wrong, he shares only a small facet of the reason ("I'm sad for my father")—because of course he can't share what he's feeling for Carmela. Tony tells him he needs to get over it, though the very next shot is a close-up of him crying about Ralphie Cifaretto's dead horse—which is also only part of the reason for the emotion that we see. He does provide Melfi with a more detailed account of the sources of his emotional state, but can't, of course, tell her that the horse was a victim of arson or that the arsonist was a victim of his own wrath—or that the fallout from his act of retribution is that a paralyzed boy is now fatherless. One element he does share is his concern about Christopher's heroin addiction; the next sequence shifts the perspective onto another character who feels this concern even more acutely: Adriana, whose misery is equally complex for a different array of reasons—including the FBI agent sitting in the car seat next to her. The episode's title is multivalent, referencing all of these characters equally: Adriana, who resists feeding intel to the FBI; Tony, who keeps his vendetta toward Ralphie a secret; Furio, who represses both his love for Carmela and his anger at Tony; Christopher, who throws punches at the intervention his *famiglia* has organized for him and storms out of the room to avoid talking about his problem.

PARALLEL ACTION

Adriana is one of several characters who move from the background to the foreground in Season Four. In the season's fifth episode ("Pie-O-My"), the opening sequence is centered on her and directed in a way that evokes everything she is feeling—resentment about Tony's business dealings in her nightclub, pressure to deliver information about him to the FBI, and terror about getting pegged as an informant. To evoke her distanced gaze

Chase uses medium telephoto lenses focused on the background. He also cuts almost subliminally to a couple of canted angles while she watches Tony on a phone call from across the room. These shots transform him into a nightmare image of her worst fear; she imagines him saying, "I'm gonna fuck her up before I kill her," while the electric guitar from the band onstage needles her ears expressionistically. When she steps outside to spy on him and his crew through a window, a porch light casts her figure in a film noir silhouette against the midnight sky. The window she moves toward gradually illuminates her harried face as she glimpses (again in a medium telephoto shot) the gangsters roughing up one of their clients. A reverse-angle shot pushes in on her eyes, flat against the window—she's just as trapped as the guy who is getting mauled.

From here the action leaps to Janice Soprano in the daytime, using a pair of binoculars to keep even closer watch on the women—who appear in long telephoto shots focused on the foreground—parading into Bobby Baccalieri's house with comfort food following the death of his wife. The editing shuttles us right back to Adriana, now getting a deluxe treatment at the hair salon and sitting in front of a mirror. This is a point-of-view shot in which she is focused on her own image, but the camera pans to a new framing when the receptionist hands her a phone and she swivels around in her chair—now we're looking at her objectively, just as she's jarred out of the illusion of her glamorous lifestyle by the sound of her FBI handler's voice. The symbolism here is beautifully subtle and thought out down to the last detail—in this moment when she's caught off guard, she's getting her hair colored and we're seeing it natural, undisguised.

The image I'm most reminded of here is from Robert Altman's *Nashville*, when Linnea Reese (Lily Tomlin), having just lived out the fantasy of sleeping with a rock star, climbs out of the hotel bed she's sharing with Tom Frank (Keith Carradine) to fix her hair at a mirror. It's a thoroughly naturalistic scene, but the imagery is poetically suggestive—we see a double image of Linnea that suggests the woman she has made herself up to be for the evening, as well as the dual reality that she knows Tom is a womanizer (the mirror reflects her reaction to a phone call he has with another woman) and that she has to go home to her husband (it also reflects her exit from the hotel room).

I'm not sure this is a direct homage, but I do think it's a relevant touchstone, because there is something about the dramatic equipoise and understated poetic detail of these mid-series *Sopranos* episodes that calls Altman's work to mind. He adopted parallel action as the organizing principle of his style and used cross-cutting in a less metaphorical way than Francis Ford Coppola did in the *Godfather* films, whose influence looms large over the earlier episodes. The poetry in Altman's work was a product of soft resonances between the lived experiences of individual characters, which evoked a feeling of shared culture within a densely populated milieu. You could say that he poeticized individual experience while simultaneously satirizing cultural experience, which is frequently Chase's strategy as well. The birthday barbecue for Carmela's father in the Season Five episode "Marco Polo" largely unfolds in a sequence of Altmanesque tracking shots that move us through a bustling scene, continuously reframing the action, shifting and sometimes splitting our point of view, placing us inside and outside the experiences of multiple characters. My favorite shot here begins as a close-up on a barbecue grill and then dollies over to reveal Tony walking over to turn the meat. He doesn't see Russ Fegoli (Bruce Kirby)—one of his mother-in-law's cavalier Northern Italian friends—at the table behind him flashing him a disdainful look, but we do.

EPIC DREAM SEQUENCES

Toward the end of Season Five, the show's primary stylistic mode shifts away from naturalism as Chase returns, in a pair of epic dream sequences, to the influence of his alpha and omega: David Lynch. The eleventh episode of Season Five ("The Test Dream") and the second and third of Season Six ("Join the Club" and "Mayham") contain the most ambitious of these sequences since the Season Two finale ("Funhouse")—which premiered in April of 2000, a year before the release of Lynch's *Mulholland Dr.* The influence of that film on these later dream sequences may account for the more matter-of-fact style. Whereas the lens distortion and angular camerawork on the boardwalk in "Funhouse" almost immediately signified that we were outside reality, the transition into dream space in "The Test Dream" is more seamless. The last shot we see before the dream begins is from Tony's POV, of an Asian call girl staring back at him from his hotel room's minibar. A smash cut shuttles us forward in time to a close-up of Tony's head on his pillow, but we take this ellipsis as a realist technique and assume we'll see the call girl lying next to him, especially since we hear her voice. The camera pans with Tony as he rolls over, but rather than revealing the call girl it shows the late Carmine Lupertazzi (Tony Lip) lying next to him. The continuity of the panning shot keeps the sequence grounded in a realist style, and so does the low angle from which we next see Carmine, as it's taken from Tony's POV on the floor after he's fumbled out of bed. As in the opening scenes of *Mulholland Dr.*—and the late movies of Lynch's great influence, the Spanish surrealist Luis Buñuel—the visually straightforward way in which these baroque details are rendered makes them all the more uncanny.

Because the next scene is consistent with the show's established convention of Tony narrating his experiences to Melfi in her office, we assume that he's woken up. But when an eyeline match reveals another dead person, Gloria Trillo, sitting across from him, we realize this was a false awakening that has opened a garden path into dream logic. The scene transitions in *The Discreet Charm of the Bourgeoisie*, Buñuel's late-period masterpiece, work in a similar way. That film also returns again and again to a scene depicting a journey without a clear destination. In Tony's dream, he twice finds himself a passenger in a car, wondering aloud where he's headed. These episodes are recurrences from the dream that bookended Season Four's eleventh episode, "Calling All Cars." The endpoint there was, symbolically speaking, his mother's house—an elegant house decorated in an old-world style, down the stairs of which descended a woman in silhouette whose figure was strongly reminiscent of Livia Soprano. This time the endpoint is his own house, or more accurately Carmela's house, since they are now separated. His chauffeur on the second trip, Artie Bucco (John Ventimiglia), makes a pit stop at a hotel where he cheers Tony on as he makes love to Charmaine Bucco (Kathrine Narducci), his wife. The image of Tony astride her gets linked by a match cut to an image of him saddled up on his dead horse, Pie-O-My, in Carmela's living room. The association between these shots leaves no doubt as to what she's really talking about when she tells him he can't come home if he's going to bring his horse into the house.

It isn't a car ride but a business trip that continues the itinerant dreamer motif at the beginning of Season Six. As in Season Four, when Tony shows up at the door of his mother's house in his grandfather's shoes (asking for work as a stonemason), he's confused about his identity. Episode 6.2 ("Join the Club") opens with the familiar bird's-eye shot of him waking up in bed, and the discontinuity here with the end of the previous episode, when he collapsed onto the floor after Uncle Junior shot him, is so extreme that we wonder if that event could have been a dream from which he's now waking. But then when he phones his family we hear strange voices on the answering-machine greeting and realize we're in an alternate reality (he's in a coma). This is the end of the road that might have been, in which he's climbed the capitalist ladder from selling patio furniture—a life choice he mused about back in Season One—to precision optics. The editing shows us how this idea worms its way into his subconscious—craning his neck toward the night sky at the sound of a helicopter, he squints at a searchlight that's actually a surgical lamp wielded by a doctor who fades in and out as a giant superimposition. Later, this same lamp burns an iris-shaped white hole in the screen and dissolves into an image of Tony's eyeball as he lies in his hospital bed. The cross-cutting between the waking world and the events of his unconscious evokes the experience of delirium: when Paulie Gualtieri (Tony Sirico) launches into a rant that sends Tony's heart rate soaring, his dream persona pounds on the wall of his hotel room for his neighbors to keep their noise down; when the surgical team revives him with defibrillators, the next shot shows him on a bumpy car ride while a thunderstorm rages around him.

This is, for my money, the most visually audacious and authentically hallucinatory of all the series' dream sequences. It ultimately leads him—by way of a beacon he glimpses on the horizon from his hotel window—to yet another house. It's an inn, actually, but an inn with a domestic atmosphere that suggests he'd be comfortable staying there for a long, long time. This is an old-world setting that siren-sings to him—the music wafting from the inside sounds at first like Italian opera (though it's actually Latin American folk music, since he's in Costa Mesa, California, after all), and the woman he glimpses standing in the doorway suggests his mother. This image recalls the woman descending the staircase in his Season Four dream; the mood here is just as mysterious, but gentler—she isn't in shadow but obscured by a porch beam. This brief scene includes a lot of back-and-forth cutting between Tony's point of view and reactions, evoking both the seduction of a final resting place and his trepidation at departing from the world that he knows—emblemized by an insert shot of the briefcase he's clutching and a reverse shot of the wind whistling through some trees against a pitch-black sky. "Don't leave us, Daddy, we love you," they seem to cry, and as Tony turns his head back to the warm light and the rustic wreath of flowers just inside the open door to the inn, that image dissolves into the harsh white light of the surgical lamp as his eyes open to reveal a two-shot of Meadow and Carmela hovering over him.

This cut to white is much less frequently discussed than the notorious cut to black at the end of the series finale. But the two shots rhyme with one another. Like the end of the dream that opens the final season, the concluding sequence at Holsten's yokes us fast to Tony's perspective, reminding us via a regular pattern of POV shots and reaction shots when we are experiencing the action through his eyes—and when we aren't. (This final sequence is worked out with the formal rigor of Stanley Kubrick.) Tony hears the door chime four times, and all four times he looks up—but he only sees someone standing in the doorway the first three times. The fourth time there is no light, no music, no voice calling out to him—just a hard cut to the dark reality that his journey is now over.

THE SOPRANOS' TOP TEN FOOD MOMENTS

#1 KAREN'S ZITI IN EPISODE 4.11, "CALLING ALL CARS"

Soft-hearted Bobby Baccalieri suffers unyielding grief and guilt following his wife Karen's death in a car accident. He's not skipping through the process quickly enough for Janice Soprano, who has designs on his ready-made family and steady income. She sees him as a more stable mark than her previous beaus, Richie Aprile (David Proval) and Ralph Cifaretto, but her patience wears thin. It's easy to empathize with Bobby. Most of us lose a loved one and realize we'll never come home to their culinary aromas or taste a bite of their food again. We want Bobby to hold on to his deceased wife's final ziti as long as he needs to, but Janice manipulates him into defrosting and ritually consuming it. It's difficult watching Bobby attempt to savor each bite while Janice looms over him. The lit candles don't feel romantic; instead they remind us of the séance his kids hold earlier in the episode to try to reach their mom. This is forced exorcism, a *mangia* macabre.
—Nick Braccia

#2 KETCHUP AND RELISH IN EPISODE 3.11, "PINE BARRENS"

There is no scene in *Sopranos* history more beloved than the one in which a disheveled, wild-eyed, wild-haired Paulie Gualtieri and a bloody and dejected Christopher Moltisanti sit freezing in the front seat of a broken-down van in the Pine Barrens. The scene is one of pure comic misery, and as the men come closer to giving up on life, the absurdity gets funnier. Valery (Vitali Baganov), the indestructible Russian super-soldier, is on the loose with vengeance on his mind; Tony will be disappointed by their

SOPRANOS CUISINE:
MY FAVORITE CHARACTER
—Eddie McNamara

Food is my favorite character on *The Sopranos*. It doesn't get an IMDb credit for any of the eighty-six episodes it starred in, but if something important is happening on the show, you can bet that food is central to the scene. It all begins in the pilot episode when Tony sanctions an arson at his childhood friend Artie Bucco's restaurant, Vesuvio (yes, like the volcano that buried Pompeii), so Junior can't arrange a hit there and ruin Artie's business. Look, some friends help you out by lending you $50 when you need it. Tony Soprano blows up your business without letting you know and thinks he's doing you a favor. And when the series wraps, it's with a plate of crispy Holsten's onion rings before everything goes black. There's no beginning and no end to *The Sopranos* without food.

RED-SAUCE JOINTS

Vesuvio—shortly after, Nuovo Vesuvio—is a red-sauce joint, an Italian restaurant in name alone. It's about as authentic as Tutto Italia Ristorante in Epcot Center, a stand-in for any of the glorious palaces of parmigiana in the tri-state area. Red-sauce joints like this one don't faithfully re-create the regional specialties that people eat on the Boot. They boldly invented the American-Italian style of cooking—enormous portions rich with cream and cheese, and more meat on the table than a butcher shop—to show that you've made it in this strange new land because now you eat like King Umberto II.

Let's get all sociohistorical about this and talk about the Italian diaspora. Our grandparents' generation took a boat from Naples, Sicily, Calabria, or some other town in Southern Italy (in my family's case, Potenza), where they lived like serfs or sharecroppers, half starving and still getting shaken down by criminal warlords. They arrived at Ellis Island, not speaking a word of English, and moved into teeming tenements in Greenwich Village and Little Italy. Some made it all the way out to Bensonhurst, Brooklyn, the second largest Sicilian city in the world behind Palermo. These formerly rural folks found themselves in an urban environment, where if they were lucky, they could plant some tomatoes and basil on their windowsill.

Their traditional diet of fresh produce from the ground they worked was replaced by heaps of spaghetti and tomato sauce—these cheap calories were an economic necessity for poorly paid immigrant laborers, ragpickers, and seamstresses to feed their large families. And they still had to kick back to a middleman called a *padrone*, a labor broker who took a piece of the meager wages of the immigrants he found work for. What started as a question of survival for Italians in America turned into its own cuisine at restaurants like John's of 12th Street, Rao's, Bamonte's, Ferdinando's Focacceria, and Gargiulo's. These were places where nouveau-riche mafiosi took meetings and working-class families celebrated weddings, communions, and confirmations. If you're going to drop a lot of

gross incompetence; and a mix of hypochondria and hypothermia is setting in. Everything changes when Christopher looks to the floor and finds leftover condiments in a Nathan's takeout bag. Paulie expresses the purest of joy as he instructs Christopher to mix the ketchup with the relish. There was such a world of hope in those condiment packets. Neil Armstrong walking on the moon might not have felt as pleased with himself as Paulie Walnuts does in that moment. And no *Sopranos* characters ever enjoy a meal more than Paulie and Crissy enjoy that one.

—Eddie McNamara

#3 ARTIE BUCCO'S *CONIGLIO DELLA FAMIGLIA* IN EPISODE 6.7, "LUXURY LOUNGE"

Artie is enraged when he spies a rabbit in his sacred garden, eating arugula grown from the seeds he's smuggled back from Italy in his shaving kit. He shoots the pest and it ends up in the Nuovo Vesuvio fridge, where it inspires him to revisit the recipes in his grandfather Angelo's notebook. It's this recipe that allows Artie to rediscover his bliss. It's also a rare moment where the show, so adept at satirizing Italian-American tradition and inherent hypocrisies, honors it in earnest. Think of Junior's boast, "We taught the world how to eat!" or Phil Leotardo (Frank Vincent) telling Ellis Island tall tales to connect his family lineage to da Vinci. Artie's silent focus in the kitchen is pride, sans puffery.

—Nick Braccia

#4 MICHELE "FEECH" LA MANNA'S DANDELIONS IN EPISODE 5.2, "RAT PACK"

Michele "Feech" La Manna (Robert Loggia) doesn't come to see his old buddy Junior Soprano empty-handed when he wants permission to operate again: "I was just dropping off some dandelions. I found a beautiful patch over near a vacant lot on 15th Street." He snatches them up and drops them off with Uncle Jun. Bobby takes the bitter greens and starts making a salad. This is old-school, off-the-boat, Italian-American eating. The gesture evokes a throwback to the old days when Italian immigrants in America foraged for dandelion greens and ate them raw in a salad, sautéed with some garlic and olive oil, or used to green up a soup. Feech is fresh out of the can and Junior sees him as a man out of time, an old rat (not in the usual Mob-rat sense) trying to jump onto a new ship. As soon as Feech is out the door, Junior pushes the plate of dandelion salad aside. Junior might be an old man, but he's not trapped in the past; he's moved on. Not Sicilian-born Feech. His last meal before going back to the joint: wine and peaches, *pesche con vino*, another old-time treat. *Cento anni*, old-timer.

—Eddie McNamara

#5 VITO'S *PASTA E PATATE* AND PORK CHOPS WITH VINEGAR PEPPERS IN EPISODE 6.10, "MOE N' JOE"

Once Vito Spatafore (Joseph R. Gannascoli) comes (mostly) clean to his new lover, Jim "Johnny Cakes" Witowski (John Costelloe), he's able to express himself with honesty and generosity. It makes sense that his language of choice is food, since he was originally drawn to Jim through his knockout cooking in a New Hampshire diner; it's sweet that Vito wants to return the favor. While Dean Martin sings "That's Amore," Vito chops onions to prep a pastoral meal of macaroni and potatoes followed by pork chops and vinegar peppers. It's a warm, charming moment, but short-lived. The food he shares comes from a life he lacks the courage to leave. Still, on this night, the kitchen—

money on dinner, there had better be meat on the table. Oversized chicken cutlets, breaded, pan-fried, and slathered with melted cheese, were served with giant bowls of pasta in thick (sometimes meaty) tomato sauce. If you were in a hurry, maybe you skipped the pasta and had the chicken sandwiched in "Italian" bread (it doesn't exist in Italy). Artie Bucco's Vesuvio is the cousin of these legendary mansions of marinara.

Like the title of the series finale, the vast majority of "Italian" food eaten on *The Sopranos* was Made in America. Baked ziti is omnipresent, served by the tray at Sunday dinners. This quintessential dish is so loaded with notions of family and warmth that it's used by Janice Soprano as a vehicle of manipulation to tug at Bobby Baccalieri's heartstrings when his wife Karen (Christine Pedi) dies. She urges him to summon the strength to eat the final tray of frozen ziti—among all the other trays of mourning ziti—made by his newly deceased wife. That cringeworthy meal gives Bobby closure. Sharing it with Janice allowed her to move into his life. Soul food healed the soul. The point is, you won't find baked ziti in a home freezer in Italy, nor would an Italian ever serve it. The closest you're likely to find to baked ziti is *pasta al forno*, which is only similar in that it's baked in an oven.

Most of the *Sopranos* characters are Nescafé Italians, not espresso Italians. Third- or fourth-generation Americans with an understanding of Italian culture warped by a century of assimilation and Americanization in the isolated Little Italies of northern New Jersey. You can see it reflected in the rebuilt Vesuvio, whose interior appeals to diners without passports but with a mythical Italy in their mind's eye. It's represented by "classy" Corinthian columns, bellowing music, and marble everything.

When Tony and his crew speak Italian, they're mangling the language with a dialect specific to the northeastern United States. With the notable exception of legit Napoletano Furio, they're doing this to distinguish themselves from Wonder Bread "white guys" like the assimilated Dr. Cusamano (Robert LuPone). These men wouldn't be able to carry on a conversation with a five-year-old in Italian and don't know how the offsides rule works in soccer, either, but they assert their sense of Italianness by performatively talking about food: "bro-shoot" instead of *prosciutto*, "gabagool" instead of *capicola*, "moot-za-dell" instead of *mozzarella*, "galamad" instead of *calamari*, and "sazz-eech" as a double *va fangool* to the English sausage and the Italian *salsiccia*. "Proper" Italians would turn up their noses.

In fact, their Southern Italian ancestors probably drew similar sneers from speakers of standard Italian. The vast majority of Italian immigrants on America's East Coast spoke in Neapolitan and Sicilian dialects. When my grandmother spoke in the Lucanian subdialect of Neapolitan, she dropped the vowel at the end of words and pronounced the letter "c" like the letter "g"; and it's easy to see how *capicola* becomes gapicol and eventually gabagool. When Meadow says, "Grandma, don't eat the gaba-

and Jim's heart—belong to Chef Vito.

—Nick Braccia

#6 HUGH'S BIRTHDAY PARTY SAUSAGE IN EPISODE 5.8, "MARCO POLO"

The DeAngelis family thinks they're hot shit, especially Carmela's mother, Mary, played brilliantly by Suzanne Shepherd, in a role very familiar to her "what kind of people are these?" performance in *Goodfellas*. It's Hugh's seventy-fifth birthday party and Mary is delighted that her daughter is separated from her mafioso meatball husband, meaning he won't be there to embarrass her in front of her fancy Italian friends with his goombah ways and low-class lineage.

Mary makes a point to talk about how much Livia and the whole Soprano bunch disliked Northern Italian cooking and then plants a big *beso* on the *culo* of her *paisana* when she says, "But those recipes you used to send me from Tuscany. My God they were a revelation. *Bolito misto, osso bucco*." If you know anything about Italy, it's probably that Northern Italians look down on Southern Italians. Tony arrives late to the party, and in an act of aggressive buffoonery, he wears sausage links like a boa around his neck and sings to Hugh (Tom Aldredge), "Happy birthday to Hugh, I got *sazaleechi* for you," while Mary dies of embarrassment in front of her cultured Italian-American friends who look on in disgust. (Hugh loves the gesture and is all smiles.) Tony continues to play the clown when talking with Mary DeAngelis's angel Dr. Fegoli about his audience with four popes. Tony jokingly asks, "What section did you sit in?" and while Mary is cringing hard, the birthday boy soaks up all Tony's spiciness.

—Eddie McNamara

#7 CARMELA'S PINEAPPLE-RICOTTA PIE IN EPISODE 2.8, "FULL LEATHER JACKET"

Carmela gives tough-minded Newark attorney Joan Cusamano (Saundra Santiago) a pie she can't refuse. Her pineapple-ricotta dish is a transactional gesture, but the lawyer—neighbor Jeannie's twin sister (also Santiago)—doesn't accept the high-caloric currency. Carmela, obsessed with Meadow's college prospects, keeps her tone friendly enough, but the subtext of her words is, "Don't you know who my husband is?" Unlike Tony, she's a polite extortionist. The pie looks great, but I doubt Joan will eat it. Nothing tastes good when you're being force-fed.
—Nick Braccia

#8 INDIAN FOOD AND *ZUPPA DI MUSSELS* IN EPISODE 2.13, "FUNHOUSE"

The great *Sopranos* mystery has nothing to do with the fade-to-black ending—we all know what happened there. The real mystery is: What caused Tony's food poisoning? What we do we know for certain:

1. Tony and Bonpensiero went out for Indian food and had different entrees, but shared popadams.
2. Tony and Bonpensiero had the *zuppa di mussels* at Nuovo Vesuvio following their Indian dinner.
3. Artie Bucco reveals that he personally checks every piece of shellfish himself and blames the Indian restaurant for using rancid ghee.
4. Tony reveals that he was able to inspect the undigested mussels himself after they came up, proving that his body shut down as a means of self-protection.
5. Bonpensiero had a touch of diarrhea, while Tony had Old Faithful coming out of both ends all night long.

gool," she's expressing herself as part of a culture within a culture, trying to preserve their traditions with her assertive overpronunciation. Her willingness to say "gabagool" with a straight face shows her as proudly Jersey-Italian; maybe she knows better, but she doesn't give a rat's ass because fuck you.

When the Sopranos crew takes a trip to Naples, Paulie Gualtieri's identity is called into question when he asks the Italian waiter, "Can I just get some macaroni and gravy?" The waiter doesn't understand, so his mafioso dinner companions have to translate: Paulie doesn't want the authentic Italian food he's been served. Like a child, he just wants pasta with tomato sauce. They tell the server in a mocking tone and call Paulie a piece of shit in Italian, which he doesn't catch. I find it difficult to believe that Paulie didn't understand *pezzo di merda*, but you can take that up with David Chase. Upon arriving back in New Jersey, Paulie tells "Big Pussy" Bonpensiero that he "felt right at home" in Italy despite being the comedic fish out of water for an entire episode.

Paulie's entire sense of identity revolves around an idealized notion of being Italian, but actual Italians don't view him as a *paisan* coming back to the motherland. They see him as a North Jersey goofball who commits the cardinal sin of calling sauce "gravy." The Italian language is clear: it's *salsa* if it's a sauce with no meat, *ragu* if there is meat, and *sugo* can mean either with or without meat (it also means pan drippings or cooking juices). Anthony Russo, the owner of Gargiulo's and a red-sauce authority, once told *Brooklyn Paper*, "I always know it as sauce. . . . Gravy, I always thought of as brown sauce."[1] Gravy is a term of assimilation used by Italians eager to fit in because Americans understood what gravy is. But Jersey people love to think of themselves as scrappy underdogs in the shadow of New York, so if New Yorkers try telling them that only *cafones* say gravy, it's going to make them double-down on gravy in spite of all the evidence that tells them they're wrong. Ralph Cifaretto is the embodiment of doing the wrong thing for the cultural good. In the scene where he gives Jackie Aprile Jr. (Jason Cerbone) a gun that will set off a chain of events leading to his demise, Ralphie is far more concerned with teaching Jackie the right way to cook macaroni and gravy (he uses those words) than keeping the kid out of trouble. Ralphie knows what he's doing, though—adding the pat of butter is a nice touch.

The thing is, American-Italian cuisine is as complex as any other world cuisine. Vodka sauce is delicious. Try it on a slice of New York–style pizza and it's even better, and both the pizza and sauce are distinctively American creations from Italian immigrants. Order Alfredo sauce in Italy and they'll ask you, "Who's Alfredo?" but in New Jersey it's the richest, creamiest sauce you'll ever have. My love for red-sauce joints is honest and deep. I've eaten in four of the current top ten restaurants in the world and I'd rather have dinner at Don Peppe (Queens) or Joe's of Avenue U (Brooklyn) than any stuffy fine-dining restaurant. When my friends' cousins from Naples or Sicily visited

6. Dr. Cusamano thinks it's a case of *E. coli*.

So was it the Indian food or Artie's dodgy mussels that took Tony out? In my opinion it was neither. Tony knew what had to be done about Pussy and the stress about the whole ordeal manifested as physical symptoms.

—Eddie McNamara

#9 TONY'S WRONG ORDER IN EPISODE 4.13, "WHITECAPS"

Part of the comic genius of Tony Soprano's character is that he's millions of miles away from us morally, while exhibiting perfectly relatable behavior in everyday situations. That's why his furious but helpless reaction to a mixed-up Chinese food order is so hilarious: "Motherfucking goddamn orange peel beef!" Even better, it builds on his Chinese food tantrum in "Army of One," when he discovers that somebody's eaten the lo mein he stashed in the Bada Bing fridge. Takeout karma's a bitch.

—Nick Braccia

#10 ATLANTIC CITY DINNER, $1,184, IN EPISODE 5.1, "TWO TONYS"

Christopher is the low man on the DiMeo totem pole so as part of his hazing, Paulie (his captain) makes him pick up the checks after their meals. Paulie torments Christopher by running up a $1,184 tab and even sends a bottle of Cristal to a table of "skanks." After the meal, the two start squabbling outside, with Christopher digging into Paulie about not even touching the lyonnaise potatoes he ordered. The guys are about to come to blows when their waiter (Omar Chagall) interrupts, inquiring if anything was wrong with the service . . . they left a (crappy) $16 tip. Instantly, the two gangsters put their differences aside to team up against a working man who's just trying to support his family. Christopher smashes the guy in the back of the head with a brick, and Paulie finishes him off with a gunshot. I almost forgot there was a sinister side of those wisecracking clowns who were lost in the Pine Barrens. That clueless waiter wasn't in "the life"—he was a civilian. No amount of funny lines about Czechoslovakian interior decorators can ever make up for what they did to that waiter in the alley. After this, Christopher and Paulie were as dead to me as the waiter. The scene ends with Chris shouting to Paulie to grab the money from the dead man, and he does. There is no honor among thieves.

—Eddie McNamara

Brooklyn, their minds were blown by L&B's hefty slices of square pizza and they fell in love with our run-of-the-mill shrimp parm heroes from Lenny and John's pizzeria. When they said, "I wish we had this kind of food in Italy," it challenged everything I learned about Italian food from the crabby, old-neighborhood Italians who always talked shit about American-Italian food. Our food's as good as anybody else's, and we shouldn't be ashamed of it.

Give me the lobster *fra diavolo*, the giant meatballs with a mountain of spaghetti, the garlic bread, the muffaletta and the hero sandwiches, the deep-fried calzones, the meat-filled stromboli that burns the top of your mouth while molten cheese lava runs down your chin, pizza with a crispy crust and three different toppings, baked clams casino, shrimp scampi, porchetta, chicken marsala, chicken Francaise, sausage and peppers, and a potato and egg sandwich, and shove your amuse-bouche up your ass.

CHECKERED HISTORIES

In addition to being the best places to eat, red-sauce joints tend to either have a checkered history or be glamorized by the fact that gangsters ate there. Everybody knows that "Crazy" Joe Gallo was shot at Umberto's Clam House and "Little Nicky" Scarfo loved to eat at Dante & Luigi's in South Philly, and unfortunately for him, it was widely known that Paul Castellano was a big fan of Sparks. The lore for these places is as delicious as the food. One time, I was eating with the great Geno Durante (Hollywood's go-to wiseguy consultant) and indie filmmaker

Ricky Viola when they blew my mind by bringing up the urban legend of Gargiulo's spaghetti with bacon and eggs. Ricky described it as "breakfast, but with spaghetti. And the spaghetti is coated in bacon grease."

See, gangsters wake up whenever they want, so a made guy might be hungry for breakfast sometime after noon. And that guy might go to Gargiulo's (one of New York's oldest red-sauce joints, which hasn't changed since 1907 except now the servers take orders with iPads), give the waiter a wink, and enjoy the most Italian-American interpretation of the classic NYC deli bacon, egg, and cheese you can imagine.

Long story short, I marched in there and ordered "the spaghetti with bacon and eggs," but let's get real. I'm no wiseguy. I shouldn't have been surprised when the waiter stared at me like I'd asked to sleep with his wife. He continued to rattle off specials. I asked again, and he said, "We no have that." Like Jesus Christ, I was denied three times; like a real wiseguy, he refused to rat. Either that, or this dish is a Brooklyn myth. Tail between my legs, I did the only thing left to do—go to my kitchen and refuse to leave until I cooked the best breakfast spaghetti you'll ever eat.

Breakfast Spaghetti

Ingredients:

12 ounces spaghetti (about 3/4 of a box)

10 strips of bacon

1 cup cheddar cheese

2 tablespoons butter

Salt and pepper

2 egg yolks

2 whole eggs

Tabasco sauce

Directions:

1. Get a big pot of salty water boiling. Add your pasta and cook for one minute less than directed in the box instructions.
   Reserve 1 cup of the pasta water before draining.

2. Line a cold nonstick pan with your bacon slices. Cook over medium-low heat. When the bacon starts curling, give it a flip. Keep doing that until you've got your bacon the way you like it. Transfer the bacon to a paper-towel-lined plate. Keep the pan greasy.

3. Return the pasta to the pot and heat over medium. Add the cheese, butter, reserved cooking water, and a punch (that's like 3 pinches) of salt and pepper. Stir that up until it melts and becomes a sauce. Take it off the heat and stir in the egg yolks to make the sauce richer. Add the bacon to the pot and mix well.

4. Fry the two whole eggs in a small pan.

5. Divide the pasta into two bowls. Top each with an egg. Hit them with a little Tabasco sauce to get that authentic NYC-deli bacon, egg, and cheese flavor. Mangia!

SOPRANOS STYLE
—Meirav Devash

These guys today, they want to be buried in a jogging outfit.
—Corrado "Junior" Soprano (Episode 1.6, "Pax Soprana")

Now officially a period drama, in terms of style *The Sopranos* isn't a time capsule representing 1999–2007 at large. It's painstakingly curated for a very specific subculture—the Italian-American Mafia's B-team at the turn of the millennium. Mob fashion has devolved from *Esquire* cover boy Joe Bonanno[2], dapper in a double-breasted suit and fedora, to Tony Soprano in Fila tracksuits and New Balance sneakers[3], and for this we can thank folks like costume designer Juliet Polcsa, who navigated the fashion space between tacky and sophisticated by scouring local Jersey malls and niche boutiques; manicurist Maria Salandra, who did nails for everyone down to the strippers at the Bing; hairstylist Mel McKinney; and makeup artists Kymbra Callaghan and Stephen Kelley, who won an Emmy for their spot-on work on the show. Callaghan told *W* magazine, "Every time I thought I'd gone overboard, I'd look around at the women in my Hoboken neighborhood, and my work was completely validated."

The Sopranos seduced middle America with the guilty pleasures of New Jersey style, and left them hungry for more. How else can we explain the subsequent success of MTV's *Jersey Shore* and our national obsession with Snooki's poof[4], *The Real Housewives of New Jersey*, the

MUSIC IN *THE SOPRANOS*: TOP 40 SONGS—ANDY CAMBRIA AND MARK DELLELO

#1 "DON'T STOP BELIEVIN'," JOURNEY (EPISODE 6.21, "MADE IN AMERICA")

It's distinctly a product of baby-boomer America, rife with ornamentation brought on by the desire for excess (the fake-sounding digital piano, the overdriven arena-rock guitar shredding, the reverby drums—these are the results of isolating individual parts of a musical arrangement and producing them to within an inch of their lives). Even Steve Perry's vocal phrasings are directly lifted from Sam Cooke. This whole song could be something Cooke would've done—with a lot more warmth and soul—in the early '60s, when Johnny Boy and Junior Soprano ran North Jersey. It's not a very good song. Yet . . . it's a great song that makes you feel the way you might if you jettisoned your diet to go out and wolf down onion rings. Like America itself, the song is unconventional and oddly satisfying: it doesn't get to its chorus until the very end, but when it does we love to sing along. Though we want to believe in the small-town girls and city boys in the booth at Holsten's, cracks in the facade of this cozy scene start to appear when we hear lines about a singer in a smoky room: *The smell of wine and cheap perfume / For a smile they can share the night / It goes on and on and on and on.* And we start to remember: for every night Tony's taken his family out to dinner, there's likely been a night he's spent in the back room at Bada Bing. As A.J. complains about the tedium of his new job, and Tony tells him to buck up, we hear the lines: *Some will win, some will lose / Some were born to sing the blues / Oh the movie never ends / It goes on and on and on and on*, right before we learn Tony has forgotten the optimistic speech he gave at Nuovo Vesuvio years ago. The native Soprano cynicism is alive and well, and now we can only hear "Don't Stop Believin'" as a bitingly ironic commentary on the cheerleading it espouses. As the man in the Members Only jacket enters the bathroom to a wailing guitar solo and the onion rings arrive at the table, the song's volume has overtaken Tony's voice on the soundtrack. And when it ceases, along with everything else in the infamous cut to black, we know why. You don't hear it when it happens.

—Andy Cambria

#2 "LIVING ON A THIN LINE," THE KINKS (EPISODE 3.6, "UNIVERSITY")

Ralph Cifaretto is one of the looniest psychopaths we meet in the series, and this episode is the one where we learn just how fucked up he is. When he dominates conversation at the Sopranos' dinner table by tag-teaming with A.J. to describe all the gory details from *Gladiator*, he just seems juvenile. But then in the back room at the Bada Bing when he playacts a scene from the movie, whirling around a heavy chain like a morning star (and accidentally blinding Georgie, the bartender, with it), his capo Gigi Cestone says what everyone in the room is thinking: "They're gonna find this piece of shit in the trunk someday." The Kinks' song used as a theme for this episode refers on one level to his foolhardiness, and on a deeper level to the deterioration of a Cosa Nostra in which a homunculus like him would ever qualify as a made man. And Tony himself is no Marcus Aurelius—he's in the bathroom getting his "weasel waxed" by one of the "University" coeds while Ralphie is pulling his Commodus

rise (and fall) of the Juicy Couture tracksuit, and the return of French-tipped nails?

The closets of North Caldwell tell a story about the dark side of the American Dream and what people will endure to fit in, to stand out, and to stay on top. Tony may lack the polished elegance of John Gotti, but he makes up for it by truly owning his unique brand of goombah existentialism and slovenliness. You don't need a degree from Tufts like Dr. Melfi[5] to decipher the clues in the characters' style choices. A.J.'s Hot Topic nu-metal shirts are a visual cry of teenage rebellion (Pantera's pot leaf) and resentment (Slipknot noose). Carmela tries to live up to everyone's expectation of the mom-slash-moll and creates the Mafia version of Martha Stewart. Adriana La Cerva and *Sex and the City*'s Carrie Bradshaw both wear Jimmy Choo stilettos, but they live worlds apart—much further than the sixty miles from Long Branch, New Jersey, to Manhattan's Upper East Side.

There are a few reasons for this. One, because insecurity (specifically the kind that sounds like, "Whaddaya think, you're better than me?") is one of the foundations of the New Jerseyan character. New Jersey's entire identity is based on being situated next to New York. It provides a certain type of success and a provincial life in the shadow of the city, with a reasonable commute. Secondly, there's the issue of class. Even with stacks of money in the bank—or hidden in the birdfeed—Ade, Carmela, and even Jennifer Melfi are blue-collar broads at heart. Their outfits are the costumes of strivers, telegraphing that they've climbed the social ladder.

ADRIANA'S SINGULAR STYLE

When we meet Adriana in the series pilot, she's a restaurant hostess wearing a simple black dress and sleek center-parted chignon. The viewer barely registers her. But once her character is allowed to evolve as Chris-tuh-fuh's gangster moll, so does her oddball sex appeal. She's so tacky, so skanky, so Freehold Raceway Mall that it's déclassé to admit just how smokin' hot she actually is. She mixes bridge-and-tunnel sensibilities with a rock 'n' roll streak, and somehow winds up looking more like Madonna circa 1985 than a woman of the Noughties. Both Madonna and Ade have a thing for crosses, but Madonna's are about igniting controversy. Ade wears hers on a gold chain because that's what a "good girl" in Italian-American culture does. Even if she is also wearing a black PVC minidress and snorting blow at the Crazy Horse with Tony Soprano.

Her fashion faux pas know no bounds. In Season Three, Episode 1 ("Mr. Ruggerio's Neighborhood"), instead of tennis whites she hits the courts in a tomato-red fringed halter and booty shorts. Even household chores turn to cringe—she irons shirts in ultra-low-rise denim and a crop top that shows off her belly-button ring. Ade's style swan song? Two animal prints in a single episode—Season Five, Episode 12, "Long Term Parking," her last: after meeting with the FBI in a spangled white zebra-print jacket, she brings Christopher a Heineken in a body-skimming tiger-striped catsuit, knee-high leather boots, and a mane of voluminous curls highlighted to within an inch of their lives.

act. There's a triple resonance here between the song lyrics, which describe the crumbling of the British Empire, with the allusions to the fall of Rome and the episode's title, which suggests not a kingdom but a place of opportunity. The episode's victim, Tracee, is beginning her adult life in a strip club presided over by degenerates with lots of money to throw at their dancing girls but no chivalry, despite the oaths of honor they've sworn before an imaginary Round Table. Tony's outrage over Ralph's inhumanity when he murders Tracee is too little, too late. "You're looking at them, asshole," was his answer to the Hasidic Jew who asked him, in Season One, what had become of the Romans whose oppression his people survived. And in this episode we hear Ray Davies sing, *Now another leader says / Break their hearts and break some heads.* What was it that Tom Hagen said at the end of *The Godfather, Part II* when Frank Pentangeli told him the Corleone family was like the Roman Empire? "It was once." And that was in 1960.

—Mark Dellelo

#3 "BAD 'N' RUIN," FACES (EPISODE 5.8, "MARCO POLO")

Mother, don't you recognize your son? howls Rod Stewart as Faces' barreling rocker "Bad 'N' Ruin" kicks into high gear atop Ronnie Wood's juicy, overdriven electric guitar. There's no better theme song imaginable for Tony Blundetto, who has grown tired of waiting for his big cousin, Tony Soprano, to grant him a substantial hand in the family business, and whose descent back into Mob life is cemented by his assassination of Joe "Peeps" Peparelli. When Peeps and an unlucky prostitute exit a New York City brothel to the tune of New Jersey's arena-rock poster children Bon Jovi playing "Wanted Dead or Alive," a jittery point-of-

view shot shows them stepping onto the street as "Bad 'N' Ruin" overtakes the soundtrack. We're looking at them through Blundetto's eyes. He's nervous. He hasn't done this in a long time. But things even out as a Steadicam pushes in on Peeps getting into his Cadillac, and we hear Stewart shout: *So, Mother, when you've seen me, don't forget I'm your boy too / I know my brother has done you proud, he's one foot in the grave / Mother, don't you recognize me now?* The tragedy, of course, is that we recognize Blundetto perfectly. This is the only possible conclusion to the feud of the Two Tonys; and it's the event that seals Blundetto's doom. After completing the execution, and getting his foot run over in the process, Tony B limps off into the night to the wailing strains of Wood's bottleneck guitar. It's as if he's crying out in pain, while the credits roll and we hear: *I'm a burglar in the first degree / But it don't seem to worry me.*
—Andy Cambria

#4 "COMFORTABLY NUMB," ROGER WATERS W/ VAN MORRISON AND THE BAND (EPISODE 6.18, "KENNEDY AND HEIDI")

A cue borrowed directly from Martin Scorsese's *The Departed* is used to give Christopher Moltisanti an exit worthy of a place in the gangster movie hall of fame, while underscoring the sense of arrested development that has plagued Tony and Christopher's relationship since its inception. There's a triple irony at work when Christopher pops a copy of *The Departed* soundtrack into his CD player and "Comfortably Numb" begins: the filmmakers are subtly hinting at their own dependence on Scorsese's technique, while Moltisanti fidgets in the throes of a heroin relapse and Tony pontificates as though he's a desktop-calendar optimist. Watching Christopher

QUEEN CARMELA

If there was a First Lady of northern New Jersey, she would look like Carmela Soprano. As the boss's wife, Carm has access to the best of everything, but she puts it all together with pure New Jersey *joie*. To be fair, she has the difficult task of straddling several archetypal roles—the soccer mom, the good wife, the vixen, and the queen bee. For a lesser woman, this balance of passion and restraint might be impossible, but Carm never lets 'em see her sweat.

She does let 'em see her pastel velour sweat-*suits* and swishy windbreakers, however, often running errands in matchy-matchy sportswear. Don't think for a second that Carm's casualwear means she's let her guard down. We've probably spotted Dita Von Teese out of hair and makeup more often than Carmela Soprano. Even when her life is exploding, she always appears put-together. Her rich-bitch blond hair, perfect blow-outs with volume at the roots, and squared-off French-tipped acrylic claws are time-consuming and expensive to maintain. (The only time we see a chink in her armor is when Tony's in a coma.) This is Carmela's life's work—smoothing over the rough edges until the cracks are no longer visible.

Whether she's all-business in a silk blouse and blazer or relaxed in a ribbed tee, the neckline always flashes a bit of cleavage and a lot of gold. Like a low-key Mr. T, she layers a triumvirate of jewelry—the delicate choker, the diamond-set cross pendant, and the fashion link necklace. Carm's not the type to follow youthful fashion trends like tube tops or low-rise pants. Her love language is luxury.

If Tony stumbles and needs to get back into her good graces, the solution requires reaching deep into his pockets. When Carmela receives a stunning sapphire ring as a birthday gift, she later asks him, "Is there anything you need to tell me?" In the Season Two finale, "Funhouse," we discover that nothing gets her in the mood for romance like a fluffy fur coat. She's a class act, and Tony knows it. "Now this is the real Louie Vitoon," he says in Season Six's "Cold Stones," as he hands Carmela a Louis Vuitton wallet stuffed with hundred-dollar bills. Did it fall off a truck? Maybe. But he wants her to know it's the real deal, just like his love for her.

DR. MELFI'S WORK WARDROBE

Contrast Carmela's multifaceted wardrobe with Dr. Jennifer Melfi's upscale yet one-note look. Just try imagining her wearing anything other than a monochromatic skirt suit, understated makeup, and milky pink nails. Yeah, didn't think so. When Tony Soprano calls her "hon" in their first session, she sets him straight immediately, insisting on "Doctor Melfi." She wears these boundaries on her well-tailored sleeve. She might hail from New Jersey (and still lives there), but she's not of the Sopranos' world. Dr. Melfi is a Bard College girl who graduated from med school and, for Chrissakes, she drives a Saab.

Buttoned up in an endless parade of boring blazers, she works tirelessly to maintain a professional distance from her clients, downplaying her looks with a sensible bob and academic glasses. But those legs. *Marone!* With her bare legs crossed and high heels dangling, it's no

breathe irregularly and shift in his seat, realizing he's high, Tony momentarily stares out the window, trying to convince himself it's not true, but looks back to have his suspicion confirmed to these lyrics: *The child is grown / The dream is gone.* This moment is the end of the dream Tony had for Christopher. We can see the frustration and anger beginning to choke him, his own numbness getting the better of him, as he tries to revive the conversation with small talk: "So how was your party that day at the house?" But Chris swerves, and Kennedy and Heidi (teenage girls armed with a learner's permit) are heading right for them. We remember what happens next, and there's no music to cover the ghastly sounds of Christopher choking to death on his own blood as Tony suffocates him. From Tony's point of view, an impaled car seat in the back of the Escalade reminds us of the way he's learned to use sentimentality to justify his atrocities, and some unheard lyrics from "Comfortably Numb" seem to creep into the scene like a ghost: *I do believe it's working, good / That'll keep you going through the show / Come on it's time to go.*
—Andy Cambria

#5 "MY RIFLE, MY PONY AND ME," DEAN MARTIN AND RICKY NELSON (EPISODE 4.1, "FOR ALL DEBTS PUBLIC AND PRIVATE" AND EPISODE 4.5, "PIE-O-MY")

Season Four is bookended with episodes featuring Dean Martin's voice. The performances used in the premiere and the finale are from different periods of his career. It's the carousing Las Vegas entertainer, affiliated with the Rat Pack, whom we hear at the conclusion, ringing out over the Jersey Shore and replete with a bombastic big band arrangement—the soundtrack Tony has chosen to browbeat the Jewish lawyer Alan Sapinsly into refunding his beach house deposit. (He rants

back, "Fucking goombah trash! This whole shoreline is turning into the Gulf of Sorrento.") But it's an altogether different Dean Martin who graces the opening episode ("For All Debts Public and Private"), heard singing a cowboy ballad in a scene from Howard Hawks's *Rio Bravo* (1959). This period of Martin's career lies between his clownish partnership with Jerry Lewis and his slick reign as a nightclub crooner. The dignity of both his acting and his role as a heroic Westerner here provide Tony with an aspirational model that I've written about in a separate essay. Martin's bass-baritone never resounded with such homespun masculine virtue as we hear in this spare arrangement, supported by Ricky Nelson's guitar and Walter Brennan's harmonica with simple folk harmonies that are as old and authentic as the American pioneer spirit (notwithstanding Ricky's doo-wop stylings on the final chorus). There's a pathetic irony in the fact that we don't hear the song play out in full until the end of "Pie-O-My," in which Tony has alienated himself from every living being except for a horse and a goat.
—Mark Dellelo

#6 "LEAVING CALIFORNIA," SHAWN SMITH (EPISODE 5.12, "LONG TERM PARKING")

It's likely no *Sopranos* fan will ever be able to hear "Leaving California" without thinking of Adriana La Cerva—it's the soundtrack of the moments leading up to her death, and a brilliant audio edit incorporated into it provides one of the most memorable moments in the entire series. After the fateful phone call, wherein Tony tells Adriana that Christopher has attempted suicide, manipulating her into staying put so Silvio Dante can pick her up, we see a car driving down a sunny highway to the song's blissed-out, acoustic-guitar introduction. For a moment, we

wonder Tony has a hard time keeping his mind on therapy. Her sex appeal is all about the unattainable and what remains unseen. It makes her irresistible to Tony, a man who believes nothing should be off-limits to him. Yet fantasy is often best left to the imagination, which is apparent (in the Season One episode "Pax Soprana") when Tony asks his *comare* Irina to role-play as a sexy Melfi substitute:

"I'm just sayin', maybe wear somethin' a little more professional. You know, like you're in business," he says.

"Fuck you. I'm no whore."

"No. That's not what I mean. Not like you're in the whore business. Oh, forget it."

MEN'S APPAREL

As a rule, menswear isn't nearly as interesting as women's fashion, dad bods don't inspire mad lust, and cigar smoke doesn't double as cologne. But this is *The Sopranos* and rules no longer apply. Take Paulie Walnuts, Tony's long-suffering captain and a genuine '50s throwback. From his audacious skunk-striped pompadour to his double-breasted Italian suits to the way he flashes his pinky ring when pointing—extending his index and little fingers simultaneously into the *mano cornuto*—he's got old-school cool down pat. Or Silvio Dante, the most flamboyant member of the gang, with a bulletproof helmet of hair and shirts patterned after Atlantic City casino carpeting. Or Furio Giunta, freshly imported eurotrash in a ponytail and Versace-like silk shirts otherwise reserved for hip-hop stars or whoever is dealing coke in Ibiza.

With ambition to spare and the attention span of a gnat, Christopher Moltisanti is the family's worst dresser and, in retrospect, the most accurate. His look is a confused mélange of Mafia tropes with the weather-inappropriate touches of a junkie. To bury a Russian in the snow-covered Pine Barrens, he dons a red silk shirt, pinstriped slacks, a black leather jacket, and derby shoes. For warmth, he wraps dirty carpeting from the van's interior around himself like one of André Leon Talley's capes. When he goes casual in a black Nike tracksuit unzipped to the navel to frame his undershirt and St. Christopher pendant, he tops it off with a khaki bucket hat punctuated by fishing lures in what can only be described as a Jay-Z/Gilligan mashup.

Christopher looks sharp exactly once—on the day he gets made. Keep in mind that Paulie has to call with a fashion heads-up to "look sharp and meet him at Modell's in half an hour." He really pulls it together in a blue herringbone suit with matching cream-colored shirt, tie, pocket square, and Cartier wristwatch. We never see the suit again.

As for Tony, a narcissist ill at ease in his own skin, he seeks out comfort in casualwear. He's not a fashion guy, which makes sense considering he likely shops in the Big & Tall section. His belly expands along with his power, limiting his options to flowing cabana shirts, boxy paneled bowling shirts, and cozy tracksuits. Somehow, his growing waistline and normcore dad clothes don't chip away at his confidence in the slightest. He's as self-assured as Brad Pitt in the bedroom, love handles and all. Despite all the fancy

think this is finally it: Adriana is in the car alone, driving away with her suitcase in the passenger seat, having realized her only chance to survive is to flee. When we hear the lines _Maybe in another life you like to stay / And the devil may call you when he thinks it's time,_ we're cheering Adriana down the road. But then, that edit. There's a smash cut to a close-up of Adriana's eyes, and now the song sounds mid-rangey and filtered, like it's coming out of a radio speaker. In this instance, the music starts working for us the same way it does for her: our horrified realization that we've shifted to her point of view, that she's a passenger in a car being driven by Silvio, hearing this song through a car stereo being played by someone else, coincides with the line _You know that he'll be knocking if you're still here,_ and we realize she's about to die. Adriana has her own moment of terror as the song's mood shifts again. In contrast to the up-tempo, poppy groove of the verse used to score what we now know was a fantasy, the chorus breaks down into a bluesy, half-time feel and utters a cryptic warning: _Don't wait too long, 'cause you're almost there._ But all Adriana can see are acres of barren woodlands rolling past her window. There's only one reason someone gets taken deep into the forest in this world. _Don't want too long, till you see it undone._ This line is for us. Our entire concept of the North Jersey milieu we'd grown to love is about to be shredded to bits. Adriana has started to cry, and we wish we could pounce through the screen and comfort her in this moment of reckoning. What we get instead is the sight of Silvio, sensing her fear, and monstrously relishing the thought of what's about to happen. Mercifully, we don't see it when it does.

—Andy Cambria

#7 "IF I WERE A CARPENTER," BOBBY DARIN (EPISODE 5.9, "UNIDENTIFED BLACK MALES")

The series had to include a Bobby Darin song, of course, but this one was in some ways a surprising choice, as it's from the stage of his career when he took a detour from the nightclub circuit (he famously sold out the Copacabana in 1960 and then became a fixture in Vegas) into something resembling folk-rock (this song was written by Tim Hardin, who performed it at Woodstock). Moved by the civil rights movement, Darin spent time with Martin Luther King and Bobby Kennedy and considered a career in politics. There's surely some irony in the fact that the song's persona is here identified with Tony, who's just confessed that he made up a racist story to save face when he didn't turn up for the job that landed Tony Blundetto in the can. (He wasn't jumped by two "unidentified black males"; he had a panic attack after his mother berated him.) At the end of the episode, Carmela is putting away some of her fancy jewelry when Meadow calls her to announce her engagement to Finn, telling her mother that he's using his graduation present to buy her a ring. Carmela begins to cry as any mother would, but these aren't tears of unalloyed joy: in the next beat she looks out the window and sees Tony sunning his beer belly in the swimming pool. *If I were a carpenter, and you were a lady / Would you marry me anyway, would you have my baby?* Well, she did, even though she had another suitor who was a pharmacist. And now her baby is about to marry a Columbia graduate headed off to dental school, and the last shot of Carmela reveals a silent, painful sob.

—Mark Dellelo

luxury goods that fall into his lap, clothes don't impress him much. When Richie Aprile gifts him "the jaaacket," a brown silk-lined "Corinthian leather" trench formerly belonging to Rocco DiMeo, "the toughest prick in Essex County," Tony reluctantly accepts it before ditching it later. Sure, Tony throws on a sports coat and Rolex when necessary, but he's never as comfortable as he is in an A-shirt and boxer shorts, cocooned in that ratty white bathrobe. *Capisce?*

THE JERSEY MOB MAKEOVER
—Meirav Devash

When FBI special agent Deborah Ciccerone-Waldrup is chosen for an undercover assignment befriending Adriana La Cerva, her boss at the Newark Organized Crime Task Force asks, "How big can you make your hair?" Bureau Chief Cubitoso (Frank Pellegrino) knows digging for information on the Soprano family is the easy part. The hard part is getting Little Miss Priss over here in the slicked-back bun and single strand of pearls to nail a believable Jersey girl beauty look. She just joined Forever 21 Jumpstreet, and she can't show up with *facia brutta*. A makeover of this magnitude is a complicated and time-consuming affair, requiring a spray tan and two hours' prep time. Here's what it takes to become sexy personal shopper Danielle Ciccolella from Whippany.

GIANT, BOUFFED-OUT HAIR

A real Italian-American princess can call any of ten cousins who went to beauty school. When all you've got is a cover story and a blow-dryer, it's a whole other story. First, the secret to big hair is to start in the shower. Use a volumizing or clarifying shampoo to remove any product residue and skip conditioner—it'll only weigh your hair down. Next, rough-dry your hair with the blow-dryer until it's 80 percent dry. Flip the hair upside down and use a round brush to dry it. Gravity and a final blast of heat should do the trick. For even more height at the crown, set the still warm hair on top with large rollers until cool. Still want more? Tease the shit out of it at the roots and hairspray ruthlessly from about six inches away. Don't light any cigarettes during this stage. Smooth down the top layer of hair with a comb, spray it again, and place sunglasses on your head like a headband.

BRONZED SKIN

The most legit look requires a summer at the Jersey Shore or serving time in a tanning bed, but the quickest way to get all-over Sunkist skin is with a faux tan. Book a spray tan with a professional who will douse your cold, naked body like you're in a prison movie with the stinky active ingredient DHA. If you've got some lead time, use a foolproof gradual formula at home for a few days, which will still smell slightly of yeast and gym socks but not as bad.

DAYTIME SMOKY EYES

Why save smoky eyes for an evening soiree when you can wear them to "sit with a Starbucks"? For her first meeting with Adriana, Danielle skips sooty black eye shadow and tries something a little softer. To get the look, apply metallic champagne color to the lids and tightline the eyes with grayish brown powder. Starting at the outer third of the lids, layer on the gray-brown shade and brush it beyond the outer corners, blending up and in to a hazy point.

FALSE LASHES

What God gave you is never enough. The right length and thickness is approximately Bambi lashes + Kim Kardashian + tarantula legs. Ardell makes great ones, available at drugstores. Consider stacking two sets of lashes, one on top of the other, for more drama. Tip: apply lash glue to the outer edge of the eyelash strip—not your eyelid—or you'll glop on too much glue and seal your eyes shut.

CONTOURED CHEEKS

Contouring can fake the look of chiseled cheekbones no matter how much spaghetti you eat. First, suck in the cheeks to see where the natural hollows are. That's how you'll know where to brush the color. Using a neutral or cool-toned bronzer and a Kabuki brush, sweep from your ear under each cheekbone, stopping at the center of the cheek. Blend in a circular motion and add blush to the apples.

BROWNISH LIPSTICK

When red lips seem a little too try-hard, the appeal of brown lipstick can take hold. The guidette code respects blinginess over earthiness, so the obvious choice here is a frosted beigey-mauvey-brown color that will spark

'90s flashbacks. The mouth should look and feel irresistible, particularly when perking the lips around the word "Whippany."

LONG, FIERCE CLAWS

Jersey girls talk with their hands as much as they do with their mouths, so your manicure had better be on point. Your long, skinny tips should make banal tasks like washing dishes or pressing your numeric keypad a zillion times to text nearly impossible. If you're too busy for acrylic tips at the salon (say, you're an FBI agent with a double life), press-on nails are a godsend. French tips with crystals or chromed-out metallics are ideal—they're both attention-getting and neutral, so they match any outfit. Use quality nail glue from the beauty supply store instead of whatever comes in your nail kit. That will stop them from popping off at an inopportune time, like when removing a wandering hand from your thigh.

#8 "GLAD TIDINGS," VAN MORRISON (EPISODE 5.13, "ALL DUE RESPECT")

In the Season Five premiere Tony was in exile from his home, but the last image of the finale shows Carmela welcoming him back. *And the princess will wake up from her slumber,* Van Morrison sings, backed by an R&B horn section that blasts out like a fanfare for a king at his castle. *And we'll send you glad tidings from New York,* whose sovereign, Johnny Sack, has just held an audience for Tony, who made his escape when the FBI showed up: the king is dead, long live the king. Earlier in the episode we heard the same verse with irony, just before Tony blew away his cousin Tony Blundetto with a shotgun and Van Morrison sang: *Ask you not to read between the lines.* And before then we heard it filtered through Christopher's envy, as it played on his car stereo while he voiced his resentment about the boss's favoritism toward his other cousin. There's Christmas snow on the ground and two out of three of these characters get a big gift: *Don't it gratify when you see it materialize / Right in front of your eyes / That surprise.* But when Van Morrison sings, *And they'll lay you down low and easy,* he's not addressing either of them. It may not exactly be low and easy, but when you think about the kind of hit a rabid Phil Leotardo might have pulled on Tony Blundetto, Van the Man's benediction sounds about right.

—Mark Dellelo

#9 "BLACK BOOKS," NILS LOFGREN (EPISODE 3.7, "SECOND OPINION")

This song plays softly in the background at the start of a sequence where Carmela visits Meadow in her Columbia dorm, but then shifts into the foreground once a shot from Carmela's point of view identifies its source as a stereo in an adjacent room. The first lyric

ON THE COUCH WITH DR. HASTINGS:
HOW PSYCHIATRY AND PSYCHIATRISTS ARE PORTRAYED IN *THE SOPRANOS*

Over the years, pundits—professional and otherwise—have argued over Dr. Melfi's effectiveness. Is she a lousy shrink? Is Tony an impossible patient? It's easy to forget that she's one of multiple shrinks who appear on the show—all treating members of Tony's immediate family—with most appearing in at least three episodes.

We're sitting down with my friend Dr. Jonathan Hastings, a New Hampshire psychiatrist who also attended NYU for graduate studies in cinema, to discuss Dr. Melfi's professional techniques and her overall performance. We'll also consider the work of the other mental health professionals we meet on the show.

NICK: Thanks for agreeing to be part of our book, Dr. Hastings. First, tell us a little about your background.

DR. HASTINGS: I'm just finishing up my training in psychiatry. I'm a longtime film buff, and, before going back to medical school to become a doctor, I worked in the bowels of the entertainment industry (emphasis on "industry"). Arguing about movies and TV is my favorite pastime.

NICK: And you've mentioned to me that one of the doctors who trained you had something to do with *The Sopranos*. Can you expand on that?

DR. HASTINGS: Our course on how to conduct a psychiatric interview was run by Dr. Ron Green; his sister, Robin Green, was one of the writers on the show, and she'd ask him for recommendations about which medications a psychiatrist would likely recommend for Tony.

NICK: So Dr. Green is actually responsible for the lithium that gives Tony delusions of a voluptuous Italian dental student who house-sits for the Cusamanos in "Isabella"! To kick off our discussion, I'd like to hear your perspective on David Chase's view of therapy and its value.

DR. HASTINGS: I think the show takes psychotherapy very seriously, and we do see that it has value: Chase has Tony, during that first session with Dr. Melfi, lamenting the culture of therapy, invoking Gary Cooper as an earlier generation's ideal of the strong silent type. But that doesn't seem to be a view endorsed by Chase, or the show in general. On the contrary, we see Tony start to get better—less depressed, less prone to panic attacks.

Stepping back, though, it becomes a little more complicated: there's a

that's likely to grab our attention is something about *tender times long past*, which could describe the mother-daughter relationship, but then we hear the second verse loud and clear through Carmela's ears and watch her reflect on the lines, *She wants to see other guys / Get lost in other eyes*. After two scenes in which Tony has demonstrated his aloofness, she is highly susceptible to these lyrics. "He reports to a strip club; who knows how he spends his days," she tells Melfi. Carmela's moment of reflection while the song plays may be what convinces her, in the next scene, to set up a private therapy session with Melfi's mentor, Dr. Krakower. "You can make that plural, yes—my husband sees other women and I sort of look the other way," she admits to him. The therapist shows chutzpah and speaks to her very candidly, landing a body blow that sends her flat out on the living room couch. When Tony enters the room she tells him, "Everybody else in this family sleeps all day, I thought I'd try it." We hear a reprise of the song and listen to Nils Lofgren's intricate fingerpicking and shimmering fretboard tapping as Carmela manipulates Tony into agreeing to a sizable donation to Columbia: "You have to do something nice for me today and this is what I want." Judging that acquiescence is the better part of valor in this moment, he tries to seal the conversation with a sly smile and an invitation to dine out, but Carmela's face doesn't soften as she rises to get dressed and Lofgren goes on to sing: *The hardest truths don't have a why / Often true love will just die.*

—Mark Dellelo

#10 "ALL THROUGH THE NIGHT," TRADITIONAL WELSH AIR (EPISODE 1.3, "DENIAL, ANGER, ACCEPTANCE")

The electric baptism scene in *The Godfather* marking Michael

Corleone's ascension to Don features wailing blasts of a church organ while we watch his soldiers execute their enemies—underscoring the irony in his pledge to reject Satan and live a moral life. As Meadow's high school choir sings, *Soft the drowsy hours are creeping / Hill and vale in slumber steeping* and Tony looks on lovingly, director Nick Gomez cuts away to Junior Soprano taking his revenge on Christopher and Brendan Filone. Chris is humiliated at gunpoint, and Brendan is shot through the eyeball while zonked out in the bathtub: the latter act of violence is a particularly juicy allusion to Moe Greene's murder. Cutting back to the performance, we watch Meadow and bestie Hunter Scangarelo take their solos as they sing: *While the moon her watch is keeping / All through the night / While the weary world is sleeping / All through the night.* Tony is moved to tears by what he perceives as a vision of purity and innocence, underscored by the lyrics, which have the feeling of a lullaby. His business has been making him feel devoid of human feelings or goodness, and watching his daughter make beautiful music gives him the euphoric sense that his life has meaning. The fact that Meadow and Hunter are propped up by crystal meth during their performance is lost on him. He sees what he wants to see—just as the business he conducts all through the night, every night, remains unbeknownst to his daughter. Even if *The Godfather* made its bones while *The Sopranos* was going out with cheerleaders, it certainly makes up for lost time by doubling down on the ironic use of music in the famed baptismal sequence and involving both sides of the family.

—Andy Cambria

bigger question that the show starts to wrestle with through Dr. Melfi's own conflicted feelings about helping Tony. If therapy makes Tony a better gangster (which, I think, we might argue, it does), is that really a good thing?

NICK: I would definitely agree that it makes him a better gangster. I also think we'd agree that it's through engaging completely in the therapeutic process with Dr. Melfi that he reaches two of his most chilling decisions: to kill his cousin Tony Blundetto and his honorary nephew Christopher Moltisanti. But let's discuss Dr. Melfi, and her professional performance throughout the series. For the uninitiated, how would you describe Melfi's practice—her style, beliefs, training, and approach?

DR. HASTINGS: She's very much the traditional private-practice psychiatrist, of a kind that's probably not as common today as it was twenty years ago. Her approach as a therapist is "psychodynamically" informed, which broadly means that the therapist works with the patient to gain insight into the unconscious conflicts that may be causing symptoms of psychic and emotional distress. This isn't to be confused with "psychoanalysis," when the patient meets with the analyst daily, not weekly, and lies down on a couch and free-associates. That's a much more intensive style of psychotherapy, and requires a great deal of extra training, whereas all psychiatrists who finish a residency training program in the U.S. have had experience with psychodynamic therapy.

NICK: Why isn't her style of practice as common in 2020 as it was in 2000?

DR. HASTINGS: Since then, comparatively fewer psychiatrists have been practicing primarily as therapists. They are more likely to focus on treatment with medications, leaving therapy to psychologists and social workers (who, as of now at least, still can't prescribe medications). Part of the issue is that being a good therapist takes much more practice than most psychiatrists will get in their medical training (a few training programs excepted) and so it makes sense to work in a way that plays to your strengths.

NICK: In "The Sopranos," Chase uses Tony's appointments with Melfi as a structural device. He has four appointments in the episode and skips one of them. Does their initial dynamic and chemistry ring true to your experience of the intake and "getting to know you" phase?

DR. HASTINGS: Overall, it rings completely true. On her part, a mix

#11 "IT'S ALRIGHT MA (I'M ONLY BLEEDING)," BOB DYLAN (EPISODE 6.21, "MADE IN AMERICA")

Advertising signs that con you / Into thinking you're the one / That can do what's never been done / That can win what's never been won / Meantime life outside goes on / All around you. Though Dylan wrote that lyric during the Vietnam War, as the girlfriend sitting next to A.J. in his SUV says, "It's amazing it was written so long ago—it's about right now." And in the next scene A.J. will announce to his parents his intention to enlist in the army and join the fight in Iraq! Is it unfair to say that his interest in the song doesn't extend beyond his hormonal desire to shag the teenage girl who turns him on to it? I think so, but not by much. The aspect of Dylan's lyrics that A.J. identifies with is the existential one that we'd expect any antiauthoritarian adolescent to latch on to: *But though the masters make the rules / For the wise men and the fools / I got nothing, Ma, to live up to.* And he probably also thinks that any girl who gets this song gets him: he makes eyes at her while listening to the verse *When a trembling distant voice unclear / Startles your sleeping ears to hear / That somebody thinks they really found you.* But if any part of Dylan's critique of consumerism registers with him, it's short-lived: surely the irony that the song caused the spontaneous combustion of his luxury car (because of a reaction between the battery powering the stereo and the dead leaves on the ground) is lost on him. And he quickly trades in his misbegotten idea to fight for truth, justice, and that other thing when his parents offer to buy him a BMW and get him a job in the movie industry, anyway.

—Mark Dellelo

#12 "MY LOVER'S PRAYER," OTIS REDDING (EPISODE 2.9, "FROM WHERE TO ETERNITY")

It's as perfect a pairing as one could imagine, when "From Where to Eternity" opens on anguished Adriana La Cerva keeping vigil at Christopher Moltisanti's bedside in the ICU to the tune of "My Lover's Prayer" by Otis Redding. His fiery, pained vocal phrasings and the fundamental power of his voice represent Adriana's unwavering love and devotion for Christopher. In the morally bankrupt Sopranosphere, Adriana stands as an outlier: she looks for the good in everyone, and always places her own needs second. The bold desperation Redding is unafraid to showcase in his performance could be a mirror for the way Adriana clings to the dream of sailing into the sunset with Christopher at her side, especially since his survival looks uncertain at best. The song surges to full volume when she breaks down as he lapses into cardiac arrest. Its reference to prayer is echoed by the episode's overarching theme—the moral hypocrisy displayed by the Soprano family in relation to the teachings of their Catholic faith. Adriana rests a charm inset with the image of the Pope on Christopher's chest in the hospital; and a major subplot centers around Carmela's insistence Tony get a vasectomy after a family friend's *comare* gives birth to a child. At first Tony refuses. But after realizing the damage he's already inflicting on his own kids (let alone what the presence of a child born to a mistress would do to them), he acquiesces—only to discover that Carmela, who doesn't want to rule out the possibility of another baby after Meadow leaves for college, has changed her mind. As the Soprano bed is consumed by their lovemaking, "My Lover's Prayer" returns to close out the

of trying to draw him out and also, appropriately, tentatively challenging him makes sense. On his part, a little defensiveness as he gets used to how therapy is supposed to work also rings true. The sentiment he expresses— that therapy is really just a kind of whining—is something that I've seen brought up at the beginning of treatment. People are still ambivalent about therapy during that early getting-to-know-each-other period.

I do think it's a bold move on her part when she questions the possible placebo effect starting Prozac has had on him. Melfi is doing it to call attention to the benefit Tony is getting from the talk therapy, but she's also putting that improvement at risk by making him conscious of it. (Incidentally, I think it's now better understood that people do start to feel better from medications like Prozac relatively soon after starting it, though it's true that it takes several weeks to enjoy their full benefit from it.)

NICK: In the series' earlier therapy sessions, we see Tony vacillate between kvetching about his mother, Livia, and defending her. "I'm the ungrateful fuck, because I come here and I complain about her and I let my wife exclude her from *my* home," he tells Dr. Melfi. I'd presume this is a common theme in therapy: a patient complaining, only to shift their tune once the therapist validates the feeling. Can you tell us about the techniques a therapist like Melfi might use to help a person accept their feelings, and evaluate how she manages this with Tony through the first couple of seasons?

DR. HASTINGS: That's a fundamental therapy dynamic. The idea is that the symptoms come out of an unconscious conflict between different beliefs or emotions: so it's very common that someone will have negative feelings towards a person that they feel they should only have positive feelings about. It's the therapist's job to help patients feel safe in expressing, consciously, those negative feelings, while at the same time realizing that their reaction is likely defensive, as we see with Tony. At that stage of therapy, the technique is mainly to call attention to that shift in tune.

NICK: Melfi deals with both physical threats and romantic overtures from Tony. She's clearly frightened when he flips the table and looms over her, enraged, after a comment Melfi makes about his mother in "I Dream of Jeannie Cusamano." How do you assess her professional judgment following these sequences?

DR. HASTINGS: Any single instance like that might be legitimate cause for some

episode, this time reminding us of the spiritual compromise undertaken by Carmela in the face of loneliness. That's desperation of a sort, but it stands in stark contrast to the purity of conviction displayed by Adriana in the face of, what was then, certainly her darkest hour.

—Andy Cambria

#13 "STATE TROOPER," BRUCE SPRINGSTEEN (EPISODE 1.13, "I DREAM OF JEANNIE CUSAMANO")

On a brutally stormy night, trapped in a torrential downpour that's made the roads impassable, the Soprano family takes refuge at Artie Bucco's Nuovo Vesuvio, where they find that Silvio, Paulie, Christopher, and Adriana have done the same. They're among friends and family. Artie knows just what cabernet to send over. And even though he's only got candlelight and gas with which to cook, he's able to rustle them up a pasta dinner that looks absolutely heavenly in the warm, amber-tinged flickers of the trattoria. As A.J. digs in prematurely, Tony smacks the back of his hand and proposes a toast: "Someday soon, you're gonna have families of your own. And if you're lucky, you'll remember the little moments. Like this. That were good." Carmela holds back tears and we're right there with her. This tender moment is interrupted by the low groaning of a tree branch threatening to buckle under the gales outside; and lightning flashes as Springsteen's chugging, palm-muted acoustic guitar fades into the scene, filling us with a sense of ominousness and dread. There's nothing anthemic about the vocal delivery as we hear the lyrics: *License, registration, I ain't got none / But I got a clear conscience 'bout the things that I done,* and we see that the joy at Nuovo Vesuvio is fleeting. These are the thoughts of a paranoid man, and a reminder that even when Tony is at his most vulnerable and charming the serpent lies just beneath the skin.

—Andy Cambria

#14 "CORE 'NGRATO," DOMINIC CHIANESE (EPISODE 3.13, "ARMY OF ONE")

Uncle Junior, his narcissism in full bloom, gets up to perform this Neapolitan song (written by an Italian-American composer in 1911 as a showpiece number for Enrico Caruso) at Jackie Aprile Jr.'s wake. Everyone in the room projects his or her own feelings onto it (which we see in a sequence of close-ups), and in most cases it has the anticipated sentimental effect. But the irony of singing these lyrics at this moment appears lost on everyone except for one character who may actually be the least likely to understand the Italian. Meadow has just finished giving her mother an earful about the ways in which Jackie's parents neglected him. It's she who grasps the callousness of Junior's grandstanding and the whole *famiglia*'s sentimental indulgence of it at this moment when the Mafia culture they're all a part of has devoured one of its own. She throws hunks of bread at Junior as he thoughtlessly sings, *Heart, ungrateful heart / You've taken my life / Everything has passed / And you don't think anymore.* In the final moments of the episode Junior keeps singing in Italian while sentimental songs in other languages overtake his voice in the sound mix: the tragic irony of the Mob boss performing this song at this occasion is no clearer to his audience in their ancestral language than it would be if they heard it in French or Spanish.

—Mark Dellelo

#15 "RETURN TO ME," BOB DYLAN (EPISODE 3.12, "AMOUR FOU")

When it becomes clear that talk and physical intimidation aren't

therapists to cut ties with a patient. The romantic overtures may be something she's expecting, based on the kind of therapy she's providing and the kind of topics they are exploring. From a professional, "being-a-good-therapist" point of view, she'd want to consider the feelings Tony develops for her and focus on them as part of the therapeutic process. The threats of violence (and actual violence) shows, perhaps, overconfidence on her part; though it's hard to say because, as those scenes are written and as they play out with Tony pouncing but never injuring her, her confidence is justified. There's not much detail about her background with other patients who reacted violently towards her; it may be just something she's used to and is comfortable with (though it doesn't necessarily play that way in the scenes). But either way, she would have been perfectly justified, from a professional standpoint, for terminating Tony's care after any of those violent outbursts—but her decision not to is also understandable.

NICK: At the beginning of Season Two Melfi has to "lam it" and set up shop in a local motel to see patients. When Tony tracks her to a diner and confronts her, she's filled with rage—one of her patients committed suicide while her availability was compromised. She asks him, "How many more people have to die for your personal growth?" And yet she decides to take him back on as a patient. As a doctor, what do you think about her decision? What would you do?

DR. HASTINGS: It's tough. It's easy to think that if she really felt that way, she would not take a patient back on who was potentially a danger to her other patients. On the other hand, the desire not to abandon someone who is reaching back out is also very strong. I hesitate to be too judgmental, even about a fictional psychiatrist. I've certainly seen treatment decisions made by other people that, looked at from afar, seem to be suboptimal (to put it mildly), but, most (not all) of the time, if you go back and ask the other doctor or therapist why they did what they did, it makes sense in the context of everything that was going on with that patient at that time. If I were in Melfi's position, I would want to get feedback from a supervisor, just to make sure my own ego wasn't getting in the way of what was really best for my patients. I don't think her decision is terrible, though, and it certainly isn't unbelievable.

NICK: How do you think Melfi handles the fact that two of her patients, Tony and Gloria, are dating behind her back and lying about it?

going to get Gloria Trillo to back off from her relationship with Tony, Patsy Parisi is dispatched and gets her alone under the guise of taking a new Mercedes for a test drive. Stopping the car, he pulls out a pistol and presses it to her chest in what's undoubtedly Dan Grimaldi's most chilling scene of the series. As Gloria trembles in terror, Patsy calmly tells her, "You call or go anywhere near him or his family, and they'll be scraping your nipples off these fine leather seats. And here's the point to remember: *my* face is the last one you'll see. *Not* Tony's. We understand each other? It won't be cinematic." Patsy reappears in the episode's final shot, strolling to his car, groceries in arms, chatting on his cell phone, telling his wife he'll be home in twenty minutes with reheatable stuffed shells. As Dylan croons, *Hurry back, hurry back, hurry home / To my arms and my heart*, there's a chilling link made between the comfortable banality of end-of-day American life and Gloria's agonized plea for affection that prompts the death threat against her. For Tony Soprano and his crew, casually threatening to murder someone you're done using is no big deal. It's all in a day's work.

—Andy Cambria

#16 "SPOSA SON DISPREZZATA," CECILIA BARTOLI (EPISODE 3.11, "PINE BARRENS" AND EPISODE 3.12, "AMOUR FOU")

This Italian opera aria is a lament by the wife of an unfaithful husband. Naturally, it's associated with Carmela's point of view, though we first hear it in reference to the object of Tony's adulterous affair: Gloria Trillo. The song plays in the background during Carmela's visit to the Metropolitan Museum of Art with Meadow. There's some dramatic irony in its use, as she doesn't know that Tony is sleeping with Gloria, though she certainly knows he's been unfaithful to her. It isn't the song that triggers an emotional response from her in this moment, but rather a Renaissance painting: Jusepe de Ribera's *The Mystical Marriage of St. Catherine*, which depicts the wedding of a virgin saint with the baby Jesus. "She's marrying a baby?" Meadow asks. "We all do," Carmela answers. The synergy here among song, narrative, image, and the naked intensity of Edie Falco's performance, and even the rather theatrical staging—Carmela stops short when she spots the painting from across the gallery, then glides over deliberately to get a closer look—summons up the sensory ka-pow of opera. And the scene gets at the mysterious nature of genuine confrontations with great art, dramatizing the way in which aesthetic stimuli can, in our most receptive moments, set loose all sorts of feelings we haven't fully sorted through. Carmela sees innocence, serenity, beauty, and youth in the painting as thoughts of her own tumultuous romantic life and hopes and fears about her daughter dance through her mind.

—Mark Dellelo

#17 "MOONLIGHT MILE," THE ROLLING STONES (EPISODE 6.12, "KAISHA")

An unconventional Stones song that is largely free of Keith Richards's bluesy, distorted guitar playing, "Moonlight Mile" is bookended by a plaintive acoustic-guitar intro and string-section outro that—coupled with the subtly poetic lyrics—make it one of the truly epic rock-star songs about missing home. Capitalizing on this structure, Chase uses "Moonlight Mile" to begin *and* end "Kaisha." As that acoustic guitar plinks in the background, Carlo Gervasi enters the garage of a darkened beach house, shuttered for the winter, and extracts the obnoxious "Fat Dom" Gamiello's frosty severed

DR. HASTINGS: She's in a difficult situation. She knows they're lying, but she still has to respect her doctor-patient confidentiality with each of them. I think she does a good job of pushing them, without being overly confrontational. She gets a lot of therapeutically useful information out of Gloria, just by asking those questions and seeing Gloria's overly defensive response. For example, when Melfi raises the delicate issue of overhearing a man's voice when she last spoke to Gloria on the phone, Gloria jumps into a lie about her car having broken down, saying the voice was the mechanic's. Some therapists might have wanted to avoid this kind of confrontation, but Melfi's instincts are right to bring this up: the question—the confrontation—brings out Gloria's borderline personality traits. She's too easily wounded emotionally to be able to lie effectively! She's too upset to say something like "I can see you're trying to look out for me," which would be a reasonable response to have. Instead, she goes on the attack and accuses Melfi of being unprofessional. Gloria can't help but to sabotage herself. Ideally, Melfi would be able to come back to this interaction later, though that's not something we see in the show.

NICK: Does a private practice therapist like Melfi have a supervisor? Or just a therapist like Peter Bogdanovich's Elliot Kupferberg? Is that a professional mandate? Tell us a little about their professional relationship (and is it strange that they have a personal one?) before we get into the specifics of the dynamic and how it relates to her relationship with Tony.

DR. HASTINGS: A private practice psychiatrist like Dr. Melfi wouldn't be required to have a supervisor, though it's a good and common practice. The difference between a supervisor and having your own therapist is that the supervisor, by definition, is also concerned about the supervisee's patients, whereas someone acting solely as the therapist for the psychiatrist would be more focused on the psychiatrist herself. Kupferberg does seem to be acting in a supervisor's role at some points, though the line is blurry. Their personal relationship probably makes more sense if they're supervisor/supervisee and less so if they're therapist/client. Interestingly, when therapists have criticized the show, the main target for their criticism has been Kupferberg's behavior and choices, more so than Melfi's, especially his decision to break all sorts of ethical standards of confidentiality when he reveals that Tony Soprano is Melfi's patient.

head from a freezer. He drives away while Mick Jagger sings, *When the wind blows and the rain feels cold / With a head full of snow,* and then has trouble disposing of it in a drain, kicking it and yelling "Motherfucker!" Cut to Sheepshead Bay, where Phil Leotardo's wire room has itself been wired with explosives planted by the Sopranos. While Jagger sings, *Made a rag pile of my shiny clothes / Gonna warm my bones,* Phil and his *comare* are knocked off their feet by a thunderous fireball that seems to envelop half a city block. At the end of the episode, during a Christmas Eve gathering at the Sopranos' home, "Moonlight Mile" resurfaces. Carmela pauses as she rests her hand on Tony's knee right before the camera tracks backward and the seasonal hearth seems to swallow everyone gathered around it (a cozy fire harking back to Sheepshead Bay). Until this moment, we've been listening to Frank Sinatra sing "Silent Night," but a brilliant audio crossfade brings The Stones back and Jagger sings, *My dream is fading down the railway line / I'm just about a moonlight mile down the road.* All that's left in the song's wake is our memory of the clandestine body disposal in the intro—the murder, lies, and duplicity that have financed the palatial Soprano estate and made the happy holiday gathering possible.
—Andy Cambria

#18 "THIS MAGIC MOMENT," THE DRIFTERS (EPISODE 6.13, "SOPRANO HOME MOVIES")
While there's a complex family drama playing out under the surface of Tony and Carmela's trip to Bobby Baccalieri's lakeside cabin, the episode's main event is the sequence where Bobby commits his first murder. We hear "This Magic Moment" for the first time as Bobby scans the dial of a

late-model portable radio, tying the song to a relic of simpler times and linking it to the conversation he and Tony have about how gangster life used to be under their fathers. Tony recalls that Bobby's never "popped his cherry"—old man "Bacala" shielded his son from violence the same way Tony shields A.J. Later, after a drunken Monopoly game turns into a fistfight in which Bobby emasculates Tony in front of Janice and Carmela, Tony is eager to subjugate Bobby and knows what a vengeful blow it will be to his good-natured soul. So he assigns Bobby the hit on René LeCours, the boyfriend of their Québecois drug supplier's sister. After the agonizing scene in which Bobby carries out the killing (recall how we see his face reflected in the windowed door of a laundry-room dryer, as one Bobby disappears and another is born), he returns to the cabin at sunset while "This Magic Moment" plays on the soundtrack. A string section quietly swells while the camera pushes in, suggesting how the world Bobby knew is closing in around him. As he walks into a joyous, sun-drenched backyard cocktail hour, with kids playing at the picnic table, we hear Doc Pomus and Mort Shuman's lyrics: *This magic moment, so different and so new.* His daughter Domenica gleefully leaps into his arms, and he clutches her desperately, gazing out over the lake as we hear the lines *Sweeter than wine / Softer than a summer night / Everything I want to have / Whenever I hold you tight,* before a fade to black shutters the scene. "This Magic Moment," with its story of the fairy-tale feeling we experience discovering a new love, is a devilish underscoring of Bobby's realization that there won't be any more magic for him. He's crossed a line, and blackened a part of his heart in the process. As we watch

NICK: Let's dig deeper into that. Before he (unethically) blows up Melfi's spot, we understand Kupferberg's fascination with the Mob through his conversations with Melfi (where he often drives her back to the topic), as well as in his home life ("I called this Santoro thing a year ago"). What's happening with this guy—professionally and psychologically—and how does it come to torpedo Melfi? Can you speak to this both as a drama lover who understands the character and as a professional who's repelled by his actions?

DR. HASTINGS: I think he loses sight of his ability to stay objective. Or, rather, he thinks he's staying objective but, throughout the series, we see both that he gets too sucked into Tony's story as a spectator (he seems to, at least in that private moment, get off on having insider knowledge) and that he starts to see himself as saving Melfi from Tony, leading to his unethical behavior in the end. He probably needed to work some of those issues out with his own shrink.

NICK: It's Kupferberg's action at the dinner party and Melfi's decision to revisit the Yochelson and Samenow research paper that lead her to cut ties with Tony in "The Blue Comet." During this appointment, she's curt and conveys zero empathy; her passive-aggressive tone borders on aggressive-aggressive. How do you rate her professional performance in firing her patient? And what do you think of the study's hypothesis? Is it still well respected?

DR. HASTINGS: The research has come into question, by psychologists and criminologists. It does seem that cognitive behavioral models of treatment—learning to recognize negative thinking patterns and learning new skills for dealing with frustrations—are probably more effective than the kind of psychodynamic work that Dr. Melfi is doing with Tony.

As to her behavior at the end: it seems a bit cold and comes out of nowhere. It doesn't necessarily make that much sense in terms of why then and not earlier, and it does seem to be driven by the dramaturgical desire to give things closure rather than based on an attempt to draw an accurate picture of the therapist-client relationship.

NICK: We've talked a lot about Tony and his treatment. Let's discuss Carmela and hers. She initially meets with Melfi, but is referred to her colleague, Dr. Krakower. A lot of Sopranos fans believe Krakower to be the best shrink depicted on the show and the scene where she meets with him to be one of the most pivotal for Carmela. What do think of the scene clinically and dramatically?

him hold his loving daughter, we can't help but feel he's trying to recapture the part of himself he knows he's just given away forever.
—Andy Cambria

#19 "GLORIA," THEM (EPISODE 3.11, "PINE BARRENS")

There's nothing, really, in this song's lyrics that provides a hint about the kind of character its namesake, Gloria Trillo, will turn out to be. But everything about the music does. After a couple of shimmies from the Hammond B3 organ, Van Morrison comes in snarling like the pup child of Howlin' Wolf, singing so far off pitch and off beat that you practically want to slap your palm on his muzzle and cry out, "Down, boy!" The perspective is that of a randy teenager who's had a little taste of satisfaction and is yelping and pleading for more, and the source of the music is the stereo system on Tony's yacht, the *Stugots* (Italian for "this dick"). Gloria turns the music down when she climbs on board with her high heels, fur coat, and designer sunglasses—a model of elegance and grace (we think). But she turns out to be coiled as tightly as a cobra, and after she lashes out at Tony over a perceived slight and abruptly exits, leaving him unsatisfied, when we play back the song in our minds it no longer seems like the singer is the one who needs to be tamed.
—Mark Dellelo

#20 "RECUERDOS DE LA ALHAMBRA," PEPE ROMERO (EPISODE 6.7, "LUXURY LOUNGE")

The soothing, rolling tremolo of "Recuerdos de la Alhambra" is said to suggest composer Francisco Tárrega's visions of the water fountains inside the Spanish fortress. Pepe Romero's recording is used to conclude "Luxury Lounge," a love letter to Artie Bucco. Artie is the embodiment of the immigrant dream the Soprano crew professes to defend: he's an Italian American who works hard, owns a small business, honors his heritage, and remains loyal to his friends no matter the cost. As the episode's final sequence begins, he grudgingly agrees to serve a couple who've come into Nuovo Vesuvio just after closing time. Though he grumbles, we know that Artie Bucco is simply too warm and convivial a person to turn away anyone seeking the pleasure of a lovingly cooked meal (New Jersey *Zagat* agrees). He caresses his grandfather's well-worn recipe book, feeling the effects time and kitchen steam have had on the pages, before cooking *coniglio della famiglia* using a rabbit he shot in his own backyard after one too many free returns to the vegetable garden. Romero's nylon-strung guitar drifts into the scene as the food simmers, its pure, soft tone celebrating Artie's provincial style and the care he takes with each element of the dish. Yet "Recuerdos de la Alhambra" is in a minor key, and underscores both a longing for the ancestral traditions lost in the industrial era and a deep sadness surrounding the perversion of those traditions in the name of material profit. He is alone in his kitchen, working only because he believes it's the right thing to do, as we fade out to an airplane where we see the Italian hit men (aka "cousins") hired to murder Rusty Millio on their return trip to Naples. They're marveling at how inexpensively they've been able to purchase Fossil watches and Mont Blanc pens in America and there's a change in the music's mood ("Recuerdos" shifts to its parallel major key in its second section). The lilting, airy quality it gives this final scene in the plane is a tragically ironic comment on the real-world practices of the Soprano family: while Tony and his crew love nothing more than to wax

DR. HASTINGS: I'm torn. It's satisfying to see someone tell Carmela what she doesn't want to hear, and, in a way (despite what Dr. Krakower says about the current state of mental health treatment), it's flattering that the writers let a psychiatrist be the fount of such straight-talking wisdom. On the other hand, it does feel rather convenient: the character seems like a direct mouthpiece for what the writers want us to think about Carmela's situation. It's blunt, without the nuances that come across in many of the other therapy scenes. Clinically, although it might feel good to deliver straight talk like that, he ends up not actually helping her at all. His approach doesn't allow for the idea that it would take almost anybody some time to warm up to making such a big life decision. It's a tactic that might be effective if he had taken the time to develop a relationship with Carmela and gain her trust. But as it is, I think she's right, he comes off as a judgmental outsider. She may deserve judgment in some kind of absolute sense, but the way he goes about it doesn't get her any closer to living a better life—the opposite, in fact, as it seems to drive Carmela away from seeking a way out of the gangster life.

NICK: I think we'd be remiss if we didn't discuss Carmela's subsequent conversation in "Amour Fou" with Father Obosi (Isaach de Bankolé), who is getting his doctorate in psychology from Seton Hall. She meets him in confession and subsequently in his office, where he suggests a different approach. Do you hear any wisdom in his words or logic in his advice? What's your take on him?

DR. HASTINGS: On the one hand, he does seem to be trying to meet Carmela where she's at: he isn't telling her something that puts her on the defensive. On the other hand, his advice—to live only on the "good part" of what Tony earns—seems fairly unrealistic as actual, therapeutic advice, though I can see how it makes sense as a kind of spiritual challenge. It's likely the kind of advice that, even if followed, would only make things worse. Dr. Krakower, at least, is right: ultimately, she's going to be culpable unless she makes a clean break.

NICK: Let's break out the *DSM*. Tony's a murderer. Carmela knows damn well it's blood money that keeps her in sable furs and Roche Bobois furniture. Dish out some diagnoses.

DR. HASTINGS: Maybe nothing? Tony engages in a lot of antisocial behavior, but it isn't clear that he actually meets

poetic about the stoicism of their Italian ancestors, in this day and age their descendants are most valuable to them as mercenaries they know they can hire on the cheap.

—Andy Cambria

#21 "THE VALLEY," LOS LOBOS (EPISODE 6.17, "WALK LIKE A MAN")

They could have gone, but instead they chose to stay. This song tells the story of the first settlers in the Valley of Mexico, a far cry from New Jersey, but that lyric also describes Christopher's decision to remain in the Mob instead of entering the Witness Protection program with Adriana. His regrets surface in a conversation with his screenwriter friend: "[Sammy 'The Bull'] Gravano was living large in Arizona all on that federal tit. I like the sun—it would be closer to Hollywood, anyway." *Out of the shadows, into the light:* as he staggers drunkenly home to the sound of a wailing electric guitar, we see the McMansion he's bought now that he's risen near the top of the Mafia ladder. He straightens and replants a baby tree in the mulch as the lyrics describe a people who worked the earth with their hands "for as long as they were able." These Mexican settlers built an empire in the sunlight from work that began in the shadows, but Christopher's Italian ancestors who settled in Newark, stonemasons and carpenters, began their work in the light. It's the empire their children built that abides in the shadows.

—Mark Dellelo

#22 "I WONDER WHY," DION & THE BELMONTS (EPISODE 1.1, "THE SOPRANOS") AND #23 "I'M A MAN," BO DIDDLEY (EPISODE 1.1, "THE SOPRANOS")

Dion & The Belmonts were the first white rock 'n' roll group to capitalize (in 1958) on the doo-wop style invented by young black singers who shared the same urban neighborhoods as working-class Italian Americans. As we'll see later in the show, Tony grew up in one of these neighborhoods, and as their Italian-American contingency moved into the middle and upper-middle classes they moved out, leaving these streets to become African-American ghettos (as we'll also see). So it's fitting that we're introduced to the way in which Tony conducts the business that has enriched him with the song that sent a gang of young urban goombahs soaring to the top of the pop charts. The way in which it's used both choreographically and ironically is a direct nod to Martin Scorsese—one of the first of many. You might think of the poolroom brawl in *Mean Streets*, though the song that plays there (The Marvelettes' "Please Mr. Postman") is actually from the Motown era, which was the next stage in the evolution of doo-wop. Scorsese's *Goodfellas*, which was partly set in the late '50s, has a greater preponderance of doo-wop, though in that movie it often invokes elements of nostalgia that aren't present here. Later in this same episode, we hear some blues-sanctified pop from a black artist, Bo Diddley—it packages Christopher's first kill with a sexualized machismo (he's wearing a wife beater when he does the deed, and there are cutaways to Humphrey Bogart, Dean Martin, and Edward G. Robinson) that hark back to the filmmaker who first gave Scorsese the idea to link rock music with violence, Kenneth Anger (in *Scorpio Rising*).

—Mark Dellelo

#24 "WHITE RABBIT," JEFFERSON AIRPLANE (EPISODE 1.7, "DOWN NECK")
Ironically, the earliest episode of *The Sopranos* that clearly focused on fathers and their sons is the only one in the series directed

the diagnostic criteria for antisocial personality disorder (Ralphie is probably a better candidate for that). Carmela's troubles wax and wane throughout the series; certainly she has guilt and some bad feelings about enabling Tony's behavior, but not feeling good about making poor choices isn't a disorder.

From what we see of Livia, it's likely that she had borderline personality disorder as well as a persistent depressive disorder.

NICK: Joyce Van Patten plays Dr. Sandy Shaw, a therapist who treats Janice in the episode "Christopher." It seems pretty clear that Janice is doing her best impression of a therapy patient based on what she's seen on TV. I'm not sure Dr. Shaw's much more convincing. What's your take on these potpourri-scented sessions?
DR. HASTINGS: Dr. Shaw seems to be practicing supportive therapy, where the goal is to help support a client through a psychological or emotional crisis, rather than uncovering the root causes of persistent personality problems. In fact, for this therapy to work, the therapist needs to maintain an unconditional positive regard for the client. I'd agree it seems like Janice is putting on a show for her. It probably makes her feel good to have someone

cheerleading for her. It might seem like a strike against Dr. Shaw that she doesn't see through Janice's BS—and I think that's how we're supposed to read the scene—though it's hard to say, from just one scene, how much Dr. Shaw is really at fault. It can be hard to develop a therapeutic relationship with someone if you're always suspicious of what they're telling you. At some point, though, this kind of work can be counterproductive if the support ends up preventing any growth. It's hard to imagine Janice really wanting to grow or be honest. She may not be capable. She seems more a hopeless case than Tony.

NICK: Both A.J. and Meadow see professionals to help them navigate emotional issues. Obviously, A.J.'s are more serious, but let's start with Meadow's shrink, Dr. Wendi Kobler, who is played by Linda Lavin in "No Show." Is it normal that she would ask Meadow if her parents were molesting her? I wouldn't assume that's a boilerplate question, and it seems like a weird one to ask a patient who is suffering from the obvious trauma of her ex-boyfriend's murder.

DR. HASTINGS: It's not only normal, but professionally required, to ask about any history of sexual abuse when you're interviewing a patient

by a woman. The music's main purpose is to establish a sense of time and place—a historical setting to connect to Melfi's quote that will become this episode's theme: "He who doesn't understand history is doomed to repeat it." Jefferson Airplane's music, with its clearly defined elements of psychedelia (the echoey sound effects, the brooding intervals, the surrealist references to drug use), is firmly rooted in the late '60s, as are Tony's disorienting memories of the realization that his father was connected to La Cosa Nostra. During his sessions with Melfi, we flash back to "Down Neck," the working-class neighborhood in Newark where Tony came of age, and watch through his eyes as Johnny Boy Soprano beats a neighbor senseless (and later as the police cart him away in handcuffs for conducting Mob business at an amusement park). There are plenty of eerie parallels between Johnny Boy and Tony: the ever-present slick, romantic charm, the proud doting on the firstborn daughter, and, most notably, the use of ice cream to cover up misdeeds. When Johnny Boy returns home after the aforementioned arrest, he's got Tony's and Janice's favorite cherry-and-vanilla ice cream in tow—a little sugar to help the medicine go down. And when Tony finishes his workout on the elliptical machine as the episode's dénouement begins—fittingly, he's watching The History Channel—he indulges a sullen A.J. with a mountainous, fudgy sundae. "White Rabbit" plays again, overtaking the soundtrack, as Tony squirts whipped cream in A.J.'s mouth and we fade to black on the image of father-and-son's sweet-natured horseplay. But using Jefferson Airplane to close the scene gives it a dizzying, multilayered texture: even though Tony admits his reluctance to communicate with A.J. in therapy, the music ties him directly to the cycle of paternal whitewashing begun a generation ago. Perhaps for all the damage Livia did Tony, what he inherited from Johnny Boy was immeasurably worse.

—Andy Cambria

#25 "NINNA NINNA," TRADITIONAL (EPISODE 6.19, "THE SECOND COMING")

This song begins to play as Tony walks A.J. down a corridor of the hospital where he's been committed after his suicide attempt. It's a Calabrian lullaby with a minor-key melody that is haunting enough on its own—but when you consider the story the lyrics tell, the moment becomes profound. A woman sings to her son about his father, a bandit who has fled to the mountains, telling the boy she'd rather see him dead than become a bandit himself. This certainly isn't anything Carmela would ever say to A.J. But remember the moment when Livia threatened to gouge out young Tony's eye with a meat fork? "She wasn't really going to do it," he assured Melfi. But that was before he found out she asked Uncle Junior to whack him.

—Mark Dellelo

#26 "FISHERMAN'S DAUGHTER," DANIEL LANOIS (EPISODE 3.4, "EMPLOYEE OF THE MONTH")

There are lyrics at the end of this song, but we don't hear them, because it plays after a moment when Melfi can't find any words to communicate adequately with Tony. He asks, "You wanna say something?" After a beat, she replies, "No," and there's a cut to black, followed by silence, followed by the long pedal tone that forms the harmonic foundation of this song. Over that we hear a spare bass line and an antique, modal strumming pattern on an acoustic guitar. There's a feeling of stasis and boundless extension—it's like being adrift on an endless sea.

during an intake visit. Having said that, the way that scene plays out does suggest that Dr. Kobler could use some interviewing tips. I think she's right to follow her instinct and dig deeper into Meadow's feelings about Tony (which are obviously of major importance to Meadow's own internal, psychic conflicts), but instead of jumping to "Did your father molest you?" she might have asked a few more open-ended questions to get a better sense of why Meadow is reluctant to talk much about her father before jumping to such a charged question. Doing so risks sabotaging the therapeutic relationship. I'd question a number of things she says: for instance, saying it's okay for Meadow to have gotten sick after drinking and smoking weed as long as it's not "a deliberate purge" is quite judgmental and, again, would likely put Meadow on the defensive if she did have an eating disorder. And then she very quickly and completely aligns with Meadow's desire to stop school, without really having a full sense of what may be driving that desire. Perhaps Meadow is driven by anxiety or PTSD, so avoiding the stressful situation would only end up making the anxiety symptoms worse.

NICK: A.J. sees professionals both in and out of private facilities. He's a troubled kid, but I feel like his perspective, his problems, and the treatment he gets are all pretty standard. Am I missing something? Is this a case of just not giving much of a damn about A.J.?

DR. HASTINGS: I don't think you're missing anything. His intake with Dr. Vogel (Michael Countryman) plays out much like I'd expect an actual intake to play out, with Vogel screening for the signal symptoms of depression. However, prescribing medication without talking about other options (like psychotherapy), and without talking about what to expect to happen if the medication is working, suggests a kind of thoughtlessness on the part of the doc.

NICK: Which character would you most like to treat?

DR. HASTINGS: I think from a treatment perspective, Carmela sort of gets shafted. Throughout the series she makes several attempts to seek help, but she ends up reaching out to people who either have their own agenda (like Father Phil) or who aren't willing to meet her where she's at (like Dr. Krakower). Maybe she'd still be resistant to ever taking a hard look at her own role in Tony's crimes, but I think she at least deserves a chance.

NICK: Who is the best shrink and why?
DR. HASTINGS: Easier for me to take

And this after Tony himself has just proposed an ending to their professional relationship, saying that he's ready to follow her advice and start seeing a behaviorist. She tells him simply, "No." Why, when this was advice that all of her medical colleagues agreed on? Working through her own trauma, she probably doesn't fully know, though she clearly has something she feels that *she* needs from this therapeutic relationship with a sociopath. She considers, and rejects, the idea of asking him to retaliate against her rapist, Jesus Rossi—a man who is, like Tony, an otherwise functioning member of society. (She saw her assailant's "Employee of the Month" plaque on the wall of a fast food restaurant.) There is something about this knowledge that makes it impossible for her to subtract Tony from her life at this moment. Though damned if she knows where they might be headed from here.

—Mark Dellelo

#27 "KID A," RADIOHEAD (EPISODE 4.2, "NO SHOW")

Most of this episode is about Meadow (Tony and Carmela's firstborn star child, a cheeky tie-in to the title of Radiohead's song), whose despair after the death of Jackie Jr. prompts familial conflict when she tells her parents she's dropping out of Columbia to work on an independent film in Europe. As the dénouement begins, Tony enters the Soprano master bathroom to find a sullen, deflated Carmela soaking in the tub. Sensing her exasperation, he throws her a bone and offers to start talking to her cousin, Brian, about the estate planning she's been eager to get into process. She responds, in an unimpressed monotone: "You have nothing to feel guilty about. It's me she [Meadow] blames." After Tony confusedly shoots back "What for?" Carmela closes her eyes and zones out as director John Patterson cuts to a brilliantly composed wide shot before fading to black. It's all negative space and angles—Carmela sequestered in the tub on one side of the frame, facing us, and Tony standing at the sink in a noirish spot of light, with his back to the camera, on the other. As the credits roll and "Kid A" starts to play, the at-first-seemingly-random keyboard tones emanate from nowhere before a carefully crafted electronic drumbeat kicks in. We're reminded of that final shot of Tony and Carmela, and of the distance growing between them in the wake of Meadow's depression. The beautiful, contemporary bathroom and its furnishings link up perfectly with Radiohead's music: nothing is here by accident, and even the things that seem trivial are part of a larger, precisely woven pastiche of darkness where words aren't necessary to get the point across.

—Andy Cambria

#28 "HEAVEN ONLY KNOWS," EMMYLOU HARRIS (EPISODE 5.1, "TWO TONYS")

We don't hear many country songs in *The Sopranos*, and the ones we do hear are as unsentimental as they come. This is a heartbreak song, but a resigned and acrimonious one. The first time we hear it is remarkable due to the absence of anyone on-screen who could ground it in a point of view: all we see are the exteriors of a deserted house. The season is late fall and there are dead leaves blowing around on the patio, where the barbecue hasn't been touched for months, the cushions have been removed from the furniture, and the swimming pool has been covered tight. There are a few details that have remained constant: the landscaping around the driveway, with its evergreen tree and hedges, and the daily copy of the *Newark Star-Ledger*

shots at the ones I don't like. Dr. Kobler seems to me to be the worst. Dr. Shaw I actually have a lot of sympathy for— she's not doing anything obviously wrong or harmful; it's just that Janice is so terrible. Kupferberg is, I think, too full of himself, not a bad thing in and of itself, but I think it gets in the way of his judgment on a number of occasions, and he has terrible boundary issues.

I've seen Melfi criticized by other professionals, for some of the reasons we've talked about here. Should she have terminated with Tony once she fully realized the extent of his violent side? Was it a mistake to jump so quickly into a psychodynamic theory for his depression instead of exploring more biological reasons, like genetic risk factors or possible contributions from head injuries due to the fights he had been in? Would he have responded better to cognitive behavioral therapy? In the real world, these would all be reasonable criticisms, but, then, we wouldn't have a show. Psychodynamic therapy might not actually be the best choice for a real-life Tony, but it's probably the most dramatic kind of therapy that you can put on-screen, partly because it's bound up so closely with exploring the kinds of stories we tell ourselves about who we are and who we want to be.

Having said that, and at the risk of my answer being too obvious, I think Melfi is the best shrink. Maybe by default, because she's really the one we get to see the most. We watch her handle crises and push Tony to uncover and take responsibility for his emotional problems. That she doesn't succeed isn't necessarily a strike against her. She's good enough. And he's a tough patient.

NICK: Thanks for sharing your professional insights, Dr. Hastings. One last question: You've rewatched all the psychiatry and counseling scenes and are in a unique position as both a psychiatrist and arts critic. Do you have any final thoughts on Chase's achievement as it relates to the human condition? And what are your thoughts about what makes the practice of psychiatry so central to the show?

DR. HASTINGS: While the show shares much of its DNA with Martin Scorsese's gangster movies, in some ways I think Chase's sensibility is closer to that of the Coen Brothers. Chase and the Coens give us characters struggling to find meaning in their lives, but that struggle is presented with a profound ambivalence. Even if it's possible to figure out "what it all means"—a big if—it's not clear that that's even something that ultimately

at the bottom of the driveway—though instead of Tony arriving in his bathrobe to scoop it up, Meadow speeds over it with her car. The next time the song plays, Carmela is listening to it on her kitchen radio. This cues us to listen for it to evoke her emotional mood, but it's so soft that we can barely hear the lyrics—giving Tony the cold shoulder as he enters, she reveals nothing and everything (the song plays from her point of view but the scene is directed from his). He's just had his advances rejected by Melfi and has nowhere to go but out onto that barren patio in the cold November night air, brandishing an AK-47 to guard the house he no longer lives in from a wild bear that's been marauding the neighborhood. As Carmela closes the screen door and leaves him alone in silhouette, the song kicks in again: *I'm going to turn and walk away / There's nothing left for me to say / It wouldn't change things anyway.*
—Mark Dellelo

#29 "OH GIRL," THE CHI-LITES (EPISODE 4.7, "WATCHING TOO MUCH TELEVISION")
"Sometimes I feel like I should be punished," says Ronald Zellman, the state assemblyman who's just done a deal with Tony to evict some black families from an urban crackhouse and develop it as real estate using government welfare funds. Zellman gets his wish at the end of the episode. Once the deal is done the power dynamics in his relationship with Tony have shifted, and Tony can no longer stand the thought that Zellman is sleeping with his former *comare*, Irina. He hears the R&B song on his car radio that night: *Oh girl, I'd be in trouble if you left me now*, and knows it's ridiculous when he starts crying over a Russian ex-stripper whom he dumped. But when the Chi-Lites sing, *All my friends call me a fool*, his machismo gets the

better of him. When he makes a detour to Zellman's house and begins flogging him with his belt, it's like an attempt to pass along the song's bluesy point of view to him like an infection. And Zellman discovers that guilt isn't the only unpleasant feeling when you're in bed with the Mob.

—Mark Dellelo

#30 "SISTER GOLDEN HAIR," AMERICA (EPISODE 3.5, "ANOTHER TOOTHPICK")

As Bobby "Bacala" Baccalieri Sr., Burt Young's broad smile and easygoing, grizzled visage have us in his corner before he utters a word. And when he does, we feel for him instantly: he can barely speak between coarse-sounding fits of a hacking cough brought on by lung cancer. He's in New Jersey to attend the funeral of Carmela's uncle, Febby Viola, and volunteers to carry out the hit on his perfectly detestable godson, Salvatore "Mustang Sally" Intile, who's been marked for death after a senseless golf-club bludgeoning of Vito Spatafore's brother, Bryan. "It'll feel good being useful for a change," he implores Tony. Against the wishes of Junior and Baccalieri Jr., Tony grants old man Baccalieri's wish, and this deliciously twisted setup—the godfather begging for the privilege of killing his own godson—pays off in one of the most graphically violent murders perpetrated over the course of the series. After a struggle that ends with Intile's brains being blown across a kitchen wall from hand-to-hand range, Baccalieri Sr., hands caked in blood, grabs the remainder of a pack of cigarettes from the table, lights one up, and inhales like he's taking in the flowers of spring. Driving away from the scene, still smoking that orgasmic cig, covered in huge streaks of dried blood, he cranks up the car stereo and we hear "Sister Golden Hair" swell up

has value. Psychiatry is the perfect fit. It's a discipline that, historically, has promised answers to some of the biggest, most important questions facing human beings and, despite its many successes, stops short of being able to fully address those fundamental issues.

A COUPLA *PAISANOS* TALK ITALIAN-AMERICAN LIFE

We can't have a chapter called "The Craft of *The Sopranos*" without discussing its approach to Italian-American culture and language, and so we're chatting with Fred Gardaphé, Distinguished Professor of English and Italian American Studies at Queens College, CUNY and the John D. Calandra Italian American Institute. A Chicago native, Gardaphé grew up around the Outfit and its associated violence, which claimed both friends and close family members. As a teen working in a Mob-associated restaurant supply business, he stood face-to-face with Tony "The Ant" Spilotro, the basis for Joe Pesci's Nicky Santoro character in Scorsese's *Casino*.

NICK: Thanks for taking the time to chat, Professor. Let's learn a little more about you and your work before we apply it to *The Sopranos*. What fuels your drive and dedication to the study of Italian-American culture and specifically Italian-American masculinity?

FRED GARDAPHÉ: I've written a lot about this, and the long story can be found in what I call my "breakthrough" essay, "Breaking and Entering: An Italian-American's Literary Odyssey," which opens with "If it were not for reading, I would have become a gangster. . . . Once, while I was being

to cruising volume while he hums along. But the inescapable cough begins to overtake him, and the car begins to swerve wildly as he fumbles for a dropped inhaler to the soaring chorus: *Will you meet me in the middle, will you meet me in the air? / Will you love me just a little, just enough to show you care?* There's a hilarious irony baked into the usage of this song: it's a fist-pumping sendoff to a character we hardly knew (who among us doesn't crank up "Sister Golden Hair" when it comes on?), whose final request for affection has been granted, killing him in the process.

—Andy Cambria

#31 "I'M NOT LIKE EVERYBODY ELSE," THE KINKS (EPISODE 5.10, "COLD CUTS")

The first time we hear Dave Davies sing the title of this song, it sounds like a lament, but then his voice takes on a crazed intensity that makes it sound like a boast. Listening to Janice and Bobby make benign small talk with their kids at Sunday dinner, Tony glowers and begins needling his sister about her neglected son, Harpo: "I wonder where he's having his Sunday dinner?" He can't allow her to enjoy any solace from the misery that's plagued their family since they were kids, won't indulge the illusion that her family could be like other, normal families, provokes her to release all of the rage that Bobby has done his damnedest to tame. The irony of the verse we hear as we watch him storm away from the family dinner he's ruined is that, although he's not like *everybody* else, we understand that he's absolutely like *somebody* else: his mother, Livia, who never allowed her family a moment of enjoyment, either.

—Mark Dellelo

#32 "I'M GONNA MOVE TO THE OUTSKIRTS OF TOWN," RAY CHARLES (EPISODE 6.8, "JOHNNY CAKES")

"What the fuck is happening to this neighborhood?" Patsy Parisi wonders out loud when he learns Tony sold the poultry shop that's been on the corner forever to a real estate developer for a Jamba Juice. This is after he's tried and failed to strong-arm the manager of a new nearby Starbucks to kick up some revenue to the Mob in exchange for neighborhood security—to keep anyone from throwing a brick through the window or, God forbid, assaulting the manager. But he might as well try negotiating with an absent king: corporate, as the manager explains, has about ten thousand stores in North America. *I don't need no iceman, I'm gonna get you a Frigidaire*, Ray Charles sings to his girl in the song that plays over the credits. When Charles and B. B. King performed this song in the '50s, they were describing affluent families making their move to the suburbs, away from diverse urban neighborhoods and onto private plots of land. Accumulating wealth by regulating crime in poor urban neighborhoods, the Mafia kingpins also moved to the outskirts of town. But they're beginning to see the trend that began in the '50s reverse itself and their income stream dry up as these urban neighborhoods become gentrified. "I've got a kid in college," Patsy snaps back at the poultry shopkeeper when he hears that it's closing. "Where are my fucking eggs?!"

—Mark Dellelo

#33 "LAYLA," DEREK & THE DOMINOS (EPISODE 4.13, "WHITECAPS")

"Layla" made its bones in the ranks of gangster-movie music cues long before "Whitecaps" aired in December of 2002. It was used to now legendary effect

chased by the police for disturbing local merchants so my partners could shoplift, I ran into the public library. I found myself in the juvenile section and grabbed any book to hide my face. Safe from the streets, I spent the rest of the afternoon reading, believing that nobody would ever find me there. So, whenever I was being chased or just wanted to be alone, I'd head straight for the library. The library became my asylum."

Over the past fifty years, Italian-American culture has been the center of most of my research, scholarship, and teaching. The masculinity focus comes from all the shit I took for being an Italian-American male, and because I needed to understand why violence seemed to be such a strong and normalized articulation of manhood growing up.

NICK: What kind of shit did you take for being an Italian-American male? When did you see a shift in how Italian Americans were perceived in this country?

FRED: I grew up in a Little Italy of sorts in the Village of Melrose Park, Illinois. It wasn't until I went to high school, in 1966, a good distance from my neighborhood, that I began to be treated differently because I was Italian. Until then I had thought that my grandparents were Italian and I was American.

Outside of Melrose it was a whole different world, one in which people would drive by while I was walking and yell out things like "Dago, Wop, get outta here." I had a door shut in my face when I went to the house of a non-Italian girl I had asked out on a date. In high school, we were under surveillance constantly. On the day of my graduation, I asked the dean of discipline how he always caught us breaking the rules; he replied, "My good man, because we were always watching you." I noticed things began to change in 1972, just after *The Godfather* came out. People were still suspicious of us, but they were less likely to yell at us. By then, I had shifted to a more countercultural look, and blended in better with the crowds on the streets and at concerts, but as soon as people found out I was Italian, I'd get the usual questions about the Mafia.

NICK: I get the sense that in the mid to late '70s, when *Rocky* and *Saturday Night Fever* hit, the Italian-American male quickly went from marginalized to lionized. Suddenly, it was the coolest thing to have four or five vowels in your last name. Did you notice a shift, and how did you feel about it?

in Martin Scorsese's *Goodfellas*, during the montage where we see the murderous fallout of Jimmy Conway's post-Lufthansa heist greed. "Layla" is used briefly, but memorably, to set the stage for Tony walking into a buzzsaw after his ex-*comare*, Irina, calls his house in a drunken stupor, sending Carmela into a horrified rage. As Tony cruises home in his SUV, blasting "Layla" on the stereo and whistling along gleefully to Duane Allman's wild slide-guitar solo, he bounds up the driveway to encounter an unexpected bump: he's run over his golf clubs, which Carmela has thrown out the window along with a batch of his clothes. Allman's frenzied, high-above-the-fretboard playing could be a stand-in for Carmela's inner monologue here; and just as Tony's been contentedly unaware of her intimate relationship with Furio, so, too, is he satisfied to cruise along until reality smacks him in the face. There's a neat connection between the usages of "Layla" in *Goodfellas* and *The Sopranos*: its presence ends with a scene that will begin the undoing of the main character's family. The difference is that Tony Soprano is aware of the music in "Whitecaps," a subtle, searing comment on the machismo of the gangster archetype: for all his epic bravado, Tony hasn't a clue that the spoils from one family have infected the other. In fact, he's still whistling while he works.

—Andy Cambria

#34 "NO SCRUBS," TLC (EPISODE 2.3, "TOODLE-FUCKING-OO")

The image of Meadow Soprano and Hunter Scangarelo singing along to TLC's "No Scrubs" while making a complete mess of the Soprano kitchen ranks among the most enduringly hilarious in history of the series. It was just a season earlier (in the premiere episode, to be precise) that Meadow was scoffing at Carmela—

"Get outta here with that fat!"—when offered some *sfogliatelle*. But teenage haughtiness has brought out the rebel in her; and she's now content to gobble up a butter-soaked grilled cheese, wash it down with hot chocolate, and leave half the ingredients strewn about the countertops while singing, *I don't want no scrub / A scrub is a guy that can't get no love from me.* TLC's message of empowerment and independence is blissfully lost on Meadow and Hunter, whose self-presentation as badasses is just false posturing. In contrast to the ladies of TLC—bastions of the wave of fashionable, creative, and tuneful '90s hip-hop that paved the way for the chart-toppers of the modern era—Meadow and Hunter come across as clueless kids. And all we can do is smile during the episode's heartfelt coda, wherein Tony discovers Meadow literally scrubbing vomit from the floor at Livia's house after she's trashed it with her friends. Perhaps she gets it after all, and the act in the kitchen was born from adolescent insecurity. She's far from the first one to "live at home with her mama" and long for something more.

—Andy Cambria

#35 "LA PETITE MER," TITI ROBIN (EPISODE 5.4, "ALL HAPPY FAMILIES . . .")

French multi-instrumentalist Titi Robin's style is heavily influenced by his home country's gypsy jazz, but also borrows phrasings and modes from traditional Arab music (Robin is equally at home on the nylon-string guitar and the oud). His multitextured playing and unpredictable tones are a reflection of Carmela's complicated and deeply moving relationship with her son. She's everything Livia Soprano was not, and anyone watching "All Happy Families . . ." with the hindsight of parenthood will likely feel they're looking into

FRED: I think *The Godfather* did more to elevate the last-name vowels than any other film. Both *Rocky* and *Saturday Night Fever* complicated the earlier conceptions and receptions of Italians in America, but at the same time, the focus on the working class did little to help those who, by that time, had reached the middle class. Without any type of representation in the media, those folks began to speak out against stereotypical portrayals such as those found in the two films we're talking about. They were trying to move away from this, and the media kept them close to it all. My shift came when I moved away from my Little Italy and went to college.

NICK: *The Sopranos* premiered on the cusp of the new millennium, once again putting Italian Americans—and specifically the Italian-American male—at the forefront of popular culture. Where do you think we were just before this point? To give our readers some context, New York had its second Italian-American governor. Scorsese's most recent theatrical movie had been a Dalai Lama biopic. *Goodfellas* was nearly a decade old, and Gotti was in the slammer for good. Had the perception of Italian Americans in culture largely evolved, melting into the greater American one by then?

FRED: Before *The Sopranos*, the Italian American as gangster figure had been receding from the U.S. imagination. Nothing new or better had come up since Scorsese's and Coppola's works, and while Italian Americans did achieve success in other areas of American culture, nothing documented those experiences in any way that matched the power of the earlier films. This created a great gap.

The stories of the Italian-American working class, so well told by John Turturro in his film *Mac*, and in Nancy Savoca's film *True Love*, never got the exposure that could have countered those earlier depictions, and without any major documentaries about Italian-American life and culture, other than the many made by independent filmmakers, the arrival of *The Sopranos* brought out the fear that we were a people with one story.

Chase, in a smart way, used the gangster as a vehicle to tell the story of the suburbanization of U.S. culture, but middle-class Italians were largely unable to read between the lines and understand what he was really saying about American life in the 1990s.

Italian Americans may have seemingly melted into Americans on the streets, but in their homes they were still very much Italian, hanging on to traditions and styles that not even Ital-

a mirror thanks to the tenderness, anger, and desperation Edie Falco projects. We hear "La Petite Mer" for the first time when Carm settles in for a candlelit bath, alone in the house after A.J. goes to the Mudvayne concert in New York. And at first, we think the mysterious sexiness of the song might be an appropriate backdrop for a little intimate quiet time. But of course, she can't relax. Robin's frenzied, heavily syncopated downpicking underscores her nervousness, and after a minute she's out of the tub, calling Meadow to try and get a bead on A.J.'s whereabouts. The music returns at the conclusion of the episode, after Carm insists that A.J. leave to live with Tony in the wake of A.J.'s debauched night at Hudson Suites, his lying and disrespect beginning to eat at her mental well-being. There's a beautiful touch as Carmela pulls up the driveway in her Mercedes wagon, and we remember the episode's first image: A.J. speeding back and forth, up the driveway and down, in that same car. As she unlocks the front door, she flashes back to a vision of a post-toddler A.J. careening down the driveway in his Big Wheel. She screams out in terror, "Anthony!" And we see her as a young woman, in simple jeans and a white T-shirt, nothing more than a mother scared to death for her child. She snaps back to reality and enters the Soprano foyer alone, a reverse tracking shot making it appear as though she's disappearing into the house while "La Petite Mer" swells to full volume on the soundtrack. There's nothing to mistake for eroticism this time around. All that comes through is the space in the arrangement and the darkness of the melody. Although the song's title references a *little sea*, Carmela seems adrift in something much larger—with no lifeboat in sight.

—Andy Cambria

#36 "CON TE PARTIRÒ," ANDREA BOCELLI (EPISODE 2.4, "COMMENDATORI")

Andrea Bocelli's sentimental pop anthem "Con Te Partirò" seems to follow Carmela Soprano wherever she goes in "Commendatori," the David Chase–penned episode typically remembered for the portions filmed in Italy. It's about false Italian-American pride in the age of conspicuous consumerism—and what could be a better tapestry for that theme than Bocelli's gilded bathroom faucet of a song, which he infused with so much pillow-whispering and soaring vibrato that no self-respecting member of the *Oprah* set could go a day without hearing it after its premiere in the late '90s? He's also very handsome, as Carmela notes at a lunch with Angie Bonpensiero and Rosalie Aprile. And he's blind. Translation? Not only can the guy hit the high notes, he's marketable—a near-perfect Mediterranean commodity that made people shopping at the mall feel like they were finally understanding opera. "Con Te Partirò" is used several times in "Commendatori," as a transitional element between scenes in New Jersey and scenes in Italy, linking the new and old worlds with sound the same way a visual cross dissolve would. But its most significant placements are in the aforementioned ladies' luncheon and the conclusion. At a local N.J. restaurant, Angie Bonpensiero opens up to her friends about her desperate unhappiness: just the sound of her husband, Sal, saying "I'm home!" when he reappears from the lam makes her want to vomit. At the conclusion of the episode, when Tony returns from Italy, bags full of presents in hand, and proclaims "I'm home!," Carmela hears him from their upstairs bedroom and instantly recognizes Angie's feelings of revulsion. She knows what's

ians in Italy kept alive. Italian scholars were coming to the U.S. to study their culture's past as Italian Americans preserved their version of being Italian in the sanctuaries of their homes and clubs. This failed to attract the younger Italian Americans, many of whom were finding their ways to a new Italy, giving them new tools for expressing their Italian backgrounds.

NICK: That's really interesting—the idea that Italian Americans maintained traditions and styles that the Italians in "Commendatori" would have abandoned. Can you think of a few examples exhibited by Tony and Carmela, or others inside their circle? Aspects of this behavior that Chase conveyed through the craft brought to the show?

FRED: Throughout the series there is a touch here and there of maintaining traditions such as the religious *feste* and family dinners, but that's the extent of it. There is a mention of the role of Italian-American organizations like Joe Colombo's Italian-American Civil Rights League in "Christopher" and by [Dr.] Melfi's perception-obsessed ex-husband, Richard La Penna (Richard Romanus). The smattering of Italian that appears in the series is another example of losing the vehicle that transports culture pretty well. The uses of food throughout give hints as to the importance of nourishment to the Italian, but again, it's just a symbol for something that once was more central to the Italian in America. Like many Italian Americans of their era, Tony and Carmela have largely abandoned traditions such as how to name the children (usually after the grandparents, starting with the paternal side, and then with more kids going to special saints' names). My grandmother would have said something like "What kinda name is Meadow? She has no saint to protect her." Then she would go on to call her by a saint's name that came closest to the sound of her name or started with the same initital: Madeline or something like that. The Season Two episode "Commendatori" is a great example of what happens when a disconnected Italian American visits the homeland; there's no attempt to go back to the hometown of the ancestor.

NICK: I only just discovered (from a 1999 *New York Times* piece) that Chase—though Italian on both sides— wasn't Roman Catholic. His father was a Baptist, and his mother was raised by a "socialist atheist." There are moments when he seems fond and respectful of the faith, but plenty more where he seems to satirize it, especially aspects that evoke the supernatural or fuel the superstitious. We

waiting for her when she walks down those stairs—an expensive trinket meant to assuage her feelings of resentment and excuse whatever indiscretions come along with "the business." She's living a lie, and in that private moment must feel nauseated that she asked Angie to remember the teachings of the Catholic Church before initiating divorce proceedings. If anything, she's envious of Angie's willingness to speak truthfully about her status as a doormat—and she knows her response to her friend's plea for help was as phony as an Andrea Bocelli song.

—Andy Cambria

#37 "OVER THE MOUNTAIN, ACROSS THE SEA," JOHNNIE & JOE (EPISODE 5.6, "SENTIMENTAL EDUCATION")

This doo-wop song paints an idyllic mood of anticipation. It's sung from the male point of view, with the suggestion that the girl he's pining for is as elusive as a dream. We hear it playing on Carmela's kitchen radio as she's staring out the window with a dreamy look in her eyes, thinking about her date with Robert Wegler the night before. She appears to be pining for him, but the irony is that she doesn't need to, at least as far as he's concerned—he phones her to say that he's already made plans for their next date. Tony pollutes the fantasy by barging into the kitchen and making a crass remark about Wegler (a cultured and sensitive man he assumes is a "fag"). And ultimately the transactional world he's made Carmela a part of will sabotage their affair, when she takes advantage of Wegler's role as A.J.'s guidance counselor. *Into each dark and starry night / Oh, what a mystery that's sealed so tight.*

—Mark Dellelo

#38 "SCENES FROM AN ITALIAN RESTAURANT," BILLY JOEL (EPISODE 4.6, "EVERYBODY HURTS")

As Tony and Carmela hold court over a dinner out with family and friends, "Scenes from an Italian Restaurant" is used to establish the overriding joviality of the evening: though we can see the characters talking and laughing, the only thing we hear on the soundtrack is Joel's song. The music is a mask for what's going on beneath the surface of these *bei tempi*, just as its volume obscures all the other possible sources of sound in the restaurant. This song, with its famous piano-accordion intro, and Joel crooning, *A bottle of red, a bottle of white*, is ersatz Italian romanticism—all we need is a bowlback mandolin playing tremolo in the background and we'd be in Epcot Center. Though the gang is assembled to attend a Billy Joel concert on the night in question, Tony's gregariousness is driven by the episode's central event—the off-screen suicide of Gloria Trillo. That news hits Tony like a sledgehammer, and he sets about doing good deeds in order to overcompensate for the guilt he feels about his own toxicity in the wake of her death. These are not acts of friendship or love, they're the misgivings of a sociopath throwing money at his problems and buying enough goodwill to temporarily fill the void inside himself. Tony knows cousin Brian is a fashion plate and hooks him up with Patsy Parisi, who deals in designer suits. When Brian leads the toast at dinner, sporting a sharp-looking black-and-red ensemble straight out of *GQ*, he pronounces Tony a great guy—one he's proud to call a friend. It's a little tough to stomach. But as the lyrics of "Scenes from an Italian Restaurant" remind us, if you're Tony Soprano, *it all depends upon your appetite.*

—Andy Cambria

certainly see this with Paulie Gualtieri, a character you've written about extensively. How do you respond to Chase's integration of the Roman Catholic faith into the show and its characters?

FRED: Regardless of where Chase situates himself personally with organized religion, his work captures the range of relationships Italian Americans have with the Catholic Church and religion in general. Many real-life gangsters I knew were close to the Catholic Church, in spite of how they lived their lives. How they dealt with the obvious conflicts was their business. Some bought their way into Catholic cemeteries, others were banned. What Chase did best throughout the series is deal with the struggle humans have in dealing with the spiritual life; whether it was the priest who was attracted to Carmela or the nun who was Paulie's real mother, Chase's characters reflected the consequences of trying to reconcile the spiritual and material worlds of human life.

NICK: The show really has a knack for conveying a perspective on faith that feels simultaneously dead serious and hilarious. Like when Paulie sees the Virgin Mary appear on a Bada Bing stage. I think that scene perfectly captures the paradox of the reconciliation you describe. The show has true believers, like Carmela, Paulie, and Christopher—people who really believe in heaven and hell—mingling, or even married to, secular materialists. Is this dynamic a tradition in Italian or Italian-American art and literature? Where else does it show up that might have informed Chase?

FRED: There is a very strong anticlerical tradition in Italy, which is the reason why the Vatican is its own nation today.

During the period of the Inquisition, if you made fun of the Church, you'd get burned at the stake, like Giordano Bruno—my candidate for the patron saint of humor. Bruno was a sixteenth-century Italian philosopher whose book *l'Asino*, or *The Ass*, taught people how to laugh at authority. There's a statue of him in Rome's Campo dei Fiori that strategically places his rear end toward the Vatican. Chase might have gotten this sense of humor about Catholicism from the Protestant strain in his background. Carmela, Paulie, and Christopher get their notion of religion from being conditioned by the Church.

NICK: I spent a little time in Italy in the late '90s when I was in Rimini for a sporting competition. I've never visited Naples or Abruzzo, where my family is from, so my sense of Italian

#39 "FIELDS OF GOLD," STING (EPISODE 2.8, "FULL LEATHER JACKET")

It's hard to imagine sympathizing with Richie Aprile, but watching him endure Sting's "Fields of Gold" as his olive branches are snapped like twigs in front of his nose is as close as we get. Arriving at the Soprano house, thank-you dish of tripe and tomatoes in hand, Richie finds Carmela sipping coffee and doing a little daytime sketching while "Fields of Gold" plays from the stereo. She's whiling away the hours without a care, and the vanilla-sounding Muzak underscores the lull of suburban complacency (we could just as easily be strolling through the produce aisle here). Every material comfort is available—*We'll forget the sun in his jealous sky as we lie in fields of gold*—including a surplus television set that's been promised to Soprano housekeeper Lilliana. And when her husband, Stasiu, shows up to collect it, Richie sees just how disposable one man's treasure can be: Stasiu is wearing the leather jacket Richie gifted Tony in an effort to garner favor with his new family (Richie views himself, not Tony, as the rightful heir to the DiMeo throne and has also begun dating Janice Soprano). As Stasiu crosses the frame in front of Richie, unknowingly rubbing the jacket in his face, we hear a softly plucked reprise of the vocal melody, its saccharine, adult-contemporary reverb acting as counterpoint to the bitter feelings of rage and embarrassment welling up behind Richie's eyes. The fealty he thinks he's displayed by giving the boss Rocco DiMeo's old jacket has been stuffed into a donation bag, along with everything else the Sopranos have used up. In the moment when Richie gets up and leaves in a huff, Sting's voice must ring true: *Many years have passed since those summer days among the fields of barley.* Thanks a lot, old-timer, but we've already got everything we need.

—Andy Cambria

#40 "COMES LOVE," ARTIE SHAW (EPISODE 6.1, "MEMBERS ONLY")

"Who's down there?" Uncle Junior cries out when Tony calls him for dinner. "Artie Shaw," he answers. He probably put on this record hoping it might help break through Junior's dementia by calling up happy memories from his youth. Instead, Junior comes down with a different kind of love: he's packing a pistol in fear that his old nemesis, Gennaro "Little Pussy" Malanga, has invaded his home. Maybe because he'd originally planned to kill Little Pussy in Artie Bucco's restaurant, Vesuvio, and that first name teleports his disease-addled brain back to the moment he hatched that scheme in the pilot? With a bullet hole in his stomach, Tony crawls toward the phone while Shaw's clarinet swings cheerfully (though in a minor key) and Helen Forrest sings her refrain: *Nothing can be done.*

—Mark Dellelo

culture—whether at the time of *The Sopranos* or today—is limited. I'm curious: How would Italians, both civilians and Camorra, have viewed Tony (or anybody) seeing a shrink in the '90s? Would their perspective be different today? And do notions of masculinity play into this perception?

FRED: There is only one way I know by which a man can be made into a soprano, and metaphorically this is what is happening to Tony Soprano, who happens to be a gangster in a time in which manhood is changing. Like many male baby boomers in the throes of middle age, Tony is trying to figure out who he is and why he does what he does. He has come to realize that he is not the man his father was and that his son will not be able to carry on. Trapped between the past and the present with an unimaginable future, he begins to feel weak, and after a couple of incidents in which he loses consciousness, he visits a doctor. When his doctor suggests he visit a psychologist to help him deal with stress, he stumbles upon a way of feeling better, but for Tony Soprano, it comes with a cost, and that cost is betraying the tribal code of keeping silent, especially to strangers.

Tony Soprano begins to lose a traditional sense of manhood by first talking about his work, and second by talking about it with a woman. Hesitant at first, he finds that as he continues to talk, he begins to question the traditional order of things, and this leads him to question his role as a husband, a father, a son, and a gangster. After Tony Soprano there can be no Mafia, in the traditional sense. When Tony breaks "*omerta,*" he is no longer behaving the way a man should. "*I fatti sono maschi; le parole sono femmine,*" goes an Italian saying: "Actions belong to men; words to women."

NICK: The erosion of Italian and Italian-American masculinity makes me think of an adjacent issue—the erosion of the close-knit family. When my parents grew up—and even when I grew up—entire families lived on the same block. As I grew older, there was a clear hope that I would spread my wings, *but not too far!* On *The Sopranos* we see Meadow choose Columbia for a school and, eventually, a New Jersey gangster's son for a husband. We see Livia Soprano become murderous by the prospect of leaving her home. Vito Spatafore, who would clearly be happier living the life of a gay New England antiques shopper, can't bear to be himself. What do you make of this push-pull? The drive to succeed in America, but the inability to accept what that means for the Italian-American idea of family?

FRED: Through the examples you cite, Chase gets it right without making a big deal out of it. The Italian immigrant, who knows what it's like to leave the family behind, and sometimes never see them again, is very wary of the distance that might come between his/her children and him/herself. Once they get settled in the U.S. and begin to raise a family, their old notions of family return and guide the way they conduct their relationships with their children and grandchildren. Italians believe that in family we are strong; they avoid being dependent on outsiders or institutions for their well-being. In the U.S., where the culture of the independent individual is prime, the idea of sticking close to the family for support goes by the wayside as individuals succeed in school and work. This individual success, more privileged and accepted in the U.S., becomes the explanation for family moving away. In my family, one of my uncles moved to California for work and, though I was young, I remember how terribly my family reacted. Another of my uncles dared to move to a suburb about twenty miles away from my extended family. This prompted mourning-like behavior by his mother (my grandmother), and we even had a big going-away party for him. I believe the experience of leaving family forever created a trauma for those immigrants and so they did everything they could to keep the new family they had created as close to them as possible.

NICK: One of the aspects of Italian-American culture that people love most in the show is the language, the "gabagools" (*capicola*), "goomahs" (*comares*), and "shvooyadells" (*sfogliatella*). I grew up hearing a few Italian-American colloquialisms, usually in a teasing way, like "ugatz," "stunod," and didn't think much of it. Why do you think the lingo was so infectious in Italian-American culture? And can you speak a bit to the etymology—generally—of how and why real Italian words evolve into these (appealing) bastardizations?
FRED: English is full of words from other languages, and fortunately we haven't tried to keep them out. Whether it's Yiddish, German, Spanish, French, or Italian, or any other language from immigration cultures, words stay with us because they work—they work through catchy sounds, unique denotations, and interesting connotations.

I did a study of the use of Italian language in Italian-American literature and found that the words used in later writings—from the 1970s to the 1980s, for example—are rarely the same ones used in earlier works. And as Italian Americans lost their language, this lessened some of the tension their search for identity could have created. Essentially, they lost one of the main ways of being identified with and connected to Italy.

Think of the family as the sentence and the individual as the word and you will have a clear picture of how Italian-American literature reflects its culture. To be an American is to be dispersed, to move quickly and fragmented, and to emphasize the individual in society. This is the Italian language used by younger Italian-American writers. To be an Italian, on the other hand, means remaining integral, to move slowly, to maintain the solidarity of the sentence, like the Italian used by the earlier Italian-American writers. If Italian identity comes from name only, then individuals are nouns, just words rather than sentences, disconnected from time and heritage.

Along with this decline in quantity, there is also a decline in quality; that is, writers tend to hang on to the *parolacce*, or bad words, and words that refer to food items, because these are still useful in everyday life. These are not so much bastardizations, but variations based on differences in geographical pronunciations. These are the words you find peppered throughout the show by Chase.

NICK: Of the bevy of Italian-origin slang words used on *The Sopranos*, do you have a favorite? If not, an example used in culture that doesn't appear on the show?

FRED: Of the ones Chase used, my favorite is *ciuccio*, often pronounced "chooch," which can mean dumbass or jerk, usually referring to someone who hasn't a clue of what's going on around him and will do whatever someone tells him to, often screwing it up in some way. Someone who's rather harmless, and whatever harm is caused is usually from not thinking clearly.

One word that's interesting is usually spelled *mericani*, short for "Americans," but the way my grandfather used to pronounce it, *merde di cane*, means "dog shit." Whenever I did something wrong or stupid he would say, "*Frederico, non fa l'americano!*" which means "Don't act like an American," or "Don't do it the American way."

UNDERSTANDING THE OUTLAW STATE

Jersey-born movie producer Heather Buckley and I spent a rainy Sunday driving around Paterson, Bloomfield, and Secaucus, New Jersey, hitting famous locations like Paterson Falls and eating onion rings at Holsten's. Later, we met some cast members at SopranosCon and sat down for a chat about what it means to be from North Jersey and how the location's texture and spirit permeate the show.

NICK: Heather, you're a lifelong Jersey native who loves the show. What is it about *The Sopranos* setting and texture that rings most true to you?

HEATHER BUCKLEY: When people ask me what is the most Jersey—I tell them it's Bruce Springsteen's "Atlantic City" and *The Sopranos*. These works speak to the struggle of just getting by and the alternate fatalistic route to the American Dream in one of the toughest cultures in the United States. You pull a job to feed your family, you feed your kids. You become a provider and not a bum. Goods fall off the truck so your kids will have something to open for the holidays. There is no union or benefits for you anymore—you don't have a pension. There is a sense of cultural heroism to give your family the best life, the best things, though there may be some blood on it.

Why did we have frozen shrimp and lobster tails growing up? My grandfather would get them from his job at the National Cold Storage in Jersey City. The pallets would break and the men would take them home to their families. It was what he could do to give us a little taste of prosperity. He was second generation from Warsaw and a World War II vet. He fought for the American Dream—he killed Nazis as part of the 101 Airborne—but when he got home, the system never afforded him much of it. My grandmother used to cry that the VA would not cover his medication and she could not afford it.

But why is New Jersey the best place for this story? Because you are forced to make your own way here. You have to be tough—not put up with anyone's bullshit. New Jersey politics was notoriously corrupt and you rarely had anyone to go to—consider Newark assemblyman Zellman (Peter Riegert) in the show. There is no faith in the system—only faith in yourself and your family. There's a nihilism here that you're never gonna move forward, because the system is rigged against you. So you work around the system, and champion those who build their own, and you make peace with it. If anyone helps you or is loyal to you then you stick by them until the day you die. New Jersey shows up for New Jersey. You show up for your crew.

NICK: Talk a little bit more about your family. Can you give me some detail about their background and your experiences growing up?

HEATHER: My father's Sicilian/Irish American from the Heights of Jersey City, and my Mother's Polish American from Downtown Jersey City. It seemed like everybody came to Ellis Island and decided: "I'm not going any farther, I'm gonna live here."

We grew up watching organized crime movies, and my father would make comments about the guys he grew up with. "Dad, why don't you have friends?" "They are all in jail." I have heard stories that the tough guys used to wait for the trucks out of Port Newark, and the driver would get paid to leave the truck to get robbed. They called stolen property "swag."

NICK: On *The Sopranos* we see the square world and the criminal underworld rub elbows fairly comfortably. A lot of the time when you think about noir and gangster pictures, you think about these elements being very separate from one another. Did you feel like there was a lot of commingling going on?

HEATHER: Throughout Hudson County everyone knew who "the boys" (my father's term) were and who was in charge out of Bayonne (John DiGilio) and the Lucchese crime family. The boys' headquarters were on Palisade and Newark Ave (Ducky's Restaurant, where the politicians hung out). "Everybody knew what was going on, even the cops," my mother says. "The Mob was like the police for the crooks and thieves," my father adds. It was very low-key, no shooting out in public. And you did not go into the Italian section unless you were Italian. You never robbed from the church. In the late '70s a Saint Jude statue was lifted in Jersey City. It was returned the next day.

NICK: When you look at some of the locations that we went to today, Paterson Falls, Holsten's, Bloomfield Avenue, driving around Nutley and Belleville, what is it that you see, think, and feel about those locations? What makes the vibe of the streets so inherently Jersey, so *The Sopranos*?

HEATHER: The landscape in New Jersey is very compressed. You have the cities, the suburbs, the shore, the endless Pine Barrens, and all manner of class divides in one state. And everything is fifteen minutes away.

I remember when I first watched *The Sopranos*, just the opening—the Turnpike, the city, the Goethals Bridge, the Skyway, Wilson's Carpet guy, Newark, Kearny, the Meadowlands—was everything I grew up seeing riding around from Central Jersey to North New Jersey.

Seeing the industrial landscape and the girders, the different layers of highway and New York City in a distance—it's like looking at the insides of America spilling out. Then the urban landscape gives way to houses with tailored grass, no sirens and no cities, but you take a bit of the Old Country with you (Pizzaland, Satriale's), the mom-and-pop shops (Holsten's) like there used to be in Hudson, Essex, Union, and Bergen counties on every corner.

Those areas, Nutley and Belleville, have that history—Italian immigrants who clustered near New York City to try and build their lives on the outskirts of it. Tony was born in Newark and his momentum brought him to the suburbs. My parents left Jersey City for Old Bridge in the late '70s. The next generation moved away from the mean streets; these little shops and the North Jersey locations they moved to signify that leap.

NICK: Let's talk a bit about neighborhoods and class distinctions because where Tony lives in North Caldwell seems very wealthy. I know that Junior's house is in Belleville and seems more modest.

HEATHER: The American Dream is the lawn and white picket fence—it is not the cities. Throughout North Jersey you have the counties with lots of little towns within them. These towns are dotted with little shops and strip malls—fewer sirens. Along the northern east coast of Jersey is where you find wealth (Edgewater) and, moving west, Jersey's idea of class and sophistication with new money—the prefab housing. Here, there's not a great depth of taste and elegant style like with old money. Nouveau riche has always been seen as gaudy, unlike old money, which is understated. They don't "need" to flaunt it, though they do, of course.

In the case of Tony vs. Uncle Junior—the class distinctions might also be generational. Uncle Junior was part of the Depression-era generation where, even when they finally had money, there was a real wariness about spending it; after all, it could go away at any time. And if you're already comfortable living where you are, why move?

For Tony it was different. Having a wife and kids added pressure to live and maintain a certain lifestyle.

NICK: It's the nouveau-riche thing. We see the freshly constructed Sacrimoni house go up and the McMansions in progress behind it . . .

HEATHER: It's a little tacky. Gaudiness is New Jersey. Like Adriana with her big hair, big earrings, and lots of makeup; some people would look at that and laugh. To me it's the most beautiful thing on the face of the earth, because that's a Jersey girl. Tom Waits and Springsteen wrote songs about Jersey girls. Jersey girls are strong and fierce. The houses in *The Sopranos* are the same way. It's not going to be "classic," it's going to be a bit off. It is unpretentious and unapologetic. And it ain't holding back.

NICK: Right, and I guess part of that is getting something from Hermès and saying it's a "Hermeez." Or as Tony says, "This is the real Louis Vitoon." It's about how much he paid for it, not any degree of style.

HEATHER: It's having money to flash it. The universal symbols of success—the house, the family, the kids, the car, the big house— this is what success looks like, this is what it means to "look" rich. The look is wearing too much gold, giving people the evil eye, and yet being super old-country Catholic. But with the Sopranos, and like most of America underneath that perfect lawn, everything is fucked up—they're suffering.

NICK: It's kind of interesting how Jersey geography plays into the death of Jackie Aprile Jr. and the way people process his murder, shifting all accountability away from the gangster life and towards African Americans. He's obviously killed on the orders of his mother's boyfriend Ralph Cifaretto and he gets shot in the head by Vito Spatafore, but because he'd been hiding out in the Boonton projects, in this housing project, it's described as a tragedy, something that happened *to* the Apriles and to the Sopranos and the other members of the extended family, not *because* of them.

HEATHER: You're talking about the implicit racism of these characters?

NICK: Kind of. The characters are ignorant of what happened, but it's implicit: you're dealing or buying drugs in the Boonton projects, you're gonna end up shot and killed, when really, the person who had him murdered is sleeping in his mother's bedroom.

HEATHER: Yes, part of the factionalization of different ethnic backgrounds—there's racism within that. Looking at ethnic cultures as gangs pitted against each other definitely includes the inherent classism and racism. People punch down and grind their boots down on those below them on the ladder of success. The Irish and the Italians that lived in the Jersey City Heights had lived in the United States long enough, and had enough money, to earn them the right to look down upon the Eastern Europeans who settled in the cold-water flats Downtown. When my father got engaged to my mother, my Sicilian grandmother said, "Why are you marrying a Polack?" and never talked to us again. Then everyone would discriminate against African Americans and Hispanics. There's inherent racism in all of these Mob characters—they strongly identify with their ethnic backgrounds, and class status is based on where they live (and if you were from NYC, who are these goddamned Jersey guys telling us what to do?). It is nearly impossible to be a made man if you are not of full Italian descent. You are either with us or with them. You either live here or live there. You use it as a tool to build yourself up and to rip people down.

NICK: The last immigrant group in always wants to slam the door behind them.
HEATHER: Yes, and that's very much the culture of that area.

NICK: Walking around SopranosCon, you seemed both proud and moved. Do you feel like Jersey was represented really well in there?
HEATHER: It's like a *Star Trek* convention, only with heroes and creatures from the mythical universe of New Jersey. It touches my heart that someone would care this much for something made in and about New Jersey. People are always making fun of New Jersey—the reality TV shows, that we're bridge-and-tunnel people—but there's also this incredible fascination with what the hell goes on in New Jersey. What moved me about SopranosCon was the idea that fans would get together and celebrate something that is so singularly Jersey—inspired by *our* organized crime families, *our* infamy. They showed up with their outfits and accents. They showed respect. New Jersey is so much about respect because we live in a state of disrespect. Thanks a lot, New York City.

NICK: True, there's an immense amount of pride, coming from New Jersey.

HEATHER: Yes, because someone has to love it, and I don't think it's an external love; it's us. When I meet anyone from Long Island or Staten Island and I'm from New Jersey, we just nod, because we're brothers and sisters—in this unofficial war against NYC (though we do love NYC and go there often).

NICK: You feel a kinship with other places you would define as underdog places.
HEATHER: Exactly, and so we stand by them.

NICK: Do you think there's a bit of a distinction between being on the hustle and being a hustler?
HEATHER: You just want to do good for your family. Do good for your community. That's why I think my family was fascinated by the presence of organized crime in Jersey City—they talked about the block parties they threw, helping the churches and the poor. We all knew someone who was very infamous or was gun-running.

People were never horrified to know these people. They were legends, bigger than life. It was like knowing Billy the Kid. They represented the struggle to survive. Jersey forced you to be an outlaw because you couldn't survive otherwise. I think that's why people are fascinated with the Mafia: they're entrepreneurs that have done it outside the system, and they're anarchists in a sense.

NICK: Do you think that by the time of the show (because in the pilot Tony says, "I feel like I'm comin' in at the end"), the ethos stuck around longer than it was needed? Like there are plenty of successful square characters on *The Sopranos*, but Tony still is gorging himself and juicing people.
HEATHER: It's the song "My Way"—by Sinatra *and* Sid Vicious. There is pride and there is fuck-you—gallows mockery even in the pride. Maybe it started—or people tell themselves it started—out of a certain necessity, but lessons learned about the world from

the circumstances of that necessity remain even after certain things may have improved and other opportunities appear. All of the square people struggling within the rigged system, and outlaws, who only know how to do it their way, it gives working-class Jerseyites a more nihilistic view of the world that, like, we're all suffering, what does it matter that people are suffering, like in the famous Mafia quote: "What does it matter if we kill people who are gonna die anyway?"

NICK: That's dark. There's a difference between a tax cheat who commits crimes against The Man as opposed to the commission of crimes against your fellow man. But you're saying that regionally, as part of the Jersey ethos, a distinction isn't made. There's no real guilt about juicing a guy, taking his business, and busting him out.

HEATHER: Contrast that bleak point of view with this: No one's looking out for us, so what else are we going to do? What is fair? What is just? People saw a system that was overabundant and wanted a piece of it—whatever fell off the truck. You were taught not to feel bad about that or to feel like you were dishonest or stealing—you were just trying to make it. In spite of New Jersey's cultural cynicism that believed you can't fucking make it and you can't fucking win, you did make it and you did win.

But beyond philosophy and social situation, you've also got to acknowledge the presence of sociopathy and the sometimes perversely inventive tendency to rationalize all sorts of behaviors, choices, and targets—which is one of the themes of *The Sopranos* as a show. Codes of honor and opportunism are frequently at war—and opportunism tends to win, at all levels. Big business and the government can always shake down one another. At the street level you can only target yourselves, and whoever you can reach in your crosshairs. It is what it is.

CHAPTER IV

WATCH LIST
The TV AND CINEMATIC DNA
of THE SOPRANOS

I f you've picked up this book, we probably don't need to tell you to check out the *Godfather* movies, *Goodfellas*, or the rest of Martin Scorsese's oeuvre. This chapter is designed to introduce less obvious television shows and movies we believe influenced David Chase. We'll really dig in to uncover themes, scenes, cadences, and textures that became part of Chase's expansive palette, whether he was conscious of it or not.

In the following pages, you'll find short essays on shows and movies by Phil Dyess-Nugent and Scott Von Doviak, two great contemporary television and movie critics. Writer and director Matthew David Wilder has contributed pieces on two movies he and I love from John Cassavetes and Elaine May. I've added my thoughts on the influence of two shows from producer Stephen J. Cannell, *The Rockford Files* and *Wiseguy* (Chase worked on the former) as well as Peter Yates's *The Friends of Eddie Coyle*. These pieces are presented in chronological order according to the release or airdate of the work.

Deeper into the chapter, you'll discover a piece from Dyess-Nugent on Chase's pre-*Sopranos* work, and one from Mark Dellelo on how the Western genre manifests in *The Sopranos*. Near its end Joe Mader writes on the influence of painting on the show's visual style, and finally, I consider how the world of movies influences the life and actions of Christopher Molti-santi (Michael Imperioli), who can't separate Method from madness.

LITTLE CAESAR (1931); *THE PUBLIC ENEMY* (1931); *SCARFACE* (1932) —Phil Dyess-Nugent

These pre-Code Hollywood films form the Holy Trinity of gangster classics. *Little Caesar,* the first one released, starring Edward G. Robinson as the fast-rising thug Rico Bandello, is the least substantial, though nothing can stop Robinson from making direct contact with the audience. Mervyn LeRoy's stodgy, stagy direction can't smother the freshness and vitality of Robinson's performance; close to ninety years later, countless imitations and parodies have scarcely put a scratch on it. (A caricature of Robinson in gangster mode went head-to-head with Bugs Bunny in the Warner Bros. cartoon *Racketeer Rabbit,* and Robinson himself made fun of his image in such movies as *The Little Giant* and *A Slight Case of Murder.*)

The Public Enemy, starring James Cagney as Tommy Powers—a lonely Irish American in this sea of mostly Italian-American stereotypes— was directed by William Wellman, who could do things with a camera that would have made Mervyn LeRoy blush. The screenplay, credited to Harvey K. Thew, was adapted from an unpublished novel by Kubec Glasmon and John Bright, a pair of Chicago newspapermen who had witnessed Al Capone's rise firsthand. Cagney was famously cast as the best friend of the hero (originally played by Edward Woods) until Wellman got a load of the rushes and had the two actors swap roles. Cagney had a special rapport with the audience that enabled him to do mean things—as in the famous breakfast-table scene, where he hits his girlfriend (Mae Clarke) in the face with a grapefruit—without losing the viewers' affection. Rico Bandello, whose cockiness was born of insecurity and who can't bring himself to kill his best friend, is more of a sweetheart, but it's Tommy Powers's charm, his electric energy, and the glamour of his gangster life that audiences were more likely to want to see themselves in. It is, as Pauline Kael once summed it up, "a good picture, even if its theme music *is* 'I'm Forever Blowing Bubbles.'"

Compared to these first two movies, *Scarface,* directed by Howard Hawks and written by Ben Hecht, is the Mr. Toad's Wild Ride of the gangster genre. Hecht, another Chicago reporter on his way to becoming a legendary screenwriter, wrote in his autobiography of being visited in his hotel room one night by associates of Al Capone: "They had a copy of my

Scarface script in their hands. Their dialogue belonged in it." Hecht assured them that the story was in no way inspired by the career or personality of Mr. Capone, but was instead based on some folks Hecht had taken notice of in Chicago before Big Al came along and remade the city in his image. ("'If this stuff ain't about Al Capone, why're you callin' it Scarface? Everybody'll think it's him.' 'That's the reason,' I said. 'Al is one of the most famous and fascinating men of our time. If we call the movie *Scarface*, everybody will want to see it, figuring it's about Al. That's part of the racket we call showmanship.'")

Hecht admits that when he said this to his guests from Chicago, he was lying. But although *Scarface* benefits from its journalistic detail about the construction and working of a large criminal organization, it has a baroque madness to it that sets it apart from torn-from-the-headlines melodramas. Case in point: the movie's implied love that dare not speak its name—and "love" is the politest possible word for it—is between Paul Muni's demented, near-simian Tony Camonte and his sister, played by Ann Dvorak, whose bulging eyes and crazy smile generate enough electricity to power the Las Vegas Strip. The movie is also blissfully uninterested in whether the audience likes its protagonist or cares about him. Tony wants the world's attention—brandishing his first tommy gun, he cries, "Some typewriter, huh? I'm gonna write my name all over town with it, in big letters!"—and the audience will give it to him, or else. God forbid we should find out what he'd do if he felt ignored. This is a movie where the only hope for a relatively stable, sensibly run criminal underworld is played by Boris Karloff.

In his classic essay "The Gangster as Tragic Hero," Robert Warshow wrote that the movie gangster is "what we want to be and what we are afraid we may become." Warshow also suggested that the average person who sometimes feels like a success may take comfort from seeing a Rico or a Tommy Powers or a Tony Camonte enjoy his ill-gotten position of power only to fall to the gutter, rationalizing that it's only possible to become a success by becoming a monster. Becoming a monster is something Tony Soprano (James Gandolfini) has made his peace with, and a part of him may always be waiting for the fall. When he watches these movies, it's with a rueful element that must border on jealousy: these are the guys who were there at the start, who laid the foundation for this thing of theirs and were able to have their kicks without that terrible sense that the best has already happened. There were giants in those days, and that includes both the giants who created organized crime in America and the ones who made movies about them.

THE FRIENDS OF EDDIE COYLE (1973) —Nick Braccia

We don't spend much time with "Philly Spoons" Parisi (Dan Grimaldi) before he's killed by Gigi Cestone (John Fiori), but he gets in a good line when he describes Boston as "Scranton with clams." That's sure how it feels in Peter Yates's adaptation of George V. Higgins's novel *The Friends of Eddie Coyle*. It's easy to see how the film influenced *The Sopranos*. First, there's the setting: the blue-collar and middle-class outskirts of a big city. The streets of Coyle's Dedham, Sharon, and Dorchester could easily be the DiMeo crew's Nutley, Verona, and Belleville. But it's the men who operate within the leafy streets and rendezvous in the abandoned lots (the types of spots Johnny Sack [Vincent Curatola] might call "undignified") that really interest him.

I mean, just look at the faces! Of course, there's Coyle, played by Robert Mitchum, who sports one of the most lived-in mugs in movie history. And Alex Rocco, hot off his Moe Greene moment playing bank robber Jimmy Scalise. Rocco was a real associate of Whitey Bulger's Winter Hill Gang and helped school Mitchum for the part. His legitimacy is equaled in Chase's cast by Tony Sirico, who plays Paulie Gualtieri. The details of Sirico's pre-acting career are well documented, especially in James Toback's documentary *The Big Bang*. It's also fun to see Joe Santos's face, icy, mustachioed, and beady-eyed here, contrary to the warm, open face he displays in his performances as Detective Becker on *The Rockford Files* and as retired Lupertazzi consigliere Angelo Garepe in *The Sopranos'* fifth season. His steeliness in Yates's film is matched only by Peter Boyle as Dillon, a barkeep and small-time crook who plays all sides against each other, a rat who rats on other rats.

Let's be clear that these gangsters aren't Tony. And they're not Christopher or Silvio Dante (Steven Van Zandt), either. They're not anywhere near that level. These are the expendable bottom-feeders. Losers, addicts, ex-cons, and hustlers mostly dealing in petty cash, unless they're doing risky bank jobs. When we see gun dealer Jackie Brown (Steven Keats) meet with his contact from the arms depot, we discover the guy's a drug addict who had to sell his car. He reminds us of Christopher Moltisanti's friend Corky Caporale (Edoardo Ballerini), the Italian-speaking junkie who helps fit imported Camorra killers with their toolkits. Jackie Brown drives a flashy car, like Mikey Palmice's (Al Sapienza's) associate Donnie Paduana (David Wike), who dies in his Firebird on orders from Junior Soprano (Dominic Chianese). These guys spend it as soon as they get it and are on to the next hustle. Like Brown says—and this could be the *Friends of Eddie Coyle*'s mantra—"Life's hard, lover." Truth is, nobody's going to miss most of these guys. And why would they? Coyle, with his matronly Irish wife and brood, is the exception.

The cops aren't much nicer. We watch Richard Jordan's cagey ATF agent Dave Foley play both Dillon and Coyle and we're impressed with his skills. He's willing to barter with the hoods and pretends to want to help them, but he doesn't care if they live or die. They're sources or collars to him, not people. This dynamic is expressed on *The Sopranos* with federal agent Robyn Sanseverino (played by the underappreciated Karen Young; watch her amazing work in Laurent Cantet's movie *Heading South*), who counsels Adriana La Cerva (Drea de Matteo) when they're trying to flip her. In one fantastic scene, Adriana's in a bathroom stall and we can see Sansaverino's apathetic face—invisible to Adriana—betray her true (lack of) feelings, even while her voice remains compassionate. When Adriana emerges from the stall, the agent's face fills with feigned compassion. We hurt for Adriana, even though we're not surprised; we've already heard Sanseverino mock her, back in "Irregular Around the Margins," when she impersonates her asset to the delight of her colleagues.

Yates, like Chase, loves to color in the details around these broken or breaking guys. What they eat for breakfast, and how they take their coffee, make their phone calls, decorate their homes, and talk to their wives and girlfriends. Eddie Coyle's easy. He's an over-fifty guy looking at a prison sentence. He loves his wife and kids and needs to catch a break. He tells Jackie Brown he's sick of watching everybody else make bank and eighty-six it to Florida. This time, he wants to be the guy to retire down south. Sounds a lot like Eugene Pontecorvo (Robert Funaro), who does everything Tony asks and more, but can't seem to get that ticket out. If Tony thinks it's lonely at the top, he should try out the flip side. This movie's title is meant to be taken as seriously as that of David Chase's upcoming *The Many Saints of Newark*. With friends like these, indeed.

THE FILMS OF PAUL MAZURSKY —Phil Dyess-Nugent

The writer-director Paul Mazursky has concrete ties to *The Sopranos* as an actor: not only did he appear on the show as the dealer Sunshine at Tony's poker games (until his character is shot dead by the dependably useless Jackie Aprile Jr. [Jason Cerbone]), but he also played Morris Levy, the notoriously mobbed-up music executive who served as a model for the character of Hesh Rabkin (Jerry Adler) in the 1998 movie *Why Do Fools Fall in Love*.

But in the details of its squabbling family scenes, and its bonding rituals and culture clashes between Italian Americans, Jews, blacks, Russians, and starchy WASPs, the show also exhibits the influence of the teeming canvasses of Mazursky's best films. Mazursky started writing movies to break away from the limitations he faced grinding out sketches for *The Danny Kaye Show*, then moved into the director's chair. The looseness and improvisational rapport the actors displayed in his best early movies (*Bob & Carol & Ted & Alice* [1969], *Blume in Love* [1973], *Harry and Tonto* [1974], *Next Stop, Greenwich Village* [1976]) seemed to liberate them to demonstrate previously unexplored facets of their talent. In a period when America was at its shaggiest, Mazursky's shaggy-dog encounters—between an old man traveling cross-country with his cat and a Native American salesman, in a jail cell; between a divorce lawyer still in love with his ex-wife and the ex-wife's hippie musician lover, whom he cannot help but like; between every conceivable variety of aspiring bohemian in '50s Greenwich Village—felt like snapshots of the country where you couldn't tell for sure whether everything was unraveling or coming together in a better way.

Mazursky's directing career quietly fizzled out in the '90s, after his masterly 1989 screen version of Isaac Bashevis Singer's *Enemies, A Love Story*. But whenever the Sopranos house fills up with people on some family occasion, with Adriana piling cocaine on her fingernail just to get through it, or Tony's attempt to compliment Hesh by addressing him as "You crafty old Jew," it would not be inappropriate to insert a shot of the dealer at the poker table, sagely nodding his head.

THE KILLING OF A CHINESE BOOKIE
(1976) —Matthew David Wilder

"And if you have any complaints, any complaints at all, please notify the management . . . and we'll throw you right out on your ass." As Cosmo Vittelli, a lowlife who thinks he's a king, Ben Gazzara creates one of cinema's most indelible characters in John Cassavetes's *The Killing of a Chinese Bookie*. Like De Niro's Jake LaMotta, or Keitel's Bad Lieutenant, Cosmo is a walking aria of male self-annihilation. This strip joint owner finally pays off the mobsters he's in hock to for his place—the Crazy Horse West (a more portentous monicker than the Bada Bing, and a likely inspiration for the Crazy Horse venue Christopher buys for Adriana), then celebrates with a gambling spree that puts him right back where he started. To pay his debts, Cosmo agrees to murder a Chinese kingpin the L.A. Mob has marked for death . . . but that only gives the barest indication of the strange, ecstatic poetry of Cassavetes's greatest and furthest-out-on-a-limb movie. The picture is a strangely crumpled form of film noir; a classic Cassavetes character portrait, with more than the usual romanticism and self-disgust; a super subliminal essay on Vietnam and Watergate; and an example of a kind of lyricism that's closer to *2001* than a gangster movie.

The Sopranos absorbed Cassavetes's masterpiece every which way— not least of which in its very American conception of *King Lear* in the gutter, a "skipper" who's run into the shoals, a shot caller who has no control of anyone around him. Cosmo laughingly sniffs the flower in his own lapel, dispensing nuggets of hard-earned wisdom to knuckleheads who wouldn't know sage advice if it kicked them in the ass. Though "Crazy Horse West" has a lot of connotations, the main one is that for Cosmo it is a kind of Sunset Strip Moulin Rouge, a place where tits beneath purple gobos are—in Cosmo's mind at least—a unique art form.

For Tony, his Crazy Horse West—the Bing—is a much more meat-and-potatoes proposition. When we first see him there, he is concerned with cash flow and keeping the workers in line; the place is not a glorified hang, it is a real money-dispensing instrument. Over time, the place, mostly because of its volatile mix of sex and mind-altering substances, becomes a danger zone for Tony; but in any case the appropriate code floats over the top at all times. One of David Chase's great moments of moral ambiguity has Tony pummeling Ralph Cifaretto (Joe Pantoliano) after he has butchered the young stripper Tracee (Ariel Kiley) behind the Bing—in maybe the most sheerly ghastly set piece of violence in contemporary U.S. picturemaking. "You disrespected the place?!" Tony half declares, half questions Ralphie—and in a classic Chasean manner, we have to split this idea down the middle. Tony is unable to say what he means—you murdered an innocent and defenseless girl—but he also means what he says: the cold hard fact here, folks, is not the dead hooker but the misbehavior in a captain's joint, and the chain of command that should be strictly followed at all times. In a kind of perverse flip on the Howard Hawks code of professionalism, everyone standing outside the Bing on that grim night knows that this is the bottomest of lines.

The character in *The Sopranos* who is perhaps most closely related to *Bookie*'s Cosmo is not Tony but his namesake Tony Blundetto (played with quiet gravity by Steve Buscemi). While less grotesque than Gazzara's Cosmo, he is similarly grandiloquent and feels thwarted. He feels Tony Soprano's life is his, as he went out on a crime spree where Tony was supposed to accompany him; the panic attack that kept Tony home that night saved him from getting pinched and doing hard time, as Tony B did. Like his archenemy, Phil Leotardo (the great Frank Vincent), Blundetto is a ziggurat of resentment, smoldering in rage on many different levels. Like Cosmo Vitelli (who is still bleeding out when last we see him), Blundetto perishes in a state of incomprehension, of blissless ignorance.

MIKEY AND NICKY (1976)
—Matthew David Wilder

Elaine May was doing toxic masculinity when toxic masculinity wasn't cool. The far outlier among the acerbic wit's four features to date, *Mikey and Nicky* was often mistaken upon its release as a film directed by its star, John Cassavetes. While it's hard to know how much Cassavetes and his costar Peter Falk contributed to the script, the film certainly resembled the great man's anguished psychodramas—but with a cool irony all Elaine

May's own. In it, a midlevel Mob functionary Nicky (John Cassavetes) is on the run, hiding out in a skeevy downtown L.A. hotel. Did he rip off the bosses (acted, dreadfully, maybe on purpose, by acting-teacher giants William Hickey and Sanford Meisner)? Did he fuck up some other way? He calls his only dependable friend in the world, Mikey (Peter Falk), the epitome of the square nine-to-five schnook. As a long night drags into day, a lifetime's worth of resentments and humiliations get aired, and Nicky's petty abuse of his friend is repaid by Mikey with Greek-tragic power.

To be sure, *The Sopranos* channels every sort of '70s movie antiheroism, but one can see David Chase leaning on *Mikey and Nicky* in the relationship between Tony and would-be-slick restaurateur and childhood buddy Artie Bucco (John Ventimiglia). In a novel wrinkle on *Mikey and Nicky*'s seesaw of male power, Artie doesn't just impotently envy Tony's wallet and his power with the ladies; he has reinvented himself as something Tony can never be—not just a hustler but *upscale*, aspirational, a pasta slinger who a couple years post the series' conclusion will be designing his trattoria to look like a start-up, with Pinot Noir served in mason jars. The earring-sporting entrepreneur is hoisted on the petard of his own libido—especially when he falls in love with Adriana, a move likely to get him killed by her volatile fiancée, Christopher. In a profoundly *M&N*-like scene, Tony clutches Artie, about to deck him, then bursts into laughter at Artie's protest "I love her." Clutching his pate, Tony tells him, "Even if you had a head of hair like Casey Kasem, it's not going to happen."

The Tony-Artie relationship explores the depths of childhood bonds—nowhere so deeply as in a scene where Artie, incensed by his own many problems and the literal and spiritual debt he has to Tony, races around the Nuovo Vesuvio floor and screams a tirade of abuse at Tony. The audience's jaw hangs for a moment, expecting Tony to go violently berserk, but instead he responds with a touching "what'd I do?" open-mouthed expression. From anyone else, this eruption would merit two slugs in the head. From his childhood buddy, it prompts chuckles and a reflex thought: Wait, am I actually guilty of something? The relationship between Mikey and Nicky is more abject—"You only call me," Falk's Mikey tells Cassavetes's Nicky, "when you need something." Artie and Tony's friendship is more uneven. Artie needs Tony's power, sometimes his wallet, but Tony needs

Artie for something more intangible: a reminder of what his life might have been like if he had not been part of "our thing," if he was just a clever guy hustling in the just-post-millennial, so-called "real" world.

THE ROCKFORD FILES (1974–1980), "THE JERSEY BOUNCE" AND "JUST A COUPLA GUYS" —Nick Braccia

It's common knowledge David Chase had been around the block prior to selling *The Sopranos* to HBO. Phil Dyess-Nugent tackles the larger scope of Chase's TV career and its relationship to his magnum opus later in this chapter, but I'd like to dive into two specific episodes of *The Rockford Files* written by Chase, "The Jersey Bounce" and "Just a Coupla Guys." Watching the episodes today through a *Sopranos* lens, the pair seem like trifles, but to the informed, they provide a unique look into Chase's doodle pad and are full of tonal experiments, half-formed ideas, and characterizations recognizable to any *Sopranos* fan.

First, some quick background on *Rockford* for readers born after 1970. TV and film star James Garner had a big hit with the TV Western *Maverick* in the late '50s and early '60s, and his second act is characterized by his turn as affable Malibu private investigator Jim Rockford. The setup is simple enough: after a stint in prison under a wrongful conviction, Rockford sets up shop in a beach-adjacent trailer and takes cases as he must (he'd prefer to be fishing or doting on his elderly father, Rocky [Noah Beery Jr.]). His prison pals sometimes help him with contacts and muscle, as he's forever bumping up against L.A.'s nastier element as part of his work. For the most part he's an even-keeled, deadpan straight man navigating a wild city. And more often than not, he plays tattered-suited champion to the city's victimized, like guest star Rita Moreno, who plays a resolute but trouble-plagued prostitute in three episodes and a television movie. *Rockford* ran from late 1974 to early 1980 but continued on periodically in the TV movie format until 1999, the same year *The Sopranos* debuted. Chase acted as producer from 1976 to 1979 and wrote twenty episodes. "The Jersey Bounce" and "Just a Coupla Guys" suggest that during this time Jersey hoods were never far from his mind.

The Rockford Files' Season Five episode "The Jersey Bounce" and Season Six's "Just a Coupla Guys" seem like they should be narratively connected since they feature the same duo: Newark menace Eugene Conigliaro (played by Greg Antonacci, aka Butch DeConcini in Season Six of *The Sopranos*) and his buddy Mickey Long (Gene Davis, brother of actor Brad Davis) but there's no continuity—the characters don't mention their past and seem to have never met Rockford. In fact, the episodes have a completely different feel from each other. "The Jersey Bounce" feels like a regular episode of *The Rockford Files* (the thugs frame Jim for a murder they commit), whereas "Just a Coupla Guys" is more Keystone Krooks. Eugene and Mickey are back, but defanged—they're more feckless than frightening—and there's no recollection of the murder, the framing, or the fact that, at the end of "The Jersey Bounce," Eugene tries to kill Mickey. And while it makes no sense to today's viewers, there was a legit reason for rebooting the goons. "Just a Coupla Guys" was designed as a backdoor pilot for a spinoff series starring Antonacci and Long as a pair of harmless schemers. NBC passed, and it's not all that hard to see why. Their schtick is enjoyable enough for an episode, but one has to squint pretty hard to see a fully fleshed-out series. But I get why the network invested in the experiment. It must have seemed like a shrewd business move to cash in on peak *paisano*. "The Jersey Bounce" aired on October 6, 1978, and "Just a Coupla Guys" on December 14, 1979. Italian-American culture had never been hotter. *Rocky* won best picture in 1977, and *Saturday Night Fever* ruled the box office. It'd probably never been better to look and sound like Greg Antonacci. I laughed aloud when a pretty female character who carries Conigliaro's child wistfully tells Rockford, "As soon as I saw him dancing, I knew he was Italian." Apparently, I was born twenty years too late.

Both episodes are peppered with germs of ideas that would later be developed, recycled, or remixed by Chase for *The Sopranos*. Spotting them all makes for a fun game: there's low-hanging fruit, like characters named Artie and Carmela. Also, Antonacci's Conigliaro is always ready with a malapropism. He dishes out several between the two episodes that would impress even Carmine Lupertazzi Jr. (Ray Abruzzo): "It would do us a grave honor," "As they say, you don't look inside the Trojan horse," and my favorite, spoken upon examining a case of goods that fell off the back of a truck: "The beauty shops and the chicks are nuts for these Style Air Blowers on account of Gore Vidal and all the famous haircut guys use them."

And he drops guido slang like he gets paid by the vowel. He's good for an "Oh, *Marone*," a "Bah bah bing!," an "Oogatz," plus several applications of "scungilli," which is delivered as an insult synonymous with pipsqueak.

Tucked into one scene in "Just a Coupla Guys" is a scenario awfully close to the premise for *The Sopranos*. Conigliaro and Long stumble into a war between a retired and reformed Jersey boss (Gilbert Green) living in Short Hills as a born-again Christian—a crime boss who really did change!—and his angry associate, Tony Martine (Antony Ponzini). Martine has a son, Anthony Jr. (Doug Tobey) who plays the drums and sees a psychologist. "He's gonna transition his way right into military school!" Martine exclaims. This episode also features a scene with Simon Oakland (who played the mercurial Tony Vincenzo on *Kolchak: The Night Stalker*, another show that benefited from having Chase on staff) as Eugene's uncle, Beppy, the proprietor of a Newark sandwich shop next to an adult bookstore. The salt pork on the menu and private back office for hoodlum hijinks make one wish for a Satriale's sandwich.

There's a lot of shared texture and test-driven ideas, but there's also a couple more refined aspects of *The Rockford Files'* New Jersey experiment that evolved into meaty aspects of *The Sopranos*. Chase has an obvious interest in guys six or seven rungs down the Mob ladder who scurry and tweak around, looking for ways to make an impression on the Cosa Nostra brass. In their more treacherous "The Jersey Bounce" incarnation, Eugene and Mickey murder a chubby L.A. wife beater named Mac Amodeus (Walter Olkewicz) on spec to impress a porn-king gangster, Artie Nodzak (Luke Andreas). Their reckless initiative mirrors the acts of ambitious morons like Matthew Bevilaqua (Lillo Brancato Jr.) and Sean Gismonte (Chris Tardio) who shoot Christopher Moltisanti in Season Two's "Full Leather Jacket," and Jackie Aprile Jr. and crew's card game heist gone awry in Season Three's "Amour Fou." Chase loves nitwit wannabes and their ill-advised schemes to make their bones. There's something that tickles him about the way Italian-American men fall for how they're depicted in the media and take on the affectations. *The Sopranos* has lots of characters like Eugene; they've all seen the movies and believe the hype.

Another thread is really just a throwaway in "Just a Coupla Guys." It's a backdoor pilot, but it's still James Garner's name atop the credits, so they had to do something with Rockford while working to ingratiate Eugene and Mickey to the audience. Rockford—relegated to the sidelines for much of the episode—finds himself a comic-relief fish out of water. At the beginning, as he traverses Newark International Airport, a mustachioed local tells him "Jerseyites are among the most friendliest people that you are ever gonna meet!" Rockford subsequently gets his watch torn from his wrist and his car and luggage stolen, then survives a drive-by shooting before enjoying a second mugging. Watching this *Looney Tunes* gauntlet of black comic woes conjures images of the shoeless Paulie Gualtieri, at the mercy of the Pine Barrens. Chase didn't invent fish-out-of-water comedy, but he's a helluva practitioner.

WISEGUY (1987, THE SONNY STEELGRAVE ARC)
—Nick Braccia

I deeply love *The Sopranos* and James Gandolfini's performance, but I'm not certain it's my favorite show about the New Jersey Mob, or that Tony Soprano is the greatest portrayal of a New Jersey gangster to appear on television. Sacrilege? Maybe. But hear me out. Stephen J. Cannell's show *Wiseguy* premiered in 1987 with a ten-episode arc about the infiltration of the Steelgrave family's Atlantic City crime empire by undercover agent Vinnie Terranova (Ken Wahl). These episodes include Sonny Steelgrave (Ray Sharkey), a complex, emotionally combustible Jersey gangster whom we can't help but care about, even as he garrotes his enemies. *Wiseguy* aired for four seasons and is largely terrific, with supporting performances from actors like Stanley Tucci and Jerry Lewis, but it's the first ten episodes that share DNA with *The Sopranos*, and it's largely thanks to Sharkey's Steelgrave.

Before we dive into what makes *Wiseguy* and Sonny great and influential, a little background: *The Sopranos'* creator David Chase and Cannell have history. Chase worked for Cannell on *The Rockford Files*. When his former boss died in 2010 Chase shared some of what he'd learned with the *L.A. Times*: "His characters had weaknesses—they were fallible human beings. . . . That was the beginning of viewers seeing a TV protagonist as someone like themselves."

Watching *The Sopranos*, it's clear Chase admired Cannell. *The Sopra-*

nos is sprinkled with Cannell Easter eggs, from Adriana's *A-Team* viewing, to the appearance of *Rockford* regular Joe Santos as Angelo Garepe. *The Sopranos* and *Wiseguy* share similarities beyond the Jersey setting. Both series cast Warhol superstars in supporting parts (Patti D'Arbanville appears in both shows, Joe Dallesandro in *Wiseguy*) and include Annette Bening in a single episode. *The Sopranos* twice mentions the Moody Blues song "Nights in White Satin," a number that appears in *Wiseguy*'s greatest scene. I don't believe any of these choices are coincidence, but they are superficial. The shows have very different styles and tones—*Wiseguy* is played as a straight crime show, hard-boiled; *The Sopranos* is an American satire masquerading as a Mob drama. Ultimately, it's the unconventional depiction of vulnerable gangsters who are filled with self-doubt and honest about their fears that unites the two shows.

Traditionally in gangster stories, we live vicariously through the charismatic criminals; we get the kicks without committing the crimes. Then, when they receive their comeuppance and are busted or dead at the end, we get to go home. *The Sopranos* and *Wiseguy* subvert this convention. We like Tony and Sonny *because* we relate to them, not only because they satiate our ids. And we often recoil when they commit violence and sacrifice more of their soul.

Chase and Cannell apply similar techniques to get us emotionally invested in their embattled crime bosses. When we meet Sonny Steelgrave in the pilot, he's second fiddle to his older brother Dave, a gangster in the Gotti mold who is dapper, confident, and steely. To add to his grandness, Dave's played by gangster movie royalty: actor Gianni Russo, Carlo Rizzi in *The Godfather*. At first, Sonny seems to share his qualities, but when Dave is killed in a gun deal gone bad, we quickly discover how much of his swagger comes from the confidence his brother's presence instilled. Sonny takes over the family, but he doesn't have his brother's stature or coolheadedness. He's vulnerable, emotional, and easily wounded. Insecure and without anybody he trusts, he bonds with Terranova. Of course, Sonny doesn't know his surrogate brother is an undercover Fed. In early seasons of *The Sopranos*, Tony—just a capo at the time—loses one best friend, Jackie Aprile Sr. (Michael Rispoli), to cancer while another, Big Pussy Bonpensiero (Vincent Pastore), is wired for sound by the Feds. He'll discover this betrayal just as he's acclimating to the responsibilities of bosshood. Like Sonny, his ascent is an unsteady one.

To help build affinity for Sonny, Cannell and his cowriter Frank Lupo create a world that consistently keeps him vulnerable to threats from other crime families as well as his own. Sonny's adversaries are always more vain, grotesque, or frightening than him. While we root for Tony Soprano against mercenary scumbags like Richie Aprile (David Proval), Ralphie Cifaretto, and Phil Leotardo, Sonny's got to deal with brutal Cretan killers, an escaped homicidal mental patient, and entrenched big-city mobsters who possess more turf and greater power. Compared to these ogres and nutjobs, Sonny consistently comes off the charmer. It's easy for us to root for him (and Vinnie) to outwit the opposition.

Like *The Sopranos* with its final scene in Holsten's, *Wiseguy*'s Steelgrave story ends with a jukebox selection. It's not Journey. Instead, The Young Rascals' "Good Lovin'" and the aforementioned Moody Blues song reverberate through an abandoned theater where Vinnie is alone with Sonny, who now knows his best friend is an undercover Fed who's betrayed their friendshp. Since Sonny can't escape Vinnie or the locked theater, he treats the jukebox like a kind of time machine, bringing him back to an era where he had a firm grasp and a bright future.

Despite my adoration of *Wiseguy*, however, I do think *The Sopranos* is a greater achievement. Maintaining such a high level of quality for six seasons and eighty-six episodes is unprecedented. But in the ten-episode Steelgrave arc of *Wiseguy*, Ray Sharkey burns so brightly that I'll put it up against the best ten episodes of any show set in Jersey or anywhere else.

TWIN PEAKS (1990–1991; 2017) —Scott Von Doviak

David Chase has never been shy about expressing his general contempt for the medium of television, at least as it existed prior to the "it's not TV, it's HBO" era *The Sopranos* helped birth. One exception to his wrath over the years has been *Twin Peaks*, the cult-classic ABC series co-created by David Lynch and Mark Frost, which Chase has often cited as a prime influence. As he told Matt Zoller Seitz in 2015, "As surreal as *Twin Peaks* could be, and as particular as it could be, as it was, it felt more like real life to me than the average hour-long television show. It has always been important to me to feel the geography of a place. When I first went to work on *The Rockford Files*, they showed me three episodes of it, and I thought, Boy, that really is Los Angeles. It's not just Los Angeles as someplace, it's Los Angeles. And that made me want to take that job. I really felt the same way about *Twin Peaks*, oddly enough."[1]

No one would argue that *The Sopranos* isn't grounded in a sense of place (though some New Jerseyans would dispute the veracity of their homeland's depiction). In *Twin Peaks* terms, Nuovo Vesuvio is the Double R Diner, Bada Bing is the Roadhouse, and the back room of the pork store is where the Bookhouse Boys convene. Both series also share a flair for absurdist humor and non sequiturs. (Think of Silvio and Christopher dropping in on a bizarre collection of Providence gangsters in "Whoever Did This," or Christopher asking, "Is this about the Easter baskets?"—a question Tony refuses to even entertain—in "Two Tonys.")

It's not the external geography that most strongly connects *The Sopranos* to *Twin Peaks*, however; rather, it's the internal exploration of the main character through the realm of dreams and alternate realities. Although other characters would have Lynchian nightmares throughout the show's run (notably Christopher being haunted by his first kill "Email" Kolar [Bruce Smolanoff] and Carmela's [Edie Falco's] encounters with a posthumous Adriana), Tony's dreamworld is both crucial to the show's probing of his psyche and reminiscent of Special Agent Dale Cooper's (Kyle MacLachlan's) visions and visitations. Just as a dancing dwarf (Michael J. Anderson) and a dead woman (Sheryl Lee) provide Cooper with the answers he seeks (albeit in veiled terms, such as assuring him that the chewing gum he favors will soon see a resurgence in popularity), a talking fish swimming up from the depths of Tony's subconscious forces him to confront what he knows to be true: Big Pussy is a rat. *The Sopranos* would return to Tony's dream life throughout the series, much to the dismay of a segment of the fan base. (See "The Test Dream" in Chapter 7 for more on this.)

When *Twin Peaks* returned in 2017, did Lynch and Frost extend a tip of the hat the other way? In the final episode, Cooper finds himself in a strangely underpopulated purgatorial netherworld, with a name he doesn't recognize—a scenario reminiscent of Tony's "Kevin Finnerty" odyssey in Season Six. Of course, Lynch has done this sort of identity switcheroo before, and may never have watched *The Sopranos* (though he was a huge fan of *Mad Men*). You can be sure Chase was watching when Cooper and company returned, however. In 2017, Chase shared his enthusiasm for the revival with Matt Zoller Seitz, proclaiming it "even greater" than the original.

TREES LOUNGE (1996) —Scott Von Doviak

David Chase was so impressed with this '90s indie film centered on a seedy Long Island bar that he hired its writer-director to helm one of the most beloved episodes of *The Sopranos*, "Pine Barrens." Not only that, he hired its star to play the pivotal role of Tony Soprano's cousin (also named Tony) in the show's fifth season. As it happens, both men were Steve Buscemi. And that's only the beginning of the influence this naturalistic, shaggy comic drama had on the series.

Chase extolled the virtues of *Trees Lounge* at a 2017 screening of "Pine Barrens" at the IFC Center's Split Screens Festival. "I love that movie. I thought it was so well directed and so clear and not baroque or anything like that," *Variety* quoted Chase as saying. "And from that movie we got our casting people: Georgianne Walken and Sheila Jaffe." Walken and Jaffe took their extensive Rolodexes with them to *The Sopranos*, and populated the show with a number of veterans from the impressive *Trees Lounge* cast.[2]

Among the familiar (if slightly younger) faces in Buscemi's film are regulars Michael Imperioli and John Ventimiglia, recurring players Suzanne Shepherd (Carmela's mother, Mary DeAngelis), Elizabeth Bracco (Vito's wife, Marie Spatafore, and yes, sister of Lorraine Bracco), Joe Lisi (Dick Barone), and one-timer Steven Randazzo (Vincent Rizzo in "46 Long"). In addition, the cast contains two alternate Tony Sopranos: Anthony LaPaglia, who was the front-runner for the role when Fox considered making the pilot, and Daniel Baldwin, who played the thinly veiled Tony stand-in Sally Boy in Christopher Moltisanti's movie *Cleaver*. (The Cleaver himself was played by LaPaglia's brother Jonathan. Small world!)

It's easy to see what Chase found appealing about *Trees Lounge*, even aside from the cast. Long Island and New Jersey share the looming shadow of New York City, and while Buscemi's film doesn't delve into the criminal underworld, the communities in both works are largely made up of descendants of Italian immigrants. Debi Mazar's Crystal, with her leopard prints, big hair, and poor choices, is a proto-Adriana, while the relationship between Baldwin's Jerry and his daughter Debbie (Chloë Sevigny) prefigures that of Tony and Meadow. He may not like her talking shit around the dinner table, but he's violently protective of her when the time comes.

It's a bit surprising that Buscemi never did any writing for *The Sopranos*, as the working class/drinking class rhythms of his *Trees Lounge* script suggest a good fit, right down to the malapropisms ("Now I got it embezzled in my head"). Although Buscemi proves to be an able actors' director, it's the casting that's most impressive, with Carol Kane, Samuel L. Jackson, Eszter Balint, and Mark Boone Junior all delivering strong performances. One casting mystery: How did Kevin Corrigan, who appeared in both *Goodfellas* and *Trees Lounge*, never turn up on *The Sopranos*? If anyone was born to play a knucklehead working with Christopher, it's him.

EZ STREETS (1996–1997) —Phil Dyess-Nugent

EZ Streets is the missing link between *Wiseguy* and *The Sopranos*, an ambitious crime serial created by a major TV network for a writer-producer, Paul Haggis, who had worked his way up from dreck (*The Facts of Life*; *Walker, Texas Ranger*) and had cinematic ambitions. Set in a nameless American city on the Canadian border, it uses a revenge-driven crime-story template and an ensemble cast to paint a dense mural of urban corruption high and low. In the pilot, which Haggis wrote and directed, the audience is introduced to police detective Cameron Quinn (Ken Olin), who aims to set a counterexample to his father (Rod Steiger), a bent cop whose shady activities finally got him thrown off the force. Quinn's own life and career unravel when he loses his partner on an undercover job gone wrong. (He also loses $10,000 in cash, which Quinn improperly liberated from the evidence room for his partner to use as a prop.)

Targeted by Internal Affairs and shunned by the rest of the police department, Quinn is scooped up by a maverick police captain (John Finn), who explains that if he's really "a cop who looks dirty" (as opposed to a dirty cop), he might be just the warhead to point at Jimmy Murtha (Joe Pantoliano), a calculating mobster who rules the city's "alphabet streets."

Richard Portnow, who plotted with Kevin Spacey's Mel Profitt on the second arc of *Wiseguy* before getting his lawyer's license and representing Uncle Junior on *The Sopranos*, has dubbed Murtha's gang "the Easys," because they control the action all the way down from E Street. When Quinn points out that there is no Z Street because W Street is the last stop before the river, Pankow explains that "the Ewies" just doesn't roll off the tongue the same way.

The cast of *EZ Streets* also includes Carl Lumbly as the mayor; flat-faced, dead-eyed R.D. Call as a menacing power broker to whom the mayor is in thrall; Mike Starr as a violent thug sutured to Jimmy Murtha's hip; and Jason Gedrick, '90s TV's answer to Billy Crudup, as a good kid who accidentally got mixed up in one of Murtha's impulsive robberies and did three years in prison rather than roll on him. Either Olin's obsessed but honest cop and Gedrick's tortured innocent could be considered the show's hero, as they both have a claim on the viewers' sympathies, and it's a measure of the show's unhurried pace and long-range narrative strategies that the two of them don't even meet until the fifth episode.

The most prominent woman character is Murtha's lawyer, Theresa Conners (Debrah Farentino), who is also his lover. Pantoliano's performance as Jimmy Murtha often suggests a rough sketch for Ralph Cifaretto, and he's never more Ralphish than in his sparring with the silky, painfully beautiful Farentino. Ralph likes to hold a gun to women's heads when he has sex with them. Theresa, who's smarter than Ralph's girlfriends, keeps a gun in bed with her when she's alone. But is it there in case Murtha wants it when he comes over, or in case she needs it if he shows up in the wrong mood? It's clear from our first sight of her, applying makeup to a black eye, that her attraction to him is based on the threat he poses. That may also explain why she comes to the window in her negligee to "extend an invitation" when she knows Quinn is parked outside with his camera, watching her. Sensing a threat to what he thinks of as his, Murtha engages in witty romantic repartee, saying charming things to her like "You must really like wearing those dark glasses."

Aside from Pantoliano, *EZ Streets*'s strongest connection to *The Sopranos* is Haggis's sheer ambition, his drive to extend what's possible in the medium. It's also a cautionary tale. Less than a decade earlier, CBS had been willing to take a chance on an unusual genre show like *Wiseguy* and give it the time it needed to develop a cult following. Even though *EZ Streets* attracted more press attention from the beginning than *Wiseguy*, after the feature-length pilot and the first regular episode were broadcast to crummy ratings, CBS pulled the show from its schedule in what critic Joyce Millman called "an extreme instance of network panic." The network brought it back four months later, but without bothering to re-air the first three hours, a self-sabotaging move that practically amounted to daring first-time viewers to tune in for some moody neo-noir confusion. Haggis, reading the writing on the wall, went on to co-create a more conventional, less memorable show—*Family Law*, which ran for three seasons—and then focused his attention on movies. (He worked on the scripts for the Clint Eastwood pictures *Million Dollar Baby*, *Flags of Our Fathers*, and *Letters from Iwo Jima* and the James Bond movies *Casino Royale* and *Quantum of Solace* and wrote, produced, and directed *In the Valley of Elah* and the Oscar-winning *Crash*). As for David Chase, the fact that *The Sopranos* wound up at HBO after failing to land at a commercial network has got to feel like one of the luckiest quirks of fate of his career.

ON DAVID CHASE, PRE–*THE SOPRANOS*
—Phil Dyess-Nugent

Whatever arguments we can have about the merits of individual shows, most people would agree that in the 1990s, between the premieres of *Twin Peaks* and *The Simpsons* in 1990 and *The Sopranos* in 1999, American TV got objectively better—the median standard was smarter, more sophisticated, more technically polished, better acted, and *less embarrassing*. A big part of this came about thanks to the efforts of veterans like Mark Frost and James L. Brooks, who brought in creative talents from outside the industry, including David Lynch and Matt Groening, as well as the sudden appearance of a new generation of creators such as Chris Carter and Joss Whedon. These talented creators had grown up watching TV and simply weren't as mortified to be working in the medium as older writers, who believed TV was a step down from moviemaking. Embracing the medium of TV, they chose to not dumb things down for the audience because they saw themselves, without embarrassment, as part of the audience.

But that's not David Chase's origin story. In 1999, Chase was an industry veteran in his fifties who wanted to break into movies but remained shackled to television. He was a talented and capable guy with a strong track record of good work on good shows, but I don't know that anyone thought of him as a potential auteur. Except there's evidence that is how Chase saw himself. In 1988, he co-created (with Lawrence Konner, a screenwriter who later worked on *The Sopranos* and *Boardwalk Empire*) a CBS series called *Almost Grown*, a drama set at various points in the lives of a man and woman (played by Tim Daly and Eve Gordon who were lovers in the 1960s, married in the 1970s, and were now divorced but still inextricably intertwined with each other's lives. Although it didn't stay on the air very long—it was promoted as if to poach *thirtysomething*'s audience, an audience that remained pretty much un-poachable—it was a good show, with smart use of pop music from the different time periods and noteworthy for Gordon's remarkable, open-hearted performance. It was also noteworthy for a commercial in which Chase himself appeared on-camera, explaining what he and his collaborators were trying to do. It was a strange thing to see at the time, not just because so few people knew who David Chase was, but because it was such an unusual idea to present to a network TV audience: hearing what the person who had made the TV show had to say about it.

Let's backpedal. Chase's TV career began in earnest in 1974, when he was hired as a staff writer for *The Magician,* a short-lived action-mystery series starring Bill Bixby as a stage magician who uses his powers for justice. Later that year, he joined the cultishly beloved horror show *Kolchak: The Night Stalker.* (Two years earlier, Chase had racked up what, for forty years, would remain his only writing credit on a theatrical movie: *Grave of the Vampire,* a not-half-bad horror movie starring two grindhouse titans of the day, Michael Pataki and William "Big Bill" Smith.) Chase was credited as "story consultant" on *Kolchak*'s full twenty-episode run and had his name on six of its scripts, though looking at the credits on some TV shows from that era tells you only so much about who did what: Chase is one of the six names on "Chopper," a semi-legendary *Night Stalker* script that's famous partly because it started out as a spec script sent over the transom by then-beginners Robert Zemeckis and Bob Gale. But Chase's connection to both *The Magician* and *The Night Stalker* should probably earn him a passing mention in the obituary of Chris Carter, since he was a fan of both shows and worked homages to them into *The X-Files.*

Chase next served as a story consultant on *Switch,* a lighthearted crime caper starring Eddie Albert as a retired cop and Robert Wagner as a con man who is persuaded to help the good guys. *The Magician, The Night Stalker,* and *Switch* were all genre shows with something off-kilter about them, not a bad way for a young TV writer to learn the game and do what he can to attract attention to himself. But *The Rockford Files,* Chase's next port of call, was just a little something more: a genre show, but the TV apotheosis of its genre, the private-eye thriller. It looms large in Chase's back catalogue in relation to *The Sopranos*: it shows his first attempts to capture a criminal milieu (including an organized-criminal milieu) that might actually seem convincing, the first full flowering of his humor in such scripts as "The Queen of Peru" and "Irving the Explainer," the ambitious narrative stretch of double-sized two-part episodes like "To Protect and Serve" and

"Black Mirror," his interest in rock 'n' roll and the music business in "The Oracle Wore a Cashmere Suit" and "Only Rock 'n' Roll Will Never Die," and one character—the hit man Anthony Gagglio, played by George Loros in "To Protect and Serve" and "The Man Who Saw the Alligators"—so believably sociopathic as to be more terrifying than anything Darren McGavin's Kolchak ever drove a stake into. (Loros, grown positively cuddly with age, would go on to play the long-lived rat Ray Curto on sixteen episodes of *The Sopranos*.) Chase's association with the show would continue into the '90s, when he wrote two *Rockford* reunion TV-movies and directed one of them.

Between *Almost Grown* and *The Sopranos*, most of Chase's non-*Rockford*-related work was done under the umbrella of the team of Joshua Brand and John Falsey, creators of *I'll Fly Away*, a sort of *To Kill a Mockingbird: The Series* and the kind of show that exists to win awards for people—Chase was given one from the Producers Guild of America—and the funkier *Northern Exposure*, where he wrote one episode and served as executive producer during the show's last two years, which were not its two best. A distant observer during that period might have assumed that his greater ambitions had cooled and he had entered a phase of working retirement, but subsequent events show that this distant observer had his head up his ass.

PURPLE LIGHT IN NEW JERSEY:
TIME FOR A GANGSTER TO DREAM
(UNDER THE INFLUENCE OF WESTERNS)
—Mark Dellelo

"Whatever happened to Gary Cooper? Now *there* was an American. The strong, silent type. He did what he had to do." The first time Tony makes this reference is in the pilot episode, as a way of raising his defenses in his first therapy session with Dr. Melfi (Lorraine Bracco): "Nowadays, everybody's got to go to shrinks, and counselors, and go on *Sally Jessy Raphael* and talk about their problems." He brings it up again in the fourth season, on a car ride with Silvio and a few other members of his crew who have just disrupted a Native American demonstration on Columbus Day in a gesture of Italian-American pride. "They discriminate against all Italians as a group when they disallow Columbus," Silvio tells Tony. "Group!" Tony answers with contempt. "Would Gary Cooper belong to some victims' group if he were alive today?"

Though Tony is an inveterate movie fan, we only once see him watching a gangster film, and that's mostly to save face: he fires up *The Public Enemy* when the "*mulignan*" Meadow (Jamie-Lynn Sigler) is dating identifies it as ground zero for the genre. We know, of course, that he loves the *Godfather* films, particularly the scene (as he tells A.J., played by Robert Iler) where Michael avenges the attempt on his father's life in *Part I* and the scenes (as Carmela tells Father Phil, played by Paul Schulze) where Vito returns to Sicily in *Part II*. But one afternoon when the guys in the back room at the Bada Bing are about to put on these movies, he protests, "I can't watch these again." Maybe because they hit too close to his work life (this is, after all, not long after a gunshot shattered the bottle of juice he was holding, echoing the bag of oranges that Marlon Brando dropped when he was gunned down in *Part I*). Instead, his idea of escapism is crashing out on the couch in front of *Rio Bravo* (1959)—specifically the scene where Dean Martin and Ricky Nelson duet on "My Rifle, My Pony, and Me." This bucolic dream of cowboy life is, as Walter Brennan quips to John Wayne at the end of the scene, "better than being out in the street and getting shot at."

But there's more to it than just that. There's an ethical code behind the actions of the Western heroes Tony admires, just as there's an ethical code behind what Vito Corleone does when he returns to Sicily, or what Michael Corleone does when he comes out of the men's room at Louis Italian-American Restaurant with a gun. These are men doing what they "have to do," much like Colorado, the cowboy played by Ricky Nelson in *Rio Bravo*, does what he "has to do" by joining forces with the local sheriff and deputy in the town where his wagon master is gunned down.

Rio Bravo was made in response to *High Noon* (1952), which starred Gary Cooper as a sheriff about to hang up his badge when he gets word that an outlaw he sent away for murder is coming back to town after a pardon. Tony sees an image from this movie as part of his nightmare in the Season Five episode "The Test Dream," and it's the movie's most harrowing moment: the camera cranes up to show Cooper completely alone in the public square. Despite his efforts to marshal up a posse of deputies to face off against the outlaw and his brothers, the townsfolk have all shuttered their doors in the hope that the problem will go away when Cooper does. He does what he "has to do," but he has to do it alone.

Tony's nightmare is brought on in part by his anxiety after hearing the news that his cousin Tony Blundetto has just escalated hostilities with New York by wounding Phil Leotardo and killing his brother Billy (Chris Caldovino). He's worried that he's losing his grip on his *famiglia*, a fear that will be borne out a couple of episodes later when Silvio tells him that a lot of the crew are unhappy with his management of the Tony Blundetto situation. His answer to Silvio is one of his most direct expressions of the existential isolation that haunts him throughout the series: "You've got no fucking idea what it's like to be Number One. Every decision you make affects every facet of every other fucking thing. It's too much to deal with almost. And in the end, you're completely alone with it all."

The shot from *High Noon* that appears in Tony's dream is a nightmare image of that existential isolation. And its inversion is the scene in *Rio Bravo* that Tony watches on his couch at home: though the four men in it (Dean Martin, John Wayne, Ricky Nelson, and Walter Brennan) are enjoying only a brief respite from the high seriousness of doing what they "have to do," they aren't alone in doing it. This is the posse that Gary Cooper failed to pull together. For Howard Hawks, who made *Rio Bravo* because he didn't like *High Noon*, they form a more convincing image of the Western ethos, in which rugged individuals unite for the common good, honoring the leadership and emulating the values of the strong, silent type.

This epithet happens to be the title of a Season Four episode, and it's the way in which Tony would like to see himself. But this ethos is contradicted by the corrupt moral universe he inhabits. When the minor-key cowboy ballad "Ghost Riders in the Sky" plays in a makeshift casino bar to underscore a moment of tension between Tony and Ralph Cifaretto, it's a burlesque of a showdown between gunslingers in a Western saloon because there is no honor on either side. The chip on Ralph's shoulder (he turns down Tony's peace offering of a drink) comes from a perceived ethical transgression on Tony's part: you don't raise your hands against a made man in your own family, as Tony did after Ralph savagely beat one of the club's dancing girls to death. Tony's moral outrage over the murder of this innocent girl may have been enough for him to momentarily disrupt this perverted ethical code, but it wasn't enough for him to castigate Ralphie in any consequential way—and there ended our empathy with him. In a sense, he failed here to do what he "had to do." The incident reverberates with an earlier Gary Cooper Western, *The Virginian* (1929), in which Cooper oversaw the hanging of a member of his posse for stealing cattle. He could have spared his friend but instead did what he felt he "had to do"—what his very identity as a Westerner presented as an inexorable choice. In the 1950s the film critic Robert Warshow wrote about both this movie and *High Noon*, comparing the characteristics of the Westerner to those of the gangster, and it's not difficult to imagine that David Chase had read this essay, particularly given that Tony's line about Cooper doing what he "has to do" appears repeatedly throughout it. Warshow writes:

> The gangster is lonely and melancholy, and can give the impression of a profound worldly wisdom. . . . He is lonely and melancholy not because life ultimately demands such feelings but because he has put himself in a position where everybody wants to kill him and eventually somebody will. . . . The Western hero, by contrast, is a figure of repose. He resembles the gangster in

being lonely and to some degree melancholy. But his melancholy comes from the "simple" recognition that life is unavoidably serious, not from the disproportions of his own temperament.[3]

In *Rio Bravo*, when Wayne tells a friend that his posse includes a drunk and a cripple, the friend asks, "Is that all you've got?" Wayne answers, "That's *what* I've got." Ralph is Tony's top earner; he's what Tony's got. And he's surrounded by people who remind him of this—like Johnny Sack, the New York underboss who has a stake in the Esplanade development project that Ralph's assigned to, and to whom Ralph turns for support. Even Silvio suggests that Tony made a mistake when he manhandled him. But Tony gets his best advice from his Uncle Junior, of all people, who provides an objective look at the consequences of passing Ralph over for captain and counsels Tony that there isn't an easy answer, that as boss "you steer the ship the best way you know—sometimes it's smooth, sometimes you hit the rocks."

Eventually Tony's pragmatism wins out over his pride and he does promote Ralph to captain (though only after forcing Ralph to grovel for it). He may not be a member of the posse that Tony wanted, but he's a member of the posse that Tony's got. In "Pie-O-My"—a Season Four episode centered on a horse—you can see an attempt to whip up the kind of camaraderie the cowboys in *Rio Bravo* enjoy. In a tracking shot as the posse approaches the horse's stable, Ralph (the owner of the horse) walks at the head of the pack and looks the most dashing in a Burberry coat. But Tony knows that Ralph realizes the thin ice he's skating on, after a string of bad judgments that culminates with the whopper of alienating his erstwhile ally Sacrimoni by making a laughingstock of his wife. Ralph's learned enough to pay respect to Tony by offering him a taste of his winnings, but Tony takes narcissistic pleasure in making him squirm and holding out his hand for more. Despite the overtures toward a recreational mood, and despite the fact that Ralph owns the racehorse, this is still the same high-stakes gambling the gang traffics in during their workday, and the same pecking order applies.

At the end of the episode Ralph thinks he can gain the upper hand with Tony by dodging a call about the horse's bad health and sneakily routing it to him. He's then forced to go out in the rain in the middle of the night to pay the veterinarian (Bruce Barney) Ralphie has stiffed. (Ralph's gall here foreshadows what will turn out to be his worst mistake, as Tony's affection for the horse and fury over Ralph's sabotage of it will ultimately spell his demise.) As Number One, Tony can't pass the buck to anyone else; the burden to do what he "has to do" is on him, and we might expect a reprise of the mood of existential isolation he's so often fallen victim to. Yet when he steps, alone, into the barn, it looks like there's no place he'd rather be. The horse is sprawled on a bed of hay that radiates golden light, bouncing off the deep turquoise walls that form a sanctuary from the gray rain we see in the background. (This is one of several closing shots in the series that evoke Edward Hopper; see page 174.) With no one to nag him but a goat, Tony lights a cigar and the song that Carmela switched off in their living room plays out in full: "Purple light in the canyon . . . it's time for a cowboy to dream." The pathetic irony of this moment is that he's not a cowboy but a gangster. To return to Warshow: "The gangster's loneliness and melancholy are not 'authentic'; like everything else that belongs to him, they are not honestly come by. . . . He is wide open and defenseless, incomplete because unable to accept any limits or come to terms with his own nature, fearful, loveless." A horse and a goat are the closest he'll ever get to the easy rapport of Dean Martin and Ricky Nelson trading verses.

PAST AND PRESENT:
ARTIST INFLUENCE IN *THE SOPRANOS*
—Joe Mader

The visual arts play an important role throughout *The Sopranos*: the frozen and severe figurines in Dr. Melfi's office, Carmela's emotional reaction to a Renaissance painting in the Metropolitan Museum of Art, the ridiculous portrait of Tony as Napoleon that Paulie appropriates, and my favorite, the painting in Tony and Carmela's bedroom that's obscured by their bed's headboard. (The painting is identified by various internet sites as Pontormo's *Visitation*.) Is there a more apt metaphor for Tony's and, especially, Carmela's relationship with Catholicism and morality in general? Animal appetites (symbolized by the bed) and willful ignorance cover up a large part of a representation of God's grace and mercy, the worst kind of cafeteria Catholicism.

But paintings also have a different kind of influence in the show, as visual inspiration for the look of the series and its cinematography and art direction. There are obviously myriad influences on chief cameramen Alik Sakharov and Phil Abraham and main art directors Scott P. Murphy and Henry Dunn's brilliant work, including the work of many other film artists and innumerable painters, but I want to bring up two particular artists whose style recurs in the series.

The great Renaissance painter Caravaggio, a bad boy in a time rife with bad boys, brought an astonishing humanism to his paintings of divine subjects. In his painting of the deposition of Christ's body from the cross to the grave, *The Entombment*, outstretched hands serve the place of halos, and the fleshly pallor of Christ's body erases the strength of the musculature Caravaggio expertly renders. There are no angels, no hint of the supernatural or the miraculous, just the contrast of the death of the main subject to the undeniable life and vigor of the other figures (which include St. John and Joseph of Arimathea). Life itself is divine to Caravaggio, as he demonstrates in painting after painting.

Caravaggio's use of chiaroscuro (the interplay of light and shadow) was (and is) peerless (although you could make an argument for Vermeer and a few others), and you can see his influence in the very first episode of *The Sopranos*. A scene between Junior and Tony in Artie Bucco's restaurant is as carefully composed as Caravaggio's *The Cardsharps* or his *Supper at Emmaus*. Shadow is used to show us where to look and where not to look, to provide perspective and mood.

A shot of Tony about to get an MRI echoes *The Entombment*, where the only light in the darkened room eerily emanates from the machine's cavelike opening. The image contrasts with the darkly comic dialogue between Carmela and Tony as they discuss whether or not he has a brain tumor. And when Christopher executes a rival gang member during a meeting at the butcher shop that serves as a front for Tony's organization, the meat and hogs' heads often have more light on them than the two actors, evoking the images of fruit and other foods in Caravaggio compositions.

The richness, depth, and complexity of Caravaggio's work stands in contrast to that of the twentieth-century American realist Edward Hopper. Hopper's great subject is the alienation of modern life. His human subjects have a brittle isolation and unknowability. They remain at a distance from the viewer, locked in their own thoughts and sorrows. The lighting is usually harsh, from artificial, fluorescent sources, and color is used in large unvarying swaths. Windows and glass are used both as sources of light and as barriers. His most famous painting, *Nighthawks*, has only four human figures, and even the two sitting next to each other are looking straight ahead. There's no conversation or communication, only individual late-night reveries, as the figures drink their coffee and contemplate the morning soon to come. The overwhelming feeling is one of loneliness, despair even, an austere vision that nevertheless has its own beauty. Similar images recur in Tony's meetings with Hesh and Christopher at the Bada Bing: the camera looks through a stripper's dancing legs at a second-floor office window where the men discuss business. Windows, electric lighting, TV monitors, and spotlights isolate figures in both the background and the foreground. And in Melfi's office, with its wooden paneling and complete lack of natural light, we get a similar feeling of isolation and alienation, as well as intimacy.

"Our existence on this earth is a puzzle," Carmela waxes philosophically at a dinner with Tony. It's a feeling Hopper made manifest in his art.

Sakharov and Abraham would probably cite any number of paintings and artists who inspired their work on *The Sopranos*, which looked unlike any series before it. So many scenes, gorgeously arranged with a painterly use of light, evoke past masters like Caravaggio and Hopper. *The Sopranos* matches spectacular storytelling with elevated image-making, borrowing from master visualists of the past to achieve something both modern and classic, another of the many achievements of creator David Chase and his team.

A REEL GANGSTER:
FIVE MOMENTS THAT SHOW HOW
THE MOVIES MADE MOLTISANTI —Nick Braccia

Christopher Moltisanti's relationship to the movies is hilarious and, at times, surprisingly moving. The young gangster has strong artistic impulses and even good instincts. While he's supercharged with creative energy (and some innate talent), he lacks the self-awareness and discipline to harness it. Whenever he expresses himself artistically, he either short-circuits and explodes in violence or creates a mess he's unable to wrangle. David Chase and his collaborators (Imperioli included, as both writer and actor) have great fun and success using Chris's artistic drive to trigger his volatility. They bring him into movie-themed moments that range from meta-throwaway gags to tragic irony. In a way, they fulfill the kid's dream of always wanting to be in the pictures. Sadly, the only one not clued in is Moltisanti. What follows are five of my favorite Moltisanti movie moments and why I believe they're magic.

THE HOMAGE
Episode 1.8, "The Legend of Tennessee Moltisanti"

"The Legend of Tennessee Moltisanti" opens with a glorious comic nightmare sequence that evokes Sam Raimi and Tim Burton. Christopher's surrealist vision speaks to the potency of his creative juice, which pumps through his subconscious following the commission of his first murder. The youngest of the crew, Christopher is struggling and frustrated that the killing didn't earn him a promotion. He tries to channel his nervous energy, guilt, and fear into something productive that might further his Hollywood ambitions, but his literary toolkit is far too primitive to convey the feelings and images dancing in his imagination. He's left feeling completely blocked just a few pages into his screenplay, entitled *Made Man*, and begins to see himself as the butt of a cosmic joke: "Where's my arc, Paulie?" He needs relief for his creative, professional, and existential constipation, but it only gets worse when a bakery clerk (Brian Geraghty) disrespects him. Pushed to the limit, Moltisanti forces the poor kid to fill a pastry box at gunpoint. In the end, Christopher shoots the kid in the foot and when he complains, Christopher tells him, "It happens." The joke is that Imperioli's character, Spider, was shot in the foot by Joe Pesci's Tommy DeVito in Martin Scorsese's *Goodfellas*. Sick of waiting for something good to happen, Moltisanti blasts a hole in reality and struts out with the cannoli. It's a meta-moment that gives him a sense of power and a minute to breathe easy, even as the nine-toed clerk screams on the floor. If Christopher can't create anything original, he'll settle for a cover.

THE METHOD
Episode 2.5, "Big Girls Don't Cry"

When his sweet, loving girlfriend, Adriana La Cerva, sees Christopher struggle with writer's block, she thoughtfully enrolls him in a class, Acting for Writers, because she thinks it will help free him up. She's right, but it doesn't go the way anybody hopes. Although he's initially skeptical we quickly learn he's a natural, much more adept onstage than on the page. The trouble is, he's an emotional geyser and so sensitive that all his expressions of vulnerability are followed by rage or violence.

Christopher impresses even when he's nervous and oblivious. He's just being honest when he tells his class, "I bought that book, *How to Write a Movie in 21 Days*. That was a year ago." His timing is perfect, but he's puzzled by their laughter. He wows his instructor (Linda Emond) with his improvisational dexterity and surprises a proud Adriana rehearsing a scene from *Rebel Without a Cause*. When he catches her responding to his talent for expressing emotion, he shuts down, bottles up, and retreats to a cocaine binge.

Dealing with Moltisanti the actor is like handling plutonium. In his big scene (he plays Jim Stark—the James Dean role—in the scene where Sal Mineo's Plato is killed) he goes full Method and floors everybody. In a moment of brilliant improvisation, Moltisanti improves on the original scene by recalling Plato "was always cold" and gently zips up his jacket. When an ignorant classmate asks, "How'd you make yourself cry like that?" the temperamental Chris storms out.

In a final class appearance Christopher, filled with shame and rage, punches out a poor classmate (Robert Prescott) during a simple exercise. Unfortunately, we don't get to see Moltisanti onstage again. It'd have been worth a homicide or two.

THE BUSINESS
Episode 2.7, "D-Girl"

The idea that Hollywood is more cutthroat than the Mob wasn't the freshest joke in February 2000 when "D-Girl" aired, but the episode has its moments as Chris, still smitten with the industry, mingles with Jon Favreau (playing himself) and his cousin Gregory's (Dominic Fumusa's) girlfriend, Amy Safir (Alicia Witt), a Hollywood development executive. It's a whirlwind fantasy escape for Moltisanti. The Los Angelenos find Chris's stories, bluntness, and his dangerous aura novel. He hangs with Favreau and sleeps with Amy, oblivious to the fact that the West Coasters are slumming it for the thrills. In the end, Favreau steals one of his stories and Amy, a social climber who never heard a name she wouldn't drop, cold-shoulders him. The mobster gets rolled.

Still, his experience is notable in that we see his strong instincts on display again: Favreau's producing a movie and needs to wrap a scene before they lose sunlight. Christopher helps actors Sandra Bernhard and Janeane Garafolo by offering some authentic slang ("buchiach") that punctuates their scene. At the monitor, with the headphones on, he's green, but not out of place.

THE MOVIE
Episode 6.14, "Stage 5"

Finally, Moltisanti's art is distributed to the masses! First in a production office and later, at the premiere, we get to experience scenes from *Cleaver*, a horror feature with a story by Christopher Moltisanti. It's not exactly the visual extravaganza from his dream in "The Legend of Tennessee Moltisanti," but it's got heart. Though the screenplay was written by J.T. Dolan (Tim Daly) and the film directed by Morgan Yam (John Wu), the movie has

Chris's fingerprints all over it (though I suspect if he had the experience and patience to direct, his style would have more *giallo* touches).

Style aside, it's the content of the feature that gets Moltisanti in hot water. His story is clearly the product of repressed anger—over the Tony Soprano and Adriana incident in "Irregular Around the Margins" and his guilt over her death in "Long Term Parking"—but he doesn't sufficiently disguise his inspiration. Carmela, and subsequently Tony, are embarrassed and angry.

Back in Season One, Christopher laments his lack of an arc: "They start out somewheres, something happens to them and it changes their life. Where's my arc? I got no identity, all I got is nightmares." The irony is, he has an arc, and it's a tragic one, as it was set in stone when he let Adriana die. This movie, an expression of his rage and his guilt, marks the beginning of his last act. With Tony clued in to Christopher's true feelings, *Cleaver* will be his first film, but his final curtain.

THE DEATH SCENE
Episode 6.18, "Kennedy and Heidi"

Christopher has many Scorsese-inspired moments in the series. From his run-in with the man himself in "46 Long" (a starstruck Moltisanti yells, "*Kundun* . . . I liked it!") and the aforementioned *Goodfellas* homage to his recognition of Sandra Bernhard from *The King of Comedy*. He's unfortunately the butt of the dark joke in "Kennedy and Heidi" when he's gravely wounded in an accident that happens because he's distracted adjusting the volume on the soundtrack to Scorsese's *The Departed*. His love for the movies—and especially Marty—essentially bookends our journey with Moltisanti, who wears his *Cleaver* hat while Tony suffocates him.

Christopher's afforded one movie moment encore, posthumously, in a homage to Brian De Palma's 1981 thriller *Blow Out*, in which B-movie sound technician Jack Terry, played by John Travolta, gets the perfect sound effect for a horror film: the scream of his girlfriend, Sally (Nancy Allen), who is strangled by a psychotic political operative (John Lithgow). We see Tony, from his stretcher, gaze at Christopher's body bag and personal effects, including his *Cleaver* hat. Off that shot, we see Christopher's wife, Kelli (Cara

Buono), who has just received the terrible news. She unleashes a blood-chilling shriek and drops the phone. Her horror-aficionado husband would have loved to use her terrific scream in his next picture. The last time we see Christopher, he's laid out in full hair and makeup. Sadly, he was unable to reconcile his artistic life and career in the pictures with his day job. It's a tragedy, as the kid had real talent.

CHAPTER V

THE SOPRANOS

in Culture

There's plenty in these pages about the text and craft of *The Sopranos*, but it's worth spending a little time examining the cultural phenomenon it was and, if SopranosCon is any indication, continues to be. *The Sopranos* essentially birthed the idea of peak TV, and what a perfect show to do it. Brutal but not as brutal as *Oz*. Peculiar with bits of surrealism, but we're not talking *Twin Peaks*. Genre pleasures mixed with relatable domestic life, *The Sopranos* was an offer that HBO's comparatively cultured audience couldn't refuse. It was middlebrow with balls! People loved the balance of whackin' and yakkin' with biting satire in a show populated with so many quotable characters. In no time, a cottage industry of bootleg shirts emerged. And soon, the HBO licensing department, which had never had a cultural hit like this, got their merchandising machine moving: DVDs, cookbooks, soundtracks. Later, pinball machines and video games. It wasn't Westeros dollars like *Game of Thrones* produced, but it was the monetization of a fandom that would change television forever.

In this chapter, I'll visit SopranosCon, and Eddie McNamara will track back to the early aughts to evaluate some *Sopranos* cookbooks. Then, USC professor Henry Jenkins, author of several books on culture, sits down for a chat with his son, Charlie, a novelist and former creative director at the L.A. content studio Chaotic Good, to discuss the show's cultural impact. We close out in a Lower East Side arcade, where I sample the *Sopranos* pinball machine after hooking up an archaic PlayStation 2 to see how the video game *The Sopranos: Road to Respect* holds up.

A WEEKEND WITH FAMILY
—Nick Braccia

Just as I'd signed on to create this book, SopranosCon was announced as taking place at the Meadowlands Exposition Center in Secaucus, New Jersey, on November 23 and 24, 2019. What a lucky break! The event was scheduled just a week before the manuscript was due, so doing my best-worst Hunter S. Thompson schtick, here is my impression of what was absolutely a gonzo event.

Walking toward the entrance, I passed by a large cartoon cutout of Paulie "Walnuts" Gualtieri (Tony Sirico) and headed up the stairs where, by 8:30 a.m., a long line had formed. It had crossed my mind that a lot of tri-state area wannabe wiseguys would show up—cigars, pinky rings, pug noses, and snarls—but I didn't see much of that. Yes, there were men in tracksuits, some worn as cosplay, some with irony, others in earnest, and a few somewhere in between. Mostly, the line—which was about 75 percent male—was just fans who were older and more blue-collar than at other pop-culture conventions I've attended, but largely polite and passionate, with a deep knowledge and reverence for the show.

Just ahead of me in the line was a couple who'd flown in from Edinburgh especially for the event. The Scotsman was well coiffed, dressed in black with a neatly trimmed beard, his companion sporting impeccably manicured glitter-gold nails. I heard him tell her, "This one's from 'Funhouse,'" and I realized The Rolling Stones' "Thru and Thru," which plays while Tony and Salvatore "Big Pussy" Bonpensiero (Vincent Pastore) eat in the Indian restaurant, was piping from the speakers. As the song ended and "This Magic Moment" started, I smiled at him and said, "Soprano Home Movies." This was a wised-up crowd, not a wiseguy one.

I've got some experience in the fan-con world: I've helped direct and manage large installations and activations at San Diego Comic-Con and New York Comic Con and BookCon, and have visited at least a dozen events. Because SopranosCon was a first-time production, I assumed the con would have an amateurish atmosphere, and it did feel a little rough around the edges. They just didn't have enough staff—or enough experience—to pull it off clean. Some examples: the woman who helped me cash in the $40 autograph credit I'd purchased didn't understand how my pre-purchase translated to the event's "boxes of ziti" currency system. I'm still not sure *I* understand. At 11 a.m., I decided to try my skills at *Sopranos* Trivia, which took place at a Bada Bing replica bar, where—twenty years later—original Bing (and Satin Dolls) dancer Diana Lynn was still doing her thing (exotic dancing is a profession known to put on the miles, but Lynn didn't look to have aged at all). The trivia host, Mike Vivalo, wasn't supplied with a microphone (at least thirty people were playing) and had to prompt participants to share pens to write their answers. Luckily, he's a quick thinker with charisma to spare and rolled with every production snafu. His bartender wasn't as gracious. He complained loudly—and hilariously—in the most authentic *Sopranos* voice I heard all weekend: "I don't get why they lettin' yous come in here before we's set up!" And "Nobody tellin' me nothin'!" He wasn't in character. He just *is* a character.

Quibbles aside, passionate fans and game cast members are sometimes all you'll need; the love of the material smooths over the rough spots. There was a makeshift "Pine Barrens" maze made from wonky eight-foot-tall posterboard with images of wintery trees and classic quotes from the beloved episode. It was fun to walk around but what really made it was the Econoline van (like the one in which Paulie and Christopher [Michael Imperioli] camp out) in the back of the Barrens. Fans had snagged ketchup and relish packets from a nearby hot dog vendor and placed them on the van's hood, adding their own props to commemorate the saddest mobster meal.

Like the forest, Dr. Melfi's (Lorraine Bracco's) office was a suitable simulation and perfect for a photo opp with your friends. The creative crew nailed the superfan touches, like adding a *Departures* magazine (from "The Blue Comet") and a basket of Tide (from "Two Tonys").

The rest of the floor was a mix of charm, mayhem, and the kind of moments you can't make up. Over fifty cast members were in attendance, sitting at their booths to sign pictures. The more famous actors, like Dominic Chianese, Tony Sirico, and Drea de Matteo, had enormous lines that overlapped with one another. Some of the talent really embraced the moment: Christine Pedi, who played Karen Baccalieri, had boxes of ziti and a Pyrex,

TEN THINGS I LEARNED DURING MY SOPRANOSCON TRIP

1. The Holsten's bathroom is small, only a couple feet from Tony's booth, and has plenty of space to hide a gun.
2. The guy who played Jesus Rossi, Dr. Melfi's rapist, thought it'd be a good idea to make "Employee of the Month" T-shirts.
3. Cannoli-eating contests are kind of depressing.
4. The bridge over Paterson Great Falls is narrow, high, and slippery when wet ("Go Jovi!"). It'd be difficult to throw somebody off and not fall over yourself.
5. Alabama 3 are English and have a ton of songs in addition to "Woke Up This Morning."
6. Attractive women love to have their pictures taken with Burt Young.
7. A "luxury e-cigar" is a real thing.
8. Agent Harris (Matt Servitto) likes Johnnie Walker Black and signs autographs with "We're gonna win this thing!"
9. A strip club stage looks very strange in the middle of a brightly lit room.
10. People at conventions love to bitch and moan like they're Livia (Nancy Marchand) at Green Grove. You know, like the woman with a Virginia ham under her arm, complaining because she's got no bread.

a homage to the ziti her character froze before her death. Tony Cucci, who played "Fat Dom" Gamiello, brought his character's severed head, a prop that Carlo Gervasi (Arthur J. Nascarella) pulls from a freezer in "Kaisha."

The exhibitors weren't the usual collection of Funko dealers; instead they offered tomato sauces, Bada Bean Cawfee, and lots of illustrators and painters doing work on the fly. There was a barber set up for cuts, fades, and shaves; a tattoo artist on the floor, inking people with their favorite character portrait; and, inexplicably, a Mary Kay representative (I suppressed my desire to tell her, "I heard you paint faces"). Back in the corner in a large pen was the horse Pie-O-My for fans to visit.

The scene was a bizarre bazaar and a very eclectic group of personalities. A team of New Jersey model train enthusiasts erected Bobby Baccalieri's (Steve Schirripa's) complete set from his garage, a prop they've maintained since the show ended. Model train guys mixing with pole dancers, capicola vendors, and Tommy James from The Shondells isn't what I expected, but just what I needed. Everybody paused to pay their respects at a large photo memorial with an image of every cast member who has died, from the lovingly remembered James Gandolfini to Brian Tarantina, who played Salvatore "Mustang Sally" Intile and passed away just three weeks before the event.

The talent mostly seemed thrilled to be there. Some of these actors are out of the business. They were excited to be celebrated and showed a lot of gratitude. There were a few bummers. It was going around that Tony Sirico took ill and had to leave early on Saturday. His exit immediately shifted into a Paulie Walnuts–appropriate myth, as I was told he yelled at the volunteer who ushered him into a waiting car, "Stop fuckin' pushin' me!" Who knows if that happened or not, but I choose to believe it did. There were several cast panels, including one with *Sopranos* actresses: Maureen Van Zandt, Lola Glaudini, Sofia Milos, and Kathrine Narducci. Narducci, who played Charmaine Bucco, was arguably the most emphatic and emotional participant throughout the weekend (Matt Servitto gave her a run for her money). She also told the best story of the weekend. She explained that when *The Sopranos* wrapped everybody was able to take home props. She rushed into the Nuovo Vesuvio kitchen and grabbed the frying pan Artie Bucco (John Ventimiglia) cooks the rabbit in—and it's her favorite one in her kitchen today.

When I returned on Sunday, I wanted to introduce our interview subject Heather Buckley to Pie-O-My. Someone who appeared to be associated with the horse had a support animal, a companion German Shepherd. The dog seemed agitated, as we heard someone repeat, "Give him some space. Give him some space." Richie Aprile actor David Proval watched the scene unfold and, ignoring the instruction, walked right over to the dog and bent his seventy-seven-year-old frame to pet and comfort it. It was amazing to watch. It beautifully echoed the scene in *Mean Streets* where Proval's character, Tony DeVienazo, enters the cage to nuzzle his tiger cubs. One only stumbles onto this kind of thing at a community event that's fast, loose, and glued together with love. A real magic moment.

STATIC CLING:
WHY THE INFLUENCE OF HBO AND *THE SOPRANOS* HAS STUCK FOR OVER TWENTY YEARS

CHARLIE JENKINS: Do you remember back in the mid-'90s when cable companies scrambled HBO? As a kid I could only glimpse the premium networks as I flicked past them with the remote. I'd go to channel 98 and press the up button. The signal would become clear and for about two wonderful seconds I could watch HBO. Then it would disappear. So I'd go to channel 100 and click the down button to try to watch two more seconds. The trick didn't always work, so I'd have to sit there ping-ponging back and forth, back and forth. I knew what was on TV. I wanted to know what was on HBO.

Sometimes they would do a free preview weekend, so I'd stay up until 4 a.m. watching *Tales from the Crypt* and *Real Sex.* There's no shame in it: I was twelve. Mature content means everything to twelve-year-olds. They find it full of intrigue (and breasts). There wasn't really a big draw on HBO—nothing that would make it worth spending money on when we didn't have a lot. So we only previewed, we never signed up.

About seven years later I went over to bother my friend at his dorm room one night and he was watching *The Sopranos.* I took one look at James Gandolfini and wanted to know Tony's story. He was a fat, middle-aged balding man who stood out in a landscape of matinee idol protagonists. He was so charismatic you'd watch him read the phone book, and here he was delivering great dialogue.

My classmates used to say, "Oh, I can't have TV. I'd get hooked on it." But for me, that "hook"—that excitement for Sunday to come so I could see the next episode—was something I wanted to feel. And so I subscribed to HBO. But also, David

Chase made such a good show that it was undeniable. How did you discover the show?

HENRY JENKINS: I ended up binge-watching the first few seasons of *The Sopranos* through Netflix. Keep in mind that at the time Netflix was sending out actual discs in little red envelopes—it wasn't the streaming service it is today. I was spending a year writing a book in a cabin in the North Georgia mountains with crappy broadcast reception, so I needed to watch DVDs. There would be three episodes, I think, per disc. Every few days I would drive forty miles to the nearest town and drop them in the mailbox, and then I'd have to wait for the next set to arrive so I would watch three episodes a night and keep three DVDs in circulation. When I got back to civilization, I watched the final seasons as they were aired.

The Sopranos reached television amidst a transition from appointment-based television to engagement-based television. I grew up in a world where you only had three networks of episodic television. You needed to be home and tune in when the episodes aired or you missed them, perhaps, we thought at the time, forever. Every week the castaways had to pretend they might get off *Gilligan's Island*, but we knew the story would end with them in the same place the episode began.

By the 1980s, *Hill Street Blues* was challenging that logic, developing stories that would not neatly wrap up every story line, and we discovered the fascination of long-form storytelling where characters and situations evolve across many years, carrying program history with them. The networks were anxious about that. They thought people might lose track of the plot if they missed a week.

By the early '90s, *Twin Peaks* (another of my faves) pushed those structures to the breaking point. This was the first series I watched along with an internet fan community. Fans were supporting each other by doing recaps. I missed an episode and was able to find a local fan willing to hand off a VHS dub. We were thinking through the mysteries together, sharing clues, making fan theories. The critics said that the show was becoming too complex for the average viewer to follow, and the fans said *Twin Peaks* was too simple to hold their collective interest. As a culture, we were changing from watching television (as something that was always on in the background) to watching specific programs we selected as we might choose a book to read.

Keep in mind that *The Sopranos* was, following *Oz*, only the second dramatic serial to be on HBO. The HBO series were aired multiple times each week, which already loosened the pressure to be home at a particular time. You couldn't yet Netflix and chill, exactly, but Netflix's deliveries of DVDs through the mail represented a fundamental change in how we accessed and watched television. You could jump into a series that was already under way, as I did with *The Sopranos*. Recaps were now being institutionalized by groups like Television Without Pity. We could seek shows that interested us, watch them on our own time, and engage with others who shared our passions. *The Sopranos* now seems emblematic of this transition and everything that has happened since.

CHARLIE: In his book *Difficult Men*, Brett Martin does an excellent job of laying out the defining characteristics of *The Sopranos* and the other dramas of the New Golden Age that directly followed it. I'll summarize Martin's list, because it's really on point: Premium dramas, like *The Sopranos*, have three-dimensional but sometimes unlikable characters. At first a lot of the protagonists were middle-aged men. That's shifted since the early 2000s. But from the beginning they also featured a wider range of female characters than had been common before. They usually have a heavy emphasis on relationships, but also an endless series of twists and cliffhangers, meaning the best of both worlds: character and plot. The shows have ruthless narratives, which offer no guaranteed protection for beloved characters. Almost any character can be killed off without warning, and viewers can no longer assume something won't happen because it's too disturbing for TV. Nothing is too disturbing for TV anymore.[1]

Premium dramas have an allergy to neatly resolved problems. Instead, the plots are radically serialized machines of disaster, with every complication unleashing two more. You can't pick them up at some arbitrary point in the middle. The seasons are generally only eight to thirteen episodes long instead of twenty-four to twenty-six, which allows producers to spend more time and money fully developing each one. And the productions are orchestrated by omnipotent showrunners—writers who have amazing discretion over multimillion-dollar budgets.

The Sopranos popularized a lot of those techniques. But, as you point out, Dad, it didn't emerge fully formed out of nowhere. I love the stuffing out of *Northern Exposure*, an earlier drama that didn't dumb things down. But it was still downright cozy. Cicely, Alaska, was a kind of 1990s Mayberry with Native Americans and moose. Quality network television series were skillfully written, but they didn't leave you feeling icky going into the commercial break. *Oz* started toying around with the HBO model. But with all due respect, very few people saw *Oz*. It's harder to have a lasting cultural impact if you're invisible. Its significance would be felt much more on other artists, and on the career of breakout star J. K. Simmons. *The Sopranos* cranked the dial all the way to the max, and did so with artistic mastery and good old-fashioned suspenseful storytelling, which placed it at the center of the zeitgeist.

My ex and I used to watch the reruns on A&E and we'd howl with laughter because the dialogue was overdubbed with family-friendly alternatives to profanity. They kept calling each other a "frig'n bloodsucker." There were 4,983 instances of profanity in eighty-six episodes of *The Sopranos*—around fifty-eight cuss words an hour. You can't change that much of the dialogue without changing the meaning. Chase was careful to capture the sound of "real world" New York conversation and the censors turned it into a farce.

Many writers point out what a big deal it was for *The Sopranos* to make a show about a sympathetic murderer. That doesn't feel weird now, which shows how much influence *The Sopranos* has had. Personally, I don't feel that bad laughing at the scenes where Tony mows a pedestrian down in the park like he's playing *Grand Theft Auto* or Paulie strangles a guy because he's whining about wanting his TV remote back.

What feels jarring today is that the sympathetic characters are unapologetically racist, sexist, and homophobic. It's not just that they make crude jokes. They also call people slurs when they beat them to death. Tony orders a black kid to stop studying with his daughter simply because he's black. That's almost certainly a realistic portrayal of the socially conservative Mafia. It's not necessarily an endorsement of the characters' actions. The teenagers I knew at the time often quoted offensive jokes and terms they'd heard on *South Park* and *The Sopranos* in order to make each other laugh. While "gay" and "retarded" had been insults long before those shows aired, I'd bet the rate with which those terms were used skyrocketed at middle-class high schools and liberal colleges when Paulie Walnuts and Eric Cartman entered the zeitgeist.

The show's creators would claim that the shows were merely satirizing a culture of ignorance and greed, not reinforcing that culture's worst habits. Perhaps my classmates didn't understand that they were the butt of the joke—they were the generation *South Park* was satirizing, and they were parroting the prejudices of their parents, who came from the generation *The Sopranos* was satirizing. That said, I'd question why both shows wrote and delivered their jokes with such clever word play and comic timing if they didn't want audiences to laugh with the characters. If David Chase, Matt Stone, and Trey Parker naively didn't realize their audiences were going to start telling their own renditions every time they were alone with friends, they clearly knew by the point the shows had been on for years. What passed for shock value in *All in the Family*'s day seems like cuddles and rainbows compared to what passed for shock value on *The Sopranos*. The types of mature content that had always marginalized HBO as a curiosity in the past quickly ignited a full-fledged paradigm shift in entertainment once *The Sopranos* hit the mainstream.

HENRY: Think about that burst of static that comes before the HBO logo. To some degree, it pays tribute to that trick you describe above, channel flipping for an illicit glimpse of HBO programming amidst the static. But it also signals that we are crossing a threshold into the outer limits of the medium. What follows is not "television" but rather "HBO."

You map some of the defining traits of the HBO drama, ending with the most distinctive one (at least at the time *The Sopranos* entered the picture): HBO was free from the regulatory constraints of the Federal Communications Commission and could show things that were outlawed on "television." *Real Sex* exploited this freedom to offer adult-style entertainment—but not porn. It's a documentary about sexuality and, like an article in *Playboy*, viewers (or readers) would be disappointed if the episode did not include boobs and butts. You did not generally see pubes. HBO sought a balance between respectability and exploitation.

The "freedom" we celebrate on HBO's dramas follows this same logic. In the '60s and '70s, Roger Corman would hire lots of new filmmakers with the promise they could make whatever cinematic experiment or explore whatever themes they wanted as long as they included nudity, sex, violence, and "strong language." Corman's hires understood these stipulations as constraints. With HBO, showrunners often discuss them as the "freedom" to tell mature stories they could not put on regular television, but it amounts to the same—an audience expectation. Can you name an HBO drama, regardless of genre, that does not include these exploitation elements? Those elements surface on *The Sopranos*: the whackings bring the blood and the WTF moments (to use a technical term) like the time Tony kills someone on his daughter's college tour or when he knocks off Christopher. Then we toss in Bada Bing—always good for some gratuitous nudity (or what fans call "sexposition"). And the characters curse like sailors or, more exactly, like gangsters from New Jersey.

With *The Sopranos* and the shows that have followed it, there were two other defining tendencies. First, most of the HBO showrunners—at least early on—came from traditional television. They knew how to work within, around, and through the conventions of popular genres. *The Sopranos* is a gangster story. It is also a family soap opera in the legacy of, say, *Dallas* or *Dynasty*, about the struggles over wealth and power, and the ways that they impact the members of a particular family. In that sense, HBO is still "television."

Second, these shows reflect trends toward "quality television." Viewers for Quality Television (VQT) was an advocacy group that wanted sponsors and networks to pay attention to audience demographics (specifically the spending power of upscale viewers) as much or more than ratings in deciding what programs to keep on the air. VQT promoted trends toward ensemble casts, rounded characters, darker worldviews, serial storytelling, and genre mixing as constituting a more intellectually engaging form of television. VQT rallied support behind two of Chase's earlier shows, *I'll Fly Away* and *Northern Exposure*. Seeking viewers with the money to pay for their subscription service, HBO embraced these same properties across most of their dramas as the basis of its exceptionalism.

Put these together and you have a winning formula that hits us in the groin and appeals to our higher thinking at the same time. *The Sopranos*—and yes, the underviewed *Oz*—were the first HBO shows to fully realize the potential of this approach. *The Sopranos* often gets described as cinematic. *Deadwood* or *The Wire* are often described as novelistic. Both descriptions gain cultural prestige through comparisons with media that already claim the status of art. But *The Sopranos* helped many to realize that television itself could be art.

CHARLIE: Television did become a higher form of art. *The Sopranos* was on for eight and a half years. By the time it ended in 2007, the balance of the entertainment industry had shifted from movies to television. I had decided back in middle school that I wanted to write for TV rather than film, because I wasn't concerned about making prestigious art. I just wanted to make a show like *Quantum Leap*. By the time *The Sopranos* ended, writers had every reason to prefer working in TV: creative control, art, long-term employment, money, and, yes, prestige.

Two years after *The Sopranos* debuted, HBO was earning as much as the six broadcast networks combined. So the networks were forced to change. Can you imagine what a FOX exec would have said if they'd read a *House M.D.* script in 1999? "The doctor can't be a drug addict. He can't depress everyone with nihilistic philosophy." *Friday Night Lights* would have taken place at a rich school in Southern California and looked as airbrushed as *Dawson's Creek*.

By 2007 channels like HBO, Showtime, and FX were running a full slate of heavily serialized, character-driven cinematic drama series. Showtime's contribution was in making shows like *The Sopranos*, but about women. *Homeland*, *Shameless*, *Nurse Jackie*, *The Big C*, *Secret Diary of a Call Girl*, *The Real L Word*, *United States of Tara*, and *Weeds* all had morally complicated female protagonists. They made a business decision to counter programming like *The Sopranos*. Some audiences—male and female—didn't relate to a show about guys who cheated on their wives and beat up prostitutes. Some didn't relate to *Sex and the City*, either. Showtime gave them choices. As *Gawker* commented, "Showtime, before anything else, has stayed away from feminine clichés—no nail salons or cosmos to be seen. Maybe that's where their success begins."[2] Making a show about women over fifty who have cancer, or even making a show that took a call girl's life goals seriously, was a huge departure from classic TV. The fact that five of those eight series had female showrunners was part of the strategy to differentiate themselves from everything else on TV. But Hollywood is always perceived as an elitist liberal institution that doesn't serve half the country, which gave FX a wide opening for *their* counterprogramming. They took the genres older viewers liked watching on network TV and approached them more seriously. *The Shield*, *Rescue Me*, and *Nip/Tuck* breathed fresh oxygen into the cop show, the firefighter show, and the medical drama.

The dramas of the early twenty-first century didn't all copy *The Sopranos* by any means. *Mad Men* isn't fast-paced and action-driven. The trailers for that show always left me in stitches because absolutely nothing happens. "People are gonna smoke cigarettes and talk on the phone. Don't ya dare miss it!" But if *The Sopranos* hadn't shown networks that it was okay to use the largest possible bucket of crayons, AMC would still have been using the same six colors as everyone else. *The Sopranos* changed the industry so completely and immediately that an HBO executive named Carolyn Strauss went to Alan Ball and requested *Six Feet Under*, a philosophical treatise about death. Before *The Sopranos*, virtually every great creative pitch was outside producers' comfort zones. A year afterward no one had to pitch a show about dead children and puppies, because HBO expected it to be popular.

If HBO had bet the farm and lost—if *The Sopranos* had been denounced by average people for being artless smut—that would have stunted the industry's creative progress. Many of the same changes would still have happened, because society has dramatically changed, but we might still be fighting to get out of a conservative creative mindset. Instead, I've never felt particularly sad that *The Sopranos* ended, because it was replaced by dozens of shows across all networks that had adopted its best qualities, and that has never changed. As long as the industry doesn't make a cowardly retreat, we'll enjoy an extravagant amount of cinematic programming.

Unfortunately, HBO may not continue to lead the way. In 2019, John Stankey, CEO of WarnerMedia, HBO's parent company, announced that they need people to watch for hours every day in order to be competitive. Perhaps because reruns of *The Office* are Netflix's biggest commodity, HBO Max paid several billion dollars for exclusive rights to stream reruns of *The Big Bang Theory*. Network sitcom reruns aren't "HBO." They're just TV.

HENRY: In *The Revolution Was Televised*, *Rolling Stone* TV critic Alan Sepinwall argues that the influence of *The Sopranos* has started to wane and *Game of Thrones* has established a new model for HBO dramas. He compares this shift to the transition between the early '70s personal films of Scorsese and Coppola (with their "intimacy and thematic ambition") to the rise of the Spielberg and Lucas blockbusters (with their "visceral thrills").[3] I would argue that those shows don't so much reject *The Sopranos'* influences as pull them into new genres: fantasy in the case of *GOT* or *Carnival Row*, zombie horror in *The Walking Dead*, science fiction in *Westworld, The Man in the High Castle*, or *The Handmaid's Tale*, and superheroes in *The Boys* or *Watchmen*. *Game of Thrones* is a very personal story for George R. R. Martin (who himself came through the training of genre television with his work on *Beauty and the Beast*), even if *GOT* sometimes, especially in its final season, feels more like work-for-hire from David Benioff and D. B. Weiss.

GOT incorporates the same basic exploitation building blocks we've seen before: Littlefinger's brothel mirrors Tony's establishment [the Bada Bing], the whores in *Deadwood*, the street walkers and porn stars in *The Deuce*, the sexy androids in *Westworld*, or the strippers in *Ozark*.

Martin pushes the shock appeal, giving *GOT* a reputation as one of the more salacious shows on television, and one remembered for the incestous relationships amongst the Lannisters. The Red Wedding, the Purple Wedding, and similar moments are much more bloodthirsty than anything in *The Sopranos*. And these are some of the reasons people talked and tweeted about *GOT*.

The show also met quality television expectations with morally ambiguous characters who are prepared to stab each other in the back in their struggles over wealth and power, philosophical conversations that come unexpectedly from prostitutes and sellswords, an ever-expanding world with many different and contradictory rules for conduct, and serialized storytelling at an epic scale.

Yes, many of these shows embrace the fantastic, whereas *The Sopranos* kept its feet firmly planted in the muddy Pine Barrens. But, in many ways, these shows still follow the same logic that generated *The Sopranos* (that balance between exploitation, genre, and quality television). And to remain competitive in the #MeToo era, these shows must incorporate more strong women, more ethnically and racially diverse casts, and a more critical perspective on toxic masculinity and sexual violence.

In an era of too much good television, fan engagement becomes a key currency. The showrunners want hard-core fans and they want those fans tweeting about the show (and the WTF moments spark public outpouring). Fans are often most engaged in the middle of these sprawling narratives, when anything seems possible, but are apt to splinter and squabble over the endings: few of these shows stick the landing as well as *The Sopranos* did. Some laughed at its final moments, others cried, some were outraged, and I scratched my head. But I never forgot that ending.

This book and the feature film *The Many Saints of Newark* are pretty good testament to the fact that people are still talking about every little aspect of *The Sopranos*.

COOKING THE BOOKS
—Eddie McNamara

As the author of the world's greatest vegetarian cookbook (*Toss Your Own Salad*) and an all-around jerk, I make a point of hating on everyone else's cookbook. And when I found out that there were two official *Sopranos* cookbooks, I was prepared to feel the same way. But I kind of love *Entertaining with the Sopranos*—allegedly compiled by Carmela Soprano (Edie Falco). What other book is going to give you Christopher Moltisanti's advice about how much cash to give at a graduation party? I shit you not, that's a real thing in this book, and it doesn't even crack the top ten most absurd elements.

While it's certainly a cookbook and the Italian-American recipes are *nonna*-approved legit (thanks to chef and author Michele Scicolone), the hosting part is a shticky guide to throwing parties tri-state style. Still, Carmela's potato pie recipe is awesome. Do regular people even know about potato pie? If they don't, they should. Carm also likes to make *polpettone*—meatloaf stuffed with boiled eggs—when she has friends and family over, and if you're not eating that with your family, you should start today.

If you ever wanted to learn how to make damn good eggplant fritters or discover Janice Soprano's (Aida Turturro's) thoughts on what makes a perfect wedding, they're in here. Artie Bucco gives some wine recos, but he's a lot more low-key in this book than I would have expected.

He does get a full page on fish and food poisoning, though.

Obviously, the weirdest part is you're supposed to suspend disbelief to the point that you accept that this book is written by Carmela Soprano and other *Sopranos* characters, not Edie Falco and the actors who play them. There's a "My Life So Far" section written by A.J. Soprano (not Robert Iler) that deals with inviting people to a Catholic confirmation party. We learn that Anthony Jr. wants to own an arena football team like Jon Bon Jovi when he grows up. Even Father Phil (Paul Schulze) gets in on the act and plugs his after-school program for at-risk youth. On page 29, Dr. Jennifer Melfi, M.D., M.A., M.F.T., writes Carmela a letter addressing her fear of hostessing.

There's a section by Junior Soprano called "When Christmas Was

Christmas." Back in the old days, things were different. He got a nickel once, they ate *caposelle* (a roasted sheep's head with eyeballs and brains) and a fish his mother cooked stunk up the whole neighborhood almost as badly as this bit stunk up the book. Still, you'd do a hell of a job of cooking for and entertaining guests if you followed the advice here.

But wait, there's more. My wish for Artie Bucco to really get a chance to shine is manifested in the *New York Times* #1 bestseller *The Sopranos Family Cookbook*, where he tells a surprisingly interesting Ellis Islandish story about his family history through food. Michele Scicolone provides the recipes again, but the focus here is Neapolitan-inspired, family-style cooking. Marinara and Sunday Gravy are the first two recipes, and they lay the foundation for this style of cooking. There's also a fantastic essay called "Cooking the Neapolitan Way" from Natalie del Greco from the Newark Public Library. (Her name translates as Greek Christmas.)

You could open a restaurant with these recipes just by scaling up. In fact, if you live in a crappy place without decent Italian-American takeout, you should buy this book and open one. This food is serious. Scungilli in hot sauce, linguine with clam sauce, pear and grappa pound cake, chicken Francaise, and even a homestyle pastina with ricotta are here, and the instructions are easy enough for any home cook to follow.

While there's some of the same in-character fan service that was on full display in the entertaining book, this one doesn't make you feel like you're losing your grip on reality.

People literally ate this stuff up when the show was in full swing. The suburban mafioso mystique took hold of the nation. People were buying blueprints of the actual house *The Sopranos* was set in so they could live like them; it's no shock that they were attempting to eat what the characters ate and entertain like Martha Stugatz.

Somehow the American Dream as seen by working-class East Coast white ethnics became aspirational to the culture at large. Would there even be a Kardashian family if the Sopranos didn't drop tacky luxury into America's living room and make it seem socially acceptable? I don't think so. The effect of *The Sopranos* was major.

Before *The Sopranos*, an imaginary celebrity chef having the number-one cookbook was out of step with Gen-X culture. Cookbooks attached to an intellectual property might seem completely normal now. *A Feast of Ice and Fire: The Official Companion Cookbook*; *True Blood: Eats, Drinks, and Bites from Bon Temps*; *Wookiee Pies, Clone Scones, and Other Galactic Goodies: The Star Wars Cookbook*; *World of Warcraft: The Official Cookbook*; and *WWE: The Official Cookbook* (written by the brilliant Allison Robicelli) are commonplace, popular, and add to the immersive experience of a consumable showbiz brand. But at the turn of the millennium there was no such thing as franchises for adults; all that *Star Wars* bullshit was for kids.

It seems quaint to imagine a world where average schmucks on the street didn't talk about cinematic universes and culinary cosplay didn't exist. There used to be a time when movies like *Reservoir Dogs* and *Pulp Fiction* could shape the landscape of film for a decade without a single Tarantino-inspired cookbook offering milkshake recipes, "How to Stick Up a Diner" essays, and Mr. Pink's guide to tipping. Thanks, David Chase.

THE SOPRANOS GETS PLAYED
—Nick Braccia

The Sopranos was at peak popularity in 2005 and 2006, so it makes sense that HBO and others wanted to cash in on the franchise and license their intellectual property for other media formats. Adapting popular series for gaming—specifically video games and pinball—has been a cash grab since the early '80s, and the results are mostly lousy. Tight time lines, slim budgets (a lot of the cash goes to the license holder, leaving less for production), and development teams who would prefer to work on original titles all contribute to shoddy products. Famous examples are myriad: consider the virtually unplayable Atari 2600 *E.T.* game or toy company LJN's rush to market game adaptations of comics and movies for the Nintendo Entertainment System (*The Uncanny X-Men*, anyone?). These shovelware licensed games vastly outnumber the gems, though some classics exist, like Midway's pinball game for *The Addams Family* or Capcom's *DuckTales.*

In the mid-aughts, licensed games were mostly still the pits, though the 2010s ushered a shift. Games with smaller scope for mobile platforms (Telltale Games' *The Walking Dead*) and media conglomerates with their own game studios or distribution arms (WB Interactive's *Batman* Arkham games) gave franchise products a better shot at quality. Universal and their sister company Vivendi Games—both part of Vivendi Universal—were a few years ahead of this curve, having success with *The Chronicles of Riddick: Escape from Butcher Bay* in 2004.

For the games referenced, we don't have to squint very hard to see how the property might be adapted into a game. With *The Sopranos*, it's not as easy to capture the show's spirit, or imagine a game worth playing. It's a deeply nuanced satire and a meticulously designed world. Aside from the accents, T&A, and some crime details, it doesn't feel like much of a fit for the rampage and mayhem popular with genre games. Much of the pleasure comes from the comedy. Could the themes work in interactive entertainment, where the gamer has agency? I dedicated about twelve hours of my life to find out, and, surprisingly, the more abstract approach—the *Sopranos* pinball game—is much more successful than the narrative-driven Play-

Station 2 game, despite the latter's having hours of terrific voice work from the show's cast.

To understand why the pinball machine works, it's helpful to understand why the PlayStation 2 game doesn't. *The Sopranos: Road to Respect* for PlayStation 2, developed by 7 Studios and published by THQ, entered a very busy market in 2006, especially for games set in the criminal underworld. The remarkable success of Rockstar Games and Take-Two Interactive's *Grand Theft Auto* franchise created a desire for more of the same. With a four-year gap between *Grand Theft Auto San Andreas* and *Grand Theft Auto IV*, there was an opportunity in the market that intellectual property (IP) holders were eager to fill. Since the *Grand Theft Auto* series paid homage to *The Godfather* and Brian De Palma's 1983 *Scarface* remake, why not get the real thing in the hands of players? In March of 2006, *The Godfather* was published by Electronic Arts, and in October, the *Scarface: The World Is Yours* game came from Vivendi. *The Sopranos: Road to Respect* was only a month behind. Suddenly, the market was flooded with games based on the IP that had inspired *Grand Theft Auto*, the hottest franchise around. It's all interesting context and tough competition, but the success of *The Sopranos: Road to Respect* would come down to the gameplay experience.

Sopranos: Road to Respect invites you to play as Joey LaRocca (voiced by Anthony DeSando, who played Brendan Filone in Season One), the bastard son of rat Salvatore "Big Pussy" Bonpensiero, who is invited into the DiMeo crime family by Tony. Through game engine cinematics and in-game dialogue, we learn that many in the family, including Christopher Moltisanti, don't like or trust LaRocca because of his father's betrayal. We also learn that LaRocca has conversations with Big Pussy's ghost, who appears in reflective surfaces throughout the game—water, mirrors, and Satriale's windows. Yes, it's as insane as it sounds. The game is modest in scale; chapter-based in a time when open-world sandbox experiences were all the rage and is, more or less, a straightforward beat-'em-up that's held together by two paper-thin plots. The A-plot focuses on Joey's ability to outsmart and outfight a rival mob boss named Angelo Buscetta, while the B-plot pushes you to keep A.J. Soprano alive, because Jamaican drug dealers are on his ass for ripping them off during a warehouse rave.

The basic fight mechanics and quicktime events quickly wear thin, even if Joey's maneuvers include smashing heads into toilets and knee-ing thugs in the nuts. And, man, Joey sure beats up everybody. Frat boys, dockworkers, professors, juice machine operators, personal trainers, porn directors, paralegals, doctors, and pharmacists. And he's gallant! Early on he refuses to sleep with a drugged woman and later charms porn stars and protects strippers. The narrative feels like it was written by Jackie Jr. and his friends on a crank bender. Still, the cast have some fun with their lines. For example, when Joey has to attend Hesh's nephew's bar mitzvah, Tony and Paulie give him some advice:

TONY: There's a party at Vesuvio's next week. Hesh's nephew's bar mitzvah.

JOEY: Hey, Tone, thanks. Should I bring a gift?

TONY: Fifty bucks in an envelope. Kids that age, all they want is cash.

PAULIE: Bring fifty-four. It's a sacred number. Some Jewish ka-blah-blah shit.

The core problem with the game—aside from the mediocre fight me-chanics and sparse level design—is that it's a genre game based on the least interesting part of the show: low-level meatheads committing petty crimes. As Joey, we have the ability to interact with characters using three differ-ent tones, "Smooth, Neutral, and Tough" but there's not enough nuance or narrative pathing to make it worth experimentation. To adapt *The Sopra-nos* strictly as a crime game is to miss the point of the show entirely. Still, the dialogue is funny enough that, if you want to hear some new lines from Gandolfini, Imperioli, Sirico, Van Zandt, and Pastore, you can find a play-through on YouTube. It's like hearing B-sides and rarities from a band you love. I wish I could cut the gameplay some slack, as video games don't age as well as other forms of entertainment, but even in 2006, *Road to Respect* was firing blanks.

In opposition to the crowded video game market, in 2005, when the

Sopranos pinball machine was released, new pinball games were few and far between, the bar pastime having fallen out of favor. It's worth noting that business picked up over the following decade, as bar-arcades popped up in media-centric cities like New York, Los Angeles, and Austin, and there are now several new titles released each year.

I had to track down the fairly rare pinball game (only 3,500 produced) at Two Bit's Retro Arcade on Essex Street in New York City. *The Sopranos* pinball machine, manufactured by Stern, was designed by George Gomez, who has a deep background in video games, having worked on multiple hit *Tron* titles, as well as *Spy Hunter*. His design of the *Sopranos* machine, however, looks to have been informed by his work on the 1998 Williams pinball machine *Monster Bash*, themed on the Universal monsters.

The efficiency of engineering and creativity that Gomez applies to evoke *the feeling* of Tony's life in the game is awe-inspiring. The playfield is multilevel, with the George Washington Bridge, Bada-Bing stage, and Tony's boat *Stugots* all represented. The gameplay pushes players to literally keep the balls in the air, on a playfield that could be a carnival collage of Tony's life. There's even a large talking fish to taunt you.

Narrative stressors include setting fire to Vesuvio, finding bugs in Tony's office, and helping Pie-O-My win a race. At any one time, you might be working three or four tasks at once, as these little story blips and the urgency of the pinball mechanic work in concert to drive players bonkers. Toward the back of the playfield is the Bing and a makeshift cemetery for dead characters. When the balls are in either spot, you don't have to sweat too much. In a nice touch, the flippers are positioned over an FBI agent's desk, covered in dossiers and a wire. We're looking at Tony getting busted as we try not to lose a ball. It's pinball with an extra dose of anxiety and no points to spend on Prozac.

The LED screen keeps the visuals fun and light, and the little bits of dialogue that pipe out of the machine give you the sense that Paulie Walnuts could wallop you at any time. For a couple of quarters over a few minutes, we get the full *Sopranos* experience, highly concentrated.

The question is: Could a great, narrative *Sopranos* game be made in 2020? I think at least a good one, but I'm not sure it can elucidate any aspect of the story—or to use an overplayed term, storyworld—better than the show. I can see an episodic Telltale-style game, where, playing as Tony, all your narrative choices impact both families, creating stress and danger as you continue to rob Peter to pay Paul and keep everybody happy-ish and alive. Or a game that combines the domestic homebuilding mechanics and social narratives of *The Sims* with a more zoomed-out Mafia strategy component focused on resource management and loyalty meters; the two mechanics could influence one another in interesting ways. Regardless, any *Sopranos* game needs to focus on maintaining happiness, safety, and sanity while running a criminal empire, something the show suggests is definitely not fun and probably impossible. Maybe they'd add a cheat code where we could pull a Little Carmine and simply move to Florida.

CHAPTER VI

WHACK ATTACK

Ninety-two characters meet their maker during the *The Sopranos'* eighty-six-episode run. This number—an average of 1.12 deaths per episode—excludes ambiguous outcomes like those of Valery the Russian (Vitali Baganov) and Tony Soprano (James Gandolfini); deaths that occur before the series time line (like Tony's father, Johnny Boy, played by Joseph Siravo); and animals, such as Pie-O-My, Cosette the Maltese, and that delicious-looking rabbit that Artie Bucco (John Ventimiglia) shoots for noshing on his arugula.

We're evaluating the circumstances of death for everyone left in the morgue or the mulch. For some characters, it's all about the death scene— just a mere few seconds. For others, we need to consider entire episodes or cross-episode (and cross-season!) character arcs to fully appreciate the impact of their demise. Many times, the death has almost nothing to do with the deceased and everything to do with the living.

We'll assess each death on a scale of one to ten across four categories for a possible total score of forty points. Our goal? To christen *one and only one* character with a gaudy posthumous crown to wear in the afterlife. Let's hope the winner isn't stuck in Christopher Moltisanti's (Michael Imperioli's) vision of hell: an Irish bar where it's St. Patrick's Day every day for eternity. Why choose this approach? Let's just say I come from a family that gets the paper and goes straight to the obituaries.

SEASON ONE

EMIL KOLAR

> *Shot in the back of the head by*
> *Christopher Moltisanti while sampling*
> *cocaine at Satriale's after-hours in*
> *Episode 1.1, "The Sopranos"*

Czech garbage scion Emil Kolar (Bruce Smo-
lanoff) has a dubious distinction: he's the first
character murdered on *The Sopranos*. It's a
nicely staged death that establishes a core
theme for one of the show's primary characters:
Christopher's infatuation with the movies and
his ironic inability to understand what's actually
cinematic, even as it surrounds him.

While waiting for Kolar at Satriale's, Christopher mimics Bruce Lee moves in the dark,
like he's practicing for a movie fight. Once his
victim arrives, Christopher shares his wares:
several lines of blow neatly organized on a
cleaver (foreshadowing the name of his feature
film, *Cleaver*, in Season Six). As he positions
himself to grab his hidden gun—shades of the
visit Michael Corleone (Al Pacino) makes to
the restaurant bathroom in *The Godfather*—
our eyes are drawn to a grotesque audience: a
collection of severed swine heads hanging in
a windowed pork-store freezer. They're perfectly positioned to watch Christopher's first
kill. After he pulls the trigger and Emil's blood
splatters the cleaver, he registers the pig faces
and does a double take. He's the killer in a perfectly designed horror movie scene and doesn't

even know it. The double take is Chase's sly acknowledgment that Moltisanti is always going to be one step behind in his cinematic ambitions. Less subtly, his subsequent trio of gunshots into the already dead Kolar trigger quick cuts to framed black-and-white photos of Humphrey Bogart, Dean Martin, and Edward G. Robinson. Moltisanti thinks he's among his peers, but it's clear to us (and his colleagues) that he's not. A few scenes later, when a perturbed Salvatore "Big Pussy" Bonpensiero (Vincent Pastore) chastises him for killing Kolar simply for being the garbage-business competition, a defiant Moltisanti snaps back, "Louis Brasi sleeps with the fishes." Bonpensiero corrects him on the name and sternly notes, "There's differences, Christopher, okay? Between the Luca Brasi situation and this!" Imperioli's Christopher always seems on the verge of tripping over himself; he's brash and ambitious, but also sensitive and distracted. In these early scenes, we get a sense of his paradoxical whole.

Later in the episode, Christopher explains to his boss, Tony, whom he calls his uncle, that he could make millions selling his life story to Hollywood. Apoplectic, Tony grabs him by the lapel and yells, "What you gonna do, go Henry Hill on me now?" He's referencing the gangster who told his life story in Nicholas Pileggi's *Wiseguy*, which became *Goodfellas*. But Christopher doesn't drop it—and, frankly, never does—offering, "She [his Hollywood development contact] says maybe I can even play myself." Honestly, the kid can barely do that

THE CATEGORIES

NARRATIVE IMPACT
We'll consider how each death drives the show's dramatic trajectory and punctuates its themes, as well as the effect it has on key characters.

CINEMATIC
Yeah, Patsy Parisi (Dan Grimaldi) promises Gloria Trillo (Anabella Sciorra) that her murder won't be cinematic, but plenty of *Sopranos* sayonaras are just that. We'll dole out style points accordingly.

KILLER PERFORMANCES
Does the actor who's on the way out make the most of his or her final scene? Does the killer (if there is one) give it a little extra *oomph*? This extends to any performance directly or tangentially related to the death.

ELEMENT OF SURPRISE
Do we see it coming? Not just the death, but the timing, the method, the culprit?

minute to minute in his *real* life. Christopher's cinematic sense of self is a source of constant comedy over the next six seasons. On the other hand, it's worth noting that Kolar's death haunts him emotionally (at least for a little while) and physically (for much longer), as the Czech's body needs to be moved twice over the course of the series.

NARRATIVE IMPACT: 6   CINEMATIC: 9   KILLER PERFORMANCES: 8
ELEMENT OF SURPRISE: 5   TOTAL POINTS: 28

HECTOR ANTHONY

Killed by an accidental gunshot after Special K drops his gun in Episode 1.2, "46 Long"

Hector Anthony (Manny Siverio) is a driver for Comley Trucking, a company that's been paying protection money to Junior Soprano (Dominic Chianese) for twenty-one years. He's aware of and possibly an accomplice to the series of Comley hijackings perpetuated by Moltisanti and his friend Brendan Filone (Anthony DeSando). He's also the first victim of the show's abrupt—even absurd—black-comic violence when a hijacker, Special K (J. D. Williams), bobbles and drops his automatic pistol. It hits the pavement and discharges, killing Anthony. On *The Sopranos*, there's good luck and bad luck, but it's all dumb luck because the universe clearly doesn't give a fuck. Narratively, this shitshow of a hijacking cooks Filone's goose, as he's already disliked by Junior.

NARRATIVE IMPACT: 4   CINEMATIC: 4   KILLER PERFORMANCES: 2
ELEMENT OF SURPRISE: 7   TOTAL POINTS: 17

BRENDAN FILONE

Killed by a gunshot through the eye, care of Mikey Palmice in
Episode 1.3, "Denial, Anger, Acceptance"

The odious Brendan Filone is Christopher's tweaker pal, an unscrupulous hijacker who unapologetically hits on the high school friend of Meadow Soprano (Jamie-Lynn Sigler), Hunter Scangarelo (David Chase's daughter, Michele DeCesare). He's the first DiMeo family associate to get whacked on the series when he's killed by Mikey Palmice (Al Sapienza) and Junior Soprano at the suggestion of Livia Soprano (Nancy Marchand). His crime? Ignoring an order to stay away from Comley Trucking's loads. This murder, at the end of the episode, is part of a larger sequence: a montage devised by director Nick Gomez and editor Conrad Gonzalez that's a subversive remix of the famous finale of *The Godfather*, a baptism sequence that's intercut with the executions of the Corleones' rival New York family bosses. Gomez and Gonzalez juxtapose Filone's murder (along with the mock execution of Moltisanti) with Meadow and Hunter's choir recital, and, like casino magnate Moe Greene, a famous victim of Michael Corleone's settling of affairs, Brendan's shot through his right eye. In the next episode, Pussy makes this connection explicitly, calling the murder a "Moe Greene special." In a witty twist, both Greene and Filone are caught unawares while in vulnerable positions. Greene on a massage table (initially with his glasses off) and Filone in a bathtub, eyes closed. At least they're relaxed.

The scene also offers an early example of Chase's penchant for sick jokes. In addition to the Coppola riff, there's a piece of twisted symmetry for eagle-eyed viewers. During the concert, Meadow and Hunter (certainly not innocents like baby Anthony Corleone) are clearly under the influence of crystal meth. They're sweating and fidgety, each struggling to control her hands. Their twitchiness onstage mirrors Filone's death, seconds later. As he is dying from the gunshot, his foot twitches violently before his body settles into stillness. Gomez and Gonzalez cut back to the girls, singing, *"Sleep my child and be so gently, all through the night."* Filone, we hardly knew ya and still it seemed like we knew ya more than enough. As Palmice rhymes before he pulls the trigger, "Hijack? Bye, Jack."

Though the Filone character plays a minor and speechless role in the sequence, it's one of the show's first great moments, a homage filled with menace and comedy. And from a narrative perspective, it's a dramatic hand grenade that demonstrates Livia's influence over Junior and brings Tony and his uncle to the precipice of war.

NARRATIVE IMPACT: 8   CINEMATIC: 10   KILLER PERFORMANCES: 8
ELEMENT OF SURPRISE: 6   TOTAL POINTS: 32

JACKIE APRILE SR.

Dies from stomach cancer in Episode 1.4, "Meadowlands"

We don't see a lot of Jackie Aprile Sr., played by Michael Rispoli, who (along with Steven Van Zandt) was a finalist for the role of Tony Soprano, but we do catch enough, through flashbacks and his few scenes, to understand he's a gentleman gangster, with the right temperament to be the boss. He's not a psycho like his brother, Richie Aprile (David Proval), or a fool like his son, Jackie Jr. (Jason Cerbone). Jackie Sr.'s off-screen death is more notable for its impact on the story: it creates a power vacuum and Tony must decide whether to reconcile or war with his uncle, Junior. The loss of Jackie also impacts Tony's sessions with Dr. Melfi (Lorraine Bracco), where it becomes clear that he considers death by disease a much scarier and tragic proposition than the dangers of his workplace.

NARRATIVE IMPACT: 8   CINEMATIC: 1   KILLER PERFORMANCES: 2
ELEMENT OF SURPRISE: 1   TOTAL POINTS: 12

FABIAN "FEBBY" PETRULIO

Garrotted by Tony Soprano in Episode 1.5, "College"

"College" is generally accepted to be the first *great* episode of *The Sopranos*. It has two fantastic lean-forward plotlines: Will Tony—who is on the New England college tour with Meadow—kill the rat Febby Petrulio (Tony Ray Rossi) while keeping his daughter ignorant (and safe), and will Carmela (Edie Falco) get intimate with Father Phil Intintola (Paul Schulze)? Moreover, while the episode is a nail-biter, it's also thematically rich as it dramatizes the chaos and collateral damage of Tony's dual life in some of the show's most harrowing scenes, before culminating with the brutal murder of Petrulio by Tony's hand.

After spotting Petrulio at a Maine gas station, Tony races after his car to verify his identity. He drives like a demon with a terrified Meadow riding shotgun: he's speeding, cutting into oncoming traffic, and going in the opposite direction from Colby College, their destination. The scene is frightening, and Jamie-Lynn Sigler makes us feel Meadow's panic with every swerve, as the highway line her father so carelessly crosses represents the one he tries to maintain between his two families.

When Tony finally gets to Febby, he strangles him with a bungee cord while the turncoat pleads for his life. Tony squeezes so tight, his hands bleed. It's not just a result of his anger with Febby the rat but also the anxiety and rage that are a product of managing his incongruent lives. Once Febby's dead, he looks up and sees a flock of geese flying in the opposite direction. Like the ducks in the series' first episode, they know what's good for them so they're getting out of Dodge.

Puke Rebuke: It's funny that Father Phil and Meadow both vomit in the episode. Yes, they're drunk, but they're also passengers on Tony and Carmela's wild ride, attached to a Soprano parent barreling through a deeply conflicted life. By episode's end, they're happy to have survived the storm.

NARRATIVE IMPACT: 7 CINEMATIC: 8 KILLER PERFORMANCES: 9
ELEMENT OF SURPRISE: 7 TOTAL SCORE: 31

DOMINIC AND RUSTY IRISH

Suicide from a bad trip on designer MDMA, and thrown over a bridge by Mikey Palmice and Joe Marino for selling the fatal dose in Episode 1.6, "Pax Soprana"

It's nice to see local natural wonder Paterson Great Falls and its narrow bridge again, following an appearance in "The Sopranos." In that episode, Pussy Bonpensiero intimidates delinquent debtor Alex Mahaffey (Michael Gaston). Mahaffey smells what's up and relents before any harm can come to him. Still, we could intuit that *somebody* on *The Sopranos* would eventually take a header to the rocks below.

We didn't have to wait long. Nor are we going to complain that the victim is a drug dealer named Rusty Irish (Christopher J. Quinn) who sells a bunk dose to young Dominic, who happens to be the grandson of Junior's tailor (Salem Ludwig). The kid has a bad trip and subsequently commits suicide. Disturbed by this news, Junior orders Rusty's death.

Rusty's swan-dive death scene is also a nice way to convey the old-school nastiness of Al Sapienza's Mikey Palmice, a goon with a Richard Widmark smile who really seems to enjoy his work.

> **NARRATIVE IMPACT: 2   CINEMATIC: 5   KILLER PERFORMANCES: 7**
> **ELEMENT OF SURPRISE: 2   TOTAL SCORE: 16**

GALLEGOS

Shot to death by Paulie Walnuts in a Manhattan apartment building in Episode 1.10, "A Hit Is a Hit"

One of the more inconsequential killings on the show. Gallegos (Jessy Terrero) works for Colombian drug dealers who are shipping into Port Newark against the Mob's wishes and warnings. This plot detail seems to exist so that Paulie Gualtieri (Tony Sirico) can make cracks about Pablo Escobar and Juan Valdez. The scene is notable only in that Moltisanti, Bonpensiero, and Gualtieri go undercover in goofy appliance installer uniforms. They peep from behind the large refrigerator box in an odd bit of slapstick staging that seems like a homage to '80s comedies like *Ghostbusters*. Other than that, there's not much to see here.

NARRATIVE IMPACT: 1   CINEMATIC: 1   KILLER PERFORMANCES: 1
ELEMENT OF SURPRISE: 2   TOTAL SCORE: 5

VIN MAKAZIAN

Commits suicide by jumping off the Donald Goodkind Bridge in Episode 1.11, "Nobody Knows Anything"

The late John Heard was nominated for a 1999 Emmy for his heartbreaking performance as Vin Makazian, an alcoholic, corrupt Newark detective on the hook for tens of thousands in gambling debts. To put a dent in his obligations, he does jobs for Tony, like trailing Dr. Melfi and providing intel on informants, including Sal Bonpensiero. Despite his hustle and desire to accommodate Tony, he's treated with derisive remarks, leading the pickled, broken cop to respond to Tony's insult, "Degenerate gambler with a badge," with "You know, you got an amazing ability to sum up a man's whole life in a single sentence."

Makazian's end begins with a great piece of staging. Sequestered in his bordello sanctuary, Vin takes a shower. The fogged-up glass provides a thin layer of insulation from the troubled outside world. He hears a racket and draws a porthole-size hole in the condensation to see what's happening. The barrier broken, he sees a badge. The bordello's been busted, and the johns are corralled in cuffs. This intrusion and arrest mean that Makazian will lose access to his only respite. There's nothing left for him to do, nowhere left to go. Out on bail and stuck in traffic, he pounds on his horn with the helpless fury of a man who knows he's out of options. Eager to die, he pulls over on the Donald Goodkind Bridge and leaps.

After Makazian's death, Tony chat ups Debbie (Karen Sillas), the brothel madam. This isn't a visit to mourn, though. Tony's hoping to hear more about rats inside his crew, since Makazian is the one who fingered Bonpensiero as an informer. Instead of intel, he learns that the man he mocked so frequently considered him a friend.

And when Debbie admits to playing a kind of lover-therapist to Makazian, she asks, "Who wouldn't want to sleep with their shrink?" Her question catches Tony off guard and he feels a sense of recognition, a shared understanding of depression, and pangs of empathy. In the episode's final shot Tony looks up to another bridge, Jersey City's Pulaski Skyway, no doubt thinking of Makazian's leap and pondering the choice he'd make were he to run out of options.

NARRATIVE IMPACT: 6   CINEMATIC: 8   KILLER PERFORMANCES: 10
ELEMENT OF SURPRISE: 6   TOTAL POINTS: 30

MARIOLINA CAPUANO

Dies from unknown causes in Episode 1.12, "Isabella"

The only real tribute paid to the deceased is Junior's fond remembrance: "Mariolina gave me my first handjob. Me and Vincent Maniscalco in the alley behind the chicken market." Rest in peace, Mariolina.

NARRATIVE IMPACT: 1   CINEMATIC: 1   KILLER PERFORMANCES: 5
ELEMENT OF SURPRISE: 1   TOTAL POINTS: 8

DONNIE PADUANA

Shot to death by Mikey Palmice for kidding about Soprano family affairs in Episode 1.12, "Isabella"

The death of Donnie Paduana (David Wike) is a minor scene, but a nicely directed one with some fun details. He's a low-level gangster who hired hit men to kill Tony for Junior. Donnie's what Joe Spinell's character, Willie Cicci in *The Godfather: Part II*, would call a "buffer." After the first attempt on Tony's life stalls out, Donnie shows up late in his '86 Pontiac Firebird, its stereo blaring cheeseball guitar riffs. It's a completely inappropriate entrance for a meeting so clandestine that Junior Soprano feels the need to dive down on the backseat while it takes place. From the car, he hears Donnie's quip about Tony's mother wanting him popped and that's enough. He signals Palmice to eliminate Donnie. The hood has already put the wheels in motion for Tony's demise, so he's no longer useful. Mikey casually murders him and they drive off, but not before a slow roll-by so Palmice—the up-and-comer—can admire his handiwork while, on the soundtrack, Garbage's song "Temptation Waits" plays and Shirley Manson sings, "I'll tell you something / I am a wolf but / I like to wear sheep's clothing / I am a bonfire / I am a vampire / I'm waiting for my moment." And that, dear reader, is Mikey Palmice.

Pun Fun: When Junior learns that the hit on Tony has been aborted, he vomits. This prompts Palmice's second fabulous pun of the season, as he offers, "Junior, mints?"

**NARRATIVE IMPACT: 2 CINEMATIC: 6 KILLER PERFORMANCES: 8
ELEMENT OF SURPRISE: 5 TOTAL SCORE: 21**

WILLIAM JOHNSON "PETITE" CLAYBORN

Accidentally shot by his partner, Rasheen Ray, during a botched hit on Tony Soprano in Episode 1.12, "Isabella"

"Petite" Clayborn (John Eddins) and Rasheen Ray (Touche) are Junior Soprano's hired killers and their target is his nephew, Tony Soprano. Tony's made himself an easy mark as he mopes about in his robe and lithium-induced haze, conversing with Isabella (Maria Grazia Cucinotta), an Italian dental student, in his imagination. Director Allen Coulter designs the hit (and the sequence leading up to it) to wake up Tony and propel him to action. As he rises to Tindersticks' "Tiny Tears"—a perfect sleepwalking ballad—the shot rotates so that we see him in bed, but vertically positioned. It's like Coulter is trying to force him to stand up or, if it comes to it, dump him out.

The assassination attempt, which takes place at the newsstand near Melfi's office, plays like the world's most strident alarm clock. Clayborn's bullet shatters Tony's Tropicana bottle (a *Godfather* homage, as Vito Corleone was orange-shopping when shot). The lumbering Tony is jolted into survival mode, and narrowly escapes as a bullet grazes his ear and Ray accidentally shoots Clayborn. Free from the killers and (finally) wide awake, the bloodied, maniacal-looking Tony laughs until he loses control of his car and is knocked out. His face rests on the blaring horn. Coulter's implication is: "It's about time you woke up, asshole."

Stormy Weather: The episode features an ever-strengthening wind, which rises to a crescendo just before the attempted murder scene, like Mother Nature is trying to get Tony's attention. Such fearsome gusts won't appear again until the series finale, "Made in America," where they portend a more ominous end for a man who resists a lasting awakening.

> **NARRATIVE IMPACT: 8   CINEMATIC: 9   KILLER PERFORMANCES: 8**
> **ELEMENT OF SURPRISE: 6   TOTAL SCORE: 31**

CHUCKY SIGNORE

Shot to death by Tony Soprano while on his boat moored at the marina in Episode 1.13, "I Dream of Jeannie Cusamano"

Chucky Signore (Sal Ruffino) is one of Junior Soprano's most trusted advisors, and, after the failed attempt on Tony's life, he becomes an obvious target for retaliation. Signore's caught unaware on his boat by fellow mariner Tony, who reveals a Beretta hidden inside the mouth of a giant red snapper; this is another *Godfather* twist-up, since a dead fish is usually a message sent postmortem. Tony unloads his clip and Silvio Dante (Steven Van Zandt) quickly arrives with heavy chains and a pair of cement blocks (always prepared, that Silvio) while the ghostly drums and harmonica of R. L. Burnside's "It's Bad You Know" play Chucky out to sea one last time.

> **NARRATIVE IMPACT: 3   CINEMATIC: 7   KILLER PERFORMANCES: 5**
> **ELEMENT OF SURPRISE: 6   TOTAL POINTS: 21**

JIMMY ALTIERI

Shot in the back of the head by Silvio Dante in Episode 1.13,
"I Dream of Jeannie Cusamano"

DiMeo family captain Jimmy Altieri (Joe Badalucco Jr.) is promised an evening of dalliance with Russian women by Christopher Moltisanti, but he's really just being set up for execution. Altieri is shaped similarly to portly fellow mobster Sal Bonpensiero, who is fingered by corrupt cop Vin Makazian as a confidential informant. Tony can't believe it, so he assumes Makazian, often drunk, got the two confused. Some fishy behavior from Altieri is all Tony needs to believe he's flipped for the Feds and must go.

The death itself is conventionally staged, but it's curiously edited with a prodigious use of slow motion as to give the scene an '80s Stephen J. Cannell production feel. A stock establishing shot of Times Square opens this sequence but includes a Howard Johnson's and Burger King that were long gone by April 1999, when this episode aired. The movie on the marquee is *The Milagro Beanfield War*. Maybe once they decided on that stock video, they chose to edit the scene as if it was '88? I'll give them the benefit of the doubt.

> **NARRATIVE IMPACT: 5   CINEMATIC: 6   KILLER PERFORMANCES: 5**
> **ELEMENT OF SURPRISE: 6   TOTAL SCORE: 22**

MIKEY PALMICE

Shot to death while jogging by Christopher Moltisanti and Paulie
Gualtieri in Episode 1.13, "I Dream of Jeannie Cusamano"

It's a bummer that Mikey Palmice goes so quickly in the series, since Al Sapienza plays him perfectly. The irritable Mikey is a douchebag for the ages: a contemporary yuppie (he's a jogger with an eye on upward mobility) with throwback touches like gangster suits, a son named Francis Albert, and a neo-flattop haircut. And he's a charmer. His last words to his wife are "Go take a Midol."

His murder, the last of the show's first season, is a fine piece of direction from John Patterson. As Palmice jogs away from his house, even a neighborhood dog, Nips, can't help but snarl. Once Christopher and Paulie exit their Cadillac and charge, Palmice flees into the woods. This trio of city crooks are immediately out of their element. (Paulie's trouble here foreshadows the problems he'll have a little later in "Pine Barrens.") As they sprint after Palmice, bird chirps are interrupted by gunshots and Paulie's shrieks at the prospect of contracting poison ivy. Finally, Palmice trips on a stump and lies at the feet of his enemies. His pleas for mercy go unheard. Christopher feels he's getting justice for his murdered friend Brendan Filone, and Paulie's OCD fear of skin maladies is more than enough to entice him to empty his clip. Palmice's death completes the decimation of Junior's crew.

NARRATIVE IMPACT: 6   CINEMATIC: 9   KILLER PERFORMANCES: 9
ELEMENT OF SURPRISE: 5   TOTAL POINTS: 29

SEASON TWO

PHILLIP "PHILLY SPOONS" PARISI

Shot to death by Gigi Cestone for spreading rumors about Tony in Episode 2.1, "Guy Walks into a Psychiatrist's Office"

"Philly Spoons" Parisi (Dan Grimaldi) steps up to run Junior Soprano's crew following his boss's indictment and Mikey Palmice's murder. Sounds like a promotion! As he leaves his house to pick up crewmember Gigi Cestone (John Fiore) at the airport, he should take his wife's reminder, "Philly, don't forget the pastries!" as a warning. It's a *Godfather* homage to remind us of Pete Clemenza's "Leave the gun, take the cannoli."

In the next scene, we see Paulie Gualtieri drop off Cestone at the airport with an empty bag—it's a ruse. Unbeknownst to Parisi, Cestone has defected to Tony's side, where he'll work under the Aprile crew. So, once Philly shows up to collect Gigi, we have a good idea Parisi's booked on a direct flight to eternity.

On the ride, Philly yaps, kvetches, and tells tales about Tony's psychiatry visits and his falling out with Livia. He was likely done for anyway, but his big mouth seals his fate. Cestone shoots him in the head and gets picked up by Paulie. The upside is, we're still able to enjoy Dan Grimaldi's performance, as he continues on the show as Philly's twin brother, Patsy, for the rest of the series. From a narrative perspective, Junior doesn't have anybody left, save for soft-hearted Bobby "Bacala" Baccalieri (Steve Schirripa) and a few old-timers.

> **NARRATIVE IMPACT: 4   CINEMATIC: 4   KILLER PERFORMANCES: 5**
> **ELEMENT OF SURPRISE: 7   TOTAL SCORE: 20**

UNNAMED PATIENT OF DR. MELFI

Commits suicide off-screen while Dr. Melfi is on the lam, following the DiMeo family in-fighting between Tony's and Junior's factions. We hear about this death in Episode 2.1, "Guy Walks into a Psychiatrist's Office"

We don't know this character, but what matters is that we understand what she meant to Dr. Melfi. When Tony accosts his psychiatrist in a diner, she's at first frightened, then repulsed, and finally boiling with rage. She confronts Tony with the truth that his actions cost this woman her life. An emboldened, defiant Melfi asks, "How many more people have to die for your personal growth?" We're including (and grading) this death based on Lorraine Bracco's terrific work.

> **NARRATIVE IMPACT: 4   CINEMATIC: 2   KILLER PERFORMANCES: 9**
> **ELEMENT OF SURPRISE: 5   TOTAL POINTS: 20**

FREDDY CAPUANO

Killed for spreading rumors about the Sopranos in Episode 2.2, "Do Not Resuscitate"

When Junior and Tony meet in the office of cardiologist Dr. Shreck (Matthew Sussman), Junior's incensed that Freddy Capuano ("That hairpiece motherfucker!"), owner of Green Grove Retirement Community, is gossiping about the Sopranos. Next thing we know, his prime parking spot at Green Grove is vacant and his empty Cadillac is deposited near the Passaic

River. The only thing left of Freddy is his lush toupee. It seems Green Grove is under new management.

> **NARRATIVE IMPACT: 1   CINEMATIC: 2   KILLER PERFORMANCES: 1**
> **ELEMENT OF SURPRISE: 3   TOTAL SCORE: 7**

REVEREND HERMAN JAMES SR.

| *Dies of old age in Episode 2.2, "Do Not Resuscitate"*

Tony has a secret arrangement with Reverend Herman James Jr. (Gregalan Williams). He pays James to orchestrate protests against Massarone Construction so that he can extort protection money and no-show jobs. In a brief scene, Tony meets the Reverend's father, Herman James Sr., a World War II vet played by the great Bill Cobbs. He tells Tony, "Never underestimate a man's determination to be free," but Tony doesn't get it, since he only understands the determination to consume. Spiritual freedom is an alien concept to him. In fact, Tony could have flipped the line: "Never underestimate a man's determination *not* to be free." It's a blessing that James Sr. dies ignorant of his son's scheme with Soprano.

> **NARRATIVE IMPACT: 1   CINEMATIC: 2   KILLER PERFORMANCES: 7**
> **ELEMENT OF SURPRISE: 1   TOTAL SCORE: 11**

JIMMY BONES

| *Beaten to death with a hammer by Salvatore "Big Pussy"*
| *Bonpensiero in Episode 2.4, "Commendatori"*

DiMeo Family associate Jimmy Bones (Mike Memphis) is an Elvis impersonator who would have benefited from a little less conversation. He sees Sal in Party Box, a party supply store, while he's meeting his FBI handler, Skip Lipari (Louis Lombardi). Jimmy doesn't hear anything specific, but his presence gives Pussy major agita.

The only way he can appease his anxiety is murder. He visits Bones's

Dover, New Jersey, home—filled with Elvis memorabilia, naturally—and, as soon as Jimmy turns around, bashes his skull in, spraying blood all over a framed photo of Colonel Tom Parker. From the kitchen, we hear the tea kettle—perhaps a nod to Elvis's song "A Whistling Tune" from his 1962 boxers and gangsters movie, a remake of *Kid Galahad*.

> **NARRATIVE IMPACT: 2   CINEMATIC: 6   KILLER PERFORMANCES: 7**
> **ELEMENT OF SURPRISE: 2   TOTAL SCORE: 17**

TOM GIGLIONE SR.

Blown off the roof by a gust of wind while installing a satellite dish, one day after his retirement, in Episode 2.6, "The Happy Wanderer"

Tom Giglione Sr., a character we've never met, is the father of Tom Giglione Jr. (Ed Vassallo), one we rarely see. The junior Giglione is married to Tony's younger sister, Barbara (played by Nicole Burdette in early episodes and Danielle Di Vecchio in later ones). They live in Brewster, New York, and infrequently appear on the series. Tom Sr.'s death is notable as a minor point of conversation between Dr. Melfi and Tony, who bemoans a sick twist of fate—Tom Sr. fell off a roof on the first day of his retirement. From a plot perspective, Tom's wake serves as an opportunity for Tony to chastise Richie Aprile for his aggressive and insubordinate behavior, while also suffering the histrionics of his mother, who gives a wailing performance Tony likens to Bette Davis.

> **NARRATIVE IMPACT: 1   CINEMATIC: 1   KILLER PERFORMANCES: 1**
> **ELEMENT OF SURPRISE: 1   TOTAL SCORE: 4**

WALDEMAR WYCZCHUK

Blown up by a car bomb in New Jersey in Episode 2.7, "D-Girl"

Waldemar Wyczchuk is an unseen Mob associate who dies in a car bombing. His death is an important one, as it marks the beginning of Sal's emotional breakdown. Skip Lipari and other FBI handlers push Bonpensiero to wear a wire to get information on Wyczchuk's killing from Tony. Under duress and incredible stress, Sal wears the equipment to A.J. Soprano's (Robert Iler) confirmation party. He gets no good intel, but mentors the younger Soprano, telling him, "You got your health, your family. Enjoy it while you can. While you got it all in your hand." Bonpensiero loses it. He knows that one of two endings await him and that he's on an accelerated schedule.

**NARRATIVE IMPACT: 2   CINEMATIC: 3   KILLER PERFORMANCES: 7
ELEMENT OF SURPRISE: 1   TOTAL SCORE: 13**

SEAN GISMONTE

Shot in the head by Christopher Moltisanti in Episode 2.8, "Full Leather Jacket"

Sean Gismonte (Chris Tardio) is as dumb as he is pretty. He's the only wannabe gangster I can think of who dies because he forgets to unbuckle his seatbelt. He makes the gaffe during an ill-advised attempt on Christopher's life. Gismonte and pal Matthew Bevilaqua (Lillo Brancato Jr.) think capping him will earn the respect of Richie Aprile and help them get a leg up. Sean's fate is fitting for a man who believed his path to career advancement went through Aprile.

**NARRATIVE IMPACT: 2   CINEMATIC: 3   KILLER PERFORMANCES: 4
ELEMENT OF SURPRISE: 5   TOTAL POINTS: 14**

MATTHEW BEVILAQUA

Shot to death by Tony Soprano and Salvatore "Big Pussy" Bonpensiero in an empty Hacklebarney State Park snack shack in Episode 2.9, "From Where to Eternity"

When we meet Matthew Bevilaqua and his friend Sean Gismonte, they're the first of a special breed of *Sopranos* character: the Gen-X gangster wannabe weaned entirely on *The Godfather* movies, mid-career Scorsese, and the 1983 *Scarface* remake. Okay, maybe the more studious ones also know De Palma's *Carlito's Way* (superior to his *Scarface*). Cagney, Edward G. Robinson, or Paul Muni? Fuggedaboutit. These prats are bereft of taste and brains—kind of like A.J. Soprano—but unlike Tony's son, they're turned on by violence.

Their bad movie logic first gets them in trouble when they deliver unsanctioned beatdowns in a boiler room, and it ultimately gets them killed after a misguided attempt on Christopher's life. While Sean's killed instantly, Bevilaqua—the more developed character of the pair—escapes.

Bevilaqua *does* get the best jokes. It's just that he's usually the punch line. Even the character's casting is a rib. Lillo Brancato Jr. plays the lead in Robert De Niro's *A Bronx Tale*, a lightweight *Goodfellas*-meets–*Stand by Me* movie that Bevilaqua would no doubt have seen two dozen times. This wannabe is thrilled to have a gangster nickname (it's "Drink Water") and gets flummoxed serving drinks and snacks to Frank Sinatra Jr. during a high-stakes illicit card game ("Thank you, Mr. Sinatra Jr., sir!"). And perhaps the funniest gag: *Mean Streets* costar David Proval, who plays Richie Aprile, chases Bevilaqua down the street and throws a bat at him. It's like he's standing up for the '70s classics and giving the '90s wannabes two emphatic thumbs down.

Even though the character's a moron, we can't help but feel for Bevilaqua a little when, beaten, bloodied, and strapped to a chair, he pleads for his life before he's shot to death by Sal and Tony. It's notable that, as he realizes his time is up, he cries, "Mommy!" The only other time we hear such a cry in the entire series is from A.J., when he's face to face with a large black bear near the Sopranos' pool. Bevilaqua's character and fate are exactly what Tony fears for his meek puddle of a son.

Not-So-Fun Fact: After the show, Brancato served nearly five years of a ten-year sentence on a burglary charge but was acquitted of second-degree murder after a break-in went bad and an off-duty police officer was killed.

NARRATIVE IMPACT: 5   CINEMATIC: 6   KILLER PERFORMANCES: 8
ELEMENT OF SURPRISE: 6   TOTAL POINTS: 25

RICHIE APRILE

Shot to death by Janice Soprano in Episode 2.12, "The Knight in White Satin Armor"

Richie Aprile is a man out of step. In the decade he was locked up, everything changed. He comes back to New Jersey still playing checkers, but his gangster family members—especially the Sopranos—are playing chess. Through most of his scenes, we watch his noisy, old-school moves disrupt Tony's peace of mind. As he plods forward (the only way he knows how), Junior, Tony, and ultimately Janice (Aida Turturro) run circles around him. They all think a million Machiavellian miles a minute and leave Aprile dizzy, overextended, and out of luck. While Junior signs his death warrant and Tony seals it, it's Janice who kills Richie for his virulent homophobia and violent misogyny. He just wasn't made for these times.

> **NARRATIVE IMPACT: 6   CINEMATIC: 6   KILLER PERFORMANCES: 7**
> **ELEMENT OF SURPRISE: 9   TOTAL SCORE: 28**

SALVATORE "BIG PUSSY" BONPENSIERO

Shot to death aboard a boat by Tony Soprano, Silvio Dante, and Paulie Gualtieri in Episode 2.13, "Funhouse"

Sal is killed by his friends in John Patterson's "Funhouse," one of the most daring episodes of the series. For the first two seasons we've watched him suffer: he's squeezed by the Feds, crippled by fear and guilt (which manifest themselves as debilitating back pain), and frustrated that he can't earn. We know—and he knows—he can't keep juggling. Tony, meanwhile, is alternately preoccupied or in denial regarding his friend's betrayal. As the pair enters "Funhouse," neither can avoid what's predestined. In order to protect the DiMeo crime family, Tony must prove that Bonpensiero's a rat and kill his friend, a choice that will cost him a piece of his humanity, but also show that he's willing to do whatever it takes to protect his business.

To help Tony reach this conclusion and take action, the clever writers (David Chase and Todd Kessler) send him on a surrealist vision quest where the truths he must face are encrypted with funhouse mirror distortion. The impetus for his dream journey is ambiguous. It could be an E. coli–infected chicken vindaloo or a funky mussel from Nuovo Vesuvio, but it's most likely that the fire in his belly is psychosomatic—the result of his emotional anguish over his friend's likely betrayal and the action he must take. Regardless of the cause, what Tony sees leads him to make his first deeply tragic decision of the series (he is Michael to Big Pussy's Fredo). And it's no coincidence that the boss he usurps—the imprisoned Ercole DiMeo—has a name that's nearly interchangeable with the possible cause of his illness. When Tony sprints to the bathroom, he's not just wrestling with the porcelain throne, he's poisoned by what's required of him as the sitting boss of his crime family. The episode's surrealist narrative is so intricate, precise, and full of meaning, it's worth a close reading.

The dreamscape Patterson's designed presents a real trial for Tony, but is there a better place to become "The Boss" than Asbury Park? (This magic mirror of an episode could easily be titled "Punhouse.") The first phase of his dream opens with Tony walking alone on the boardwalk in winter. He finds his crew and everyone acknowledges him through eye contact or body language except a cigar-smoking Bonpensiero, who just stares toward the ocean—his soon-to-be home.

We learn they're all waiting for somebody, but we don't know who. "Fuck this. They're never coming": this is Tony's subconscious acknowledgment that the situation is urgent and there's no cavalry on the way. Only he, the leader, can walk through the proverbial fire, which is why Sal vanishes from the dream and Tony self-immolates, a sign that he understands he'll need to sacrifice part of himself to fix this situation.

Tony's second dream returns him to Asbury. It's a virtuoso sequence that plays out as though he's in an amusement park. It leaves him completely turned around, but also offers the clues he needs. He follows the boardwalk path, which squeaks like a rickety roller coaster. His Uncle Junior pops out from a window like a cardboard funhouse ghoul. A disembodied voice taunts him, "Where you going? What are you looking for?"

In a neat visual trick, Silvio appears in the shot suddenly, as if Tony's zipping by him in a ride's carriage. Sil delivers one of his (awful) Michael

Corleone impressions from *The Godfather, Part III* like he's a fairground automaton: "Our true enemy has yet to reveal himself."

Finally, Tony looks through coin-operated binoculars and sees himself playing cards with Paulie, whom he shoots to death; Tony's unconscious is looking everywhere but where it needs to. We're made to believe he wakes, recovered. He sees Melfi, but she quickly transforms into Annalisa Zucca (Sofia Milos), the ruthless female Napoletano boss from "Commendatori." This is who he must become.

In a final hallucinatory scene, Tony hears from the man himself, when Bonpensiero, appearing as a fish like one served at their shared Indian feast, confesses his crimes against the family. Tony can no longer hide from the truth.

Now awake, he must gather his courage and prove Pussy's guilt before meting out punishment. This is the first sequence in the series where Tony—with a rudimentary understanding of dream logic from therapy—puts the work he's done with Melfi to evil use.

In Pussy's house, Tony checks—and double-checks—Pussy's cigar box (Pussy's smoking one when he appears in the first dream, remember?). He discovers Bonpensiero's wire inside the box of Cubans. This is another nice *Godfather, Part II* reference—Michael is in Havana with Fredo when *his* heart gets broken. And there's one final, more obvious allusion to the older Corleone brother. They get Bonpensiero on a fishing boat (c'mon Sal, how many times did you see the movie?) that they happened to borrow from—yep—a Cuban.

The poor cluck never had a prayer, and we wonder if he subconsciously wants Tony to put him out of his misery. Regardless, *we* know he's bound to sleep with the fishes from the episode's start, and Patterson, Chase, and Kessler deploy the motif with wit. At their second dinner (Nuovo Vesuvio following the Indian feast) he orders *zuppa di mussels*. When he appears as a talking fish laid out to market in Tony's vision, he cracks, "These guys, on either side of me, they're asleep." When Tony, Silvio, and Paulie finally shoot him dead, wrap him, and dump him, his chained body bag even flops and leaves a little wake like a whale tail. He's swimming home at last.

After Pussy's murder, Tony deflects an interrogation from Dr. Melfi and storms out. Later, at Meadow's graduation party, he holds court. Carmela, looking for him, discovers her husband in the great room. The alleged food poisoning has run its course, but the experience has forever changed Soprano. He stands tall with a cigar, smoke pluming from his mouth. He's more "boss" than he's ever been and, having tamed the fire in his belly, looks like a dragon guarding his hoard. Meanwhile, his best friend rests eternally in Davy Jones's locker.

NARRATIVE IMPACT: 10   CINEMATIC: 10   KILLER PERFORMANCES: 10
ELEMENT OF SURPRISE: 8   TOTAL SCORE: 38

SEASON THREE

LIVIA SOPRANO

Dies from complications of a stroke in Episode 3.2, "Proshai, Livushka"

The relationship between Tony and his mother is the most important aspect of the first two seasons of *The Sopranos*. She's a ubiquitous and toxic presence in this life. A powerful manipulator with a cruel streak, she's crafty enough to weave plausible deniability into her every action, including her decision to okay the assassination of her only son. Actress Nancy Marchand's unfortunate death between Seasons Two and Three robbed the show of one of its core dynamics. Though, in truth, the relationship had played out effectively and moved to the periphery for a good portion of Season Two, as Livia-induced agita is replaced by the appearance of Tony's sister Janice. And, while they seemed to be setting up Livia for a more prominent role in the third season, did anybody believe the idea of her testifying against Tony about illegal airline tickets would have been as gripping as her colluding with Junior to murder her son?

To give Tony a final scene with his mother, the production employed existing lines and computer-generated effects. The results are mixed at best, but at least we get a sense of Tony's anxiety about her potential testimony. It's a not-so-subtle joke that one of the audiobooks

he brings her is Mario Puzo's *Omerta*. The other, in a sad bit of Pie-O-My foreshadowing, is *The Horse Whisperer*.

The scenes in "Proshai, Livushka" that speak most deeply to Tony's mourning feature no words from actors on the show, but substantial dialogue from the characters in *The Public Enemy*, William Wellman's famous 1931 James Cagney gangster picture. When Tony sits down to watch the movie—before he receives news of his mother's death—he's tickled by the prologue card, which warns against the social scourge of men like Tom Powers and Rico from *Little Caesar*. He can't wait to root for Cagney and giggles at the actor's opening credits appearance. The night after Livia's death, he's sleepless and returns to the movie. He watches the infamous scene where Powers smooshes a grapefruit into his moll's face. Tony laughs, but his mood shifts the instant sweet, doting Ma Powers appears. He becomes somber, and Gandolfini shows us the longing in Tony's eyes.

After his mother's wake, Tony's mood is pensive. He watches Powers, wounded in the rain, proclaim, "I ain't so tough" before collapsing, near death. The next shot from *The Public Enemy* is Ma Powers going to visit Tom. The presence of the mother elicits a smile from Tony.

After a disastrous memorial service at the house, during which nary a good word is uttered about Livia, Tony returns to the movie to watch its final scene. Ma Powers believes a reformed Tom is coming home from the hospital, healthy and ready to live a straight life. In high spirits, she rushes to prepare his room. The tragedy is that she won't be reunited with her son: Tom is delivered home dead, killed by his enemies. It's only now that Tony Soprano allows himself to cry. And it's not because of Tom's death. It's not even because of the loss of Livia. He's grieving because he didn't have a mother that loved him as much as Beryl Mercer's Ma Powers cared for her boy Tom.

**NARRATIVE IMPACT: 9   CINEMATIC: 6   KILLER PERFORMANCES: 8
ELEMENT OF SURPRISE: 4   TOTAL SCORE: 27**

FABRIZIO "FEBBY" VIOLA

Dies from cancer is Episode 3.5, "Another Toothpick"

Febby, a previously unmentioned uncle of Carmela Soprano, receives a funeral more notable than the man. It's where we hear the titular phrase "another toothpick" evoked—Livia's description of her elderly peers felled by cancer. And it's where we meet Bobby Bacalieri Sr. (played by Burt Young), another cancer victim, but one who is determined to go out at his fighting weight.

> **NARRATIVE IMPACT: 1   CINEMATIC: 1   KILLER PERFORMANCES: 3**
> **ELEMENT OF SURPRISE: 1   TOTAL SCORE: 6**

SALVATORE "MUSTANG SALLY" INTILE

Shot in the head following a violent struggle with his godfather,
Bobby Bacalieri Sr., in Episode 3.5., "Another Toothpick"

Mustang Sally (Brian Tarantina) is a putrid sleaze, even by New Jersey underworld standards. It's like he's modeled after the most loathsome Tarantino character knockoffs. His résumé is rich: he threw a Meadowlands hot dog vendor off the second mezzanine for adding too many onions (shades of Marcellus Wallace and Tony Rocky Horror in *Pulp Fiction*). He's violent with his girlfriend, Tina (played by Vanessa Ferlito, who would go on to costar in Tarantino's *Death Proof*), and he's responsible for the appalling crime that drives the plot of "Another Toothpick." He wallops Bryan Spatafore (Vincent Orofino), brother of Vito (Joseph R. Gannascoli) in the head with a golf club, putting him in a coma. It's fitting this grubby Tarantino extra gets one of the most gruesome and gory *Sopranos* deaths.

Mustang Sally thinks it's help, not the Reaper, knocking when his terminally ill godfather, Bobby Baccalieri Sr., appears at his door coughing up blood. He doesn't suspect the old man at all when Baccalieri sneaks up behind him, gun in hand. But as in any scene that's a Tarantino homage, this kill won't be clean. Mustang Sally's friend Carlos (Michael Martochio) interrupts the assassination, and the first shot misses the mark—it only takes off an ear. There's a bloody struggle on the table before Mustang Sally's brains splatter the wall. Burt Young's Baccalieri is both covered in blood and coughing it up, but still has enough in the tank to shoot Carlos to death and enjoy, with the satisfaction of a lifelong smoker, a deep drag on one of the deceased's cigarettes.

Did You Notice? Two future events are foreshadowed in the scene where DiMeo family members (mostly from the Aprile crew) visit Mustang Sally's victim, the comatose Bryan Spatafore. Vito, seeking revenge for the attack on his brother, tells his captain, Gigi Cestone, "I want this cock-sucker to bleed from his ass, Skipper." Ironically, that's how Vito goes in Season Six—with a pool cue shoved up his rectum. And Ralph Cifaretto (Joe Pantoliano), so quick to make jokes about Bryan's being left a veg-etable, must consider the same grim fate in his own family, after his son, Justin (Dane Curley), is accidentally shot with an arrow and suffers brain damage.

NARRATIVE IMPACT: 4   CINEMATIC: 8   KILLER PERFORMANCES: 8
ELEMENT OF SURPRISE: 4   TOTAL POINTS: 24

CARLOS

Shot to death by Robert "Bobby" Baccalieri in Episode 3.5., "Another Toothpick"

Carlos is a wrong-place, wrong-time casualty, but anybody who hangs out with Mustang Sally can't be all that nice. And being killed by Bobby Bac-calieri Sr. could be considered an honor. Terence Winter's dialogue is espe-cially wry in the scene. The lung-cancer-ridden Baccalieri tells Carlos, who is smoking, to "quit while you're young." Carlos responds, "Gotta die from something, Papi." Yep, and in about five minutes.

NARRATIVE IMPACT: 1   CINEMATIC: 5   KILLER PERFORMANCES: 6
ELEMENT OF SURPRISE: 2   TOTAL POINTS: 14

BOBBY BACCALIERI SR.

Dies from complications of lung cancer and/or a motor vehicle crash in Episode 3.5, "Another Toothpick"

After he viciously executes his godson, Mustang Sally, and Sally's friend Carlos, Baccalieri Sr. embraces his true love and lights a post-killing smoke before getting in his car to escape the scene. It feels positively postcoital.

As alluded to above, this plotline has a Tarantino whiff about it. It's gruesome, it involves a guy named after a muscle car, and it showcases a beloved '70s character actor in Burt Young. Baccalieri's death scene brings this homage to its dénouement, and Young is terrific. It plays like a nihilist spin on Robert Forster in *Jackie Brown*. Forster's Max Cherry discovers hope and love when he plays the Delfonics' "Didn't I (Blow Your Mind This Time)" on his car tapedeck. Conversely, Young's Baccalieri is on a death ride and he's going out with nicotine, blood, and shattered glass while America's "Sister Golden Hair" plays on his car radio. He tosses the half-smoked cigarette out the window, but it's too late. He can't catch his breath and he's dropped the inhaler. Fuck becoming "another toothpick," and there's no way Baccalieri's meeting anybody in the middle (as the song suggests). He's just happy he was afforded one last opportunity to ply his trade and enjoy that smoke.

> **NARRATIVE IMPACT: 5   CINEMATIC: 8   KILLER PERFORMANCES: 8**
> **ELEMENT OF SURPRISE: 5   TOTAL POINTS: 26**

TRACEE

Beaten to death by Ralph Cifaretto outside the Bada Bing in Episode 3.6, "University"

We never learn Tracee's (Ariel Kiley's) last name. The way she's abused and ultimately murdered in "University," it's something of a miracle she's afforded any name at all. When we meet Tracee—a Bada Bing dancer who appears in only one episode—she engages an uninterested Tony Soprano, giving him a loaf of date-nut bread for providing medical advice for her son, a gesture Tony barely remembers. She makes other friendly overtures that he disregards. To him and the others who lech around the Bada Bing's VIP room, she's a business asset and sexual plaything: the property of Silvio and the club first, and of Ralphie, who sees her as his *comare*, second. Both take advantage of her at every opportunity. Ralph pimps her out to cops; Silvio manipulates her into taking loans for braces at shylock rates and, when she misses work, drags her outside and beats her as Ralphie laughs from the window.

We learn that Tracee, just twenty, previously lost custody of her son, Danny, but has regained it. She tortured him with lit cigarettes—the result of her own childhood abuse. This young woman is aimless and broken, reaching out to anyone who might show some concern for her, even if it's mock care that quickly shifts to cruelty. And it's her terrible luck that she's drawn to Ralphie in the midst of his cocaine-and-*Gladiator* phase.

When she confesses that she's pregnant with his child, Ralphie insults her and laughs off the idea of supporting them. She lashes out. Ralphie responds to the insult by savagely beating her to death. The scene is arguably the most horrific of *The Sopranos*. No music, just the ambient sounds of late-night Lodi, New Jersey, so we can hear every smack, every thud as Tracee's screams give way to gurgles and finally silence.

After she's dead, Paulie Gualtieri, though his stoic, pale face acknowledges the horror of the situation, can't bring himself to grant Tracee personhood. "You get a sheet Chrissy. Cover *that* up." Tony, shocked and disgusted by the insult to the Bing and the death of the girl (in which order, it's not clear), attacks Ralphie. He's a real knight in white satin armor.

As the episode winds down, the song "Living on a Thin Line" plays while Bing dancers gossip about her disappearance. It's telling that it's the death of Pie-O-My—a horse—that eventually drives Tony to murder Ralphie, and not that of Tracee, whom Silvio describes as a "thoroughbred" earlier in "University." Later in Season Four, after he murders Ralph, Tony takes a moment to pay respect to a Polaroid of Tracee at the Bing. It's the least he could do.

**NARRATIVE IMPACT: 7   CINEMATIC: 9   KILLER PERFORMANCES: 9
ELEMENT OF SURPRISE: 9   TOTAL SCORE: 34**

GIGI CESTONE

Dies from a heart attack in the Aprile crew clubhouse bathroom in Episode 3.8, "He Is Risen"

Gigi Cestone is one of the more likable members of the DiMeo outfit. He seems like a stand-up wiseguy who respects the code and plays by the rules. A loyal, mellow middle-manager, Gigi seems overwhelmed by the responsibilities of his capo promotion. His decision to outsource the killing of Salvatore "Mustang Sally" Intile to hit man and geriatric cancer patient Bobby Baccalieri Sr. proves especially egregious, as it costs Bobby Jr. his father. The stress (and probably genetics) gets to him, and Cestone is found dead on the toilet by his crew. He's surrounded by newspapers and issues of the comparatively tasteful nudie mag *Perfect 10* (perhaps a choice made to convey Cestone's relative class in comparison to his garish peers).

At his funeral, Tony, Silvio, and Paulie discuss how going "on the *piscione*" is "fucking humiliating" but has famous precedents with Elvis Presley and "Don something, producer of *The Simpsons*" dying the same way. Silvio means Don Simpson, the blockbuster producer and *Days of Thunder* actor who partnered with Jerry Bruckheimer on *Flashdance, Beverly Hills Cop*, and *Top Gun*, among others. It's worth noting that, despite his scandalous reputation, Simpson wasn't thumbing through *Perfect 10* when he died; he was allegedly reading an Oliver Stone biography.

Cestone's role on the show is a minor one. He has a limited number of scenes, but his death is notable in that it creates a vacant capo position and the opportunity Ralphie needs to get a promotion from his frequent nemesis, Tony.

NARRATIVE IMPACT: 5   CINEMATIC: 3   KILLER PERFORMANCES: 3
ELEMENT OF SURPRISE: 4   TOTAL POINTS: 15

SUNSHINE

Shot to death for talking too much by a jumpy Jackie Aprile Jr.
while dealing cards at Eugene Pontecorvo's low-stakes poker game
in Episode 3.12, "Amour Fou"

This one hurts! Not just because the robbery of Eugene Pontecorvo's (Robert Funaro's) and, by extension, Ralph Cifaretto's card game by Jackie Jr. and his friends is so misguided, but because Sunshine, the defiant dealer who taunts the methed-up bandits with old adages ("Victory has a hundred fathers, but defeat is an orphan!") is played by the director, writer, and actor Paul Mazursky. Mazursky is responsible for several of the best high comedies of the late '60s, '70s, and '80s, like *Bob & Carol & Ted & Alice*, *Next Stop, Greenwich Village*, and *Moscow on the Hudson*. David Chase cast this five-time Academy Award nominee as more than just a nod to his influence on the show (see Phil Dyess-Nugent's essay on page 150). It's a meta in-joke: the unfathomable idea that Jackie Jr., the ultimate pipsqueak, takes out a cultural heavyweight. *Ya done fucked up, kid.* I'm sure the late director got a kick out of playing the part. Sunshine, on the other hand, might not have gotten clipped if he'd known when to fold 'em.

NARRATIVE IMPACT: 7   CINEMATIC: 6   KILLER PERFORMANCES: 7
ELEMENT OF SURPRISE: 5   TOTAL POINTS: 25

CARLO RENZI AND DINO ZIRELLI

Shot and killed during the botched robbery of Eugene Pontecorvo's
low-stakes poker game in Episode 3.12, "Amour Fou"

Like Matt Bevilaqua and Sean Gismonte in Season Two, this pair of lamebrain pretenders punch way above their weight class and catch a half-dozen slugs in the head for their trouble. Following Jackie Aprile Jr. into battle is, at best, ill-advised, but that's exactly what they do when they—along with chickenshit driver and drug dealer Matush (Nick E. Tarabay)—arrive at Pontecorvo's poker game to prove their mettle, thanks to Ralph's trip-down-memory-lane story about Tony and Jackie Sr. taking down Feech LaManna's

(Robert Loggia's) card game in the '70s. The funniest part of the bit is that these guys, who aspire to be legitimate OG and made men, run out on one another the first chance they get. Matush takes off with the car when he hears a gunshot. Jackie drives right by Dino (Andrew Davoli), leaving him for dead, to save his own ass (at least for an episode). *The Sopranos* is filled with horrible, morally corrupt characters. Carlo (Louis Crugnali) and Dino? They're what my dad used to call DWEs: dicks with ears.

> **NARRATIVE IMPACT: 2   CINEMATIC: 6   KILLER PERFORMANCES: 4**
> **ELEMENT OF SURPRISE: 4   TOTAL POINTS: 16**

GIACOMO "JACKIE JR." APRILE JR.

Shot to death by Vito Spatafore in Episode 3.13, "Army of One"

Ah, Jackie Jr. The airhead apparent. A terrible Scrabble player. A mangler of Mafia movie tropes. Yes, he's a walking punch line and a jerk, but cruelty doesn't come quite as easy to him as it does to the criminal uncles (both blood and honorary) he emulates. Before he and his pals storm Eugene Pontecorvo's card game, he shows fear and tries to dissuade everyone: "Fuck it. Let's go down the Shore." His words have no power, though, as Dino and Carlo, guys without the shine of the Aprile last name, are eager to make their bones. Their misguided ambition (along with their stupidity) is their doom.

Jackie Jr. and his crew are pretenders. Perhaps it's irresponsible to describe Tony Soprano's generation as having an ethic—they're extorters and killers, after all—but they've achieved success because they're hardworking, crafty, and ruthless. Experienced. This new brood is spoiled and has learned from movies rather than the streets. And their boomer parents are so proud to have *provided* (a parental quality that extends beyond the criminal sector) that nobody's given the children any idea how ill-prepared they are for this (or any) adult life. Jackie Jr.'s cluelessness is most evident when, after dropping out of Rutgers, he considers a new life path. Not a doctor (as his dad wanted) nor a criminal, but "men's fashion. Not the faggy part, but like, *to be* Hugo Boss."

And while Jackie's entitlement and ignorance are played for laughs, his end is still tragic. In part because of his age and relationship with Meadow, but also because of Tony's hypocrisy. Tony claims that Jackie Sr. was his closest friend and promises to keep Jackie Jr. on the straight and narrow. And, while he does ride the kid—especially when he's dating Meadow—his position changes quickly after Jackie Jr.'s failed card game hold-up, where the dealer, Sunshine, is killed and Furio Giunta (Federico Castelluccio) is shot in the leg. As noted, the idea for the hold-up comes from Tony's nemesis, Ralph, and Tony deftly uses Jackie Jr.'s life as a chess piece, backing Ralph—who dates Jackie's mother, Rosalie (Sharon Angela)—into a corner.

Ralph stalls his difficult decision while Jackie Jr. lams it in a Boonton, New Jersey, housing project, the guest of Ray Ray (a strong cameo appearance by Michael K. Williams) and his daughter. Jackie Jr. kills time playing chess with the young girl. Frustrated and impatient, he quits while losing (just as he did in his Scrabble game with Meadow) and knocks the pieces across the board. Ray Ray tells him, "You should have played that out. It's the only way you're going to learn." But it's too late. Jackie Jr.'s a pawn in a game Tony's playing (and winning) with Ralph. Moments later, he's shot dead by Vito Spatafore on Ralph's command and lands facedown in a pile of snow. Jackie Jr.'s flaw is that he's never learned how to learn, and that's what elevates the character's fate from farce to tragedy.

NARRATIVE IMPACT: 7   CINEMATIC: 6   KILLER PERFORMANCES: 6
ELEMENT OF SURPRISE: 7   TOTAL SCORE: 26

SEASON FOUR

DENNIS LYNCH + PARTNER

*Killed by police in a Pennsylvania
robbery in Episode 4.1, "For All Debts
Public and Private"*

Two men die in a brazen armored truck robbery
in Pennsylvania, far enough away from New
Jersey, but the crime—and bloody results—
give Carmela extreme agita. She works hard to
get Tony to meet with a financial planner, asks
him to provide her with his account numbers,
or do *anything* that makes her feel like she'd
be able to subsist at her current one-percenter
level should Tony get sentenced to jail or the
cemetery. Seeing Mob widow Angie Bonpensiero (Toni Kalem) handing out sausage samples
at Pathmark doesn't do much to assuage her
worries.

> **NARRATIVE IMPACT: 3   CINEMATIC: 1**
> **KILLER PERFORMANCES: 2**
> **ELEMENT OF SURPRISE: 1   TOTAL SCORE: 7**

BARRY HAYDU

Shot to death by Christopher Moltisanti in Episode 4.1, "For All Debts Public and Private"

Like most of Christopher's murders, the death of retired police detective Barry Haydu (Tom Mason) has more wit and cinematic flair than a garden-variety *Sopranos* Mob killing. Tony presents the opportunity to Christopher to avenge his father, Dickie Moltisanti's, death as a gift, but it's just as much a tactic to secure the ever-distracted Chris's focus and loyalty. Christopher knows it's possible he's being manipulated. Regardless, he gets right to the point with the protesting Haydu: "It wouldn't make any difference. He wants you dead."

With that, Christopher—aware he's possibly an actor in a scene Tony wants played out—sets the stage: he turns out the lights, heightens the volume on the television, and closes the blinds. This aspiring movie mogul isn't going to sacrifice the opportunity to establish his mise-en-scène before taking his shot.

Retirement Plans: It's interesting Haydu is the second character (after Tom Giglione Sr.; see page 222) to die immediately following retirement. Putting in your thirty years doesn't count for much on *The Sopranos*.

NARRATIVE IMPACT: 5	CINEMATIC: 7	KILLER PERFORMANCES: 7
ELEMENT OF SURPRISE: 5	TOTAL SCORE: 24	

KAREN BACCALIERI

Killed in a car accident in Episode 4.3, "Christopher"

Karen Baccalieri (Christine Pedi), wife of gentle-ish giant Bobby Baccalieri, only appears in a few scenes prior to her fatal car accident. The best part of the episode is Steve Schirripa's moving portrayal of grief-stricken Bobby. Bobby's profound guilt and wish that he could have sacrificed himself in her place are decent, noble human responses, but next to the motivations and behaviors of his colleagues, he seems almost superhuman. To them, he's always been a joke who didn't even keep a *comare*.

Dramatically, Karen's death is interesting for the ways in which the Soprano siblings Janice and Tony respond to it. Janice, a master opportunist and manipulator, sees a much more malleable meal ticket than her current sponsor, Ralphie, and begins to insert herself into Bobby's life and family. Tony seems to ignore the inconsolable Bobby's blubbering, but it's obvious it irritates him. When the crew's riding back from an upstate casino visit, Tony rants (again) about Gary Cooper's emotional resilience. Tony takes expressions of grief as a personal affront.

Fun Fact: When Christine Pedi attended SopranosCon in November 2019, she adorned her autograph booth with both boxed ziti and a Pyrex covered in tinfoil to honor the last ziti Karen ever baked.

NARRATIVE IMPACT: 7   CINEMATIC: 4   KILLER PERFORMANCES: 9
ELEMENT OF SURPRISE: 7   TOTAL SCORE: 27

GLORIA TRILLO

‖ *Suicide by hanging, referenced in Episode 4.6, "Everybody Hurts"*
In a show rife with superlative performances from recurring actors, Annabella Sciorra's work as the complex and combustible Gloria Trillo is possibly the greatest. And, while Gloria's suicide occurs off-screen, it shakes Tony to his core when he hears about it in "Everybody Hurts" and haunts his dreams for much longer.

Throughout Season Three, the pair are slaves to their drives: Tony's for sex and nurturing, Gloria's for death. It's only through Tony's conversation with Melfi after the relationship's violent end that he understands "there are certain kinds of people who are drawn to fire, looking for an inevitable result, like a moth to a flame." For us, evidence of their animalistic dynamic is abundant from their very first meeting and continues until after her death.

Let's play armchair etymologist and ornithologist, since the *Sopranos'* writers love wordplay. "Trillo" includes "trill," a mellifluous bird warble. In "He Is Risen," when Tony enters Melfi's lobby and discovers Gloria on the couch, he's immediately taken by her look (she's stunning in all black with fishnets and a luminous blue necklace), but it's her cell-phone chatter that lures him in like a linnet's song. A successful Mercedes saleswoman, she's pitching a flirtatious doctor a pre-owned car and Tony deduces that she's crafty and coy—and to him, it's ear candy. And she's funny (not a quality shared by any other women in his life)—she confesses to being a serial killer: she's "murdered seven relationships." We know Tony's got a thing for "smart, sexy, and Italian," but we haven't seen him under a siren spell like this before.

What follows is a cat-and-mouse game where Tony seeks out Gloria while Melfi—the metaphorical animal wrangler here—is first oblivious, then miffed. When Tony gives Gloria his appointment, she slinks inside the office and Melfi closes the door. We can only see the side of the doctor's face, but it's clear she'd like to keep a wall between these two. But Tony Soprano cannot be denied and it's funny how sneakily (and easily) he, with help from director Allen Coulter, is able to shift Gloria from Dr. Melfi's world to his own. He whisks her from her job at Globe Motors to his boat, the *Stugots*—where they're far from Melfi's care—with the fluidity of Fred Astaire.

Their subsequent scenes in "The Telltale Moozadell" present a mating ritual set against an ominous backdrop—a collection of dangerous creatures. The ritual begins when Tony gifts her a luxury wallet, which he shakes and dangles like a carrot he'd offer a creature, but she's unimpressed. She's a rare bird and his usual tricks won't work. She counters and invites him to share one of her rituals: "Wanna go to the zoo? I try and get there once a year." The first shot we see of their zoo date is a gorilla. Soon, a simian-faced Tony playfully nibbles on her ear, his mouth mirroring the great ape's movements. Later they stop in front of a tiger's pen. We can hear the powerful cat growling, as if it could spring at any time: a hint of Gloria's hidden nature.

Away from Melfi, they're in the jungle and we get our first clue that they're utterly ill-equipped. Tony tells her, "I never met anybody like you." It's ironic when, moments later, she teases him with, "Poor you"—one of his mother's favorite daggers—and there's a split second of recognition as we feel his stomach drop. But before he can consider why, she's reengaging their foreplay and, thanks to his animal attraction, the thought of Livia is gone as fast as it came. As they make love in the reptile room, they're watched by an enormous yellow boa and we're reminded of Paulie's line to Tony, "Hey, snakes were fucking themselves long before Adam and Eve showed up, T."

Later in the episode, a giddy, glowing Gloria (the moth to the flame) explains to Melfi that her nightmares have stopped and that she had a "wonderful dream where I lit the big torch at the Olympics," just before she lies about her relationship with Tony. She thinks it's a good dream, but Melfi knows—and we suspect—that, subconsciously, she's lit the wick of the dynamite stick. Later in an elegant hotel room rendezvous, Gloria and Tony continue their dangerous dance, even as Keith Richards warns on the stereo, "Make no mistake about it / Things ain't what they seem." Gloria slithers onto him and discovers his loaded pistol. "There's nothing more useless than an unloaded gun," he says before letting her handle it. Finally, the relationship of her dreams.

It's in "Pine Barrens" that Gloria plays with fire and nearly gets what she wants. She invites Tony over for dinner, but a series of extenuating circumstances keeps pulling him away. She's lit the candles as well as the fireplace and prepared the perfect meal (London broil roasted on high heat). After Tony (finally) arrives, sleeps with her, and is called away, she's enraged and flings the meat at his head. She looks at him, longing for a violent response, but he just smiles and leaves.

At his next appointment with Melfi, he complains about Gloria's behavior. Melfi draws obvious parallels to Livia Soprano and the episode ends with an aria from Vivaldi's *Bajazet*: *"L'amo ma egl'è infidel / spero ma egl'è crudel, / morir mi lascierai?"* Translation: "I love him, but he is unfaithful / I hope, but he is cruel / will he let me die?" The last line is Gloria's deepest desire.

Well, if throwing the London broil is poking the bear, taking Carmela for a test drive in "Amour Fou" is slapping the dragon. Furious, Tony threatens Gloria at her workplace, and later, back at her place, she insults him and Carmela and he clocks her. Again, she mocks him with "poor you" and this time he recognizes Livia: "I didn't just meet you, I've known you my whole fucking life." When she threatens to tell Carmela and Meadow about their relationship, he attacks as fast as any jungle beast. With his enormous size advantage, he is quickly on top of her, constricting her breath.

He threatens to kill her, she begs him to, and he almost does, but catches himself. He won't fulfill her death wish.

Later, Tony sends Patsy to make sure it's clear to her that—should she insist on dying by his hand—her murder won't personally be fulfilled by her *amant fou*. In "Everybody Hurts," when he learns of her suicide, he asks an associate at Globe Motors if she left a note. The coworker explains that it "was just copy for a classified ad. She was selling her wolf stole." Gloria's animal games were over, so she fulfilled her wish on her own.

NARRATIVE IMPACT: 8   CINEMATIC: 8   KILLER PERFORMANCES: 10
ELEMENT OF SURPRISE: 8   TOTAL SCORE: 34

FURIO'S FATHER

Dies from cancer in Naples, Italy, in Episode 4.8, "Mergers and Acquisitions"

We don't meet Furio's father, but it's implied he was in the Naples Mafia, the Camorra. He isn't as important to the show as his son's visit home for his funeral and subsequent return to New Jersey. Furio walks through the Napoletano cemetery with his Uncle Maurizio (Nino DelDuca) after the burial. Maurizio, while also a mobster, is a practical, simple man. Reflecting on his brother's life, all he has to say is, "He had lots of women; that's the best you can hope for."

We feel for Furio, a man who wants something more. He longs for love and country, but has neither. To the New Jersey thugs, he's a "zip," and he laments the fact that he can't be with Carmela, the love of his life. His uncle hears him out and concludes the situation is hopeless. The only solution would be to kill Tony and he knows that's not really an option. It's not how things work in New Jersey, at least not for him.

When Furio returns, he spends the night at an upstate casino with Tony and the crew. He seethes as he observes Tony's unbridled lust and gluttony. In one of the show's most harrowing scenes, he contemplates pushing a drunk, urinating Tony into a whirling helicopter propeller. After this scene Furio disappears back to Italy, leaving Carmela heartbroken.

Furio and Carmela's relationship is a housewife's romance novel fantasy, but we still root for them, because their chemistry is real. And, like anything that threatens Tony's status quo, it's snuffed out.

> **NARRATIVE IMPACT: 2   CINEMATIC: 7   KILLER PERFORMANCES: 2**
> **ELEMENT OF SURPRISE: 1   TOTAL SCORE: 12**

RALPH CIFARETTO

Strangled by Tony Soprano in Episode 4.9, "Whoever Did This"

Ralph Cifaretto dodges death more than any character on *The Sopranos*, other than Tony. He's almost killed on orders from John "Johnny Sack" Sacrimoni (Vincent Curatola) for telling a nasty joke about Ginny (Denise Borino), Sacrimoni's overweight wife. He barely escapes a mauling at Tony's hand for murdering the naive young stripper Tracee. Whether or not he deserves a serious (or permanent) punishment for talking up the card game robbery to young, dumb Jackie Jr. is also debatable. What's not up for discussion is that he's a psychotic, coked-up menace with terrible taste in movies (*Gladiator*? really?) who pisses off everybody in his life: man, woman, and child. He sticks around because he's a made man and, more importantly, because he earns. And he's not without other skills. He's got the sharpest tongue—sometimes silver, sometimes forked—on the show. The talented, well-traveled actor Joe Pantoliano shows how quickly the smarmy Ralph can turn on his Eddie Haskell charm and how his quick wit allows him to insult his peers without their having any clue what hit them, especially Paulie. He's got verbal dexterity and probably the highest IQ in the crime family after Tony, but Ralph's a broken, depraved scumbag.

Of course, Ralph's real role on *The Sopranos*, like Richie Aprile before him, is as a foil for Tony. Ralph's a guy whose behavior creates constant agita, backing Tony into a corner and pushing him to do things he doesn't want to do—things that are bad for his business and his soul. When Tony *finally* kills him, it's ambiguous whether Ralph is guilty of torching the stable and killing Tony's beloved horse, Pie-O-My. It doesn't actually matter. This is capital punishment for cumulative crimes.

The common denominator in his transgressions is that he's always fucking with Tony: his living, his peace of mind, his relationship with New York, his desire to keep Jackie Jr. straight, and his place of business. He even starts sleeping with Tony's sister. It's just Tony's good luck that Janice ends up kicking him down the stairs, freeing Tony from the risk of his becoming family (again, echoes of Richie Aprile). But it's not as easy to get Ralph out of the DiMeo family. At least not until "Whoever Did This." The title of Season Four's ninth episode is a joke, because there was only one person who was ever going to wring Ralphie's neck: Tony Soprano.

In Ralphie's death episode, director Tim Van Patten and writers Mitchell Burgess and Robin Green deliver a kind of perverse twist on the three visitors in *A Christmas Carol* (it's worth noting the episode aired in November 2002). Ralph experiences a personal tragedy, which results in three scenes where he displays humility and empathy, earning our sympathy. (Superfans have noticed—and it's even included in Amazon Prime's streaming notes—that Ralphie's dialogue in this episode includes several lyrics from The Rolling Stones' "Sympathy for the Devil," a song title that might have made for a cute though too obvious episode title.)

In the inciting incident of "Whoever Did This" Ralph's son, Justin, suffers a terrible accident as he's impaled with an arrow while playing Lord of the Rings with his friend in his father's backyard. It's a cruel irony that their dangerous game echoes Ralphie's violent reenactments of *Gladiator*. Making matters worse, Ralph should have been watching the kids. Instead he was lolling in his bathtub.

With Justin in critical condition, we meet Ralph's ex-wife, Ronnie (Marissa Matrone). We get the sense that Ralph, like Tony, tried to balance his family and crime life, but his appetites and impulses won over years ago. After a dustup with his ex, the grief-stricken and enraged Ralph explodes at the boy who accidentally injured his son. Tony pushes Ralph against the wall, his hands on his shoulders and neck. He's just restraining him physically, but the shot of Tony grasping Ralph foreshadows the gruesome violence yet to come.

While sitting vigil for Justin, Ralph receives a visit from someone from his past: ex-girlfriend Rosalie Aprile, a woman he left because he was exhausted by her grief over her son's murder. Ralph shows more humanity in this scene than we've seen from him before, though we can't forget he's the guy who ordered Jackie Jr.'s murder. "I just didn't understand what you were going through, Roe," he says. "I was stupid. I'm sorry."

The next of Ralph's three meetings is with Father Phil. "Pleased to meet ya": Ralph's first words evoke The Stones and tell us all we need to know about his previous relationship with the Church. In their conversation, Ralph alludes to the awful things he's done and his belief that God's punishing his son for Ralph's sins. "I would do anything," he says, weeping, "if Justin could even walk again."

These two visits have an obvious impact on Ralph. He funds a Rutgers scholarship and asks Rosalie to marry him. Ralph, the show's requisite devil for two seasons, is suddenly Ebenezer Scrooge on Christmas morning. But he has one more stop to make.

Ralph delivers an envelope of cash to Tony and breaks down crying in front of him. Ever the predator, Tony feeds on his vulnerability and tells him he's been sleeping with Ralph's girlfriend Valentina (Leslie Bega). He then suggests Ralphie visit their horse, Pie-O-My. Ralph demurs, as she's more Tony's horse now than his. The dynamic is exactly where Tony wants it: Ralphie loses composure and expresses envy for Tony's life and in return, Tony asserts he's taken Ralphie's woman and his horse.

After this visit Tony receives a ferocious counterpunch: Pie-O-My dies in a stable fire. He crouches next to the horse's corpse, hidden under tarp and chain. It's dragged away, and the horse's adorable goat companion bleats in mourning, expressing what Tony can't.

Tony, not buying the story of an electrical fire, goes to see Ralph. Although Tony seems friendly enough, we know the signs aren't good. Ralphie offers Tony eggs (just as Richie Aprile did before he died) and there's a carton of Tropicana on the counter (there's never sunshine in Soprano-land when OJ is involved). When Tony shares news of the terrible stable fire, Ralph's reaction is hard to read: Is he feigning surprise? He's also just received positive news about his son's recovery, so it makes sense that would be his focus. Tony shares the darker details of Pie-O-My's death, and Ralph counters with affectionate mentions of his son (Justin is his Tiny Tim). Finally, Tony accuses him directly. Ralph maintains his innocence, but, because the horse's death is a financial boon, responds, "But so what?!" Compared to the situation with his son, Pie-O-My doesn't rate for him.

(Did Ralph do it? The scene was famously shot two ways: with Pantoliano being asked to play it as if he'd committed the arson, and again as if he hadn't. It's rumored that scenes from both versions were used in the finished print.)

The confrontation becomes violent following a quick-witted insult from Ralph; Tony clocks him with a sucker-punch right hook and the battle begins. In one of the series' wittiest sick jokes, Ralphie's kitchen becomes the Roman Colosseum of *Gladiator*, an arena filled with an arsenal of unconventional weapons: frying pans, salad bowls, glassware, and roach spray are all used with lethal intent by these Jersey warriors. Tony's accumulated rage from months and months of frustration spills out. When he holds Ralph against the wall, just as he did in the earlier hospital scene, he's no longer trying to pacify. He's trying to kill. When he delivers the fatal blows, he asks, "She was a beautiful innocent creature, what did she ever do to you?" He could be talking about Pie-O-My, certainly, but the words double for Tracee, the murdered dancer. And, to a lesser extent, Ralph's ex-wife, Ronnie, and his ex-girlfriend Rosalie. Hell, we can even toss in Paulie's mom, Nucci (Frances Ensemplare), whom Ralph cruelly prank-calls earlier in the episode. Ralph was an equal-opportunity bastard.

Tony calls Christopher to help him dispose of the body, and Ralph's bathtub becomes a Grand Guignol chop shop. Christopher's placing Ralph's severed head in a bowling ball bag is one final *Gladiator* joke, a reference to the movie's oft-quoted decapitation scene, when Russell Crowe's Maximus screams to the people, "Are you not entertained?" In this case the entertainment is the comeuppance of Ralph Cifaretto, a devil vanquished.

A pair of final images allude to the source of Tony's rage and suggest that Ralph got what he deserved. When Tony and Christopher take Ralph's headless corpse to the river, it's under tarp and chains, mirroring the final shot of Pie-O-My. And after the clean-up, Tony showers and sleeps at the Bing. The hardest part is cleansing the toxic roach spray from his eyes.

When he wakes up with his sight restored, he checks out his face and eyes in the mirror. His gaze lingers on a Polaroid of Tracee. It's the only memorial she'll ever get.

> **NARRATIVE IMPACT: 7   CINEMATIC: 10   KILLER PERFORMANCES: 10**
> **ELEMENT OF SURPRISE: 10   TOTAL SCORE: 37**

MINERVA "MINN" MATRONE

Smothered to death by Paulie Gualtieri during an interrupted burglary in Episode 4.12, "Eloise"

Minn Matrone (Fran Anthony). Oy vey. The queen hen. While not a Green Grove resident, she holds influence at the canasta table and, along with Cookie Cirillo (Anna Berger), makes Paulie's sweet, simple mother's transition into the expensive retirement community a painful and lonely one. Matrone boasts of her husband, Salvatore's, business success in the barber's tool trade ("precision cutlery, forty-six years"). Even worse, she cuts people down. When Paulie talks about Nucci's special moment at *Man of La Mancha* ("Richard Kiley stared at Ma the whole time he was singin'") she retorts, "Give me Sondheim any day."

Later, when Cookie lets slip that Minn keeps her ample savings stashed at home, Paulie's ears prick up and he sniffs an opportunity to make up for his recent run of light envelopes to Tony.

The resulting burglary botch and murder is a fan favorite. Possibly because *we all* know a Minn or two, and maybe because Paulie—the meanest mug of them all except when it comes to his ma—has such a difficult time dispatching this old battle-axe. She goes for her Life Alert button and knees him in the crotch. He's not as nimble as he once was. We recall his line when he sees Minn and Cookie in an earlier episode: "When I was a kid, you two were old ladies. Now I'm old, and you two are still old."

He finally wrestles her down, slippers in the air. Her last audible words are: "You were always a little bastard!" Indeed. But he gets the 'scarole he needs to even up with Tony and helps his mom rise a rung or two on the Green Grove social ladder.

> **NARRATIVE IMPACT: 3 CINEMATIC: 6 KILLER PERFORMANCES: 8**
> **ELEMENT OF SURPRISE: 8 TOTAL POINTS: 25**

CREDENZO CURTIS AND STANLEY JOHNSON

Killed by multiple gun shots at close range by Benny Fazio and Petey LaRosa in Episode 4.13, "Whitecaps"

Heroin dealers from Irvington, Curtis (Curtiss Cook) and Johnson (Universal) are hired by Christopher Moltisanti for a very high-profile job: the assassination of NYC crime boss and head of one of the five families, Carmine Lupertazzi (Tony Lip). Requested by Johnny Sack, Tony tasks Moltisanti, fresh from rehab, to take care of it. When the hit's called off (Tony gets cold feet), there can be no witnesses, so he lures the thugs under the pretense of collecting their kill fee. When the deal is done, Benny Fazio (Max Casella) and Petey LaRosa (Jeffrey Marchetti) rush each side of Curtis and Johnson's Chevy Blazer and riddle it with bullets—murder in stereo. The expendable pair represent the only deaths in what's arguably the most emotionally draining episode of the series. Unless you count the death of Whitecaps owner Alan Sapinsly's (Bruce Altman's) ego.

> **NARRATIVE IMPACT: 1 CINEMATIC: 5 KILLER PERFORMANCES: 3**
> **ELEMENT OF SURPRISE: 3 TOTAL POINTS: 12**

SEASON FIVE

RAOUL, A WAITER AT KING NEPTUNE RESTAURANT AND BAR IN ATLANTIC CITY

Hit in the head with a brick thrown by Christopher Moltisanti then shot to death by Paulie Gualtieri while convulsing from traumatic brain injury in Episode 5.1, "Two Tonys"

Tony famously defends the more unsavory aspects of his line of work to Dr. Melfi by telling her, "Everybody knows the stakes." This rationale provides the audience with a pass to enjoy the show's gangster-on-gangster violence. Sometimes we're so intoxicated by the Mob trappings and living vicariously through their lawless lives that we can forget their abhorrent sociopathology. Then scenes like the death of Raoul (Omar Chagall) arrive like an ice-cold shower to remind us of the crew's true nature.

Raoul's caught in the middle of (another) Moltisanti-Gualtieri pissing contest, this one over who covers the bill for their Atlantic City dinner of $1,184 (nearly $1,700 in 2020 money!), thanks to Paulie running up the tab to burn Christopher's buns. They're about to come to blows (or worse) in the parking lot when Raoul interrupts them. Moltisanti skimped on the tip (he left a measly 1.35 percent) so Raoul follows him out of the restaurant, first in confusion, then in protest. That's when they brutally assault him and, when they realize he's badly hurt, decide to commit murder as easily as Paulie ordered the Lyonnaise potatoes.

The next morning, the gangsters bond over their close call. Then the newly sober Chris goes back to reading Mel B.'s *My Search for Bill W.*, about the founder of Alcoholics Anonymous. Chris and Paulie can make amends, but none for poor Raoul.

NARRATIVE IMPACT: 4   CINEMATIC: 5   KILLER PERFORMANCES: 6
ELEMENT OF SURPRISE: 7   TOTAL POINTS: 22

JOSEPH "JOEY" COGO

Killed in a payment dispute in Episode 5.2, "Rat Pack"

A previously unmentioned hood, Joey Cogo (David Copeland), is brought to the attention of Adriana La Cerva (Drea de Matteo) by her handler, Agent Sanseverino (Karen Young), and another agent named Jefferies (John Viscardi). The agents show her pictures of his dead body, and Adriana admits to having recently met him. "Rat Pack" is the most noir and hard-boiled episode of *The Sopranos*, filled with clandestine meetings in parking lots on rainy nights, casual betrayals, and twitchy informants. This scene—and episode—reinforce the idea that kind, confused Adriana is all femme, no fatale.

NARRATIVE IMPACT: 1   CINEMATIC: 2   KILLER PERFORMANCES: 6
ELEMENT OF SURPRISE: 1   TOTAL POINTS: 10

CARMINE LUPERTAZZI SR.

Dies following a stroke while lunching on a golf course with John Sacrimoni, Tony Soprano, and Angelo Garepe in Episode 5.2, "Rat Pack"

Carmine Lupertazzi Sr.'s character was conceived in the tradition of Scorsese movie Mob bosses who don't move a lot or say much of anything.

That said, they style their stoicism so that the slightest pause or gesture can put mayhem in motion—consider Paul Sorvino in *Goodfellas* and Pasquale Cajano in *Casino*. When Lupertazzi strokes out with a mouthful of egg salad (too many gherkins!), his death creates a New York power struggle that directly results in seven subsequent murders.

Fun Fact: Frank Anthony Vallelonga (aka Tony Lip), who plays Lupertazzi, is the factual basis for Viggo Mortensen's character in 2019's Oscar winner *Green Book*.

NARRATIVE IMPACT: 7   CINEMATIC: 4   KILLER PERFORMANCES: 5
ELEMENT OF SURPRISE: 5   TOTAL POINTS: 21

JACK MASSARONE

Murdered on Tony's order for informing on the DiMeo and
Lupertazzi crime families in Episode 5.2, "Rat Pack"

New Jersey general contractor Jack Massarone (Robert Desiderio) is the rare *Sopranos* character who hits the trifecta: he's a patsy (he's tricked into paying off Tony to stop Reverend James's protesters in "Do Not Resuscitate"), a co-conspirator (in bid-rigging and skimming at the Newark Esplanade and other jobs), *and* an informant for the Feds. It's this last role that lands him in the trunk of a car.

The episode begins with Jack meeting Tony in a Fairfield, New Jersey, diner. Unbeknownst to Tony, Jack has a secret microphone implanted in his ridiculous Newark M.O.S.T. hat. That's the one-hundred-million-dollar Museum of Science and Trucking, as previously announced by Assemblyman Zellman (Peter Riegert). When Tony suggests Jack remove his hat, he explains that he's just started Rogaine. A thin excuse. As if this hat weren't conspicuous enough, Massarone brings Tony a large (and gaudy) painting of three Rat Packers: Frank Sinatra, Sammy Davis Jr., and Dean Martin. No Bogie. No Bishop. No Lawford. It's a telling number, because "The Rat Pack" centers on three snitches: Massarone, capo Raymond Curto (George Loros), and Adriana La Cerva. Massarone is the only one sniffed out in this episode, but Adriana isn't far behind.

While the hat and picture fail to tip off Tony, he catches a break when Patsy Parisi (Dan Grimaldi), who has a cop on the payroll, tells Tony that Feds were tailing him and Massarone. Tony's still not sure, though, even after meeting with Jack specifically to gauge his behavior. It's only after the meeting, as he stands in front of the mirror assessing his prodigious gut, that Tony recalls Jack's compliment, lifted from page one of a sycophant's playbook, "Have you lost weight?" And with that, pop goes the weasel.

NARRATIVE IMPACT: 5 CINEMATIC: 5 KILLER PERFORMANCES: 5
ELEMENT OF SURPRISE: 5 TOTAL POINTS: 20

LORRAINE CALLUZZO AND JASON EVANINA

Shot to death by Joe "Joey Peeps" Peparelli and Billy Leotardo in Episode 5.4, "All Happy Families . . ."

"My Lady D'Arbanville, why do you sleep so still?" Cat Stevens aka Yusuf Islam sings, in a song inspired by his late 1960s girlfriend, Warhol superstar Patti D'Arbanville. In her role as the lady shylock Lorraine Calluzzo, the actress's "heart seems so silent" because she's kicking up points to Carmine Lupertazzi Jr. rather than to Johnny Sack, and she pays the ultimate price. D'Arbanville has only four scenes in the series, but she makes them all count.

While on collections, Lorraine and Jason (Frank Fortunato) stop in a Brooklyn pub to pick up a payment. They're interrupted by the Leotardo brothers, Phil and Billy (Frank Vincent and Chris Caldovino), and Joe "Joey Peeps" Peparelli (Joe Maruzzo), all members of Team Sacrimoni. They duct-tape Lorraine to a chair before Phil holds a phone book to her chest and pulls the trigger. Lucky for her, the slug only reaches the R's. Vincent gives us one of Phil's best lines (and that's saying something) when he tells Lorraine, "Next time, there'll be no next time."

Of course there's a next time. Lorraine exits the shower while Edison Lighthouse's 1970 hit "Love Grows (Where My Rosemary Goes)" plays in her living room. She discovers that Peparelli and Billy Leotardo have broken in and executed Evanina. She runs naked through her house, hoping to escape, but is murdered by Billy. We can think of Lorraine as North Jersey's Helen of Troy. As the Lupertazzi-Sacrimoni war kicks off, her death launches a thousand bullets.

NARRATIVE IMPACT: 7   CINEMATIC: 6   KILLER PERFORMANCES: 6
ELEMENT OF SURPRISE: 5   TOTAL POINTS: 24

AUNT CONCETTA, VINCENT PATRONELLA, MRS. CRILLEY, THE SEVEN-YEAR-OLD SON OF SAL THE DRY CLEANER, UNCLE ZIO

From various causes in episode 5.7, "In Camelot"

Junior Soprano is going stir-crazy on house arrest and, following the death of a Soprano aunt, discovers that he's allotted a five-hour furlough to attend funerals. He embraces these windows of freedom with the gusto of a teenager off to Six Flags. He shows a complete disregard for funeral etiquette—referring to a post-burial get-together as an "after-party"—and starts scouring the obituaries for tenuous relations (the Feds only grant furlough permission if it's a death in the family). As he pushes his lawyer, Harold Melvoin (Richard Portnow), to be more creative, his behavior goes from impolite to vile, chatting up mourners about the delicious chicken ("good and spicy!") at a memorial for a young child.

But it all catches up with him at the funeral of Uncle Zio (Fred Caiaccia). Zio is the widow of Aunt Concetta, who dies at the beginning of the episode, and his death inspires an especially lachrymose eulogy from Father Phil. When Father Phil wraps up, Junior falls to pieces, the weeks of grief compounding in that moment. He ends the episode on lockdown with nothing to do but contemplate his mortality.

NARRATIVE IMPACT: 3   CINEMATIC: 4   KILLER PERFORMANCES: 8
ELEMENT OF SURPRISE: 1   TOTAL POINTS: 16

JOE "JOEY PEEPS" PEPARELLI AND HEATHER

Shot to death by Tony Blundetto in Episode 5.8, "Marco Polo"

New York gangster Joe "Joey Peeps" Peparelli is aligned on Johnny Sack's side of the battle for control of the Lupertazzi crime family. His assassination, commissioned by Carmine's allies Rusty Millio (Frankie Valli) and Angelo Garepe (Joe Santos), is a receipt for the murders of Lorraine Calluzzo and Jason Evanina. Like many killings on *The Sopranos*, Peparelli's death is less about the target and more about the man pulling the trigger, in this case, Tony Blundetto (Steve Buscemi), a paroled gangster and close cousin of Tony Soprano.

Since his release, Tony B makes an extraordinary effort to go straight but, overwhelmed with envy and seduced by vice, he slowly returns to the gangster path. He decides to take an assassination contract he's previously refused after spending a day with his two sons basking in wealth and privilege (things they lack) at the Soprano home, where the family has gathered for the seventy-fifth birthday party of Carmela's father, Hugh DeAngelis (Tom Aldredge).

After the party, Tony B sits in his mother's kitchen, stirring his Tang while the small TV in the kitchen broadcasts a cooking show. The host uses a mallet to pound meat over and over again. The hammering suggests the incessant reminders that echo in Tony B's head—of his cousin's success and the life he lost when he went to prison. A minor detail, but an important one: the Tang he makes is an ersatz substitute for Tony's ubiquitous orange juice, a motif carried over from *The Godfather*. And that's how Tony B feels, like Tony the Lesser. And so he defies his cousin Tony's wishes and accepts the murder contract.

With cold-blooded conviction, he goes for the kill, which is beautifully staged by director John Patterson. As Joey Peeps and Heather (Erin Stutland), a prostitute, exit a brothel, we can just make out the song coming from the whorehouse speakers: Bon Jovi's "Wanted Dead or Alive," which rocked America (and especially Jovi's home state of New Jersey) in 1986, the year Tony B went to prison. As the pair enters Peeps's car, Tony B makes his move.

Patterson gives us a rare first-person, handheld Steadicam shot to put us in Tony B's new Italian loafers. And in seconds Peeps and his companion are shot dead. It's not a clean job, though. We soon discover Tony B was seen and he's injured on the job—Joey Peeps's car runs over his foot, giving him a terrible limp. It seems that, seventeen years out of the game, Tony B has lost his step.

The murder of Peeps is just one of many in the ever-escalating New York turf war, but it both signals Tony B's return to his 1980s gangster life and sets him on a collision course with his cousin.

Fun Fact: We're treated to a terrific gangster blunder when Silvio's guys commission a tombstone that reads "Joe Peeps" rather than the victim's given name of Peparelli.

**NARRATIVE IMPACT: 7   CINEMATIC: 10   KILLER PERFORMANCES: 8
ELEMENT OF SURPRISE: 6   TOTAL POINTS: 31**

ANGELO GAREPE

Shot to death by Phil and Billy Leotardo in Episode 5.11,
"The Test Dream"

When the "Class of '04" gets released from prison, the most soft-spoken and easygoing of the bunch is Angelo Garepe, the former Lupertazzi family consigliere. Happily retired and eager to spend time with his grandson, he's more or less out of the mix. Joe Santos, who plays Garepe, has an avuncular presence and a rough-and-tumble résumé, with a long recurring role as a good-hearted detective on *The Rockford Files* and a part in *The Friends of Eddie Coyle* among other gangster movies (see pages 154 and 148, respectively, about the influence of these two works on *The Sopranos*).

This mellowed-out mobster has a soft spot for Tony B, who amused him in prison with his Jackie Gleason impressions. Garepe wants to help Carmine Jr. get revenge for Lorraine Calluzzo's death and help his prison buddy get paid. He arranges for Tony B to handle the wet work. This sets off a bloody tit-for-tat and Angelo, despite his desire to keep his beak out of the business, finds himself cornered by the Leotardo brothers and, shortly thereafter, in the trunk of a car, where he's shot to death.

It's another playful *Sopranos* irony because Frank Vincent famously finds himself in Angelo's position in *Goodfellas* after his character, Billy Batts, insults the wrong retired shoeshiner.

NARRATIVE IMPACT: 7   CINEMATIC: 5   KILLER PERFORMANCES: 5
ELEMENT OF SURPRISE: 7   TOTAL POINTS: 24

BILLY LEOTARDO

Shot to death by Tony Blundetto in Episode 5.11, "The Test Dream"

We first hear of Billy Leotardo's murder in "The Test Dream" when Christopher breaks the news to Tony, but we experience it through his brother's memory in the following episode, "Long Term Parking." It's easy to forget that we witness Billy's death since this episode ends with the most famous and tragic murder on the show: that of Adriana La Cerva. Billy's death and Tony Soprano's reluctance to hand over his cousin Tony B provide Phil Leotardo with motivation for making life difficult for the Sopranos at every opportunity for the rest of the series.

The images we see will haunt Phil for the rest of his life. It's a point-of-view flashback, but director Tim Van Patten positions him in front of a shop window so we can see his reflection. First, we see his brother, then, racing to the right, Tony B. But it's too late. His brother's already dead. Phil takes a bullet himself and, from his vantage point, we see Tony B race off. The final image before we return to the present is Phil's anguish reflected in the glass. We may not like him, but we certainly understand why later, he's so bent on revenge.

NARRATIVE IMPACT: 7   CINEMATIC: 8   KILLER PERFORMANCES: 8
ELEMENT OF SURPRISE: 5   TOTAL POINTS: 28

GILBERT NIEVES

Stabbed to death by Matush (with an assist from Kamal) in the Crazy Horse back office in Episode 5.12, "Long Term Parking"

Early in this episode, we see Gilbert Nieves's soggy corpse washed up on a Long Branch beach when his body is discovered by a group of young sea scouts. He's the victim of a murder committed by Matush and his friend Kamal (Homie Doroodian) at Adriana La Cerva's club, the Crazy Horse.

Dramatically, this murder—and the tragic events it sets in motion—conveys that Adriana isn't made for her fiancé, Christopher's, gangster world. She's too trusting and doesn't have the acumen. It also shows the danger in letting wannabes and hangers-on into the inner circle.

Matush has already been beaten by Furio for selling drugs at the club *and* he got Jackie Jr. and his friends killed when he abandoned his wheel-man post at the card game hold-up (see page 236). Still, Adriana does him a favor, because, as she tells the Feds, he's "nice," "not a bad person," and "very religious." Yikes, Adriana.

NARRATIVE IMPACT: 7   CINEMATIC: 4   KILLER PERFORMANCES: 3
ELEMENT OF SURPRISE: 5   TOTAL POINTS: 19

ADRIANA LA CERVA

Shot to death by Silvio Dante in Episode 5.12, "Long Term Parking"

In 2004, when "Long Term Parking" aired, audiences didn't think David Chase could show us anything more upsetting than the murder of Bada Bing dancer Tracee in the earlier episode "University." Turns out, we had no idea how far he could go. Adriana La Cerva, former restaurant hostess, Aprile niece, and Crazy Horse owner, is a naive but strong-hearted woman who deeply loves her emotional and often abusive fiancé, Christopher. She ends up a victim not of circumstance but of transactions. When all the deals are done, she's left alone to die because she had nothing to offer but her love.

From the start of the episode, Adriana's surrounded by wheeler-dealers making trade-ups, trade-ins, and value swaps in family and in business—essentially we learn there's no difference between the two in the world of *The Sopranos*. We see the shrewd Carmela eating with Tony at Nuovo Vesuvio, where she names the price for him to move back in. It's a boardroom-worthy negotiation. She nets $600,000 from her husband for a lot of land to build a spec house.

While Tony and Carmela wrap their negotiation, Adriana's pulled into her own. Thanks to the murder of Gilbert Nieves at the Crazy Horse, the Feds have her as an accessory and lean on her to help their RICO case against Tony. They're tossing offers at her and finally she bites. She believes she can flip Christopher. In the scene where she confesses to him, Drea de Matteo and Michael Imperioli give performances as strong as any on the show. She's simultaneously in love, terrified, and hopeful. He's enraged and we think for a minute he'll kill her, but he stops just short. If Christopher and Adriana's love is true, their only choice is to flip. It's unfortunate what she offers him isn't enough.

The transaction and exchange theme is ubiquitous in the episode. Phil Leotardo wants a corpse as payback for his brother's murder and, in lieu of Tony Blundetto, Christopher is suggested. And the Feds, looking to put together a package that'll sway Moltisanti, appeal to his screenwriting aspirations and put in a call to Sam Goldwyn Jr. All these dealers, and Adriana's the only person holding no chips. She thinks she's got Christopher and that's the belief that seals her fate.

When Christopher leaves to get cigarettes and think things over, he spies a ragamuffin family piled in their beater car at a gas station. He may have fantasized briefly with Adriana about moving to Lake George and writing his memoirs, but he'll sacrifice her life if the cost is a schmuck's existence.

Earlier, when Christopher is furious over his treatment from Tony, Adriana tells him, "You're a better man than he is, a better person." She's not wrong, she just futzes the math—he's only better by percentage points. He's more accurate when he tells her, "That's the guy, Adriana. My Uncle Tony. The guy I'm going to hell for."

When Tony calls her with the news of Christopher's attempted suicide, we suspect it's bullshit. In a cruel twist, we see her escape fantasy and think she's driving south toward D.C., and we want nothing more than for her to get away from these people. But the daydream fades away and it's Silvio who is doing the driving. The pompadour-sporting pimp plays easy-going, but we know that's a flimsy veneer.

We're spared the agony of watching Adriana die—we see a shot of the Ramapo trees as the gunshot explodes. The sound echoes the champagne bottle pop that christens Tony Soprano's return to his family earlier in the episode.

In the episode's final minutes, we see trees again and think maybe, just maybe Adriana escaped. But the trees are on Carmela's spec house lot. Unlike Adriana, Carm had something left to trade.

**NARRATIVE IMPACT: 10   CINEMATIC: 10   KILLER PERFORMANCES: 10
ELEMENT OF SURPRISE: 10   TOTAL POINTS: 40**

TONY BLUNDETTO

Shot to death by Tony Soprano in Episode 5.13, "All Due Respect"

Tony B is portrayed by our generation's king of the sad sack, Steve Buscemi (all due respect to William H. Macy). His performance is a masterpiece. After seasons where deplorable psychos Richie Aprile and Ralph Cifaretto are Tony's primary antagonists, it makes sense that Chase wanted to mix it up and create a more sympathetic foil for Soprano. Tony B did seventeen years in prison for a hijacking he was supposed to commit alongside his cousin, who no-showed. The secret Tony Soprano harbors is that he left Tony B alone due to a panic attack and subsequent fall, then concocted a story that he was jumped by an African-American gang. Compounding his guilt, his cousin's incarceration precipitated the demise of his marriage and his estrangement from his runaway daughter.

During this time, Tony Soprano's Mafia star has risen and his family has flourished. Tony B has a few pangs of self-pity ("If things had gone a different way back then, who knows?") but retains no obvious ill will. He wants to go straight and achieve on his own. Conversely, Tony Soprano's lie is choking him and the feelings that emerge (with Dr. Melfi's help) quickly convey that there's only room for one Tony. Throughout Season Five, we see how each unconsciously boxes the other in until there's no room left for either to breathe and one of them must go.

The two Tonys bristle against each other even as Tony B tries to make it as a legit massage therapist. Soprano takes his cousin's Jackie Gleason impression ("Hmmm boy, are you fat!") a little too personally, and gives him the business for doling out massages at Satriale's, prompting Tony B's dead-serious "You're crowdin' me." Two Tonys? The name patch on Blundetto's work jacket reads "Luis" and that's no wardrobe malfunction. Despite the bumps, we believe that Tony B might go straight. Unfortunately, he's nudged back into the business and, as we see from his discipline when he works his straight jobs, he doesn't do things halfway. Tony B makes choices both professionally and emotionally that push his cousin into a corner.

The cousins share a scene together before their final tragic meeting. Director John Patterson's construction and direction in this conflict-free exchange are brilliant. Tony Soprano visits Tony B at Aunt Quintina's (Rae Allen's) house to collect money and to kvetch about his problems. He is ignorant to that fact that Angelo Garepe, Tony B's prison pal, has been murdered and that Tony B's apoplectic. The two Tonys are totally disconnected from one another but are trying to act as though everything is fine. In the cramped family room, neither can get comfortable. Tony Soprano sits in a chair that's too small for his hulking frame. Tony B, masking his rage and hurt over Angelo's death, never stops fidgeting, collecting trinkets and trash littered around the room, yelling at his mother, and chastising his children. As Tony complains about his hospitalized *comare*, Valentina, and fantasizes about Charmaine Bucco (Kathrine Narducci), Tony B only half listens before ushering him out. These cousins, attached at the hip for so many years, can no longer fit in a room together.

After Tony B murders Billy Leotardo and shoots his older brother, Phil, to avenge Angelo, Soprano is left with no choice. The New York mobsters demand a head and so Tony betrays his cousin, but not before we see his wistful recollection of their days spent upstate, running around the Kinderhook farm with shotguns. As Van Morrison's "Glad Tidings" plays, only one Tony carries a shotgun on Uncle Pat's property, where he blasts Tony B on the front porch. Morrison sings, "Open your eyes so you may see," and while Tony B's eyes remain open in death, he never fully understood the man his cousin had become, a boss who delivers "glad tidings from New York."

Indictment for Lazy Screenwriting: Just as Tony B develops a sense of personal pride derived from hard work, a bag with $12,000 falls from the sky (actually, it's thrown from a speeding car) and funds his reentry into the gangster life. This cheapo idea doesn't jibe with the high standards of *The Sopranos'* creative team.

**NARRATIVE IMPACT: 10   CINEMATIC: 10   KILLER PERFORMANCES: 10
ELEMENT OF SURPRISE: 9   TOTAL SCORE: 39**

SEASON SIX

RAYMOND CURTO

> *Dies from a stroke while meeting with*
> *FBI agent Robyn Sanseverino in her car*
> *in Episode 6.1, "Members Only"*

Over the course of the series, we don't spend much time with Ray Curto, despite his high rank in the DiMeo crime family. In Season One, he's a captain who is offered the opportunity to take over as boss but declines, citing the responsibility of caring for his son, who has multiple sclerosis. Early in Season Three, we discover that Curto is wired for sound, a nimble rat who never comes under suspicion, even while suspected rats like Jimmy Altieri and definitive ones like Big Pussy are executed. He's lucky he gets to succumb to natural causes!

At his wake, New York capo Rusty Millio and Tony discuss a recent uptick in cooperating witnesses and lament the loss of Ray, a stand-up guy who would never betray the code. Irony.

Like many *Sopranos* deaths, there's a droll aspect to Ray's demise. Yet again, hardworking agent Sanseverino, who was Adriana's handler, loses a major player in her case against Tony. She's unlikely to get a promotion.

NARRATIVE IMPACT: 2   CINEMATIC: 2
KILLER PERFORMANCES: 2
ELEMENT OF SURPRISE: 5   TOTAL POINTS: 11

DICK BARONE

Dies from ALS (Lou Gehrig's disease) between Seasons Five and Six, as noted in Episode 6.1, "Members Only"

Dick Barone's (Joe Lisi's) company, Barone Sanitation & Cartage, plays a larger role in the series than the man himself, as the carting business is, and always has been, a major revenue driver for the DiMeo crime family. We tend to hear about the organization only when there's a problem. For example, in Season Two's "House Arrest," when Tony needs to lie low and actually show at his no-show job to keep up appearances. Or when, in the same episode, Richie Aprile jeopardizes the carting industry's relationship with the Mob by empowering drivers to sell coke along garbage routes.

Dick's off-screen death from ALS, noted at the beginning of Season Six, creates strife between the DiMeo and Lupertazzi families, as Dick's son Jason (Chris Diamantopoulos) is new to the industry and oblivious to his father's arrangements with criminal organizations. When he puts this business up for sale and, worse, sells it to a Lupertazzi family interest, it hits Tony's revenue and forces him to negotiate with Phil Leotardo.

It's also a reminder of Tony's early inclination that he's coming in "at the end of this thing." With a second generation that's either distracted (Christopher), straight-arrow (Jason), weak (A.J.), or devoid of any skills or redeemable qualities (Jackie Jr.), there's nobody left to give the keys to, and no more money-filled garbage trucks backing up to the driveway.

> **NARRATIVE IMPACT: 5   CINEMATIC: 1   KILLER PERFORMANCES: 1**
> **ELEMENT OF SURPRISE: 3   TOTAL POINTS: 10**

TEDDY SPIRODAKIS

Shot to death by Eugene Pontecorvo in a Boston fried chicken joint in Episode 6.1, "Members Only"

Christopher sends Eugene Pontecorvo up to Boston to kill a degenerate gambler on behalf of a bookie named Fritzie. Eugene hopes doing this job will persuade Tony to let him forsake his Mafia vows and retire to Florida.

We see Pontecorvo, who exhibits a range of natural and human emotions with his suburban family, go ice-cold and kill Spirodakis (Joe Caniano) with the precision and efficiency of a longtime contract killer.

On the ride back to New Jersey, director Tim Van Patten clues us in that killing Teddy isn't likely to earn Eugene his ticket out. Blondie's "Dreaming" plays on his car radio while rain pours down outside, Debbie Harry singing, "Imagine something of your very own, something you can have and hold." Eugene tries to wipe Teddy's blood from his face and smudges some on his map, but he can't wash away the blood and he can't escape his oath. It's a good thing that, as Debbie sings, "dreaming is free," because that's as close as poor Eugene can get.

> **NARRATIVE IMPACT: 5 CINEMATIC: 6 KILLER PERFORMANCES: 8
> ELEMENT OF SURPRISE: 3 TOTAL POINTS: 22**

EUGENE PONTECORVO

‖ *Commits suicide by hanging in Episode 6.1, "Members Only"*

We don't see much of Eugene Pontecorvo before his featured role in "Members Only," in which we learn he's eager to get his family out of Jersey and himself out of Tony's crew, thanks to a sizable inheritance from an aunt who married Victor Borge's agent. Still, this new focus is effective as scenes of Eugene and the Pontecorvo family—who are hanging on by a thread—are juxtaposed with ones featuring the reunited Tony and Carmela, who gorge and splurge, the picture of wretched excess.

The Pontecorvos have a forlorn teenage son with a drug problem, a sweet, quiet young daughter, and a bundle of happy memories from Floridian vacations characterized by long days at the beach collecting conch shells. Eugene and his wife, Deanne (Suzanne DiDonna), believe heading south with this jackpot inheritance will solve all their problems. He just needs to get Tony to okay an early retirement, since, as a made man, he's taken an oath. The boss hears him out, but despite Eugene's ingratiating gestures, including a selection of David Yurman watches, Tony plays coy. Over the course of the episode, Eugene frets, fidgets, and commits a contract hit he thinks will seal the deal (see previous entry), while Tony and Carmela return again and again to Nori, a new and expensive sushi restaurant, to put away mountains of tuna, flown in first-class from Tokyo. They only come up for air to buy a new Porsche Cayenne ("like the pepper," Carmela explains). With four trips to the place, it's as though Tony and Carmela are committed to sucking down every morsel in the ocean. It's no coincidence Tony weighs himself in this episode—for the first and only time—and he tips in at 280; his corpulence is in stark opposition to the wiry frame Eugene sports, as a man starving for a way out.

Despite Eugene's best efforts, Tony denies his desired retirement (Eugene hears this secondhand from Silvio) and we learn that, like the deceased Adriana La Cerva and Ray Curto, Pontecorvo has an extra burden: he's a source for federal agent Robyn Sanseverino. A trapped rat, Eugene decides to kill himself. It's unspoken but clear that his dying hope is that he can free his family and that his wife and children go to Florida without him and flourish. We'll never find out, but his son's recent upgrade to intravenous drugs makes it a tenuous proposition at best.

Pontecorvo's death scene is grueling, but it's also arguably the best-directed death in the series. In his final episode, Robert Funaro is extraordinary and makes us wish he'd been given more to do in previous ones. Director Tim Van Patten and his editor, Sidney Wolinsky, play a nasty, effective trick on us. We see Eugene looking through family vacation albums and gripping a seashell in his hand; we have no idea we're on the verge of a grim turn. There's a cut to a close-up of Funaro's silent-film face. What we don't realize is that there's been a location switch. Eugene's no longer in the living room, contemplating his family and future. He's in the basement with a noose around his neck—a grim fact we discover when Wolinsky cuts away to a stationary shot just as Eugene kicks out the box out from under his feet. For forty-five seconds we watch him struggle and die. There is no soundtrack until he is dead, urine leaking from his body and Artie Shaw's "Come Love" bleeding in from the next scene, where Tony, not a care in the world, boils pasta at Junior's house.

Tony's avarice and gluttony are boundless in "Members Only" so it makes sense that in the episode's closing moments, he's shot in his prodigious belly, the bullet fired by his dementia-afflicted uncle. In upcoming episodes, as he lies comatose with a gaping, exposed hole in his stomach, it feels like the last chance he's got for the evil to drain out.

Fun Fact: "Members Only" was nominated for an Emmy for writing.

> **NARRATIVE IMPACT: 6   CINEMATIC: 10   KILLER PERFORMANCES: 10**
> **ELEMENT OF SURPRISE: 8   TOTAL SCORE: 34**

BUILDING SUPERINTENDENT AND TWO COLOMBIAN DEALERS

| *Shot to death by Paulie Gualtieri in Episode 6.3, "Mayham"*

This nameless trio, murdered in a sloppy, bloodbath robbery planned by Vito Spatafore and carried out by Paulie Gualtieri, bears little significance for our narrative. (Though it is fun to watch the sexagenarian Gualtieri struggle in combat and take a blow to the testes.) What's a little more interesting is the million bucks stashed in the dishwasher of their apartment. The money becomes the source of bickering between the aforementioned crooks and subsequent strife for acting boss Silvio Dante. Paulie and Vito don't agree on how the money should be split up between them and are even less enthusiastic about giving Tony's share of $200,000 to Carmela, who teeters on the brink of widowhood as Tony lies in the coma.

These men, who in theory have pledged their lives to Tony, are actually greedy sycophants who, given the choice, would prefer their leader die rather than support his wife. "Mayham" includes a shot that captures their avarice and apathy in a single glance. After feigning grace and happiness at Tony's recovery, they hand Carmela the envelope with the $200k. She's very thankful. But when she looks back at them as they get in the elevator, their sullen mugs betray their true feelings.

> **NARRATIVE IMPACT: 4   CINEMATIC: 6   KILLER PERFORMANCES: 3**
> **ELEMENT OF SURPRISE: 3   TOTAL SCORE: 16**

PAULIE'S AUNT DOTTIE

Dies from natural causes related to Alzheimer's disease in Episode 6.4, "The Fleshy Part of the Thigh"

Despite his apostolic name, the idea of Peter Paul Gualtieri entering a convent seems like the beginning of a backroom joke at Satriale's. Inside, we learn that Paulie's visiting his dying Aunt Dottie (Judith Malina), a nun suffering from Alzheimer's. He's thrown for a loop when he learns she is really his mother; she hooked up with a military man named Russ during the war. Malina—the legendary cofounder of The Living Theatre, known on the big screen for her work in *Dog Day Afternoon*, Paul Mazursky's *Enemies, A Love Story*, and the 1991 movie *The Addams Family*—is terrific in the scene, winded by her illness and desperate to get out her secret. She's so riled and guilt-ridden we immediately want to absolve her. In the scene's final seconds, she shakes her head over and over, clutching her rosary and repeating, "I was a bad girl."

While we feel for her, Paulie doesn't take this news well. He goes topsy-turvy, questioning everything over the next several months, from his adoptive mother's love to his family's medical history. Even guys like Paulie, who work to keep things stupid simple, can be thrown a curveball.

NARRATIVE IMPACT: 3   CINEMATIC: 3   KILLER PERFORMANCES: 8
ELEMENT OF SURPRISE: 7   TOTAL SCORE: 21

RUSTY MILLIO AND EDDIE PIETRO

Shot to death by Salvatore and Italo, Napoletano hit men, in Rusty Millio's driveway in Episode 6.7, "Luxury Lounge"

Rusty Millio isn't the first made man from New York to get clipped in his car, but he is the first to be played by one of the most popular music icons of the twentieth century. Casting the diminutive Frankie Valli as Millio is a meta-move, even for a meta-show, as Valli (not Rusty) factors into the plot twice: one time before Rusty is killed and once after. In the first instance, casino tycoon Chief Doug Smith (Nick Chinlund) cashes in a favor, pressuring Tony and Silvio to call Valli's people to book him for his upstate Connecticut hotel. In Season Six's "Kennedy and Heidi," Nucci Gualtieri dies on the bus back from *Jersey Boys*, the jukebox musical about the Newark-born Valli's career as part of the Four Seasons.

As Rusty, Valli's fun in his small part as a politicking troublemaker, eager to pit Carmine Lupertazzi Jr. against Johnny Sack. His best scene is his nonplussed response to Tony Blundetto's Jackie Gleason impression in "Marco Polo." Later, when Lupertazzi Jr. bows out of the war, Sacrimoni bides his time, then asks Tony Soprano to make "the mayor of Munchkinland" disappear. Tony resists, but finally relents and delegates the task to Christopher. They bring over a pair of Camorra killers (men who work for Annalisa, the Napoletana don) to kill poor Rusty in his driveway. Good thing he outsourced, since no Jersey boy is going to punch Frank Valli's ticket.

Oh, want to know about Eddie Pietro (Nick Annunziata)? He's just Rusty's toadie. Collateral damage with no falsetto.

**NARRATIVE IMPACT: 2   CINEMATIC: 2   KILLER PERFORMANCES: 5
ELEMENT OF SURPRISE: 2   TOTAL SCORE: 11**

NEW ENGLAND CIVILIAN

*Shot in the back of the head by Vito Spatafore in Episode 6.10,
"Moe n' Joe"*

An unnamed man (Guy Paul), adorned in Patagonia and L.L. Bean, parks his car along the side of the road to get his mail. Vito Spatafore, drunk on cheap vodka and speeding away from the quaint New England life he half desires, slams his car into the rear of the man's Jeep Wagoneer.

The man is haughty but reasonable when he demands that they file an accident report. As he leads Vito up to his house, he's shot in the back of the head. The kill echoes Vito's assassination of Jackie Aprile Jr., also shot from behind and left to die upon a snowbank. A cowardly modus operandi for a cowardly man.

Despite his creepy and craven behavior, we were rooting for Vito and his mustachioed lover, Jim "Johnny Cakes" Witowski (John Costelloe). But our empathy and hope for Spatafore die in this New Englander's driveway. These civilian deaths count heavily against their killers, even when the deceased is unlikable. Ultimately, like Phil and Tony, we can't give Vito a pass. But for us it's got nothing to do with his sexuality; it's his lack of humanity.

NARRATIVE IMPACT: 6 CINEMATIC: 5 KILLER PERFORMANCES: 6 ELEMENT OF SURPRISE: 7 TOTAL SCORE: 24

VITO SPATAFORE

Beaten to death with a pool cue and other weapons by Gerry "The Hairdo" Torciano and Dominic "Fat Dom" Gamiello in Episode 6.11, "Cold Stones"

Vito is an oleaginous but high-earning DiMeo family captain who harbors a secret: he's gay. He has a wife, two sweet kids, and a *comare* and, aside from his sexuality, lives the mobster life. When his secret is discovered (he's spotted in a leather bar by a Yonkers goon making extortion collections) he lams it to New Hampshire. In leafy New England, he poses as a writer named Vincent, working on a Rocky Marciano biography. The quaint life agrees with him more than he expected. He has an eye for antiques, loves the local diner's grub, and falls for the short-order cook, a motorcycle-riding volunteer fireman.

But their honeymoon is short-lived. Vito misses the action too much. And despite his prowess as an electrician and his insider's knowledge of construction, it's been so long since he's done an honest day's work that he just *can't*. In one of the series' funniest scenes, we hear Vito's inner monologue as he counts the hours till lunch while doing handyman jobs. When he finally checks his watch, expecting it to be near lunchtime, he discovers it's not even 10 a.m. He grabs his stuff and blows town, without so much as a note for Jim. The likely proposition of death back home is more enticing than another day hammering nails.

When Vito returns to New Jersey, Tony wants to let him go and entertains the idea of setting him up in Atlantic City, but the pressure from Phil Leotardo (and by proxy, Phil's hideous Opus Dei–ish wife) is too much.

Tony, backed into a corner, finally orders him killed. The show's writers have some heart for Vito. He's afforded a final phone call to Jim (which doesn't go well) and a day at Rockefeller Center with his wife, Marie, and their children.

The staging of Vito's inevitable murder is a little too cute. He enters the Fort Lee hotel room where he's hiding out and is immediately accosted by Gerry "The Hairdo" Torciano (John Bianco) and "Fat Dom" Gamiello (Tony Cucci), who duct-tape his mouth. They flick on the light and Phil Leotardo *comes out of the closet,* tells the whimpering Vito he's "a fucking disgrace," and gestures to his pair of hoods to finish Vito off. There's a final cheeky irony, as the shot cuts from Phil's face as he sits on the bed, to the violence, to a close-up of Phil's hand. With a subtle clutch of the bedsheets, Phil's a Catholic soldier on the verge of ecstasy.

NARRATIVE IMPACT: 7   CINEMATIC: 6   KILLER PERFORMANCES: 7
ELEMENT OF SURPRISE: 7   TOTAL SCORE: 27

DOMINIC "FAT DOM" GAMIELLO

Beaten and stabbed to death by Silvio Dante and Carlo Gervasi in Episode 6.11, "Cold Stones"

The portly Dom Gamiello is a made man in the Lupertazzi crime family and member of Phil Leotardo's crew. Along with Gerry "The Hairdo" Torciano, he helps Phil murder Vito in a Fort Lee hotel room (see above).

A couple days later, he swings by Satriale's on his way to visit his daughter in Metuchen. There's the pretense of a payoff from a Canarsie card game, but Dom has really come by to razz the crew about Vito's homosexuality and death.

It's a tasteless (but hilarious) irony that DiMeo captain Carlo Gervasi (Arthur J. Nascarella) is cooking *fra diavolo* with an apron on and consigliere Silvio Dante is cleaning up Satriale's with a Dustbuster. They're the picture of (awkward) homosexual domesticity!

In a backwards and completely unintentional way, these two DiMeo family homophobes end up defending Vito's honor (and their own) when

Dom's teasing goes too far and he suggests maybe Carlo and Vito had a special relationship. Silvio slugs Dom in the back of his head with the Dustbuster and Carlo lunges with a large cooking knife. Despite Silvio's attempt to stop Carlo, within seconds a bloodied Gamiello lies dead on the table. Not what Tony needs as he looks to ease tensions in his relationship with acting boss Phil Leotardo.

Fun Fact: Actor Tony Cucci brought the model of his severed head to SopranosCon. It's an incredible likeness.

**NARRATIVE IMPACT: 5   CINEMATIC: 7   KILLER PERFORMANCES: 7
ELEMENT OF SURPRISE: 7   TOTAL POINTS: 26**

RENÉ LECOURS

*Shot to death by Bobby Baccalieri in Episode 6.13,
"Soprano Home Movies"*

On *The Sopranos*, so many of the most dramatically potent deaths belong to characters who were previously inconsequential to the story. Tracee and Joe Peparelli come to mind. René LeCours (Marc Bonan) can keep them company. He's a young Québecois drummer in a custody battle with the sister of a Montreal man who wants to sell expired pharmaceuticals to Tony and Bobby Baccalieri. In exchange for a better rate, Tony offers to kill LeCours.

He delegates this murder to Bobby—a passive-aggressive move, even for him—because he wants to get even with "Bacala" for flooring him in a drunken fistfight. The gentle (for a mobster) Bobby only hit Tony—his boss and brother-in-law—to defend his wife, Janice's, honor, after Tony relentlessly made jokes about her sexual promiscuity. (No family would be shocked to hear that this all escalated from a friendly game of Monopoly during a lake house vacation.) What makes this delegation doubly cruel is that, on a boat discussing Bobby's professional prospects (Tony is bullish on his future), it comes up that Bobby never "popped his cherry," Mob slang for committing a first murder.

Thanks to Steve Schirripa, one of the most underrated actors on the show, we can feel Bobby's fear and anxiety about the hit as he snaps at Janice and drives away, Montreal bound.

The murder is a beautiful piece of direction and sound design. We see the physically slight LeCours, carrying a box of detergent, walk by the massive Bobby and toward his building's laundry room. After he passes, Bobby confirms his mark's identity with a photograph. We hear the loud tumble dryers, but we could be listening to Bobby's innards as he struggles to suppress his humanity—something he has to do to maintain the status quo and set up a more lucrative future for his wife and three children. And his face, misshapen from the fight with Tony, speaks to the deeper disfigurement inside him when he's forced to take this job.

As LeCours does his laundry, Bobby enters the doorway and steps toward him. He raises his pistol and we see Bobby's reflection in the dryer window. LeCours looks up and, seeing this massive, strange man pointing a pistol at him, he's helpless and terrified. Bobby fires, shooting him through the chest. The bullet crashes through the dryer window, splattering it with blood. Bobby's reflection—the man he was—is no longer visible in the cracked glass.

Bobby walks to the confused, dying man. LeCours grabs Bobby's shirt and tears a piece. It will remain with him, just as Bobby's left a piece of himself in Montreal. Bobby fights back tears and shoots him in the head, completing his task. He heads back out the way he came and leaves behind the gun and the quality that made him different from his cohorts.

When Bobby returns to the family camp, he finds an Elysian scene where his children enjoy a tea party while bathed in a soft summer light. The Drifters' "This Magic Moment" plays. Bobby's toddler daughter, Nica, runs to him ("Daddy!") and he hoists her in the air, holding her close as he looks out onto the lake. The same lake where Tony Soprano committed an evil almost comparable to Michael Corleone's fratricide, taking his brother-in-law's soul out of spite.

**NARRATIVE IMPACT: 8   CINEMATIC: 10   KILLER PERFORMANCES: 10
ELEMENT OF SURPRISE: 7   TOTAL SCORE: 35**

GERRY "THE HAIRDO" TORCIANO

> *Shot to death by a hit man working for Faustino "Doc" Santoro in Episode 6.14, "Stage 5"*

Gerry Torciano is Phil Leotardo's right hand and seems like a reasonable guy compared to Lupertazzi family menaces like Phil, Butch DeConcini (Greg Antonacci), and Salvatore "Coco" Cogliano (Armen Garo). His death, which occurs while he and Silvio dine with their *comares* in Brooklyn and chat about the infirm Phil's likely successor, succinctly dramatizes what Bobby Baccalieri postulates in the previous episode, "Soprano Home Movies": "You probably don't even hear it when it happens."

We cut from Gerry complaining about the waiter to a shot of Silvio from over his *comare*'s shoulder. Sil's talking about wine when the sound completely drops out and we see blood splatter all over his face and suit. We watch as Silvio and the women, in slow motion, react to the attack on Torciano. The sound and normal frame speed return as they escape and Gerry's shot to death, his face finally resting atop a fine-looking cut of veal.

> **NARRATIVE IMPACT: 4   CINEMATIC: 9   KILLER PERFORMANCES: 5**
> **ELEMENT OF SURPRISE: 8   TOTAL SCORE: 26**

JOHN "JOHNNY SACK" SACRIMONI

> *Succumbs to lung cancer in Episode 6.14, "Stage 5"*

Compared to his friend Tony Soprano, Lupertazzi family boss John Sacrimoni has terrible luck. Some of it he brings on himself, as his pride and arrogance blind him and affect his ability to think with the cunning and clarity of his New Jersey counterpart. (Maybe he should have been in therapy!) But plenty of John's luck is just a series of lousy rolls: he hits snake eyes while Tony keeps rolling sevens. John loves his wife—we never see him with another woman—and his daughters and is willing to sacrifice business (and nearly his life) to defend Ginny's honor over a fat joke. Yes, he's a gangster with a temper, but from what we see he's a better man than Tony.

In the Mob life, his perseverance and chutzpah help him outlast Carmine Jr. in a battle for control of the Lupertazzi family, but he has no time to enjoy the prize: he's almost immediately arrested, indicted, and incarcerated. His lust for the boss role and the fulfillment of that dream made him a bigger prize for the FBI. And his poor luck is compounded, as his chain-smoking habit catches up with him just like his hubris when we discover that he's suffering from late-stage lung cancer.

He realizes the irony. He tells his FBI escort, "I got here [prison], I quit smoking after thirty-eight years. I exercised, ate right. And for what?"

To his brother-in-law, he reflects on being boss, "It's a thankless job."

With his dire diagnosis, Ginny tells him, "Miracles do happen."

"Not to this family they don't," he replies.

And in a cruel irony, it's the idiot prince, Lupertazzi Jr., John's nemesis, who is the sage of John's "Stage 5" death play. Tony visits him to ask him to reclaim the boss role, but Carmine demurs. He tells Tony about an allegorical dream he had (complete with a crown and an empty box) where his wife begs him to leave the life. He concludes that "it's not about being boss. It's about being happy." Tony still doesn't get it. And John Sacrimoni understands too late. It's just his luck.

**NARRATIVE IMPACT: 6   CINEMATIC: 5   KILLER PERFORMANCES: 10
ELEMENT OF SURPRISE: 4   TOTAL SCORE: 25**

FAUSTINO "DOC" SANTORO AND BODYGUARD

Shot to death by hit men working for Phil Leotardo in Episode 6.15, "Remember When"

Doc Santoro's (Dan Conte's) reign as boss of the Lupertazzi crime family is comically short, his fate sealed when he reaches with his fork to take a piece of meat from Phil Leotardo's plate. He's gunned down outside a massage parlor by a trio of hired killers who escape with help from wheelman

Butch DeConcini. Phil, fully recovered from his heart attack, takes over as undisputed boss of the family. It's worth noting that Doc gets the first Moe Greene special (shot through the eye) since Brendan Filone in Season One's "Denial, Anger, Acceptance."

NARRATIVE IMPACT: 6	**CINEMATIC: 6**	**KILLER PERFORMANCES: 4**
ELEMENT OF SURPRISE: 6	**TOTAL SCORE: 22**	

RENATA

Dies from undisclosed natural causes at the home she shares with Herman "Hesh" Rabkin in Episode 6.16, "Chasing It"

Renata (Lanette Ware) appears in only a few scenes, but, because we've all grown fond of the avuncular Hesh Rabkin (Jerry Adler), a retired record executive and loan shark, we feel this loss deeply. Most of the episode follows an awkward dance between Tony and Hesh over a $200,000 loan. Tony's unlucky streak means he can't cover the loan and subsequently starts to pay a vig, interest on the principal. In Tony's case, 1.5 percent a week to extend his credit: $3,000. Hesh implies Tony's insulting him by not paying his loan, but resists taking the vig. Tony insists on paying, but, as his losing streak continues, delivers the cash wrapped with passive-aggressive, anti-Semitic innuendo.

In desperation, Tony tries to persuade Carmela to bet some of her real estate profits on a "sure thing." When she resists and the game goes his way, he's furious at the lost winnings, blows a fuse, and unleashes a torrent of cruelty. It's only after visiting Vito's widow and emotionally broken family that he returns and apologizes to Carmela. He understands that, after all the bullets they've dodged (and the ones he didn't), they're exceedingly lucky and, in a gambler's parlance, "way up."

The terrible irony is that his much more risk-averse friend Hesh is stuck with much worse luck than Tony's bad run on football and ponies. He's lost generations of Soprano family friendship and Renata, the love of his life. And he hasn't done a thing wrong. He's just had the kind of unfortunate streak that life can deal. It's enough to make anyone chase the sure thing.

> **NARRATIVE IMPACT: 3   CINEMATIC: 3   KILLER PERFORMANCES: 6
> ELEMENT OF SURPRISE: 7   TOTAL SCORE: 19**

J.T. DOLAN

Shot in the head by Christopher Moltisanti in Episode 6.17, "Walk Like a Man"

Actor Tim Daly, who is name-dropped by Len (Michael Garfield), the father of Meadow's boyfriend Noah Tannenbaum (Patrick Tully), in Season Three's "University," later appears in person in a recurring role as J.T. Dolan, a screenwriter Christopher meets in AA. As we might expect from a relationship between a junkie gambling addict and a junkie mafioso, their dynamic is tumultuous. J.T. tries to help Chris when he's off the wagon and writes the screenplay for his debut as a movie producer, *Cleaver*. Unfortunately, he also borrows money from Chris and doesn't understand the serious nature of a Mafia loan until he's late paying and gets punched in the face. Even then, he seems a little slow on the uptake. They'd make a fun odd couple in an HBO sitcom.

The friendship meets a violent end when Chris, drunk on vodka, shows up at J.T.'s apartment. Chris's true desire is to lash out at Paulie, Tony, and the rest of the gang who break his balls and refuse to respect his sobriety. J.T., trying to be a good friend, calls him on his bullshit and insists that he stop confessing Mafia secrets (Christopher mentions the deaths of Adriana La Cerva and Ralph Cifaretto, as well as his desire to enter Witness Protection). When J.T. draws a hard line about Moltisanti's big mouth and substance abuse, Chris, not feeling sufficiently coddled, simply shoots him in the head and leaves the apartment. An ending this screenwriter who boasted of his work on *Law and Order* didn't anticipate.

> **NARRATIVE IMPACT: 4   CINEMATIC: 4   KILLER PERFORMANCES: 7
> ELEMENT OF SURPRISE: 9   TOTAL SCORE: 24**

CHRISTOPHER MOLTISANTI

Suffocated by Tony Soprano following serious injuries in a car accident in Episode 6.18, "Kennedy and Heidi"

"You deprive yourself of nothing." That's what Gloria Trillo says to Tony in "The Telltale Moozadell," a Season Three episode written by Michael Imperioli, who plays Christopher Moltisanti. This assessment reflects the essence of Tony's being and is the core reason he kills people he claims to love. If this isn't clear through earlier murders, it's made plain when he "euthanizes" his honorary nephew and former heir apparent, Moltisanti, in "Kennedy and Heidi." This is a killing that's more about relieving Tony's sense of burden and protecting his throne than ending Christopher's suffering. The tragedy is that Christopher has never been healthier than in the Season Six episodes that precede "Kennedy and Heidi," at least until his alleged friends nudge him off the wagon. He is a deeply flawed man, for whom murder comes too easily, but he's also a creator, a man with artistic impulses (and even some acting talent!), which differentiates him from Tony and makes him unpredictable. His flame must be extinguished for Tony to rest easy, and that's what he accomplishes when he holds Moltisanti's nose, stealing his breath, forcing him to choke on his own blood.

While there is always tension (usually about Christopher's cinematic ambitions or substance abuse), the irreparable schism in their relationship begins in Season Five's "Irregular Around the Margins." The title applies just as much to the story Tony fabricates to explain why he's in a car with Adriana as it does to Tony's precancerous moles. When Tony confides his lust for Adriana to Dr. Melfi, she lauds him for not acting on his desire. She praises his "growth," but she's blind to the malignancy that forms when his covetousness is thwarted. When Tony Soprano goes without, there's going to be fallout. We see it right away—after the car accident with Adriana, his first interaction with Christopher is to hand him a stick covered in dog shit to throw away.

Christopher, for his part, deals with his feelings around this betrayal the only way he really can, artistically, through his Mafia horror movie, *Cleaver*, where he processes his emotions around Tony's desire for Adriana and his role in her death (though Christopher is plenty culpable himself) by killing off a character clearly inspired by Tony. When the movie premieres in "Stage 5," Tony's mind is too literal to pick up on *Cleaver*'s themes, but Carmela's isn't and she clues him in. And once he sees it, he can't unsee it.

Reflecting on the movie with Dr. Melfi, Tony says, "All I did for this fucking kid and he hates me so much. . . . I think he fucking despises me. It's pretty obvious. Wants to see me dead."

In response, Melfi asks, "Without invalidating your feelings, is it possible on some level that you're reading into all this?" When Tony replies, "I've been coming here for years. I know too much about the subconscious now," it's one of the most chilling moments in the series. Dr. Melfi provides Tony with insights that make him a shrewder leader and more confident killer. Christopher's murder is one of opportunity, but we really see Tony make the decision to kill his nephew right here, in his therapist's office.

The timing is tragic, as Moltisanti's in recovery, a married new father who avoids his old haunts and works hard for his family, fending off the guilt and pain he feels about Adriana's death. But these strides only further enrage Tony. When Christopher's wife, Kelli (Cara Buono), chooses to host a barbecue at their new McMansion, we can tell Tony's miffed it's not his party. He can't even let Christopher man the steaks without indulging in some backseat grilling. If there's one thing Tony and his elder statesmen cannot abide, it's Christopher's outgrowing them. And so they badger him until he starts using again.

The death scene is a shock. The accident happens quickly and we witness Tony's real-time rationalization—the empty car seat for Christopher's daughter—that Christopher is too much of a danger to his family to live. But we know better. When a car passes, illuminating Tony's face for a brief second before leaving him in total darkness, the shot betrays the state of his soul. He's doing this for himself, not Moltisanti's daughter.

In the aftermath, Tony cannot abide the sadness, platitudes, and motions of grief when he feels none, so he ascends to the heavens via private plane and to Las Vegas. He's lonely at first, dining solo, losing at the tables, but soon we understand the real reason for this trip—so he can take what's his. So he can get one back. He visits Christopher's previously unmentioned Vegas girlfriend, Sonya Aragon (Sarah Shahi), under the pretense of giving her the bad news.

In no time, Tony's sleeping with her. The song that plays is "The Adultress" by The Pretenders. This is about taking what was Moltisanti's to make up for the times Tony went without. When the pair ingest peyote and Tony experiences incredible luck at the tables, he has a moment of realization (practically an illumination) and pronounces, "He's dead." The thrill is orgasmic. He is free of the burden of friendship and mentorship. The world is his to devour.

Out in the desert, high on peyote, Tony believes he's found wisdom, like a character in a parable. But when, overcome with joy, he screams "I get it!" it's not because he's processed anything, but because Tony literally gets everything. He gets to be the chief grill man, sleep with Chris's woman, and have no challengers to his throne. With no one in a position to outgrow Tony, he can indulge with bliss, forever arrested in his development. The only piece of knowledge he finds in the desert is "He who dies with the most toys wins."

NARRATIVE IMPACT: 10   CINEMATIC: 10   KILLER PERFORMANCES: 10
ELEMENT OF SURPRISE: 8   TOTAL SCORE: 38

MARIA "NUCCI" GUALTIERI

Dies from a stroke on a Green Grove bus returning to New Jersey from New York City in Episode 6.18, "Kennedy and Heidi"

Nucci Gualtieri is one of the most likable and memorable characters on the periphery of the vast *Sopranos* ensemble. When we learn from the Green Grove brass that she's a tattletale who doesn't always put her teeth in, we give her a pass because she's so kindhearted and the actress, Frances Ensemplare, is so funny, especially in the "Whoever Did This" scene where she's prank-called by Ralph Cifaretto. We're caught off-guard when we hear about her off-screen demise (on a bus back from a production of *Jersey Boys*, which she undoubtedly adored) as it comes right on the heels of Christopher Moltisanti's death. While that murder siphoned out what little humanity Tony had left, it's Nucci's death that robs Paulie of the one relationship in which he shows any redeeming qualities, even though he's quick to condemn her when he learns that she's lied to him throughout his life about his true parentage. (It's tough to feel any sympathy for him until he forgives the woman who made selfless sacrifices for him.) Throughout the series, his love for the woman who raised him shows that even the lowest contain multitudes. So we can't help but agree with him when he sees the sparse turnout for her wake—due in part to its scheduling coinciding with Moltisanti's wake—and bemoans, "What kind of testament is this to the spirit and generosity of the woman?"

> NARRATIVE IMPACT: 2   CINEMATIC: 1   KILLER PERFORMANCES: 1
> ELEMENT OF SURPRISE: 7   TOTAL POINTS: 11

BURT GERVASI

| *Garroted by Silvio Dante in Episode 6.20, "The Blue Comet"*

The death is a surprise, as we haven't heard about Burt Gervasi (Artie Pasquale) "playing both sides of the fence with New York." Burt appears in half a dozen episodes, usually in a background role, so we're caught off-guard when Silvio catches him with the piano wire inside his garishly decorated home while his wife's toy terrier yaps. There are a lot of terrible ways to go but this nears the top of the list.

The purpose of the scene is to convey the tenuous status of Tony's position and of the DiMeo crime family. Nobody is safe and nobody is to be trusted. It's also notable that, over the course of the series, we witness scenes where four associates—Eugene Pontecorvo, Christopher Moltisanti, Gerry Torciano, and Gervasi—graduate and become made men. By the end of the series, all four are dead and three have been murdered, despite traditional Mob rules deeming made guys "untouchable." Maybe that oath isn't so sacred.

> NARRATIVE IMPACT: 4   CINEMATIC: 6   KILLER PERFORMANCES: 5
> ELEMENT OF SURPRISE: 7   TOTAL POINTS: 22

YARYNA AND YARYNA'S FATHER

Shot to death by Italo, the Napoletano hit man, in Episode 6.20,
"The Blue Comet"

Everything goes smoothly when Chris Moltisanti uses the Italian-speaking Jersey kid Corky Caporale (Edoardo Ballerini) as a middleman to provide instructions and weapons to imported Camorra hit men in the killing of Rusty Millio. The second time doesn't go as well. Corky provides his Italian team with information on where to find Phil Leotardo and his *comare*, the Ukrainian maid Yaryna (yes, Phil's girlfriend cleans up after his religious fanatic wife, which is fodder for a thousand Dr. Melfis). Corky messes up and directs the killers to her home. There, they find—and kill—her father (Aleks Shaklin), who bears a resemblance to Phil. When Yaryna (Matilda Downey) screams in horror, they shoot her, too. Bloodied, she tumbles down the stairs, screaming, "They shot me, Daddy!" in Ukrainian. Only when Silvio and Paulie see the paper the next day do they realize their big move on Leotardo has been botched. It's a gruesome hit and a tragic case of mistaken identity.

> **NARRATIVE IMPACT: 4   CINEMATIC: 7   KILLER PERFORMANCES: 7**
> **ELEMENT OF SURPRISE: 6   TOTAL POINTS: 24**

BOBBY "BACALA" BACCALIERI

Shot to death by a pair of Lupertazzi family hit men in a hobby
shop in Episode 6.20, "The Blue Comet"

The moment Bobby Baccalieri kills René LeCours in "Soprano Home Movies" (see page 273), he's in another world. Certainly financially, as it helps resecure his position as Tony's heir following their dustup at the cabin, but more importantly it's a moral and spiritual shift to darker territory—a realm that's not a good fit for this mostly decent man. The perks of his new status mean that Bobby can drop $8,000 on a gorgeous antique train set, but being a top man in a crime family requires a craftiness and cynicism that he doesn't possess. For five seasons, he was a simple gofer, with a compassionate streak that made him an easy punch line for his Mafia brothers. Even the quorum of Lupertazzi gangsters who choose him as a target for murder find it incredulous: "That mortadella's number three? He used to be Junior Soprano's driver."

Bobby's death should be on any top ten list of best-directed scenes on *The Sopranos*. Director Alan Taylor and editor William B. Stich dramatize the inevitability of Bobby's fate through a visual link to the LeCours murder while also conveying the lack of guile that makes him unsuitable for his top role.

The scene opens with Bobby parking and exiting his car outside the hobby shop. He leaves his cell phone in the car—an inept move for an underboss to make, considering the violent drama happening between the DiMeo and Lupertazzi families. As he walks toward the store, the phone rings. We know it's Silvio because Tony's just ordered him to put everybody on notice that the Lupertazzi goons are coming for them. The camera pans to the right so that we can see the sideview mirror with its forever daunting message: "Objects in Mirror May Be Closer Than They Appear." This is the first indication that this scene will link to the LeCours murder, where we saw Bobby's reflection shattered in the dryer window after he shoots the bewildered drummer.

Inside the store, the first shot we see is of a fantastic and detailed model train layout, clearly the shop's centerpiece, and the locomotives— like the plan to kill Bobby—are already in motion. We hear the whistles as they pick up steam. For the rest of the scene this train display is an effective tool for building suspense, and also signals that Bobby's choices have brought this fate upon him—it's heading right for him, like a meteor. Ira Shortz (John Mainieri), the shopkeeper, shows Bobby the antique Blue Comet, a model of a train that used to run from NYC to Atlantic City, and tells him, "You never see a Blue Comet in that condition." And Bobby, being Bobby, has no ability to see what's coming. Even the choice of train is purposeful and tragically ironic, as he's in the middle of the tracks between New York and New Jersey sides of a war.

While Bobby banters with Ira, his killers enter. We see them through the store's convex security mirror, its circular shape echoing the aforementioned dryer window in "Soprano Home Movies." Bobby's engrossed and oblivious. He decides to take the train and Taylor cuts to a close-up of the Blue Comet's steam locomotive. It has reflective chrome components, but we can't see anything in them. Neither can Bobby.

We know Bobby's time is up when we return to the train set, this time from the perspective of a fast-moving model locomotive. As it turns the corner, we see four miniature people. Three are fixed in poses of surprise and terror. The fourth, a police officer, reaches for his gun. Taylor and Stich intercut the fast-moving trains and the hit men, who approach Bobby, building suspense. But their target remains unaware, examining his new purchase. When the shooting starts, Bobby doesn't make a sound.

An errant bullet hits a train, derailing it. Bobby finally succumbs to the onslaught of bullets and falls backward, into and through the elaborate model, dislodging tracks, engines, and cars. We see them fall in slow motion, raining down atop the crushed display until everything is still.

Unlike Tony Soprano, Baccalieri doesn't have the temperament or ingenuity to design and maintain a (seemingly) picturesque life through criminal enterprise. With the destruction of the carefully designed train set, we think back to the final shot of "Soprano Home Movies" when Bobby, having just murdered LeCours, believes he's made a sacrifice to help secure his family's lifestyle. He holds his toddler daughter tight and looks out to the lake with hope and a misguided belief that he committed the murder for them. On the soundtrack, we hear The Drifters' "This Magic Moment" and, like so many song choices on *The Sopranos*, we can appreciate the irony, as the moment he killed Réne LeCours, Bobby "Bacala" set his own fate in locomotion.

**NARRATIVE IMPACT: 8   CINEMATIC: 10   KILLER PERFORMANCES: 9
ELEMENT OF SURPRISE: 8   TOTAL POINTS: 35**

PHIL LEOTARDO

Shot to death by Walden Belfiore in Episode 6.21,

"Made in America"

From his first appearance in Season Five's "Rat Pack," Phil Leotardo is a vindictive menace who is a consistent source of trouble for Tony and the DiMeo crime family. Tony tries to appease him time and time again, but Phil's forever rankled by Tony Blundetto's murder of his brother, Billy, so any pacification is temporary.

It takes a veritable army to bring down Phil, who is on the lam in Oyster Bay, Long Island, while his crew, led by Butch DeConcini, tries to wipe out the DiMeo leadership. First, Tony gets a hand from federal agent Harris (Matt Servitto), who developed a cordial relationship with his adversary before being transferred to the terror division. Tony also receives an okay from DeConcini, who, after a discouraging phone call with Phil, decides to go behind his back. This happens at a meeting brokered by an impartial NYC Mob boss, where Butch gives Tony the go-ahead to dispose of Phil. "You do what you gotta do."

In staging Phil's death, David Chase has to solve a problem. The death of Tony's chief nemesis needs to be narratively satisfying, but the actor who plays Phil, Frank Vincent, also played Billy Batts, who suffers one of the most famous whackings in American movie history in *Goodfellas*. *The Sopranos* references this movie killing visually at least three times, and it's so well known that it was parodied in a British bagel commercial in 2018. Point being, expectations are high for Phil's death.

The creative solution isn't the best the show has to offer, but it's certainly memorable. It feels like Phil gets killed two or three times over, just to make sure we all enjoy it and get the point.

Chase shows Phil's SUV pulling into the Raceway gas station he's been using to make calls. He's with his wife, the monstrous Patty (Geraldine LiBrandi), who is driving, and their twin grandkids. The first words we hear him say are "Bye-bye! Wave bye-bye, Grandpa. Bye-bye Pop-Pop!" It's the start of a sick joke, but we have no idea *how* sick. As he exits the car, Chase cuts between his and Patty's POV as he barks onerous instructions. We see Patty's face register annoyance, which quickly shifts to horror as a hand—belonging to Walden Belfiore (Frank John Hughes)—holding a pistol appears and shoots Phil in the head. Then Belfiore shoots him in the chest (just to be sure) and escapes in a waiting Cadillac. The hysterical Patty leaves the car and races to Phil's body. But because she leaves the car in drive, it begins to roll. She realizes her grandchildren are locked in the car and, amidst her panic, we can see that Phil's head is directly in its path.

Chase makes the dubious decision to show us Phil's indifferent grandkids while we hear their pop-pop's skull pop under the weight of the car. The scene leaves us, like the aghast teenagers who see Phil's skull squished by the rolling SUV, a little queasy. Comeuppance can be gratifying, but less so when it's extreme overkill. It's the last on-camera death in the series and, frankly, a disappointment.

NARRATIVE IMPACT: 7   CINEMATIC: 6   KILLER PERFORMANCES: 5
ELEMENT OF SURPRISE: 8   TOTAL POINTS: 26

THE WINNER

It's probably no surprise that Adriana La Cerva, the woman with the biggest heart on *The Sopranos*, suffered its greatest, most devastating death and scored a perfect 40. She'll look fab in the crown, bejeweled and be-jazzled at the Short Hills Mall.

And it's worth acknowledging our runners-up: Tony Blundetto, Salvatore "Big Pussy" Bonpensiero, Christopher Moltisanti, Ralph Cifaretto, Bobby Baccalieri, René LeCours, Eugene Pontecorvo, Gloria Trillo, and, appearing on the main stage, Tracee!

CHAPTER VII

Favorite
EPISODES

I asked several people to write an essay about a favorite episode of *The Sopranos*. You'll find fresh takes on the expected classics appraised here and some unexpected episodes, too. The essays are in chronological order, and as a group we definitely have an affinity for the middle seasons. There are zero selections from Seasons One, Two, Four, and Six; three from Season Three; and four from Season Five. Matthew David Wilder gets us started with the harrowing "University," the episode that solidifies Ralph Cifaretto's (Joe Pantoliano's) reputation as the show's most loathsome scumbag. Joe Mader follows with his appraisal of "Second Opinion," in which Carmela Soprano (Edie Falco) is in existential crisis. Then, Phil Dyess-Nugent visits the "Pine Barrens," for Christopher Moltisanti (Michael Imperioli) and Paulie Gualtieri's (Tony Sirico's) winterland folly.

Shifting into Season Five, Hannah McGill writes on Tony Soprano (James Gandolfini) and Adriana La Cerva's (Drea de Matteo's) near tryst and subsequent car crash in the game of telephone that is "Irregular Around the Margins," and I consider Hugh DeAngelis's (Tom Aldredge's) seventy-fifth birthday party in "Marco Polo." Scott Von Doviak tackles the surrealist scenes of "The Test Dream," and, finally, Andy Cambria takes us on a long, sad drive into "Long Term Parking."

Don't sweat it if your favorite isn't covered here. It's very likely written about in the previous chapter, "Whack Attack," or another one. If you really want to know what we think of an episode, I promise, we're not hard to find.

EPISODE 3.6, "UNIVERSITY"
—Matthew David Wilder

It's not merely the most ghastly, alarming, appalling act of violence in television history, I'd place it as the most frightening violence in contemporary picture-making *period*—movies and TV both. The only thing that gets near it is the aluminum-baseball-bat killing of Joe Pesci and his brother at the end of *Casino*—a physically excruciating ordeal that is capped with a pointedly biblical live burial in a cornfield. In the episode, slickster psychopath gangster Ralph Cifaretto (a career-high Joe Pantoliano) gets into a fracas with stripper girlfriend Tracee (Ariel Kiley) behind Tony's topless bar, the Bada Bing. Chest-shoving leads to slapping leads to punches—and Ralphie winds up knocking Tracee to the ground, repeatedly pummeling her face to the point of disfigurement, then smashing her head into the metal railing on the side of the road until she looks like her face was dunked in a bucket of blood. And she's dead. Shall we continue?

The thing that made the episode "University" life-changing for me and for everyone I know who was watching that night was that metal railing. Hard to remember now, but back in the day, everyone watched *The Sopranos* on Sunday night—at eight o'clock here on the West Coast—and then would jump on the phone with friends to yell, "Can you believe . . . ?!" This episode, however, was different. No one was jumping on the phone with this one. But when people talked about it, after the fact, what I recall was the way the metal railing came up. There was something poetically inspired about using it as a sort of passive murder weapon to produce an image that was not movie violence, but that was in some way redolent of *real-world actual violence* that hurt as you watched it, and that gave a feeling of the bottomless sordidness, griminess, and grossness. (The real coup de théâtre was the cut to a wide shot of Tracee's body framed against the babbling brook behind the metal railing—which looks half movie-idyllic.

Kiley, the actress who plays Tracee, commented years after "University" aired that tons of HBO viewers canceled their subscriptions after they witnessed her death. Is that true? I've never heard any other telling of this tale, but it certainly marked a point of no return. Yes, Tony commits murder—an ugly on-screen murder—in the parallel-titled "College," but this is something far different: the braining to death of a pregnant girl on camera, in deliberate, physically plausible, largely explicit beats. Somewhere in the back of Chase's and his writers' minds must have been that scene that Paul Schrader wrote into an early draft of *Raging Bull:* Jake LaMotta kicks his pregnant wife in the belly till she aborts. Tracee's death scene was a kind of marker: the series, and indeed the kind of television *The Sopranos* represented (and invented), could never again be likable, stomach-able, or respectable in a certain way. *The Sopranos* "pioneered" something or "paved the way" for something else, but I have to imagine that Chase viewed the murder of Tracee as in some way suicidal, that there was no way audiences could hang with the show after this scene. One might see it as a form of authorial acting out. Of course, it turned out that Chase's ferocity, his complete and utter and existential not-giving-a-fuck, was what bound the audience's loyalty to the series and crowned HBO as the flagship of cable television.

Seeing "University" in the context of 2019's total societal meltdown, it seems to speak on a cellular level about the theme of the series as a whole: a certain patriarchal style that is in full retreat. We see the younger generation that will emerge and submerge the Tony-and-pals era of guys in charge. The episode contrasts two young women of roughly similar ages on different trajectories. Tracee just got braces, is fucking the Caligula-psychotic Ralphie, and has a small kid who, on occasion, she has burned with cigarettes. (The inclusion of this detail is classically Chasean. Never can a character come to appear too goody two-shoes, too in need of a white-knight rescuer. Something always makes everyone a little scuzzy.) In contrast, Tony's daughter, Meadow (Jamie-Lynn Sigler), is a student at Columbia, dating a half-black, half-Jewish kid (Patrick Tully) with the ridiculous and perfect name of Noah Tannenbaum. (In a perfectly hateful touch, Noah walks in on Tony watching a gangster picture and indelibly remarks, "Cagney! He was modernity.") Meadow's guy problems are stuff she'll forget in five years; Tracee is even worse at picking guys, but she won't survive her man.

The stage of the Bing, the runway where the dancers mill about, showing their goods, occasionally climbing a pole to do tricks, is at first surveyed with a lateral tracking shot, accompanied by The Kinks' "Living on a Thin Line" ("All the stories have been told / Of kings and days of old / But there's no England now"). Tracee is first seen giving Tony a gift of date bread as thanks for his recommendation that she take her kid to a doctor—clearly there are some fundamentals that she didn't learn from probably absent parents. Tony and Bing supervisor Silvio Dante (Steven Van Zandt) are wary of Tracee's getting too close to Tony. In another day—hell, five minutes before *The Sopranos* existed—it would be explained that this was because powerful Tony was a fine, ethical guy who didn't want to go too far with this helpless, just-off-the-bus girl, and he didn't want to pick a fight with her made boyfriend Ralphie, either. Since Chase is a more wised-up character, we see it a different way.

In a spot-on performance Kiley gives Tracee a flat, Midwestern voice and a kind of dented, bruised white-trash quality. She registers as sexy precisely because her vulnerability is so far from what we see in the hoods' wives and their *comares* in their finery and feathers. There is something ordinary and everyday American about her that you can see would drive these guys nuts. A few are honestly protective of her, but mostly they know themselves and view her as nitroglycerine.

As Tracee is on a death trajectory with Ralphie, the episode takes a largely comic turn in depicting Meadow's adventures with the children of the urban gentry at Columbia. Meadow's roommate, perfectly named Caitlin (a succulent comic performance by Ari Graynor), has a panic disorder, pulls out her own hair distractedly, and sees doom on every horizon. The last straw—in terms of Caitlin's working Meadow's last nerve—comes when she sees a homeless black woman muttering to herself in a park at midnight. When the woman's pants fall and we see that she has bits of the *New York Post* stuffed up her ass, Caitlin responds with abject horror. The improvised toilet tissue is the stuff of full disintegration. (This is a good time to notice something I always thought was pretty brave of Chase, even in this less hysterical period: there are no entirely positive black characters in *The Sopranos*—not down to the bit parts. There is something crooked or smarmy or self-deluded in each one. This is not because Chase is racist, but because he is rebelling at the cliché of the time: introducing black characters who somehow become enriching, enlightening moral instructors of the white characters.) We see that Meadow is going to attain altitude, she is going to escape the limited, provincial world of Tony and Carmela and join what today's deplorables would call "the globalist elite." We also see Caitlin as a prototypical millennial—a few years later this characterization will morph into HBO's post-Tony antiheroine, Hannah Horvath (Lena Dunham) of *Girls* (there, her neuroses will be played not for yuks but as high drama-queen drama).

The end of "University" is profoundly desolating. The dancers get back onstage at the Bing, gossiping about Tracee's mysterious disappearance. The size-XXL bouncer, Georgie (Frank Santorelli), reiterates his prices for strippers to enter his big-shot card game in the back room of the Bing— "Fifty bucks, and a blow job for me"—and the beat goes on. Harrowingly, we are left to think that Tracee's death will be mourned by no one except the orphaned kid she leaves behind; an interchangeable piece of ass will take her place.

Chase was always determined to reveal the power structures hidden behind the Relatable Human Drama that television has been peddling all his life. He is also a genius at finding pathos on the wing—as in the glint of moonlight on Tracee's dead face as that toxic creek burbles like a fountain behind her. "University" was a landmark in the evolution of *The Sopranos*. Tracee's terrifyingly sordid patch of asphalt was the hill David Chase was willing to die on.

EPISODE 3.7, "SECOND OPINION"
—Joe Mader

"Second Opinion" is an episode rife with shock, especially of the moral kind, containing a stunning performance by Edie Falco. Director Tim Van Patten and writer Lawrence Konner, along with editor Sidney Wolinsky, lay out a masterful structure of twenty-eight scenes that reverberate and build off each other. The episode's title most obviously refers to Junior Soprano's (Dominic Chianese's) cancer treatment. Chianese's cantankerous, aging, and ailing Junior is half in love with his doctor (played with fatuous arrogance by Sam McMurray) because he happens to be named John Kennedy. (Junior still longs for Camelot.) Junior may dream of Angie Dickinson as he's going under the knife, but Kennedy is his savior. In actuality, Kennedy is a cut-happy surgeon who removes Junior's tumor but doesn't get all of the cancerous tissue. He wants to go back in, but Tony wants a second opinion. Junior wants to avoid chemotherapy at all costs, but Tony has his way and the second doctor recommends chemo. A tumor board is convened, and in keeping with the cynical worldview of *The Sopranos*, Kennedy's indifference leads to the board's upholding the second prescription. As Junior suffers through the various miseries wrought by the cancer-fighting poisons, Kennedy ignores his calls and refuses to schedule any appointments. Junior is now somebody else's problem.

Tony, however, through his usual combination of generosity and intimidation, interrupts the good doctor's golf game and persuades him that he needs to be more responsive to his patient: "Show that man the respect he deserves—answer his phone calls." It's a neat little subplot that shows how Tony tackles a problem, how both reward and threat play a part in his transactional world. And it's worth pointing out how great Chianese is at portraying the decline in power, autonomy, and strength that comes with age: a doctor with the magical name of Kennedy becomes his all-in-all, despite the medico's almost complete unconcern. Chianese's Junior is cranky, resigned, angry, and sad all at once as he enters his dotage. His acquiescence to Tony's demands displays a child's meekness and powerlessness, and you can't help but feel empathy for him—a murderer and criminal, yes, but also a leader who's lost the stature he once had.

Another character dealing with indignities is Christopher. A newly made man, he's chafing under the thumb of Paulie, who hazes him relentlessly. He makes Christopher strip to prove he's not wearing a wire, he barges in on Adriana and Chris at their apartment as Chris is presenting her with Jimmy Choo shoes he's "acquired," and he even sniffs Adriana's panties when he thinks no one sees him. (Christopher does.) Paulie then confiscates the shoes. Christopher complains to Tony (a second "second opinion"), but to no real avail. Paulie makes things even harder, setting him up to suffer Tony's rage, a dénouement we never see but are left to guess at, by asking him to bring a singing-fish novelty gift into the Bada Bing clubhouse, after we've already seen Tony enraged by the gag. There are procedures, there are rites, and if you endure them you are rewarded. If not . . .

Junior's physical illness presages another kind of illness the episode deals with, resulting in the hour's final unwanted and unwelcome second opinion. After Sunday family dinner, Carmela's mother, Mary (Suzanne Shepherd), reminds her clearly unhappy daughter that she could have done better than Tony, bringing up a past boyfriend who now owns a chain of drugstores. After Carmela upbraids her mother with all that Tony has done for her parents, Mary remarks, "The waters don't part for you wherever you go?" "I earn it," Carmela responds angrily.

Carmela has been accompanying Tony to his appointments with Dr. Melfi (Lorraine Bracco), but this time she visits Melfi alone and becomes frustrated by the psychiatrist's remoteness and insistence that Tony, not Carmela, is her patient. After Carmela breaks into tears, Melfi recommends a colleague for Carmela to see, a Dr. Krakower: "He was a teacher of mine."

Krakower (Sully Boyar, radiating authority and wisdom, an actor who unfortunately died before this episode ever aired) is a Jew who brings an Old Testament clarity to Carmela's messy Catholic life, and says the word "Mafia" for only the second time in the series. (Meadow, in Season One, asks Tony point-blank if he's in the Mafia.) Carmela experiences it as a physical blow. She recoils with a half gasp, half moan, and then tries to lift herself out of the overstuffed armchair that no longer provides any comfort, much like her overstuffed life. He condemns Tony, and by extension Carmela. What has always been covered, hinted at, is exposed, and the truth is devastating. Krakower uses the word "Mafia" in all its immoral authority, with a clear understanding of the evil, the violence, the sin involved. He says it evenly and quietly, but it hits Carmela with all the force of an improvised explosive device.

Carmela possesses a warmth, a clearheadedness, and an emotional intelligence that endear her to us like few other characters on the show. When she goes to visit Meadow at Columbia, she has to wait in the dorm lounge. We see her sitting, noticing other students and their activities, and we feel her gentle envy for Meadow's youth, having the world ahead of her, her nostalgia for her own interrupted college days, and her melancholy. Backed by Nils Lofgren's plaintive song "Black Books," it's a lovely moment, though we're brought back to earth later when Meadow refers to Carmela's relationship with Tony as "bullshit accommodational pretense."

Carmela is also the only character in *The Sopranos* who has an emotional response to art. Earlier in this episode, she comments upon the artwork Melfi has in her office, expressing both pleasure and censure. A few episodes later, when she and Meadow are at the Metropolitan Museum of Art, Carmela comes upon Jusepe de Ribera's *The Mystical Marriage of St. Catherine* and is brought to tears. And in the final season, when she visits Paris with Rosalie Aprile (Sharon Angela), she's transformed by its beauty. Affected and introspective, Carmela tries to talk to Rosalie about the deaths of her husband and her son, but Rosalie deals with her sorrows by burying them. She's incapable of responding to art or life the way Carmela does.

Despite this, Carmela, like Tony, is also highly transactional in her relationships. Gifts of jewelry and furs delight her. Later, in Season Five, she's separated from Tony and dating an administrator (David Strathairn) at A.J.'s (Robert Iler's) school, but he breaks up with her, calling her a "user." He's ashamed that he leaned on one of A.J.'s teachers (Karl Bury) at Carmela's behest, getting A.J. a better, undeserved grade. "How could asking someone you're with for help be using them? That's what people do," Carmela responds. She's not wrong, but she's not right, either. Love is of course about being used and being useful. We fall in love *to be* used. But there's a line between being useful and being manipulated, a line that can be as elusive as quicksilver.

With Dr. Krakower, Carmela's met her match. One of the weaknesses of Season Two is that you don't believe Melfi would take Tony back as a patient. He endangered her and her practice, and you keep waiting for her to give some sort of moral ultimatum to Tony, but she never does. Melfi didn't learn much from her teacher. Dr. Krakower, though, lays it all bare for Carmela, cutting through her delusions and hypocrisies. If she stays with Tony, enabling his crimes, benefiting from them, she is as guilty as he is. Krakower refuses payment for the session, calling it blood money, and refuses her as a client unless she leaves Tony and takes the kids with her. Carmela, in moral agony, says, "My priest says I should try and work with him, help him be a better man." "How's that going?" Krakower asks, mercilessly. At the end of this brutal, amazing scene, the doctor tells her, "One thing you can never say, that you haven't been told." "I see. You're right," Carmela says, her eyes blinded by tears; she sees *and* she's blind. Like the rich man seeking salvation, Carmela can't accept the price of atonement.

Earlier, when she had lunch with the Columbia dean of students (Frank Wood), he surprised her with both kind words about Meadow and his knowledge of the Sopranos' donation history, as he made his ask for a $50,000 gift. When she first brings this up to Tony, he scoffs that $5,000 is the most he'll give. But in the last scene, he comes upon her lying in misery on the sofa, a blanket tightly wrapped around her, the lights low, and she asks again: "Tony, you gotta do something nice for me today. This is what I want." Fifty thousand dollars is the price Carmela has set to avoid upending her life with Tony. That's the price of her soul. The cost may be unfathomable, but you can always set a price. We see James Gandolfini narrow his eyes, calculating, and then see his face as he capitulates. It's another transaction, another weighing of the costs and benefits, yes, but it's also love. He suggests, "You look like you could use a night off from cooking. Whaddya say we go out?" Carmela exchanges a long look with Tony, and everything about their love, their lives, is made manifest. Love and commerce and sin are intertwined throughout *The Sopranos*. For Tony and Carmela, it's impossible to separate one from the others. As it so often is for all of us.

EPISODE 3.11, "PINE BARRENS"
—Phil Dyess-Nugent

Fuck you, Paulie. Captain or no captain, right now we're just two assholes lost in the woods.
—Christopher Moltisanti

"Pine Barrens" is a story about what happens when Tony asks Paulie to do one thing. Not a big thing, just take a little time out of his busy schedule of ferrying his mother all over creation to visit a Russian gangster named Valery (Vitali Baganov) at his home and collect the money he owes Silvio. Paulie drags Christopher along, because getting Christopher into shit is Paulie's notion of a mentoring program. (At one point he even chides Christopher for skipping breakfast, pointing out that it's the most important meal of the day.) Things go south almost immediately, though not because Valery is looking for trouble. He is surly and makes no pretense of being thrilled to have these two yo-yos in his house, but he has the money and is willing to fork it over so that he can once again be alone with his top-of-the-line home entertainment center and whatever mood-altering substances he is looking forward to enjoying as soon as they leave.

Things deteriorate because of Paulie's need to bully and his limited ability to read a situation. A blowhard who is acutely conscious of his place in the pecking order, he doesn't get it that strength sometimes manifests itself in ways different than strutting and picking on people. Having come upon Valery at a low point, when this "Russian Green Beret" turned criminal and substance abuser may be feeling dejected about what he's been doing with his life, Paulie misinterprets his defeated air and folded-in body language as the weakness of a loser he can mess with. He makes dumb jokes and sneers at Valery's universal remote, implying that such technological marvels are wasted on this primitive foreigner and degenerate gambler. When Valery responds to the abuse by insulting his tormenter, Paulie smashes him upside the head with a glass. Things, as they say, escalate quickly, and before long, Paulie and Christopher are running through snowy woods, trying to shoot a fleeing man they'd brought out to the middle of nowhere in the trunk of their car because they thought they'd already killed him.

"Pine Barrens" provides a healthy understanding of just what an awful thing it would be to die at the hands of Paulie "Walnuts" Gualtieri. Especially if he found the prospect of your demise in any way amusing, because most of us would opt to commit *seppuku* with a plastic fork if the only other option was to spend our last few minutes with that malignant little chuckle (*Heh-heh-heh!*) scratching our eardrums. Tony is out there somewhere, on the other end of a bad phone connection, dismayed at the direction all this is going in. But when life presents Paulie with a miraculous second chance, when he opens the car trunk and sees that Valery is still alive, all he sees is a potential contradictory witness to his version of events. The good news is that now Valery can save Paulie the aggravation of ruining his manicure by digging his own grave. And while he digs, damned if Paulie doesn't mentor *him*, telling Valery that he wouldn't be in this situation if it wasn't for "that mouth of yours. You gotta learn to shut it the fuck up." In the end, Paulie shoots Valery in the head—we see the blood flying—but he and Christopher can't find the body anywhere. Then they see that somebody has made off with their car.

"The Russian," as Valery quickly came to be known in internet fan folklore, has long been one of the most famous sources of tension between David Chase and the *Sopranos* audience. Viewers couldn't believe it that the actual fate of Valery—who, like his best friend and the head of the Jersey branch of the Russian Mafia, Slava Malevsky (Frank Ciornei), had previously been seen in all of one episode and would never appear on-screen again—was not made clear. Chase, as is his wont, cannot believe these whiners who can't accept that stories aren't always like that because life isn't always like that. Isn't it more fun not to know sometimes? What the hell kind of word is "closure," anyway?

"I do know where the Russian is," Chase told an *Entertainment Weekly* reporter in 2007. "But I'll never say because so many people got so pissy about it."[1] Paulie Walnuts couldn't have said it better, partly because he probably would have said "cunty" instead of "pissy."

What Chase may never be in the mood to appreciate is that the Russian, despite his place on the relative fringes of the *Sopranos* universe and his scant amount of screen time, inspires audience curiosity and fascination because he's a very impressive figure. When Tony meets with Slava in his office and comments on a photo of the two of them together, Slava speaks movingly of their days fighting in the Chechen War. He tells Tony that Valery was "like a brother to me. More than brother," that he saved his life and personally killed sixteen Chechen soldiers when he was with the Interior Ministry. (Tony passes this information along to Paulie, who translates it as "He killed sixteen Czechoslovakians. He was an interior decorator." This gets the attention of even Christopher: "His house looked like shit.") Now he is a "tragic figure," brought low by decadent overindulgence in drugs and alcohol, and don't forget that universal remote. You get a sense that the Russians are playing by a different rule book when Tony gingerly suggests that it might be time to "send him to rehab," and Slava, while still unfailingly polite, gives him a look as if Tony had suggested that Valery dress up in something pink and frilly and carry around an oversized lollipop.

The show's recurring themes of American decline and culture shock in the global age hit a new level when Valery—Mr. "I wash my balls with ice water"—is standing in the wintry wastes of South Jersey with these two mobsters who think they've stumbled into an uninhabitable Arctic hellscape. It seems like the ultimate sporting gesture that when an opening presents itself, he runs away instead of snapping their necks after shoving their guns up their asses. It says a lot about Christopher that he never seems to notice that this tall, frosty mug of bad life choices and survival techniques is the icon of cool he's always dreamed of being. He's a better killer, a more functional junkie, and his DVD collection probably rocks. Christopher should just put a slug in Paulie and ask Valery where he wants to do lunch.

Though "Pine Barrens" was the first of four episodes of the series (masterfully) directed by Steve Buscemi, three years before he joined the cast of Season Five as the doomed Tony Blundetto, it grew out of an idea director Tim Van Patten had about Paulie and Christopher getting lost in the woods. "My father was a horse player and he used to take me and my brother to Atlantic City," he told *EW*. "On the way down, he'd always try to make an adventure out of it, so we'd stop at Pine Barrens."[2]

From the moment Paulie pitches going to Atlantic City after he and Christopher dispose of the Russian's body—"So the day won't be a total loss"—"Pine Barrens" is suffused with the feeling of disappointment that happens when a day that held out the promise of some simple, basic pleasures takes a wrong turn and just keeps heading deeper and deeper into pure clusterfuck.

But the disappointment goes deeper than that. Sitting in an abandoned plumbing van, eating ketchup packets left on the floor ("Are they clean?"), Paulie and Christopher are a pathetic sight, and they don't look much better when they set out in the morning in search of civilization and a Denny's, psyching themselves up with a fantasy of ordering five Grand Slam breakfasts. (The Russian probably eats better too.) These are men of respect, of wealth and taste? Their only triumphant moment comes by pure accident, when, shooting at what they think is the Russian, they take down a deer. ("If we were trying," says Christopher, "we wouldn't have come close.")

Meanwhile, Meadow is at college, humiliating herself over the titanically dim Jackie Aprile Jr. (Jason Cerbone). Their scenes are a reminder that, in the show's later years, there was a stubborn section of the internet where people were holding out hope that not only would the Russian yet reappear, maybe Meadow would marry him.

The waking nightmare of "Pine Barrens" might be the single funniest episode of *The Sopranos*, set in a Bizarro World America where things have gotten so topsy-turvy that the only member of the Soprano crew who manages to demonstrate any expertise at anything is Bobby Baccalieri (Steve Schirripa), Master of the Frozen Wild. The episode showcases the supporting characters to such brilliant effect that, rewatching it for the first time in years, I was surprised to see just how much Tony there is in it, and his contribution is substantial. The episode opens with a typically frustrating tryst with Gloria Trillo (Annabella Sciorra), the *comare* of his dreams; it ends with Dr. Melfi prodding him to a realization that this woman who turns him on like no other is an emotional doppelgänger of his mother. As Freud could have told him, at the end of the day, nothing is colder or crueler (or more cruelly funny) than self-knowledge.

EPISODE 5.5, "IRREGULAR AROUND THE MARGINS"
—Hannah McGill

I'm bad at picking favorites. I shrink from the "You're a film critic—WHAT'S YOUR ALL-TIME TOP FILM?" question. So it's not my contention that Season Five's "Irregular Around the Margins" is the number one tip-top objectively best episode of *The Sopranos*. Love of a TV show, like love of movies, is too shifting and contextual a thing to make that claim. "Irregular Around the Margins" is, however, an episode that for me showcases to glittering effect everything that is best about *The Sopranos*. It's a microcosm, in some ways; it holds within it so much of what the show does beautifully. The writing, by Robin Green and Mitchell Burgess, is a master class in economy and management of tone. It looks beautiful, with that rich, dark, burnished look that built up and deepened over Seasons Four and Five. It's an unabashed treat for those of us for whom the various shifting relationships among Tony, Carmela, Adriana, and Christopher are at the center of the show. And it displays the extraordinary capacity of the actors who played those roles.

We begin with Adriana suddenly beset by urgent stomach trouble while she's with her FBI contact, Agent Robyn Sanseverino (Karen Young). The theme of physical frailty develops as we move on to a squirming Tony Soprano undergoing a minor operation to remove a mole—the kind they tell you to worry about, with the ragged edges that the episode title references. We are firmly in the realm of the thousand natural shocks that flesh is heir to, here, and the segue from Adriana's health troubles to Tony's foreshadows a further and more troublesome entanglement between the two of them. Here too, in the opening scenes, is the glorious hypocrisy that's so key to Tony's character—the tough guy, the purveyor of beatings and tortures, who's as needy as a child in the face of minor pain. He is also, at this time, separated from Carmela and her brisk, long-suffering form of nurture. Consciously or not, Tony's drama-queening, which meets with starchy medical indifference, recalls a similar moment in Danny Boyle's *Trainspotting* (1996), when Ewan McGregor's career junkie Mark Renton flinches from a nurse's needle. These ironic nods to the vulnerability of otherwise very hardened men, from two cultural phenomena of the millennial period, seem to encapsulate something about that era's fondness for protagonists who were at once morally bankrupt and sensitive enough to touch our hearts.

Tony's lack of forbearance, however, isn't all that stands out in this brief hospital scene. This is also one of the show's frequent references not just to death, but to ways in which Tony Soprano might die. Adriana's complaint blurred into Tony's summons up Jackie Aprile Sr. (Michael Rispoli), whose demise from stomach cancer in Season One both preoccupied Tony and kicked off his rivalry with Uncle Junior. Yet there's a strange sense of anticlimax here as Tony registers that yes, Junior has cancer, but no, it's not that big of a deal. And don't we all experience that, as we age, the giant terrifying threat of cancer becomes a shapeshifting, mysterious monster that seems to brush against everyone we know and arbitrarily mean either everything or *nothing*?

Maybe it's this brush with mortality, underwhelming as it is, that births a recklessness in Tony when it comes to his interaction with Adriana, which, later in the episode, takes a turn toward the romantic, or at least the sexual. Adriana's tummy bug humiliates a character who gets humiliated a lot, and yet it also humanizes her—de-objectifying a character who gets objectified a lot. For Tony, Adriana has all the typical advantages of a younger woman. Beyond the gorgeousness, she doesn't know his secrets the way the arch, critical Carmela does, and she's both wild and naive in ways Carmela is not. But there's also a real connection there, denoted by the way Tony and Adriana shyly share about their health and, later, the way they gravitate together to the transgression of going to score some cocaine. It's because we feel that these two have the potential for genuine intimacy that the near hookup feels dramatically powerful, rather than just a bit of why-not puppeteering in a long-running show, as when Joey and Rachel went through the motions of getting together on *Friends*. The potential liaison also enables a fleeting but wonderfully revealing blink-and-you-miss-it scene between the FBI agents. "She's a good-looking woman, and she wants to fuck Barney Rubble?" says Agent Grasso (Frank Pando). (Fred Flintstone would seem like the more obvious avatar, but maybe the offbeat reference is to indicate how just-off-the-beam the Feds often are.) Sanseverino does a bitchy impersonation of Adriana-as-bimbo: "We really don't *know* him. He *listens*." This jams us up against Adriana's aloneness. She's betraying everyone close to her, it's making her ill, and the people she's doing it for hold her in contempt. And who really knows whom here, and who is and isn't "listening"?

So what if Tony and Adriana *had* scored the coke, and that thing had occurred where sexual tension meets narcotic disinhibition and people suddenly decide that they're soul mates? It's one of *The Sopranos'* great roads not taken. As it goes, they swerve to avoid one of those visitations from nature that pepper Tony's life, a raccoon, and turn over the car. They're both taken to the hospital and, as gossip spreads via phone lines, a question mark over Tony and Adriana being alone in a car together becomes a firm conviction that she was fellating him when the car crashed. There's an element of farce to this, and yet it's far from trivial: silly sex gossip becoming a matter of life and death reminds us of the Season One plotline in which the rumor that Uncle Junior likes to go down on his girlfriend Bobbi (Robyn Peterson) is one of the spurs for Junior's plot to kill Tony.

That rumor was true and led to the punishment of a sexually besmirched woman. This rumor isn't true—not the detail of it, anyway—and still leads to the punishment of a sexually besmirched woman. When Christopher hears the rumor, both Tony's fantasy of a new life with Adriana and the sex chat of gossiping mobsters fall away, and what remains is Adriana—in so many ways the soul or the conscience of *The Sopranos*, the character who at least tries to lead from the heart—getting beaten up. Then Christopher breaks his much vaunted sobriety, shoots up in Tony's car, and gets himself taken to a deserted place for a talking-to. What's fascinating in this fiercely intense scene is the power of Tony's adamance that nothing happened between him and Adriana. "What kind of animal do you think I am?" he asks Christopher—when we know that very probably only an animal, the raccoon, kept Tony innocent of this particular charge.

As he insists on being believed—"On everything I hold sacred, on my children . . . the thought never entered my head"—we see the preeminence of performance in Tony's life and in the lives of those around him. You don't maintain an empire of violence and extortion by being emotionally honest.

You build it by *acting*, acting so hard that people buy into not the solidity or integrity of what you're claiming about yourself, but the commitment of your performance. Does Christopher believe Tony, the known philanderer, that he's wholly blameless of involvement with Adriana, the insecure flirt with daddy issues? Perhaps not, but Tony's ferocity tells Christopher it's more expedient to submit than to insist on veracity. You've seen this. You've seen people passionately argue something that you know they don't believe or swear to the truth of something that they know to be untrue. You know they're lying, they know you know they're lying, but what they're asking you to do is join them in a pretense that's more advantageous than the truth. Appearance is everything to such an extent that no one seems quite sure if what actually did or didn't happen even matters. "Even if it wasn't true," mourns Christopher, "it's what people think." Tony, to Dr. Melfi, has another take: "I might as well have fucked her."

His sobriety apart, Christopher comes out of all of this oddly buoyed up. The energy Tony expends on not killing him is the sort of affirmation he's always looking for. Adriana, meanwhile, has embraced the false consciousness of the domestic abuse victim, convinced her partner's rage must mean that he truly loves her. When Sanseverino reacts to the bruises on her face, Adriana says, "If it had been Christopher alone in a car with a woman, I would have killed him." This closing of ranks informs the ending of the episode's final scene: a theatrical family dinner/show of strength at Nuovo Vesuvio. Tony and Carmela, though not together, are together; Adriana looks at Christopher with limpid adoration; the onlookers who sniggered at the blow job story are implicitly chastened. Everything's fine. The cancer's cut out. The performance resumes.

EPISODE 5.8, "MARCO POLO"
—Nick Braccia

"Marco Polo" is the fifth, final, and best episode of *The Sopranos* written by Michael Imperioli. His run of five idiosyncratic episodes begins with "From Where to Eternity" (where his script channels the impishness of *X-Files* writer Darin Morgan) and includes the tonally incongruent "Christopher" (this is the one that inexplicably juxtaposes Bobby Baccalieri's mourning over his wife with the gang's goofball Columbus Day counterprotests). But for every ill-advised idea, his episodes include many unexpected, welcome ones, like Tony and Gloria's date at the zoo or Artie Bucco's (John Ventimiglia's) Armagnac venture ("Jean-Phillipe, *qu'est-ce que c'est?*"). With this inventive but somewhat mixed bag, the last thing I expected from Imperioli was a twist on high comedy, but that's exactly what "Marco Polo" is: a comedy of ill-manners. In hindsight, maybe his joke in "Everybody Hurts," contrasting Carmela's Lladró figurine and Devin Pillsbury's Picasso, should have clued me in to the potential for "Marco Polo," which is his masterpiece—a *Goombah Park*.

The eighth episode of the Sopranos' fifth season, "Marco Polo" isn't remembered with the same reverence as the fan favorite "Pine Barrens" or the tragic "Long Term Parking." That's a shame, as it's the series' best episode about the prickly blurred lines of American (and specifically tri-state area) social castes—one of the show's recurring themes. Northern Jersey isn't Downton Abbey, so there's no upstairs/downstairs partition to keep things clean. And all sorts come together for Hugh DeAngelis's seventy-fifth birthday party—from ex-cons to Vatican appointees—creating the perfect petri dish of nouveau riche, gangsters, and cultural elites as well as blood relations who are split into haves and have-nots. Tony Blundetto and his immediate family are members of the latter group. And over the course of the episode, he's the victim of copious slights, inconveniences, and awkward interactions that ultimately leave him feeling so impotent and ostracized that he breaks ranks with the family. Most of these perceived insults happen at Tony Soprano's house, but his self-centered older cousin is preoccupied, and—never much of an empath—oblivious to the depths of Tony B's frustration. It's like Tony Soprano's playing the episode's titular swimming pool game and can't see Blundetto's pain, even as he stands directly in front of him.

Hugh's birthday party is the episode's centerpiece—and it's a beaut—but there's plenty happening on the periphery of the celebration that clues us in to the episode's themes and lights Blundetto's wick. It begins with a pair of comic riffs on the ostentatiousness of Carmine Lupertazzi Jr. (Ray Abruzzo) and John "Johnny Sack" Sacrimoni (Vincent Curatola), the two men warring for control of the Lupertazzi family. Carmine moves up north from Miami and settles into a palatial West Hempstead estate where he gifts his soldiers Whirlpool washing machines. Inside the house, he shows off a garish mural, a trompe l'oeil with an ocean view. As expected, Lupertazzi the Younger commits felony assault on the French pronunciation. And in New Jersey, Sacrimoni takes Tony Soprano for a spin in his brand-new $100k Maserati and fishtails right out of the driveway. He has no idea how to handle the exquisite Italian machinery—he just knows he wants it. Atop the gangster hierarchy, grand is gauche and gauche is grand.

Imperioli and director John Patterson also take us to the other side of the tracks and further down the DiMeo family food chain. We spend time with Angie Bonpensiero (Toni Kalem), widow of Sal "Big Pussy" Bonpensiero (Vincent Pastore). The body shop belonging to her dead (or, as she believes, in Witness Protection) husband is now her fledgling enterprise. Tony owes incorrigible ballbuster Phil Leotardo (Frank Vincent) for repairs, so he leans on the vulnerable Angie to accommodate them. As fickle Phil runs up the bill, we see her start to fall apart—she can't afford to eat the money. Her anxiety is palpable: she fears bankruptcy *and* Tony. But the kicker is that we see Tony's *joy* in sticking it to her. It's a disgusting act of lordship. He's pissed her husband flipped and that Angie's sometime friend Carmela has kicked him out (he's living at his mom's house in Verona). Tony gets satisfaction from putting his heel on her head.

Tony's pre-party interactions with his cousin Tony B are less cruel, but clearly convey the pecking order. First he rebuffs Tony B's candid request for more responsibility. Later, he calls Tony B and catches him mid-coitus with his girlfriend Gwen (Alison Bartlett) to give him the onerous task of policing Phil and Angie's interactions. Chores galore.

Tony B's time at the party isn't much better as Carmela's always looking for a hand. He's directed to set stuff up, capture home videos of the hors d'oeuvre tables, guests, and gifts, and, later, help carry the inebriated Hugh. Eventually, he feels so put-upon, he shoots footage of Tony's belly and Carmela's rump. The usually mild-mannered Tony B is so put off by one of Carmela's requests that he exclaims, "What am I, a fuckin' slave?"

Though the Blundetto thread is the most important one to the plot, Patterson deftly explores awkward class interactions and observations. Carmela's mom, Mary, fawns and dotes over her friends Russ and Lena Fegoli (Bruce Kirby and Barbara Caruso), an uppity pair. Russ has a PhD in international affairs and worked for years as a midlevel bureaucrat in Italy. Mary's so mortified of her *gavone* son-in-law's behavior she'd tried to get Tony disinvited. Russ comes off like a humorless prig and condescends to everyone. Mary, in her chats with Lena, finds opportunities to put down Southern Italians (like the Sopranos) while lauding Northern Italian Lombardy cuisine like *osso bucco*. We glory in her mortification when Tony, sausage rope around his neck, joins the party singing, "Happy birthday to Hugh, *sazaleechi* for you!"

While Hugh opens gifts, the shot lingers on the Blundetto family table with Tony B's mom, Quintina (Rae Allen), and cousin Joanne (Christopher's mom, played by Marianne Leone). Quintina, who lives in a small house with her ex-con son, flatly remarks, "Nice to have money." But not all the working-class guests feel such envy. It's one of the show's most beloved characters, the benign Artie Bucco, who has the best time. He's not "the help" on this day—Carmella explains that he's attending "more as a guest." And we can see him enjoying every second, with a drink or in the pool. He falls asleep on a deck chair and wakes in the sunny morning, smiling and satiated. He puts on his hat and wanders blissfully from the Soprano compound and back to his life.

It's fun to drink in all this interplay, but the episode's most powerful moments are the nearly silent ones that linger following awkward interactions between people of mixed status: a blank stare from New York capo

Rusty Millio (Frankie Valli) following Tony B's loud "Mama Loves Mambo" Jackie Gleason bit that disrupts diners in a posh restaurant; the crestfallen look on Hugh's face after the arrogant Fegoli belittles the Beretta shotgun Tony gives him; and Tony B's anguish as he sees the love between Tony and Meadow, knowing that his own daughter, a former straight-A student, is a runaway.

The most emotionally brutal moment occurs after the party at Quintina's house, when one of Tony B's twin sons (Dennis and Kevin Aloia), sad they had to leave their cousin A.J.'s house, tells his dad, "I love where he lives. I don't wanna come back here." While Tony Soprano and A.J. do cannonballs back at the pool, Tony B looks like he's been shot by one. It's these words from his son that drive Tony B to accept Rusty's wet-work contract and go full gangster by killing Joe "Joey Peeps" Peparelli (Joe Maruzzo) and Heather (Erin Stutland). If only Tony and Carmela had let him enjoy the party.

"Marco Polo" works like gangbusters due in large part to the attention to narrative detail and the amount of story Imperioli and Patterson are able to communicate with remarkable economy. Anybody who's hosted a backyard BBQ or pool party will recognize the verisimilitude in small moments, like Meadow arriving, she says, to help but creating more work for her mom and feeling anxiety over whether opening gifts is appropriate or "mercenary." Or the discovery that a guest suffers from an obscure allergy—and it's an ingredient in 90 percent of your dishes. Everybody in the Northeast knows the glory of the summer-night swim in an in-ground pool and the tipsy shenanigans it provokes. Imperioli's Moltisanti attends the party with Adriana, but has no lines. He's soaking it all in, just like us. Imperioli should be very proud of the work he's done here.

EPISODE 5.11, "THE TEST DREAM"
—Scott Von Doviak

Twitter didn't yet exist when "The Test Dream," the eleventh episode of Season Five of *The Sopranos*, premiered on May 16, 2004. It's easy to extrapolate the meltdown that would have occurred on that social media platform from the reactions on message boards of the time, notably the late, lamented Television Without Pity. Those forums are long gone now, but I recall logging on after the episode aired and seeing post after apoplectic post decrying David Chase's decision to devote the bulk of a pivotal late-season episode to a bunch of stuff that didn't really happen.

Dreams were nothing new on *The Sopranos* by then, of course. Chase often spoke of his fondness for the work of surrealist filmmakers Luis Buñuel and David Lynch, and a series about a mobster in therapy provided ample opportunities to explore the character's subconscious. The show had already staged a climactic episode rife with dreamworld visitations in the Season Two finale, "Funhouse," so it's not as if "The Test Dream" was an unprecedented diversion from the norm. The initially hostile reaction from a segment of the fan base was largely forgotten by the time "Long Term Parking" aired the following week and became one of the most beloved episodes of the entire series.

Written by Chase and Matthew Weiner and directed by Allen Coulter, "The Test Dream" actually spends its first twenty-one minutes in the real world, although what unfolds there is sometimes more overtly bizarre than the dream itself. In the opening scene, Tony's latest *comare* Valentina is so intent on getting his undivided attention that she fails to devote hers to the stove burner she's lit to cook him some egg beaters. The sleeve of her kimono catches fire and she goes up in flames, just like Tony's plans to dump her. Tony's appearance at her bedside in a hospital johnny and scrub cap rivals Bobby Baccalieri's orange-and-camo hunting ensemble from "Pine Barrens" as a spit-take sight gag.

For Tony, Valentina's life-changing accident is just the first in a series of irritations that spur him to book a room at the Plaza in New York to get away from it all. When he tries to make Tony B the latest receptacle for his endless litany of complaints, he notices his cousin is distracted but is too wrapped up in his own issues to pay much attention. Only when he checks his messages later and learns that Tony B's prison pal Angelo (Joe Santos) has been whacked ("Probably Phil," Silvio suggests) does his radar go up. Still, Tony limits his response to making a few phone calls and telling the troops to keep him in the loop if they hear anything. He's already committed to an avoidance strategy, and his evasion of responsibility begins to gnaw at his subconscious.

The fifth season is probably the strongest overall, but Tony B's arc has some issues, and his relationship with Angelo is one of them. Basically we have to take their closeness on faith, because there's not much on the screen to support it. Angelo has a line about being best buddies with Tony B in the season premiere that was clearly added in postproduction to justify later developments. Consequently, Tony B's rage over his death and thirst for revenge falls a little flat, even as they serve a narrative purpose in the episode.

As in "Funhouse," Tony's subconscious is trying to tell him something he desperately wants to avoid thinking about. In that episode, directed by John Patterson, Tony's dreams are overtly weird and colorful. There are no talking fish in "The Test Dream," which mostly unfolds in the shadowy, muted palette the series settled into in the second half of its run. It's more subtle in its stylistic choices, setting it apart from the scenes taking place in reality for the most part.

We've all had the test dream, right? For me, it usually involves suddenly remembering I have an exam scheduled in a class I've forgotten to attend all semester. Only occasionally am I also naked. Tony's test dream is a little different, although he does eventually find himself back at school, confronted with a task for which he hasn't prepared. If we agree that it begins with him waking up in bed with deceased New York capo Carmine Lupertazzi (Tony Lip) at about the twenty-one-minute mark and ends with Coach Molinaro (Charley Scalies) shouting, "You'll never shut me up!," Tony's dream takes up a little more than 40 percent of the episode's fifty-minute running time.

Carmine is just the first in a long line of dead people Tony encounters during the dream. His victims adhere to him like Jacob Marley's chains, most often surrounding him in a car, driving him somewhere. Well, where would the dead be taking you? There's only one destination, right? In his call with Carmela at the end of the episode, Tony asks if Artie is all right, noting that "he was the only alive guy in a car full of dead guys." But he seems to have forgotten someone: himself.

"You know, douchebag, I realize I'm dreaming," he tells the long-gone Mikey Palmice (Al Sapienza), but it's a recognizably fleeting realization. There are moments during a long, involved dream where we recognize what must be happening, but the feeling usually passes quickly. The way people in our lives bleed into one another is another familiar aspect from our own night journeys. Melfi becomes Gloria and the pain of their relationship becomes a ghastly *Honeymooners* routine. At a meet-the-parents dinner, Meadow's feckless fiancé Finn (Will Janowitz) is replaced by A.J. as Carmela confirms that he won't amount to much. (After the episode initially aired, a still on the HBO website showed the dead stripper Tracee, long ago killed by Ralph, in Meadow's place at the table. That never happens in the episode, so perhaps Chase and company decided that particular transformation was a bridge too far.)

Identities blur even when they don't physically shift. Finn's father is introduced as Mr. DeTrolio, but he's clearly long-dead corrupt cop Vin Makazian (John Heard). As for Mrs. DeTrolio, Tony eventually recognizes her as Annette Bening. When Gloria reappears as a reporter and asks Bening about Tony, she replies that "there's something *Bugsy* about him." Tony has absorbed the gangster and crime movies he loves so deeply that they are inseparable from his real life. *Chinatown* plays on television, and Tony finds himself reenacting a scene from *The Godfather*. It rings true for me; more than once I've dreamed of watching new episodes of *The Sopranos*.

Everyone Tony encounters, living or dead, has the same message for him: it's time to take responsibility and be prepared to tackle the hard task ahead. When talking to Carmela, Tony describes the experience as "one of my Coach Molinaro dreams," so it's clear this isn't the first time he's felt unprepared for the task ahead. The coach, or at least the version who lives in Tony's head, saw a different path forward for him if only he hadn't taken the easy way out. "It hasn't been easy!" Tony argues, and he's got a point.

Near the end, the dream becomes more overtly nightmarish. Tony B kills Phil with a finger gun. Lee Harvey Oswald takes a shot at Tony, who is pursued like Frankenstein's monster by an angry mob. His walk through the dark, abandoned hallways of his high school feels like a journey to the deepest hidden part of himself. Tony's first waking moments perfectly capture the disorientation following a particularly intense dream, as Christopher arrives to confirm what Tony already knows—to a point. (It's Phil's brother, Billy [Chris Caldovino], who has been killed by Tony B, not Phil himself. Turns out Tony is no Quasimodo.)

Perhaps the most intriguing aspect of the dream is the suggestion that on some level, deep in his subconscious, Tony realizes he's a character on a television show. *Hear me out!* After waking up with Carmine, Tony answers the phone and speaks to "the man upstairs." Maybe it's God, maybe it's a more mundane sort of boss, but he clearly has power over Tony. "Our friend," he says, "he's gotta go." The man's voice belongs to Tony's creator, David Chase. Television sets appear throughout the dream. Melfi/Gloria points to one that appears to be playing Tony's dream from the Season Four episode "Calling All Cars." In the Soprano kitchen, Tony watches himself get dressed on another screen. In the locker room, Coach Molinaro says, "I see you on TV." Sure, maybe he means the evening news. But Tony's dreams so often tell him things he doesn't want to think about and delve into his deepest fears. What could be scarier than the suspicion that you're someone else's fictional creation?

Okay, maybe I'm too far out on a limb with that one, but that's part of the fun of an episode like this. Dreams were meant to be analyzed, and no two interpretations will be exactly the same. "The Test Dream" isn't as pivotal as "The Knight in White Satin Armor" or as heart-wrenching as "Long Term Parking" or as funny as "Pine Barrens," but it's the deepest dive into the psyche of our protagonist, and a whole lot of fun to watch and write about.

EPISODE 5.12, "LONG TERM PARKING"
—Andy Cambria

"Long Term Parking" is the third in a string of episodes marking points of no return in *The Sopranos*. In "Funhouse," Salvatore "Big Pussy" Bonpensiero is murdered by his friends after an agonizing stint as an FBI informant, cementing Tony Soprano's status as the de facto boss of the DiMeo crime family. In the unforgettably heavy "University," we witness Ralph Cifaretto's psychotic bludgeoning of his girlfriend, Bada Bing employee Tracee. Tony's refusal to confront this killing's moral depravity (he views it, mostly, as an affront to his business interests) leaves us with an acrid taste in our mouths—we want to believe that this ghastly act of violence, perpetrated against a civilian outside the ranks of La Cosa Nostra, would inspire outrage in the man we'd come to love. But it doesn't, because everything in this world is a transaction.

"Long Term Parking" is about the transactional nature of the two longest-standing romantic relationships on *The Sopranos*, each of which ends in a different way after characters confront their nihilistic worldviews. It's a stand-alone film noir that marks the beginning of the end of everything we'd wrapped ourselves up in while watching the show and makes us wonder: What the hell were we thinking?

There's a cold legalese that invades the Carmela-Tony dynamic in "Long Term Parking" and it stands in stark contrast to the hellfire she unleashed a season earlier in "Whitecaps." We know that even when he grandstands, Tony is a very conventional man. But an early scene reveals the coin's other side. Despite Carmela's sincere anger, humiliation, and attempts to "live on the parts that are good," the truth is that she craves Tony's presence in the house and the financial boon it provides. She faux-summons him to fix the family TV and shows her hand, announcing that any *theoretical* reunion would need to be based on honesty and fidelity. Sensing vulnerability in compromise, Tony knows he's won. And when they rendezvous for dinner at Nuovo Vesuvio to discuss more hypothetical specifics of his reentry into the home, there's an agenda on the table. Everything about their behavior and wardrobe suggests a meeting between two colleagues—the sharp-looking suits, the perfectly coiffed hair, and the polite little bites of food underscore the mannered feel of the evening. Each one of these parties has something the other one wants, and proper appearances must be maintained to seal the deal.

The eye contact between them at the meeting is minimal and Carmela often has to avert her gaze to the other side of the room (an anxious tic brought on by the feeling she knows what she's doing is a betrayal of her own ideals). When she tells Tony she'd like to buy land on which to build a spec house with her father, she's half chewing with eyes on her food when she announces the price: "Six hundred thousand." Edie Falco gives Carmela's Jersey accent an extra high-nasal twist here, emphasizing the feeling of tension when the moment of truth arrives. And after Tony accepts the overture—all that's left is the handshake—Carmela insists one last time that his philandering must end if he moves home. When Tony looks her in the eye and says, "I swear to you, *on our children*, that my . . . *midlife crisis problems* will no longer intrude on you anymore," it's a promise as empty as the request for him to make it. Nothing is sacred in this relationship, and the invocation of their children before the perfunctory kiss that brings them back together undercuts the feigned dignity they both think they possess in this moment.

On the night of Tony's return to Casa Soprano, its foyer is cloaked in dense shadows that reinforce the underlying sense of despair in the house, regardless of the faces put on by its inhabitants. Tony presents Carmela with a scarf (a "Hermeez"), another in a series of expensive gifts meant to offset the cost of his affairs. And her nonchalant acceptance of it is a tacit permission for him to resume his standard behavior. These are the superficial charms of a loveless marriage and director Terence Winter shows us the void between Tony and Carmela by framing them from a distance, allowing negative space to occupy the setting around them. When the camera finally pushes in closer, they're staged between two architectural columns, suggesting the double-sided nature of their life and the way it has pinned them in a place where they're unable to change. This idea is echoed after an uneasy family dinner. As Carmela rinses plates and loads the dishwasher, Tony reclines in front of a movie with a bowl of ice cream. The TV's working again. Everyone's respective roles have been restored. And all it took was a call to his financial advisor to "free up a down payment." They're home, and that's where they'll stay.

Adriana is beset on all sides when "Long Term Parking" begins. The episode's first image shows her on a black-and-white surveillance monitor as the FBI watches her remove something from a dumpster outside the Crazy Horse. Her ulcerative colitis, brought on by the stress of her cooperation with the Feds, will require steroids that may make her face swell up even though she's planning a wedding. And Christopher has relapsed into drinking, which relegates her to dartboard status when they're around other people. In the world of *The Sopranos*, Adriana is as close to a purely tragic character as we get. She indulges in the spoils of Mob life and makes foolish decisions but she's entirely motivated by love and loyalty (recall that her inner monologue when Christopher lay in the ICU was voiced by Otis Redding's "My Lover's Prayer"). When she's entrapped by the FBI, it eats her alive from the inside not because she's scared, but because she knows what she's doing is dishonest. Adriana is a way for all of us to take a foothold in the gangster milieu because we identify with her desire for reciprocated love so clearly. And Drea de Matteo's effortless charm and access to huge, flowing emotions as an actor have their hooks in us from the first time we see her on-screen.

When she is called into the FBI field office and we learn what we were seeing on that surveillance camera's tape is evidence of her attempting to cover up a murder, the episode does a sickening pivot. This cruel twist of fate—that blood is now on her hands because of a crime committed at the club Christopher gifted her so he could have a clean spot to discuss business—is lost on her. That sort of manipulative thinking has no traction in Adriana's head, and she asks for a lawyer when given an ultimatum: wear a wire or go to jail. It's hard to know who's more willing to trample her to get what they want, the Sopranos or the FBI. And we've never been more firmly in her corner than we are when she bargains for a last chance—convincing Christopher to turn and enter Witness Protection alongside her. This means making the soulful gamble that his love for her will outweigh his sense of allegiance to Tony. She believes he's a better man than his uncle—and so do we. But when she banks on love, the only currency she has left, and tells Christopher about her status as an informant and the evidence stacked against her, he lashes out, punching her in the face with a closed fist and choking her to within an inch of death. The scene is shot almost entirely in close-ups, which makes us feel every twitch of stress, pain, and anxiety like a jolt from a live electric wire until Christopher relinquishes his grip and they crumble into each other's arms, sobbing in desperation. Fans may recall the bedroom scene in *Goodfellas* where Henry and Karen collapse in tears, but that sequence's reliance on set dressing to provide a diorama-style backdrop to its pathos neglects the human element. Watching Adriana cling to Christopher, even in the face of his abject abuse, leaves us feeling gutted.

For a glowing moment, it seems paradise isn't lost. Chris warms to the idea of a life in seclusion and the aspiring writer in him reappears (Adriana always made him feel better about himself than anyone else). He stands up to go out for cigarettes, gently reminding her, "I love you, baby." Those are the last words she'll hear him speak. Gassing up his Hummer minutes later, he sees a schlubby-looking family piling into a late-model wagon with mismatched panels. This is how the other half lives, and just a glimpse of what could await him living like a schnook is enough to set the gears in motion. Tony calls Adriana from a strip-mall payphone and tells her Chris has attempted suicide—but we know why Tony makes a call from a strip-mall payphone. When she's in the car with Silvio, Adriana's point of view tells us we're heading into desolate woodlands—and we know why people are driven to desolate woodlands. The Pine Barrens vanishing before her eyes suggests her disintegration from the Soprano family and, by proxy, ours as well—where once there was black comedy, now there's only darkness. As she crawls away from the car begging for her life, the camera tracks over dead leaves on the forest floor, pushing past her and panning up to the sky as we hear a gunshot, dramatizing her ascension to a more peaceful place and drawing a stark contrast between her and the countless other victims of Soprano family fallout.

When Adriana dies, it's a body blow like we haven't experienced watching *The Sopranos* before. It's a shock, but it's not a surprise. We should have known better. We want to believe that she's different because of the way the FBI preyed on her, because of her anguished beliefs in love, family, and devotion, because she represents all the values that *this thing of ours* was begun to protect. But in the end, none of that matters. She's nothing more than a poker chip, cashed in to keep the game going, her life stuffed into a red suitcase and discarded in a weathered field full of rotting computer parts near an industrial plant in suburban New Jersey. That is the value of human poetry in this modern America. And when Chris abandons her car in the long-term parking lot at Newark Airport, the camera panning slowly across hundreds of similarly nameless vehicles left in the night while a robovoice drones, "*This is long term parking,*" the image draws an unremittingly bleak link between Adriana and every one of us. We're pawns in a game being played by guys who will sacrifice anything when there's an envelope to be padded. And they're winning.

We see dead leaves one more time in "Long Term Parking," as the camera tracks across a different forest floor to reveal Tony and Carmela touring the lot where she'll build her model home. The foliage and the camera movement intone a haunting lament for Adriana's spirit (as well as a link to the Shakespearean sense of doom surrounding Michael Corleone's Nevada property in *The Godfather, Part II*). Extolling the virtues of the land, Carmela deems it "*well worth* six hundred thousand." And in a rare private moment, Tony allows himself to be victimized by the knowledge of what he's done. He realizes Adriana died alone in a spot just like the one where he's standing, and he knows that his complicity in her murder is a by-product of the ruthless profiteer's lifestyle he has chosen to live. Unlike Michael Corleone, Tony doesn't see himself as a stoic; he's the sad clown who has to conceal his emotions but takes no pleasure in doing so. The natural world, and Carmela's mention of its price tag, elicit the realization that he's a fraud whose ethos is baseless, and that he's an active participant in the degradation of everything he claims to cherish. He breaks down in sadness, sitting on a stump, looking like the withered old man in Shel Silverstein's *The Giving Tree*. And although we're tempted to interpret Shawn Smith's song "Wrapped in My Memory" in an ironic manner as it opens with the lyric *It couldn't have happened to a better man*, its use here is elegiac. This is a swan song for Adriana that gives us a brief moment to grieve for her in its lyrics: *And you're wrapped in my memory like chains / Oh I say that the flowers will always be there in my heart /*

Like an old-fashioned movie with all of you playing the part / I'll never forget your part.

Tony and Silvio once dared to reminisce about their friend "Big Pussy"—"because him, you loved. And, he made a great Santa Claus." But Paulie was there to remind them "The world don't run on love. In the end? Fuck Santa Claus." After watching "Long Term Parking," we're left with an ethereal despondency similar to the one experienced by a child who's just learned Christmas is a sham. The world has had the magic sucked out of it, and there's no going back.

CHAPTER VIII

"MADE IN AMERICA"
A CONVERSATION

O n June 10, 2007, the world changed. People rocked out to Journey, Members Only jackets were back in the public conversation, we all wanted a basket of onion rings, and everyone thought their televisions broke. *The Sopranos* final episode was a major cultural event. Here, seven of us will debate the still polarizing series finale and make a case for the fate of Tony Soprano (James Gandolfini).

WHAT MADE *THE SOPRANOS* FINALE SO BRILLIANT?

NICK BRACCIA: "Made in America" aired over thirteen years before the publication of this book. I remember how pissed I was with my girlfriend at the time, who, despite not being much of a fan, kept saying, "He's dead. He's dead. Just accept it."

ANDY CAMBRIA: I watched "Made in America" complete with antipasto, red wine, and feeling like my cable had gone out during the infamous *cut to black*. Chase's direction, to me, showed that "Made in America" is about vanishing spaces: the decline of the American dream (and immigrant experience) brought on by ruthless profiteering and the commodification of every aspect of American life in post–World War II society.

Chase gets a visceral effect out of bitter, whipping, pull-your-coat-tight-around-yourself windstorms that's hard to mistake for anything other than a tempestuous Shakespearean hint of doom lurking beneath the surface of Tony Soprano's world. Take the phone call between Butch DeConcini (Greg Antonacci) and Phil Leotardo (Frank Vincent). Butch talks as he walks against the gales and throngs of New Yorkers, and after Phil hangs up on him, he stops in his tracks and stares forward, realizing he's in Chinatown engulfed by strangers. Quite literally, he ain't in Little Italy anymore, and figuratively, his way of life is coming to an end.

Similarly, Junior Soprano's (Dominic Chianese's) confines in that bleak-looking asylum with high ceilings and a sparsely populated sitting room remind us of the generational decay at hand. When Tony tries a "Remember when?" of his own, reminding Junior he once ran North Jersey alongside his brother, Johnny, all his uncle can muster is "We did? Huh. That's nice." There's a brilliant cut to a wide shot of Tony and Junior right after this exchange, showing the distance between them.

MARK DELLELO: I love your observations about the wind imagery, which make me think of the dead leaves blowing around in that great shot near the end of *The Godfather, Part II*, right before Michael Corleone (Al Pacino) does to his brother Fredo (John Cazale) what Junior attempted to do to Tony. And there may be a further homage around Junior's posture in that wheelchair—think of that immobile final image of Michael, rotting alone in his lawn chair.

What Gandolfini does in Tony's final scene with Junior rhymes with what he did in the episode when his mother died, but the emotion is bleaker because of the nature of the connection between the two men, summed up with the phrase "this thing of ours." Tony has at least as many reasons to feel unsentimental about the old man's fade-out into dementia as he had about Livia's (Nancy Marchand's) death. In both moments the emotion that chokes him up is quickly followed by anger—at the hold these two family elders still have over him, at his weakness giving in to it, at his lot in life. I've listed these sources in decreasing order of Tony's consciousness of them. When Tony exits Junior's life forever, he storms out rapidly and keeps up that pace all the way into the next shot—his entrance into the diner, where his own fate awaits.

NICK: The entire series is a tapestry of rhyming motifs and patterns—sometimes within a scene or an episode. Other times, we have to zoom out and consider the entirety of the eighty-six episodes. The wind, for example, makes an appearance in the Season One episode "Isabella." An ominous, Bradbury-esque wind blows—while "Tiny Tears" plays—up until the moment the sleepwalking Tony is nearly killed. I've wondered if the wind at the newsstand induces his incredible luck, blowing the Tropicana-blasting bullet off its course.

PHIL DYESS-NUGENT: TV series work by accumulation and familiarity. If you remember watching the show's first season in real time and then rewatch the finale years later, you might be struck by the degree to which all the color and fun had been leached out of Tony's life. For much of the finale, the message is in the sets and locations. The miserable-looking houses Tony and his family hole up in; the vast, dark garage where he and Phil Leotardo's fickle confederates have a parley; the abandoned interior of the Bing, where Carlo Gervasi (Arthur J. Nascarella) fails to show up for his meeting with Paulie Gualtieri (Tony Sirico); the nighttime gas stations; even the leaf-strewn stretch of wintry nothingness where A.J. (Robert Iler) parks his SUV and nature fights back— they all look like they were picked up at a yard sale at Samuel Beckett's place. The wintry boardwalk where he once had a chat with a fish looks like Carnival in Rio by comparison.

Tony's business may be thriving, but the life it pays for has shrunk to a choice between hiding in closets or stepping into open fire. No more barreling his car across a verdant area to beat up some welcher. His revels now are ended. This is clearly intolerable for Tony, who had many sides to him but was never kept at arm's length from the viewer. From his first appearance, James Gandolfini brought him practically into your lap, and endowed him with some of the most wonderful totally-average-guy-in-the-world charisma without pulling away from his dark side.

I'm grateful to Agent Harris (Matt Servitto) for serving as this episode's audience surrogate. His professional focus has shifted from organized crime to terrorism, but he's still sentimental enough about this thing of theirs to put his thumb on the scale and slip Tony the info that helps him take out Phil Leotardo. "Damn," shouts Harris when he gets word of Phil's assassination, "we're gonna win this thing!" For this, he is rewarded with his second dirty look from a colleague in this episode. Collectors of Mafia trivia will recognize the line as a homage to Lindley DeVecchio, an actual FBI agent who handled Mafia informants and got so into his job that he was indicted.

FRED GARDAPHÉ: It may not be coincidence that the final episode is number 86—a restaurant code that suggests the end of something, as in "86 the cold antipasta," meaning we're all out of that. More than the end of the series, Episode 86 also marks the end of an era of gangster representation that has dominated the U.S. American imagination for three generations.

HANNAH MCGILL: Throughout the show, A.J. and Meadow (Jamie-Lynn Sigler) were commentators on and critics of Tony's lifestyle. Centering them in the finale emphasizes that much of *The Sopranos* is about heredity, the judgments of one's relatives, and the cyclical nature of youthful rebellion. Tony and Carmela's (Edie Falco's) lack of a moral high ground from which to preach at their kids was an ongoing source of humor, and it's a major driver in this episode. A.J. and his girlfriend listen to Bob Dylan's "It's Alright, Ma (I'm Only Bleeding)"—the title a reference to how Tony's feelings about his mother have guided the whole show, but Dylan is himself an emblem of the gestures at rebellion every teenager makes before somehow reconciling with the system. The tension between A.J. and his parents illustrates older people's bafflement at the mutable values and preoccupations of youth. It echoes observations Uncle Junior made in the pilot about the young Tony: "He was part of that whole generation, the crazy hair and the dope!"

Then there's Meadow, who, inspired by her father's tragic mistreatment at the hands of the FBI, goes into law to defend minorities. In Tony's scene with Janice (Aida Turturro), we're briefly shown how Livia's negativity and self-pity have settled into their new host. "I put Ma and all her warped shit behind me," she says. "NOT THAT I GET ANY THANKS FOR IT!"

SCOTT VON DOVIAK: It's no accident that we overhear a bus tour guide telling tourists that Little Italy, which once covered forty city blocks, is now reduced to a single row of shops and cafés. The Sopranos used to have all the time and space in the world to stretch out and explore, but now we're down to a crucial handful of scenes. The scene in front of Satriale's is poignant because of who isn't there—that is to say, everyone from the original gang save Tony and Paulie. No matter how you interpret the ending, you have to admit there are fates worse than death for Tony, and this might be one of them: Paulie, who had been passed over for the job running the lucrative Aprile crew many times before, is all he has left. Now the job is his by default. The scene is sad and funny at the same time, honoring the history of the show and all those previous foils who met with bad ends while making us longtime viewers keenly aware of every last grain of sand running out of the hourglass.

NICK: The Sopranos are alone in the world now but packed together—in a small safe house or in a Holsten's booth. And, with their most trusted allies dead, incapacitated, or ostracized, they're adrift. Safe to say this lifeboat's dock line has been cut. And yet they remain blissfully oblivious: Carmela's shopping for a beach house, Meadow is getting married, A.J. has his new job and Beamer.

PART TWO:
WHAT WOULD YOU CHANGE?
OR WHERE DID IT GO WRONG?

HANNAH: I am a big fan of this episode both as a conclusion to *The Sopranos* and as an entry into the pantheon of Significant TV Finales, so I'm not overflowing with criticism. It's an interesting choice to give so much finale time to a character no one liked, A.J. We see how A.J. is *not* shaping up to be the new Tony as both a triumph and a loss to Tony and Carmela. We see that the generation that really annoys you with its affected moralism is going to take over and ruin everything, and there's nothing you can do about it.

SCOTT: The general dismay at realizing the series finale is largely an A.J. episode is not lost on me. The recurring pattern plays out yet again: A.J. fucks up, his parents make a flailing attempt at punishing him in some meaningful way, but in the end he is rewarded in a fashion everyone involved can justify to themselves. (After parking in a pile of leaves and blowing up his SUV, A.J. rides the bus for a brief period before being gifted with a new BMW. Hey, the buses don't run out to Little Carmine's [Ray Abruzzo's] production office, and besides, it's better for the environment than an exploding gas guzzler.)

Part of the point of the finale is that these characters are caught in loops; they're never going to change in any meaningful way, and that's why we're not going to be watching them anymore. But making that point necessarily leads to some narrative repetition: How does Tony solve his problem with New York? The same way he always did. Both sides are losing money as long as they're feuding, so there's nothing to be done but sit down and hash out a deal so everyone can get back to work except for one sacrificial lamb.

PHIL: I sometimes suspect that what I will euphemistically call the trajectory of A.J.'s character arc was part of how David Chase, aspiring-filmmaker-turned-auteur-TV-revolutionary, worked out his feelings about the movies and the death of hip Hollywood. Chase famously gave Tony some of his own taste in movies, and the references to *The Godfather* and James Cagney and W. C. Fields that pepper the show are loving tributes that also serve to tag the middle-aged Sopranos as members of what used to be called the movie generation. Chase may have used the talentless Christopher (Michael Imperioli) to make fun of his own Hollywood dreams, but at least he was on a hopeless quest to express himself through art.

A.J., the next step down the de-evolutionary ladder, may be saved through the movie business, but it's hard to see it meaning anything to him but cool parties, a well-padded expense account, and more expensive and possibly even worse hair and wardrobe choices—I mean, like something that escaped from a lab in a Cronenberg movie. No wonder Chase seemed to enjoy hitting him so much. (*Look at that! The little dumbass can't even drown himself!*) He's going to end up in a front office looking at the script for a great movie about a New Jersey Mafia family and telling the ink-stained wretch, "It feels more like a TV show."

MARK: Bobby Baccalieri's (Steve Schirripa's) funeral reception is largely a replay of the one for Jackie Aprile Jr. (Jason Cerbone) in the finale of Season Three—only with more speechifying from the character who is placed there to serve as the scene's moral conscience. In Season Three this was Meadow, who drunkenly tossed breadcrumbs at Uncle Junior during his showboating rendition of "Core 'ngrato," but this time it's A.J., who goes off on a rant about the stagnation and hypocrisy of the American Dream and actually goes so far as to explicate the meaning of the episode's title. Chase makes an effort at a glancing tone here by having the adolescent truth-teller quote Yeats and get called out for mispronouncing his name, but the scene still falls flat.

But as for the rest of A.J.'s scenes, I think the finale needs them. There were always aspects of Holden Caulfield to his character, and if Chase doesn't succeed in wrapping enough Salingeresque irony around him at the funeral reception, he certainly does when his SUV goes up in flames. Chase wryly chooses Bob Dylan lyrics to begin the scene that will convince A.J. he should enlist in the army! But if he's too preoccupied by the prospect of shagging the teenage model (Emily Wickersham) seated next to him to fully register Dylan's absurdism, he intuits something like it a couple of scenes later in conversation with his therapist (Jenna Stern), when he describes the moment as cleansing. She asks him if it was because the gas-guzzling car was a polluter, but he answers, laughing, "No, it was just seeing it go. It was a huge fireball. And you have no idea of the heat. My seat melted and I had been in it just a few seconds before." It was way back in Season Two when A.J. started going on about existentialism, but for maybe the first time he's just come face-to-face with the indifference of the universe and really grokked it. Like so many moments in the finale, this one sets the stage for what will step out of the men's room at Holsten's just when we aren't looking.

FRED: Chase provides paths for those who will continue after this part of the story has been told. What's an indictment? Just another hurdle for Tony to deal with. Meadow's future is bright—she's headed for a career in law that will defend the victims of U.S. injustice. A.J. is going into the entertainment business, even if now he is just getting coffee for his bosses. Carmela's got her eyes set on developing homes for sale. Paulie, now a captain, bares his soul—but, in the end, capitulates and accepts his future by Tony's side. Janice is going to look for another husband. Life goes on. The biological family's got it together, even when the artificial crime family is crumbling.

That plug being pulled gives the impression that Chase didn't know what else to do so he just stopped the series in its tracks.

Seems like a cop-out. The last image being Tony's eyes wide
open, chomping on the best onion rings in the state, without any
hint to the audience suggests 1) that this ending was coming
and 2) that there wasn't any other possible resolution. With this,
Chase leaves it to the audience to figure out its own endings.

PART THREE:
WHAT DID WE LEARN FROM
THE SOPRANOS?

PHIL: Before settling in for his extended visit to Dr. Melfi's (Lorraine Bracco's) world, Tony summed up his dilemma succinctly as the feeling that he'd shown up late for the party, when all the potential greatness had been sucked up and there would be little to do but fight over crumbs. Twenty years after the series premiere, it's clearer than ever that those words strike a nerve in many Americans. The economy, the political culture, the movies: everything feels like Davey Scatino's (Robert Patrick's) sporting goods store, choking on debt and piling up inventory, until the stone can be bled no more and it's time to send the "owner" best wishes and a one-way ticket to bankruptcy court.

Similarly, *The Godfather* and *The Godfather, Part II*, taken together, are what Pauline Kael called "an epic vision of the corruption of America." When Vito Corleone (Marlon Brando) confesses to dreaming that his son might have grown up to be "Senator Corleone, Governor Corleone," the irony is that he isn't consciously talking about the chance to reach for a bigger payday while maintaining a respectable facade. He's expressing the immigrant's romantic dream of America as the land of golden opportunity. The Sopranos don't dare dream that big, and still they manage to be disappointed with what they get.

The world the Corleones helped build may have been attached to puppet strings, but it had more style and functioned better than this. The last thing to go might be the sense that at least there's a corner of the world that you understand and that feels like home.

HANNAH: While I don't think "Made in America" is nihilistic, I do think it's defeatist and defiantly unsentimental. I think it says,

"We're stuck with what we're stuck with." I think that reflects the mentality of its creator, who, let's not forget, had a less-than-joyous attitude to his masterpiece at times and often said his real ambition was to be making movies. Just as Tony may have given up on the idea that his life is going to resolve or transform itself somehow, via a great passion, or an escape, or power great enough to insulate him from hassle, so David Chase has achieved beyond his wildest dreams and . . . still feels like the same somewhat sad, frustrated guy.

Ultimately, Tony is a boy whose mother didn't make him feel loved, and who reacted by making people fear him. Either a sentimental ending or a stringently punitive one would, I think, have been out of keeping with the prevailing sense that *nothing is safe, every source of succor may be cut off at any moment.* It's the mentality of a neglected child. Tony's love for his mother was rejected, his not-unrelated advances to Dr. Melfi were rebuffed, and I think the terseness of the finale can be read as the same sort of indifference to the fans' passion. You love it? So what? It's a TV show. It doesn't love you.

I think this bleakness fits the tone and intentions of the show as a whole. Plus, America developing an intense affection for not just an antihero but a nonintellectual, out-of-condition adulterer with trashy taste and brutal business practices does not seem wholly irrelevant to the Trump trajectory.

NICK: You'd have to change almost *nothing* for the show to feel contemporary. Remember the scene in "Soprano Home Movies" where Carmela and Bobby bemoan waves of American immigrants in the 2000s and articulate support for the construction of a wall? Tony and Carm, and most other characters, would most certainly be Trump voters today. Racism. No respect for law or regulations. Nepotism. Conspicuous consumption. Soprano family values are Trump family values.

MARK: Earlier in Season Six we watched as Tony lay comatose in a hospital bed, unable to wake from a nightmare in which his identity was a mystery. Way back in Season Two Christopher fell into a coma, too, and had visions of hell that Tony tried to dismiss, justifying their lot in life as soldiers by reaching back to the hardscrabble realities of Italian-American immigrants fighting to preserve values like honor, dignity, and family. Melfi asked him, "What do poor Italian immigrants have to do with you and what happens every morning when you get out of bed?"

Though it's the petulant adolescent nihilist A.J. who articulates the existentialist dilemma, Tony is the character who is living in Sartrean bad faith by always deflecting responsibility for his choices and abnegating his freedom. Phil comments above that things could have gone another way in the America, ripe with possibilities, that Vito Corleone landed in. But character is destiny and tribal warfare is what he knew. Writing about the *Godfather* films in *The Story of the Lost Reflection*, the critic Paul Coates described them as "the nightmares of an existentialist: one becomes what one does."[1] He could equally well be describing the nightmare that Tony had in his coma. "I'm forty-six years old," his unconscious alter ego said. "Who am I? Where am I going?" The answer is right there in those opening shots of "Made in America," where Tony lies in the bed that he made for himself over the arc of the past six seasons, with that semiautomatic by his side. He's hurtling toward the only absolute truth.

FRED: After Tony, there will be no more Sopranos involved in organized crime. Tony can't make A.J. into anything, nor can he do what he needs to do to keep "Our Thing" ours. Most of the guys I grew up with whose fathers were involved in organized crime were a lot like A.J.

Like the typical son of a gangster, A.J. goes through a period of wanting to follow in daddy's footsteps; then he eventually thinks about going his own way. Only without exposure to possibilities— no good work experience, no college—he hasn't a clue. Like many gangsters' sons, especially those who didn't go to college, A.J. simply settles for something family-connected that's legal and keeps him from manual labor.

A progressive writing naturalism would say gangsters' environments, their family situations, made them into what they were. A modernist writer would find the answers inside the heads of their characters. A postmodernist would focus on how these characters unmake America—that's what I think Chase created. We, the American audience, are no longer able to swallow the ideals that kept revolution at bay. The trouble is, along the way we forgot that revolution was a possibility. So we continue to live inside the world made by our fathers, forever trying to figure out how we can make it our own.

ANDY: If "Made in America" (and *The Sopranos* at large) is about the vanishing of the American immigrant experience in the wake of rabid capitalist culture, there's a grandeur about the way Tony's two families seem to be disappearing into themselves, like black holes collapsing. Think of Tony standing on Janice's deck, lamenting the encroachment of McMansions on a plot of land that used to be "all cornfield."

We end Season Six the same way we ended Season One (the rain-soaked, candlelight dinner at Nuovo Vesuvio, where the Sopranos took shelter from a storm), but so much has changed. Think of the warmly lit scene at Artie Bucco's (John Ventimiglia's) joint where Tony delivers his heartfelt speech to the family: "Someday soon, you're gonna have families of your own. And if you're lucky, you'll remember the little moments. Like this. That were good." He had them—and let's be honest, us too—wrapped in a warm blanket, feeling that everything would be all right. Contrast that with one of the biggest gut punches of the series: while bemoaning his entry-level gofer role to his parents, A.J. reminds Tony about his words at Nuovo Vesuvio. And Tony has forgotten them. This is the existentialist nightmare.

Yes, part of the American dilemma is that we've forgotten

we can change. Chase seems to be going further down a cynical path in *The Sopranos*, reminding us that the tools to change are there for the taking but we ignore them unless they can be exploited for momentary personal gain. This is the tragedy of Tony Soprano and it's why Melfi's absence weighs heavily on the finale. Tony's beyond repair, having taken the knowledge meant to help him end a generational cycle of violence and used it to justify acts of murder more heinous than anything we could've foreseen when we watched the candles flicker that night at Nuovo Vesuvio.

So it's only fitting that it all goes out to the tune of Journey's "Don't Stop Believin'," a distinctly American fist-pumping anthem of relentless optimism. Through all the choices he's made, Tony has elected to believe he's above the fray and immune from consequence. As the lyrics remind us: *The movie never ends, it goes on and on and on and on.* All of this, the old-fashioned diner, the routine parental encouragement vis-à-vis the tedium of an entry-level job, the onion rings and Cokes, is a fantasy we've created for ourselves to numb the thought that we've casually betrayed the values of our ancestors in favor of something a little easier to consume. That's Chase's vision of America.

PART FOUR:
CUT TO BLACK OR IS TONY DEAD?

MARK: Death is written all over this episode right from the opening sequence, which turns the "woke up this morning" motif on
its head. Tony wakes up and gets himself a gun (an assault rifle,
given to him as a birthday gift by his dead brother-in-law, whose
funeral he attends in this episode). The whole final season is
preoccupied with death. Tony himself barely escapes it in the first
few episodes, and later, out on the lake, he repeats to Bobby
what he told Melfi about the usual fate of guys in his position:
"Eighty percent of the time it ends up in the can like Johnny Sack
or on the embalming table." Bobby answers, "You probably don't
even hear it when it happens." And that answer haunts Tony in a
flashback after the hit on Bobby in "The Blue Comet." Sacrimoni,
of course, ends up not only in the can but also on the embalming
table, and Uncle Junior is not only locked up but also decaying by
degrees into oblivion.

The feeling of inevitability toward what Melfi called "the only
absolute truth" is so propulsive that the ending can mean only
one thing. That last close-up of Tony glancing in the direction of
the diner's front door when he hears the entrance chime is only
the penultimate shot. The final shot is what he sees next, represented by those infamous ten seconds of black.

This reverse shot is the completion of a pattern: we've heard
that entrance chime several times, and each of those times a
close-up and then an immediate POV shot have yoked us fast
to Tony's perspective. The close-up of him looking down at his
menu is as tightly framed and oblivious as the one in which
Captain McCluskey (Sterling Hayden) looks down at his veal in
The Godfather, just before Michael Corleone steps into the men's
room to pull out the gun that will blow him away. The show has
referenced this scene repeatedly. Tony even describes it to A.J. as

his favorite in any movie. He doesn't look up from the table again until Meadow walks in through the door and we're pulled into his POV for the last time. We hear the entrance chime but then nothing else: "You probably don't even hear it when it happens." **Verdict: Dead.**

SCOTT: The words echoing in my mind are Carmela's from a few episodes earlier, when she tells Tony he goes through life with a piano hanging over his head. Now here's that piano over Tony's head again, and maybe the wire snaps this time and maybe it doesn't. I wouldn't call the final scene unambiguous, although I would call it the most overanalyzed scene in television history. But I guess that's appropriate for a show that so often revolved around analysis. **Verdict: It's ambiguous.**

FRED: In Italian-American culture, death is a way of providing meaning to the lives of survivors. Death becomes an experience to be endured, remembered, and transcended as each new generation goes about the business of making life matter. Tony will live, of this I have no doubt, but how will he live is worth some speculation.

In "The Italian Way of Death," cultural critic Camille Paglia riffs on the end of mortal life, writing: "Death Italian style is a luscious banquet, a bruising game of chance, or crime and punishment as pagan survival of the fittest. . . . As an Italian-American, I was raised with respect for, but not fear of, death. Italians dread incapacity and dependency, not extinction. Since the dead are always remembered, they are never really gone. In rural Italy, cemeteries are like parks where the survivors picnic and tend the graves. In America, family plots are purchased like vacation condos; one knows one's future address decades in advance."[2] She's got a point here. No matter what conclusions we come to about what might have happened after the infamous cut to black, Tony as a character and Gandolfini as his actor will live as long as there is a memory alive that can recount them. *Evviva Tony Soprano!* **Verdict: He lives!**

PHIL: I don't think Chase felt that it was absolutely essential to the narrative that Tony Soprano die like this, at this point in his life. So why does the show end the way it does? I think he was winding the show down, and whatever he was going to do next, it wouldn't be a series of *Sopranos* reunion TV movies. As an old pro who had internalized some of the bad habits of the industry he helped to revolutionize, he might even have wanted to take that option off the table before he weakened. And then he indulged himself with the flourish of that cut to black, because what's the harm?

When I read that James Gandolfini had died of a heart attack in Rome, I thought it was exactly how Chase would have written Tony's ending if he'd been given the chance. Between the two of them, Chase and Gandolfini brought Tony Soprano to life. Gandolfini's death made me realize that I agree with Chase that how (or whether) Tony Soprano died is the least interesting thing about him. **Verdict: Probably dead, but you're missing the point!**

ANDY: Elements of the scene at Holsten's have been taken as red herrings, leaving the door open for it to be interpreted multiple ways, but that is not how I read them. We know that Chase intended to make *The Sopranos* as cinematic as he could, and the precision of the filmmaking in the final scene is reason enough for me to think all roads stop there. The direct nature of the editing and the total immersion in subjective point of view make sure there's no ambiguity. We see things through Tony's eyes right until the very end, and that can only mean one thing.

"Don't Stop Believin'" goes hand in hand with the dramatic irony that propels this scene (Tony on the receiving end of a Michael Corleone–style exit from the men's room). It's a fun song, in the way that scarfing down onion rings can be a fuck-it-all indulgence from time to time, and it's also a schlocky, easily digested version of something Sam Cooke would've done with a lot more soul. Even Steve Perry's vocal phrasings are mercilessly cribbed from Mr. Cooke. Can't you hear him singing *Just a small-town girl, living in a LONE-ly world / She took the midnight train goin' an-EEEE-where?* That fake-sounding piano. The shreddy, show-offy electric guitar. This is what we've made in America — a wasteland of over-the-top commodification. And with that as the backdrop, I can only see "Don't Stop Believin'" as searingly ironic: keep thinking it'll all be okay, and you're doomed.

Although it could be anyone who kills Tony Soprano (how many people from how many walks of life has he used and discarded?), it's the unnamed Only Member who does it. The jacket is an obvious allusion to Eugene Pontecorvo (Robert Funaro), who famously wore a Members Only jacket and hanged himself in Episode 6.1 (also titled "Members Only"), in which Tony refused to allow him his lifelong dream of relocating to Florida with his family. As we watch that man in the jacket (Paolo Colandrea) walk toward the bathroom at Holsten's, we may as well be watching the ghost of Gene cross the screen and take out a scythe. **Verdict: Dead.**

HANNAH: I find the cut to black brilliant and satisfying. It really makes us feel what we're losing, by cutting off the supply so brutally, like an ex-lover who doesn't glance back as they're leaving. But it also rewards our devotion by handing us the freedom to write our own ending. *You loved it? You finish it.* Once I figured out that my TV hadn't broken, I wanted to stand up and cheer!

It's a choice not showing us a corpse; the ending ensured *The Sopranos'* legacy would never be settled. It leaves us alone with what we've learned or totally failed to learn. We're Dr. Melfi, trying to fit the outrageous existence of a charming murderer into the tasteful little rooms we occupy, left staring and incredulous and *yes, a little bereft* when he suddenly storms out. Like Dr. Melfi, we still have our comfortable lives. We've profited from the association. We are enriched, we are complicit. **Verdict: Ambiguous.**

NICK: It's important to remember that when Tony enters Holsten's he's just left his uncle, who has no idea who he is, who he was, or what he's done, whether good or evil. In the facility, we see Tony's eyes tear up, as he finally understands the meaningless-ness. This is a realization that could have come from his Kevin Finnerty excursion, but didn't and now with so many deeds done and friends dead, what's the point? This is where Tony's at when he walks through the door. No impetus and nowhere left to go. First we see the restaurant interior from his POV, scanning for a booth. Then we see him sitting in the booth. Whose POV is this shot from? It's like there are two Tonys again! When Tony scans the song titles, it could be an episode of *This Is Your Life* or an inventory of his sins.

All he really has left is his immediate family and they're there with him, crammed in that booth in the center of the restaurant. Even if we can't see Meadow, he can. It's as good a time as any. Maybe better. At the very beginning of the episode, we hear the initial, funerary notes of "You Keep Me Hangin' On," but Chase cuts away before the lyrics start. If he didn't, we'd hear "Set me free, why don't you, babe," which is all Tony Soprano, his great-est character, wants from him. **Verdict: Tony Soprano is cold spaghetti.**

FINAL TALLY: 4 DEAD. 2 AMBIGUOUS. 1 ALIVE.

LIST OF OBSERVED LOCATIONS IN THE HOLSTEN'S BATHROOM WHERE THE MAN IN THE MEMBERS ONLY JACKET COULD HAVE STASHED A GUN

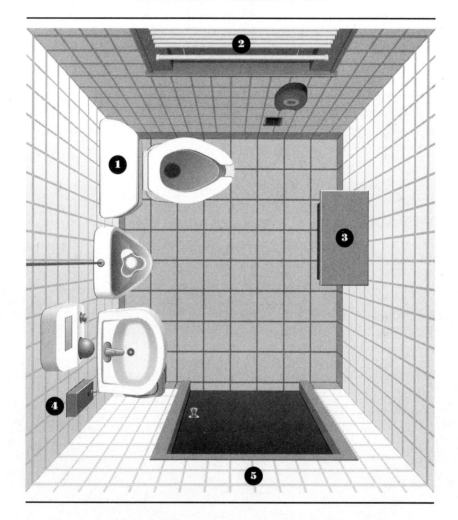

1. Inside the toilet tank   **2.** Behind the window blinds
3. Inside the radiator   **4.** Inside the soap dispenser
5. He could have brought it with him. There's no bouncer at an ice cream parlor, you stunods.

The CONTRIBUTORS

Heather Buckley is a graduate of University of the Arts with a graphic design degree and an academic focus on film history and criticism. She worked for thirteen years in New York advertising before bringing her creative and story skills into the film world. The first feature she produced, Jenn Wexler's *The Ranger*, for Glass Eye Pix and Hood River Entertainment, premiered at SXSW and played numerous festivals on an international run before its limited theatrical release in New York and L.A. Heather's work as a journalist spans over a decade, with bylines in *Vulture*, *Dread Central*, and *Fangoria*. Her background in SFX work includes *Circus of the Dead*, *Dead Still* (SyFy/Sony), and *We Are Still Here* (MPI). She is currently a Blu-ray Special Features Producer, having created documentaries for Kino Lorber, Lionsgate/Vestron, Arrow Films, and Shout! Factory releases including *John Carpenter's The Thing*, *Barton Fink*, *The Long Riders*, *Le Doulos*, and *Army of Darkness*. Heather's current feature slate includes projects from auteurs that span the spectrum of genre film, exemplary of her attraction to unique stories with strong, detailed visual aesthetics. Her favorite gangster film is *Goodfellas*.

Andy Cambria is a photographer and videographer based just outside of Boston, Massachusetts, where he's responsible for the image-making at the well-known instrument boutique the Music Emporium. Before moving to Boston in 2007, he spent six years working in New York's independent film scene—first in the acquisitions department at filmmaker Doug Liman's production company, Hypnotic, and then as a freelance production coordinator. Andy holds a BA in History and Film from the College of the Holy Cross, where he won the George Bernard Shaw Award, given in recognition of the best essay on a film or dramatic text, for a paper about Sam Peckinpah's *Straw Dogs*.

Mark Dellelo is a lecturer in Journalism and the manager of Sound and Image Media Studios at Brandeis University. He teaches media production, writes and directs short films, and researches the development of filmmaking style and technique. He holds an MFA from Massachusetts College of Art and Design.

Meirav Devash is a writer living in New York City (before that, exit 8A on the New Jersey Turnpike) reporting on everything from eyeball tattoos to probiotic skincare to goth fitness. Formerly an editor at *Allure* magazine, she has contributed to *The New York Times, The New York Observer, Vogue, Goop, CNN Travel, Ocean Drive*, and more. She is an inexhaustible wellspring of knowledge about red lipstick and heavy metal.

Phil Dyess-Nugent is a freelance writer living in Texas. He has contributed to *Nerve, The A.V. Club, HiLoBrow, The High Hat, Global Rhythm*, the *New Orleans Times-Picayune*, and the UNO Press anthology *Please Forward: How Blogging Reconnected New Orleans After Katrina* (ed. Cynthia Joyce).

Fred Gardaphé is Distinguished Professor of English and Italian American Studies at Queens College, CUNY and the John D. Calandra Italian American Institute. He is the past director of the Italian American and American Studies Programs at Stony Brook University. His books include *Italian Signs, American Streets: The Evolution of Italian American Narrative*; *Dagoes Read: Tradition and the Italian/American Writer*; *Moustache Pete Is Dead!*; *Leaving Little Italy*; *From Wiseguys to Wise Men: The Gangster and Italian American Masculinities*; and *The Art of Reading Italian Americana*. He has appeared in a number of documentary films on Italian-American culture, including *Beyond Wiseguys, The Godfather Legacy*, PBS's *The Italian Americans*, and most recently *Gotti: Godfather and Son*, on the History Channel.

Jonathan Hastings is currently a psychiatry resident, with interests in community mental health, addiction treatment, and the depiction of mental illness in popular culture. In a former life, he worked deep in the bowels of the industry part of the entertainment industry. He continues to watch movies for fun.

Charlie Jenkins is the former Creative Director of Chaotic Good Studios, a Hollywood firm that develops stories for all media. He's consulted for clients like Amazon Originals, The CW, Hulu, and Blizzard Entertainment. He was previously the Director of Research for the Alchemists Transmedia Storytelling Company and a marketing coordinator with Turner Broadcasting. He's currently shopping novels and screenplays for sale in Los Angeles, so the movie character he identifies with most is the savagely pummeled old nana in *Blazing Saddles*. Have you ever seen such cruelty?

Henry Jenkins teaches media studies at the University of Southern California. His best known book is *Convergence Culture: Where Old and New Media Collide*. You can read his blog at henryjenkins.org or listen to his podcast, *How Do You Like It So Far?* He is a member of the Peabody Award jury. He strongly identifies with Reed Richards, not because of his brain power, but because he often feels stretched too thin in multiple directions at once.

Joe Mader has written on film and worked as a theater critic for various publications including the *SF Weekly*, the *San Francisco Examiner*, Salon .com, and *The Hollywood Reporter*. He previously served as the managing director for the San Francisco theater company 42nd Street Moon. He currently works in high-tech, and writes on movies for *Critics at Large* (critics atlarge.ca) and theater for his own blog, *Scene 2* (joemader.wordpress.com).

Hannah McGill is a writer, critic, and academic based in Edinburgh, Scotland. She has provided reviews and commentary for numerous print outlets including *Sight & Sound, The Independent, The Times, The Observer*, and *The Scotsman*, and is a frequent contributor of news and culture content to radio and television programs. She is also a published author of short fiction and drama, and the cowriter of the 2014 Edinburgh University Press book *The 21st-Century Novel*. From 2006 to 2010 she was the Artistic Director of the Edinburgh International Film Festival. She is currently researching a PhD on the politics of film festival programming.

Eddie McNamara is a writer and chef in New York City, and the author of *Toss Your Own Salad: The Meatless Cookbook* (St. Martin's). Formerly, he was a police officer, 9/11 first responder, and *Penthouse* dating columnist. His crime fiction has been published in *J Journal, Thuglit, Shotgun Honey,* and more. He writes about mental health at HealthCentral.com. A native Brooklynite, he's the guy who knows a guy who knows the guy.

Steve Vineberg is Distinguished Professor of the Arts and Humanities at College of the Holy Cross, where he teaches theater and film. He writes regularly on both for *The Threepenny Review* and *Critics at Large* (critics atlarge.ca). He is the author of three books: *Method Actors: Three Generations of an American Acting Style* (winner of the Joe A. Callaway Prize), *No Surprises, Please: Movies in the Reagan Decade, and High Comedy in American Movies.* Among the greatest pleasures of his academic life has been getting to teach Mark Dellelo, Andy Cambria, Jonathan Hastings, and Nick Braccia.

Scott Von Doviak's debut novel *Charlesgate Confidential* was published in September 2018 by Hard Case Crime. It was named one of the top ten crime novels of the year by *The Wall Street Journal.* Von Doviak is also the author of three books on film and pop culture, including *Hick Flicks: The Rise and Fall of Redneck Cinema.* He reviews television for *The Onion's A.V. Club,* and is a former film critic for the *Fort Worth Star-Telegram.* He lives in Austin, Texas.

Matthew David Wilder is the writer and director of *Regarding the Case of Joan of Arc,* with Nicole LaLiberte, which debuted in the fall of 2018 at the International Film Festival of India. He wrote Paul Schrader's *Dog Eat Dog,* with Nicolas Cage and executive produced Tim Hunter's *Looking Glass,* also with Cage. He also wrote the screenplay for Robert Schwentke's *Seneca—On the Creation of Earthquakes,* with John Malkovich. In this coming year he is writing and directing an untitled vampire movie shot in Joshua Tree. He graduated *cum laude* in literature from Yale University.

ACKNOWLEDGMENTS

First, there'd be no book without my partner, Amanda Shaw, who made enormous sacrifices so that I could work on this project. And there's our daughter, Evie Blue, who at seven years old at time of publication, considers "Whoever Did This" her favorite episode.

I'd like to thank everybody at Tiller Press: my gracious and accommodating editor, Anja Schmidt, our passionate publisher and *Sopranos* superfan, Theresa DiMasi, art director Patrick Sullivan, copy editor Fred Chase, editorial assistant Samantha Lubash, Sam Ford, and Michael Andersen, all for believing in me and this book, which fell out of a completely impromptu conversation.

The many contributors in these pages aren't just fellow fans, they're friends. Some I've lived with, others I have never met but play a capital role in my life and my thinking. I'm deeply grateful for their collaboration here, but also for their enthusiasm, time, and trust. I implore any reader of this book to seek out and support their work, find them on social media, and champion their efforts. I'd especially like to thank Andy Cambria, Meirav Devash, Eddie McNamara, Joe Mader, and Matthew David Wilder for their time and attention during the larger editing process, when they each helped me to improve my own writing.

Mark Dellelo aka "Third Cat": As per usual, you went above and beyond and provided every type of support I needed, no matter how inconvenient. And this doesn't begin to cover your contributions within these pages.

Heather Buckley deserves special thanks for shuttling me around North Jersey and choosing not to toss me off the bridge over Paterson Great Falls, despite the slippery conditions that would have made for a great alibi.

To my research and editorial assistant, Noah Harper, a bright and fine young man, thank you. Paul Schrader, your loss was my gain!

Thanks to my parents, Nick and Elaine. My dad has never been to Italy, but pronounces "marinara" like he's just hopped off a boat at Ellis Island.

My mom navigated cans of scungilli for him every Christmas Eve to make a salad and thus she's the bravest person I know.

Hat tip to my brother, Chris, and sister-in-law, Karen. Their daughters, Aria and Serena, are the sweetest.

Shout out to all the Braccias, Breislers, Semiroths, and Shaws.

Andrew Green, thank you for being a founding member of the Herring Boyz and a constant source of support and hilarity. I don't know what I'd do without you.

To all the friends who have ever had my back, even when it's not easy, especially: Ivan Askwith, Rob Bennett, Kevin "Locks" Brooks, Leslie Byxbee, Michael Carlon, Bryan Castaneda, Gavin Clancy, Brendan Clarke, Sean Conroy, Doug Cummings, Eddie DeSalle, Stan Dryev, Richard Feifer, Ryan Fitzgerald, Carolyn Goldhush, Brendan Light, Amanda Kleinberg, Chris McManus, Barbara Miller, Vanessa Montes, John Paulson, Peter Field Peck, Bryan Pepi, Mary Phillips-Sandy, Ron Salvatore, Scott Stern, Nicole Waxenblatt, Lance Weiler, and Alex Weimer.

Thanks to Frank DiMatteo for his time and his candor while discussing the finer aspects of illicit activities with Eddie McNamara. It was a pleasure to meet Frank, ever so briefly, at SopranosCon. Definitely check out his books.

Ben Fisher, thank you for being an early and eager reader. And thanks to the Elysium Health family for their interest and support.

To members of my '90s Simon & Schuster International Sales crew, Maeyee Barrette, Edward Benitez, Fran Creegan, Cyrus Kheradi, Cynthia Pallisco, John Sakal, and Dan Vidra, we worked together over a year *before* this show aired. I guess this is full circle (also, we're old).

I'm very grateful for the support of my former Campfire colleagues Mike Monello, Steve Coulson, and Mike Knowlton. I'm proud to have worked beside you for so long. I'm prouder to call you friends.

I want to acknowledge the great teachers I've had in my life: Gertrude Vogt from Marvin Elementary School, Anthony Bossone from Nathan Hale Middle School, and Mike Savo and Barry Wallace from Fairfield Prep.

Steve Vineberg, my friend and favorite professor at Holy Cross, contributed to this book in many ways beyond his marvelous essay on acting. It was in and around his courses that I discovered not just my sensibility, but many dear friends including some in these pages. Steve's passion, patience, and generosity have shaped the person I am as much as anyone outside of my immediate family, and his impact on my life (and this book) is immeasurable. Steve was also an enormous help during the final stages of editing, and I am deeply grateful for his time and sharp eye.

To the cast and crew of *The Sopranos*, especially David Chase, thank you for your tireless commitment to excellence and your uncompromising, unflinching vision of tri-state area (and American) truth. Twenty-plus years later and there's still so much to discover.

Finally, I'd like to dedicate this work to the memory of two men who passed away just before this book was born, though their spirits are most certainly in its pages. They are Tom Block and Kevin Courrier. I would have invited both to contribute to this project and encourage you to seek out their criticism online. Kevin's legacy lives on through critics-at-large.ca, a site he cofounded and where you can find his work alongside several of the contributors in this book.

NOTES

Chapter II: Inspired Crimes:
Investigating the Schemes of *The Sopranos*

1. Heather Rogers, *Gone Tomorrow: The Hidden Life of Garbage* (New York: New Press, 2005), pp. 186–88.
2. Ibid.
3. Ibid.
4. "SCI Report: Corrupt Recycling of Tainted Dirt and Debris," *New Jersey State Comission of Investigation* 27 (March 2017): https://www.nj.gov/sci/pdf/Press/SCIPressReleaseDirt.pdf.
5. Albert Samaha, "Bad Rabbi: Tales of Extortion and Torture Depict a Divorce Broker's Brutal Grip on the Orthodox Community," *Village Voice*, December 4, 2013, https://www.villagevoice.com/2013/12/04/bad-rabbi-tales-of-extortion-and-torture-depict-a-divorce-brokers-brutal-grip-on-the-orthodox-community/.
6. Steve Kurutz, "Morris Levy: Artist Biography," AllMusic, n.d., https://www.allmusic.com/artist/morris-levy-mn0000599072/biography.
7. Michael Franzese, *Blood Covenant: He Quit the Mob and Lived* (New Kensington, PA: Whitaker House, 2003), p. 23.
8. Sean Egan, "John Lennon Rock'N'Roll Review," 2010, https://www.bbc.co.uk/music/reviews/rmcg/.
9. Joseph C. Self, "Lennon v. Levy—The 'Roots' Lawsuit," 1992, https://web.archive.org/web/20110921164539/http://abbeyrd.best.vwh.net/lenlevy.htm.
10. Jonathan Karp, "Review of 'Godfather of the Music Business: Morris Levy' by Richard Carlin," Academia.edu, 2016, https://www.academia.edu/27115956/Review_of_Godfather_of_the_Music_Business_Morris_Levy_by_Richard_Carlin.
11. Larry Neumeister, "Two Songwriters Win Rights to Hit Song 36 Years After Writing It," Associated Press, November 19, 1992, https://apnews.com/b542816ef44f9b73bec72c206c677184?SearchText=morris levy roulette&Display_.
12. Ibid.
13. Karp, "Review of 'Godfather of the Music Business: Morris Levy' by Richard Carlin."
14. William K. Knoedelseder Jr., "Morris Levy Gets 10-Year Sentence: Roulette Records Chief Fined $200,000 in Extortion Case," *Los Angeles Times*, October 29, 1988, https://www.latimes.com/archives/la-xpm-1988-10-29-fi-215-story.html.
15. Daniel Gross, "How to Commit a $200 Million Scam: Inside the Year's Most Shocking Credit Card Fraud." *Daily Beast*, February 6, 2013, https://www.thedailybeast.com/how-to-commit-a-dollar200-million-scam-inside-the-years-most-shocking-credit-card-fraud.
16. "Leader of International, $200 Million Credit Card Fraud Scam Sentenced to 80 Months in Prison," United States Department of Justice, January 7, 2016, https://www.justice.gov/usao-nj/pr/leader-international-200-million-credit-card-fraud-scam-sentenced-80-months-prison.

17. Selwyn Raab, "Officials Say Mob Is Shifting Crimes to New Industries," *New York Times*, February 10, 1997.

18. Alan Feuer, "Indictment Says Mob Is Linked to a Mortgage Fraud Operation," *New York Times*, March 29, 2001.

19. Robert D. McFadden, "6 Arrests Are Said to Smash Theft Ring for Car Air Bags," *New York Times*, May 5, 1998, https://www.nytimes.com/1998/05/05/nyregion/6-arrests-are-said-to-smash-theft-ring-for-car-air-bags.html.

20. Joe Goldstein, "ESPN Internet Ventures," November 19, 2003, https://www.espn.com/classic/s/basketball_scandals_explosion.html.

21. Henry Hill, "How I Put the Fix In," *Sports Illustrated*, February 16, 1981, http://temporaryehliss.blogspot.com/2014/04/henryhill-how-i-put-fix-in.html.

22. Christian Murray, "Police Bust Astoria-Based Gambling Ring, Seven Indicted: DA," *Astoria Post*, June 6, 2019, https://astoriapost.com/police-bust-astoria-based-gambling-ring-seven-indicted-da.

23. "Federal Wire Act," Wikipedia, https://en.wikipedia.org/wiki/Federal_Wire_Act.

24. Richard H. Boyle, "The Bookies Close Up Shop," *Sports Illustrated*, September 3, 1962.

25. Aaron Gray, "The Size and Increase of the Global Sports Betting Market," *Sports Betting Dime*, October 10, 2019, http://sportsbettingdime.com/guides/finance/global-sports-betting-market/.

Chapter III: The Craft of *The Sopranos*

1. Max Jaeger, "Saucy Squabble: Is It 'Sauce' or 'Gravy'?," *Brooklyn Paper*, March 19, 2014, https://www.brooklynpaper.com/saucy-squabble-is-it-sauce-or-gravy-2/.

2. Gay Talese, "The Kidnapping of Joe Bonanno," *Esquire*, August 1, 1971.

3. "Iconic Entertainment Memorabilia," *The Golden Closet News*, n.d., https://www.thegoldencloset.com/.

4. "Snooki Demonstrates How to Style the 'Poof,'" MTV, December 18, 2009, http://www.mtv.com/video-clips/txscxz/snooki-demonstrates-how-to-style-the-poof.

5. Paul Farhi, "Lorraine Bracco's Choice Role," *Washington Post*, October 21, 2001, https://www.washingtonpost.com/archive/lifestyle/style/2001/10/21/lorraine-braccos-choice-role/e8555a6a-ed87-4b61-a198-b1782ffa37e2/.

Chapter IV: Watch List:
The TV and Cinematic DNA of *The Sopranos*

1. Matt Zoller Seitz, "David Chase on the Legacy of *Twin Peaks*—Slideshow," *Vulture*, May 7, 2015, https://www.vulture.com/2015/05/david-chase-twin-peaks-legacy.html.

2. Alexa Harrison, "David Chase Talks 'Sopranos' and 'Pine Barrens' with Steve Buscemi, Terence Winter," *Variety*, June 6, 2017, https://variety.com/2017/scene/vpage/david-chase-split-screens-sopranos-steve-buscemi-1202455300/.

3. Robert Warshow, "Movie Chronicle: The Westerner," *Partisan Review* (March–April 1954).

Chapter V: *The Sopranos* in Culture

1. Brett Martin, *Difficult Men: Behind the Scenes of a Creative Revolution: From* The Sopranos *and* The Wire *to* Mad Men *and* Breaking Bad (New York: Penguin, 2014).

2. Richard Lawson, "Showtime Cornering the Market On 'Ladies with Prob-

lems' Shows, *Gawker*, March 24, 2010, https://gawker.com/5501286 /showtime-cornering-the-market-on-ladies-with-problems-shows.

3. Alan Sepinwall, *The Revolution Was Televised: How The Sopranos, Mad Men, Breaking Bad, Lost, and Other Groundbreaking Dramas Changed TV Forever* (New York: Simon & Schuster, 2013), p. 433.

Chapter VII: Favorite Episodes

1. *EW* Staff. "Sopranos: A 'Pine Barrens' Oral History," EW.com, May 13, 2007, https://ew.com/article/2007/05/13/sopranos-pine-barrens-oral-history/.
2. Ibid.

Chapter VIII: "Made in America":
A Conversation

1. Paul Coates, *The Story of the Lost Reflection: The Alienation of the Image in Western and Polish Cinema* (London: Verso, 1985), p. 110.
2. Camille Paglia, *Provocations: Collected Essays on Art, Feminism, Politics, Sex, and Education* (New York: Pantheon, 2018).